NAOKI URASAWA'S

MONSTER

volume 2

Naoki Urasawa's
Monster
Volume 2

VIZ Signature Edition

STORY AND ART BY NAOKI URASAWA

English Adaptation/Agnes Yoshida
Translation/Satch Watanabe
Touch-up Art & Lettering/Steve Dutro
Design/Courtney Utt
Editor/Andy Nakatani

Managing Editor/Annette Roman
Director of Production/Noboru Watanabe
Vice President of Publishing/Alvin Lu
Sr. Director of Acquisitions/Rika Inouye
Vice President of Sales & Marketing/Liza Coppola
Publisher/Hyoe Narita

Printed in the U.S.A.

Published by VIZ Media, LLC
P.O. Box 77010
San Francisco, CA 94107

VIZ Signature Edition
10 9 8 7 6 5 4 3 2 1
First printing, April 2006

www.viz.com
store.viz.com

Naoki Urasawa's
Monster
Volume 2
Surprise Party

Story and Art by Naoki Urasawa

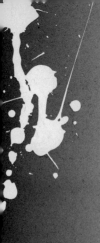

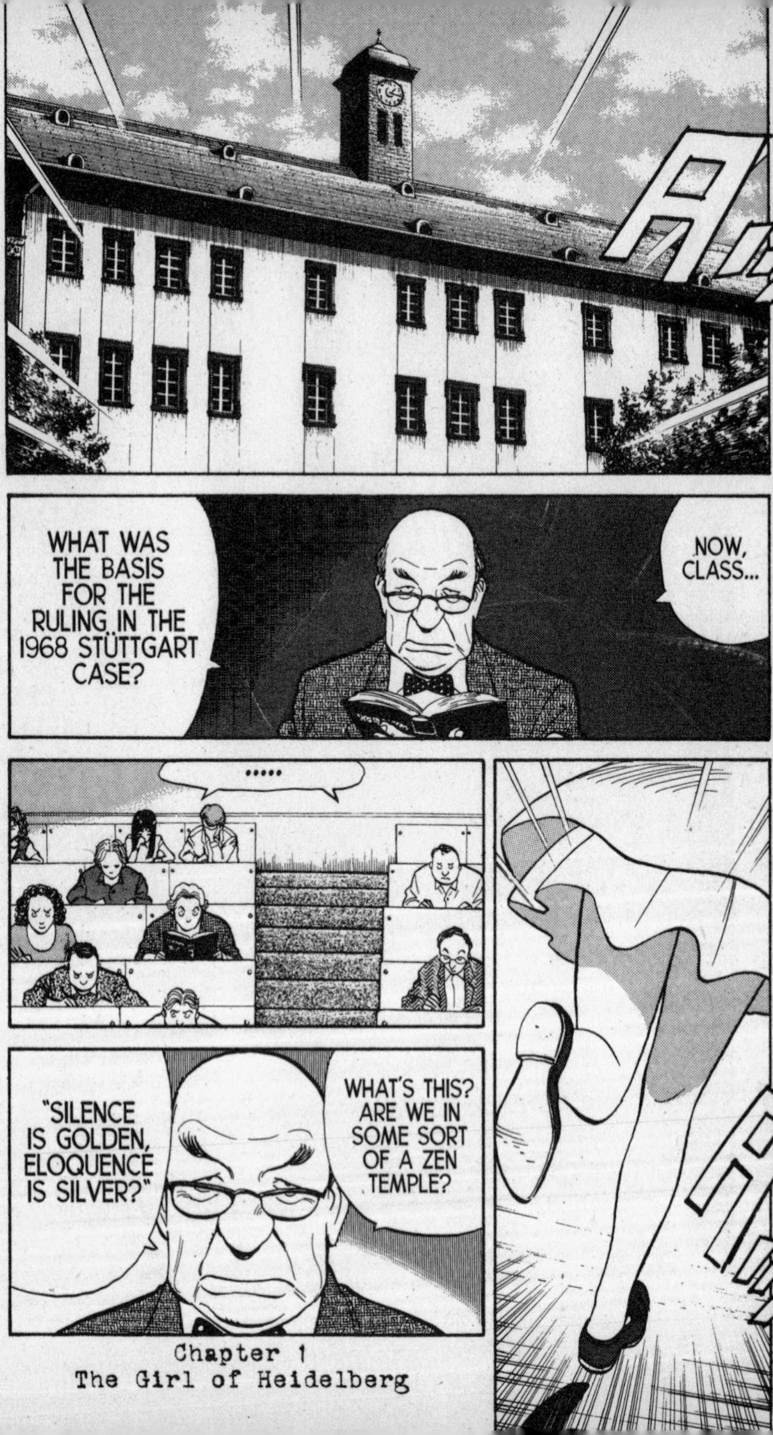
NOW, CLASS...
WHAT WAS THE BASIS FOR THE RULING IN THE 1968 STÜTTGART CASE?
.....
WHAT'S THIS? ARE WE IN SOME SORT OF A ZEN TEMPLE?
"SILENCE IS GOLDEN, ELOQUENCE IS SILVER?"

Chapter 1
The Girl of Heidelberg

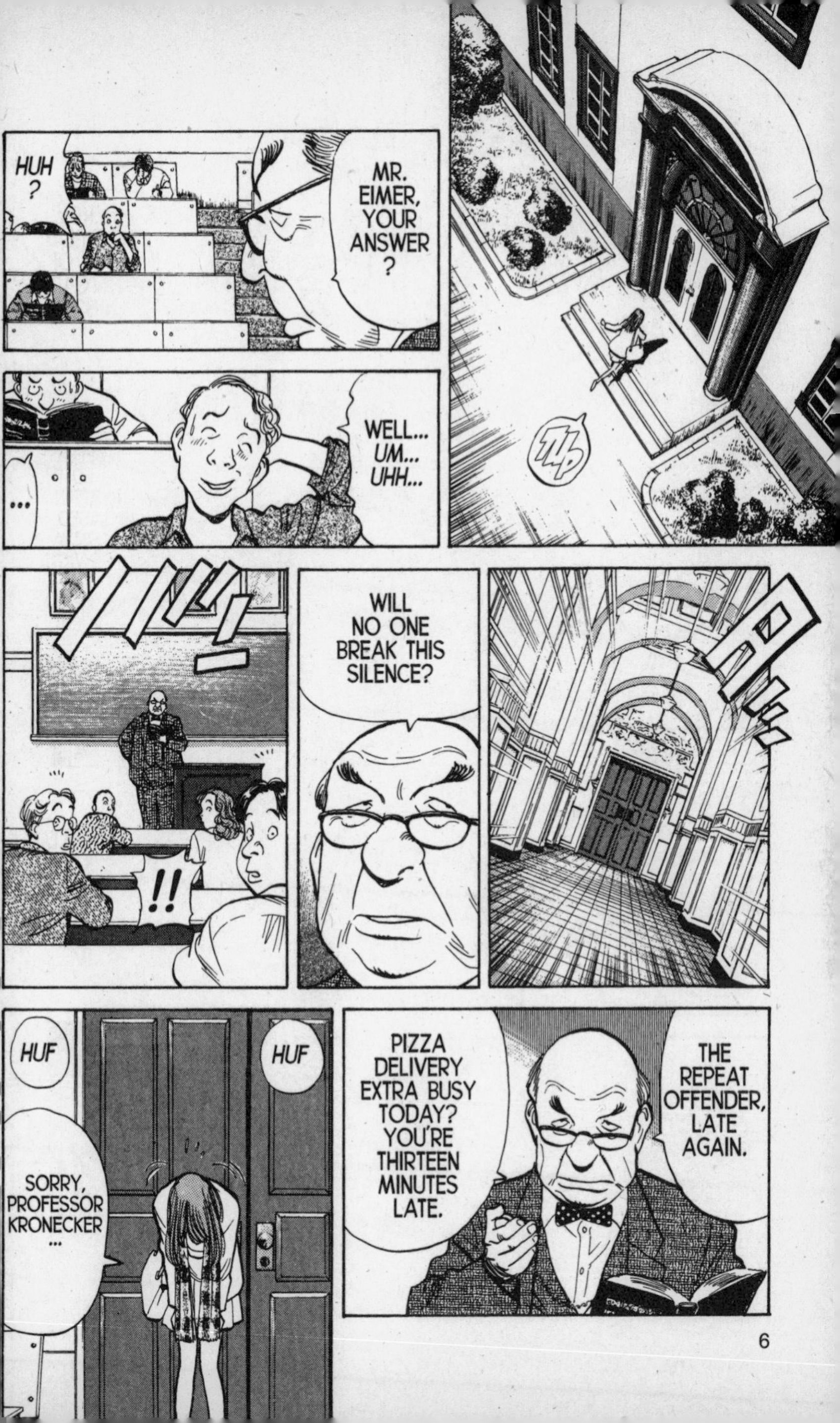
MR. EIMER, YOUR ANSWER?
HUH?
WELL... UM... UHH...
...
WILL NO ONE BREAK THIS SILENCE?
!!
THE REPEAT OFFENDER, LATE AGAIN.
PIZZA DELIVERY EXTRA BUSY TODAY? YOU'RE THIRTEEN MINUTES LATE.
HUF
HUF
SORRY, PROFESSOR KRONECKER...

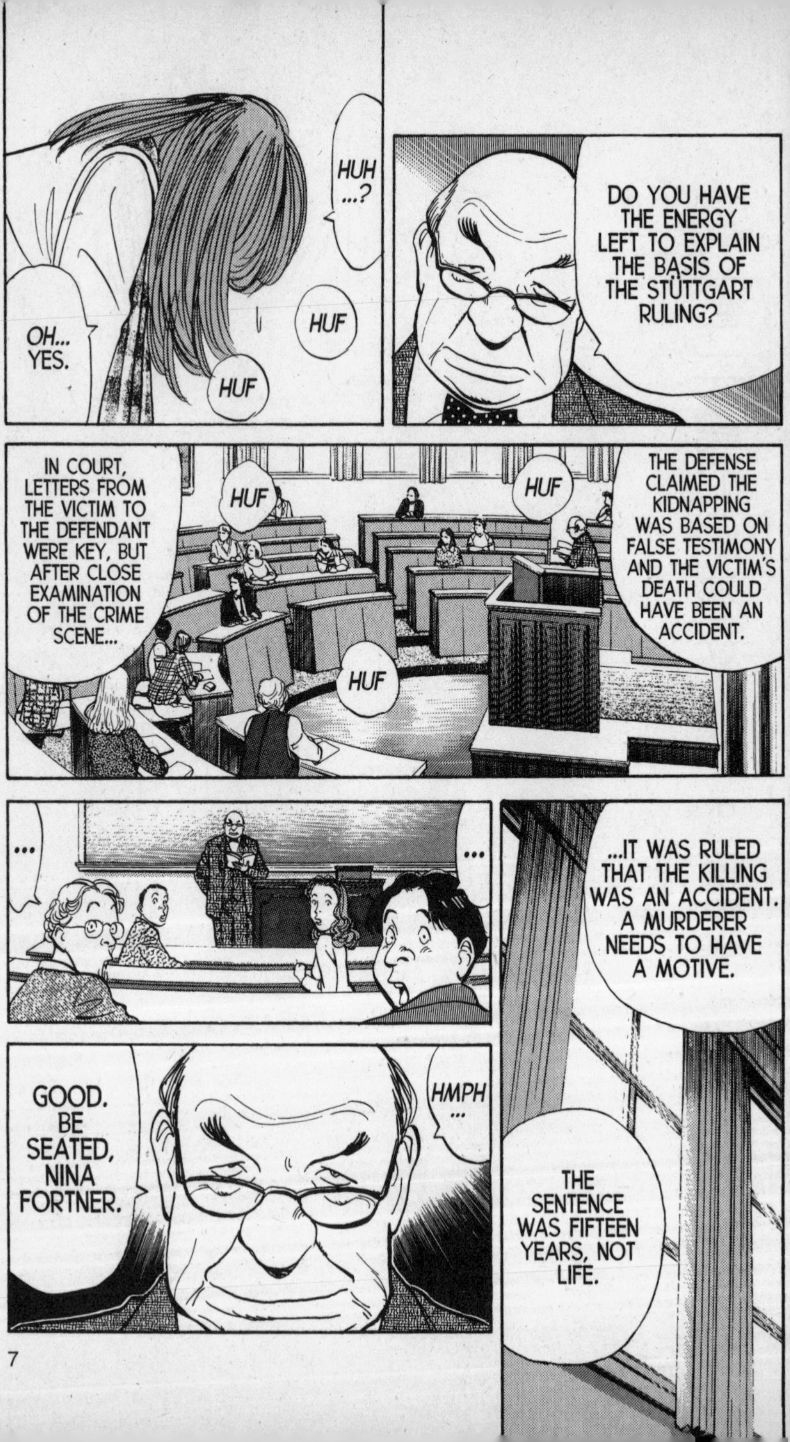
DO YOU HAVE THE ENERGY LEFT TO EXPLAIN THE BASIS OF THE STÜTTGART RULING?
HUH ...?
HUF
HUF
OH... YES.
THE DEFENSE CLAIMED THE KIDNAPPING WAS BASED ON FALSE TESTIMONY AND THE VICTIM'S DEATH COULD HAVE BEEN AN ACCIDENT.
HUF
HUF
IN COURT, LETTERS FROM THE VICTIM TO THE DEFENDANT WERE KEY, BUT AFTER CLOSE EXAMINATION OF THE CRIME SCENE...
HUF
...IT WAS RULED THAT THE KILLING WAS AN ACCIDENT. A MURDERER NEEDS TO HAVE A MOTIVE.
THE SENTENCE WAS FIFTEEN YEARS, NOT LIFE.
...
...
HMPH ...
GOOD. BE SEATED, NINA FORTNER.

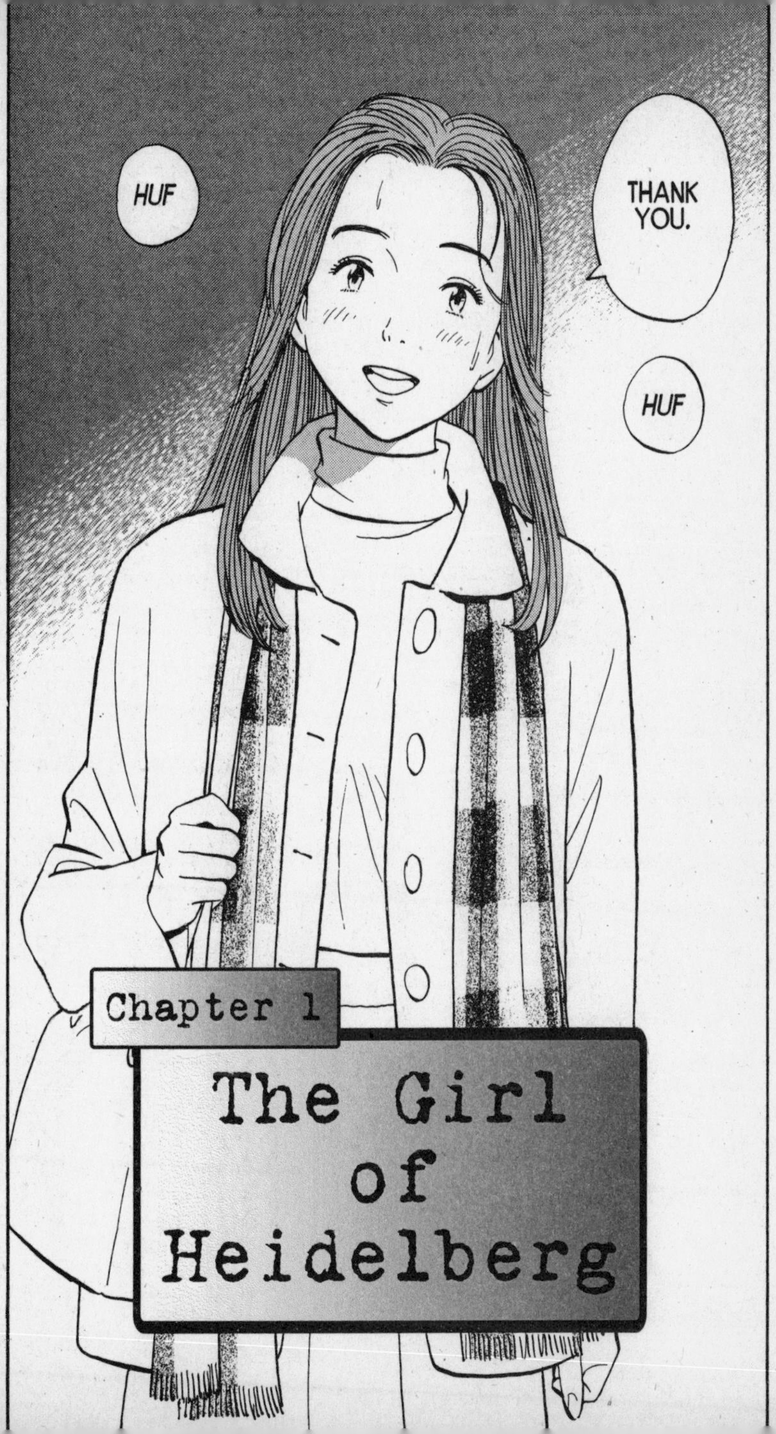
THANK YOU.
HUF
HUF
Chapter 1
The Girl of Heidelberg

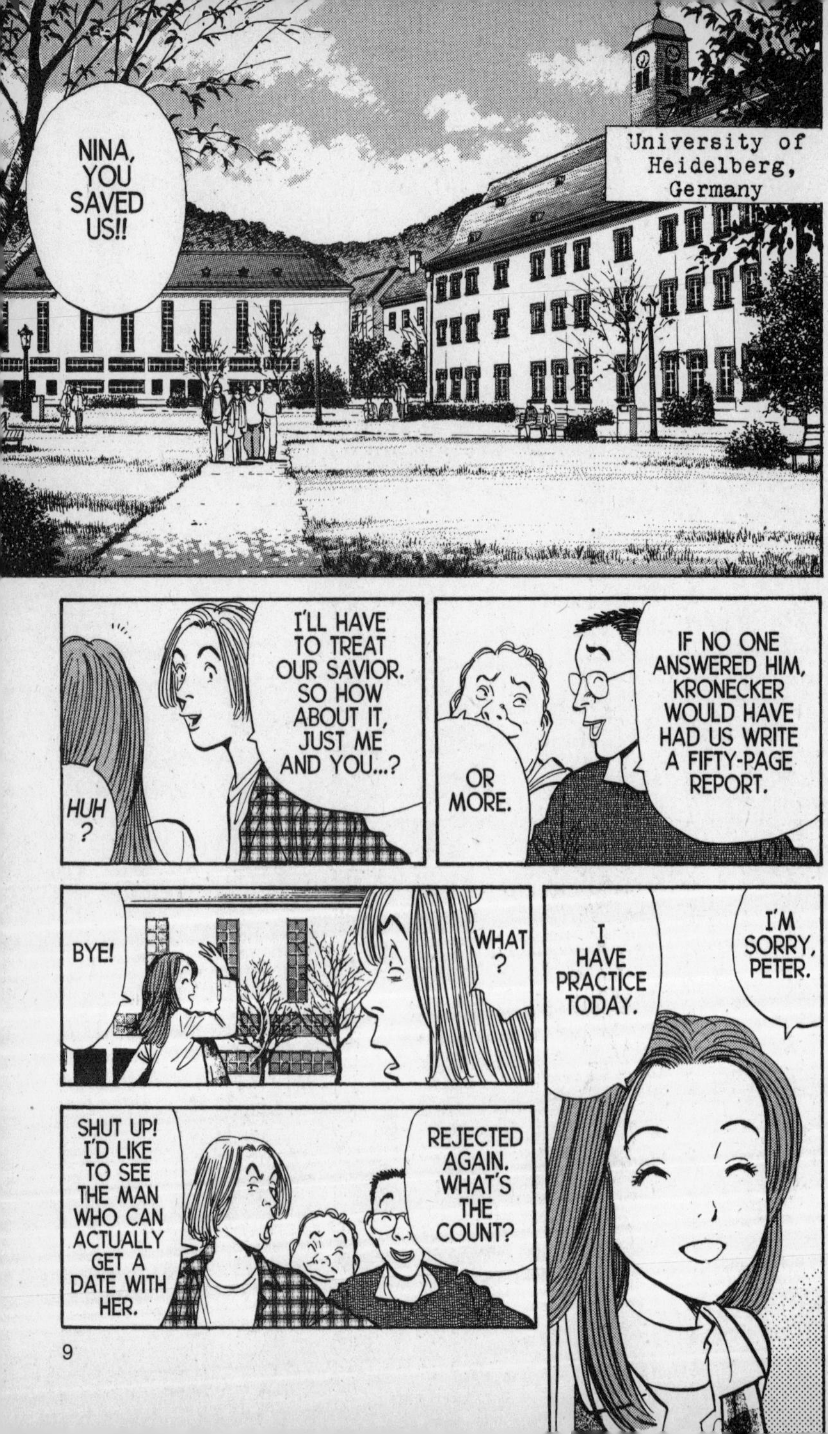
University of Heidelberg, Germany
NINA, YOU SAVED US!!
IF NO ONE ANSWERED HIM, KRONECKER WOULD HAVE HAD US WRITE A FIFTY-PAGE REPORT.
OR MORE.
I'LL HAVE TO TREAT OUR SAVIOR. SO HOW ABOUT IT, JUST ME AND YOU...?
HUH?
I'M SORRY, PETER.
I HAVE PRACTICE TODAY.
WHAT?
BYE!
REJECTED AGAIN. WHAT'S THE COUNT?
SHUT UP! I'D LIKE TO SEE THE MAN WHO CAN ACTUALLY GET A DATE WITH HER.

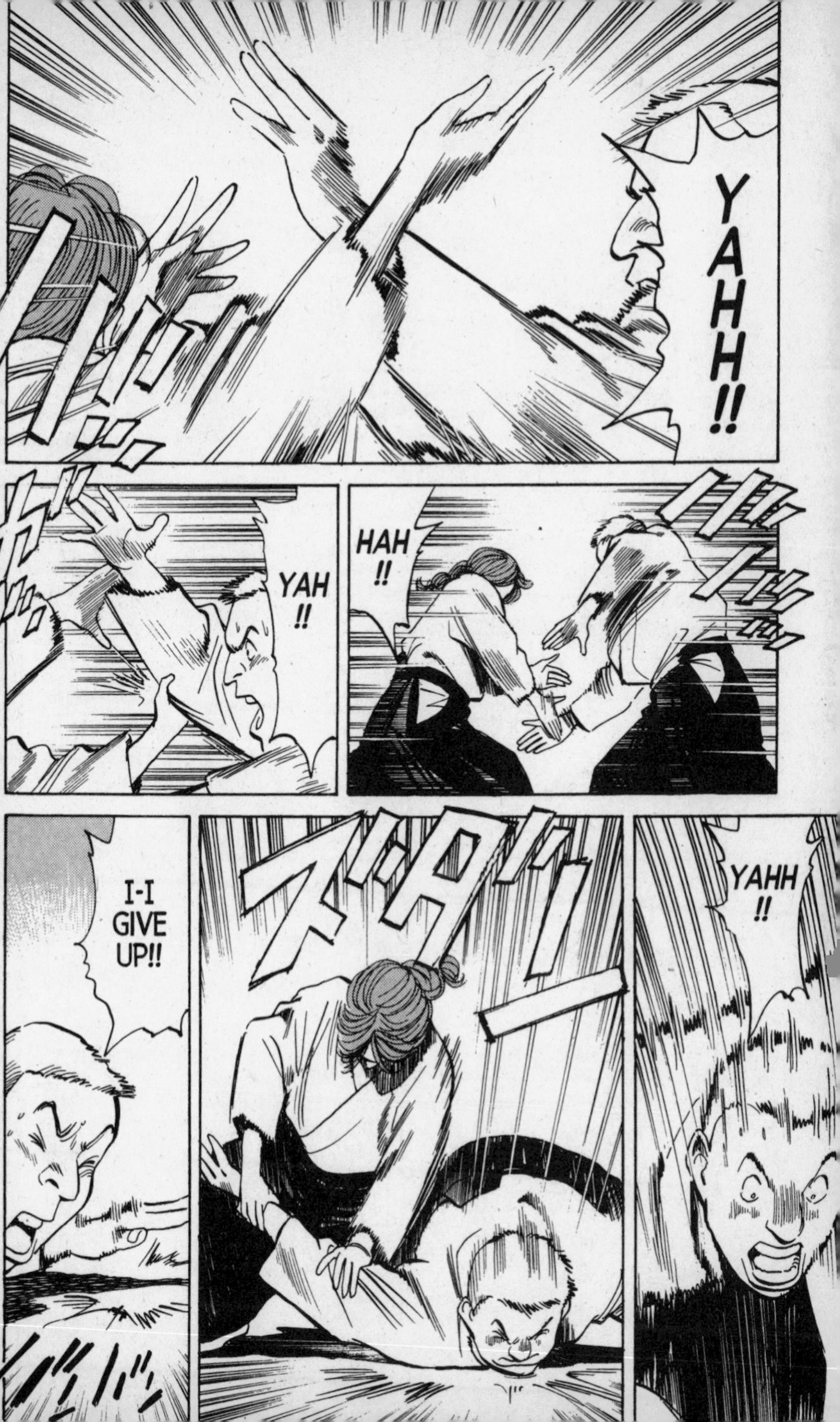
YAHH!!
HAH!!
YAH!!
YAHH!!
I-I GIVE UP!!

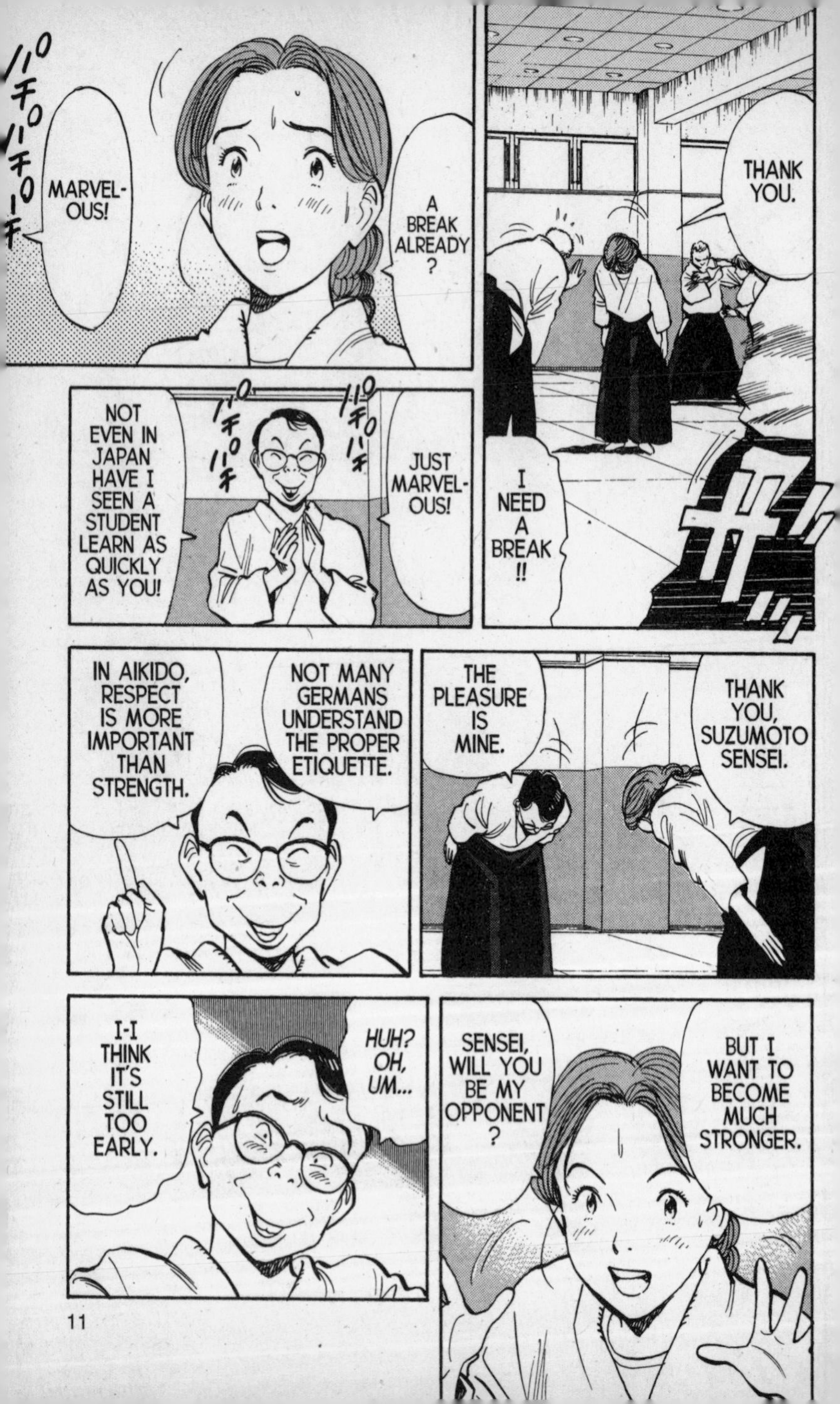
THANK YOU.
I NEED A BREAK !!
ザッ
A BREAK ALREADY ?
MARVEL-OUS!
パチパチパチパチ
JUST MARVEL-OUS!
NOT EVEN IN JAPAN HAVE I SEEN A STUDENT LEARN AS QUICKLY AS YOU!
パチパチ
THANK YOU, SUZUMOTO SENSEI.
THE PLEASURE IS MINE.
NOT MANY GERMANS UNDERSTAND THE PROPER ETIQUETTE.
IN AIKIDO, RESPECT IS MORE IMPORTANT THAN STRENGTH.
BUT I WANT TO BECOME MUCH STRONGER.
SENSEI, WILL YOU BE MY OPPONENT ?
HUH? OH, UM...
I-I THINK IT'S STILL TOO EARLY.

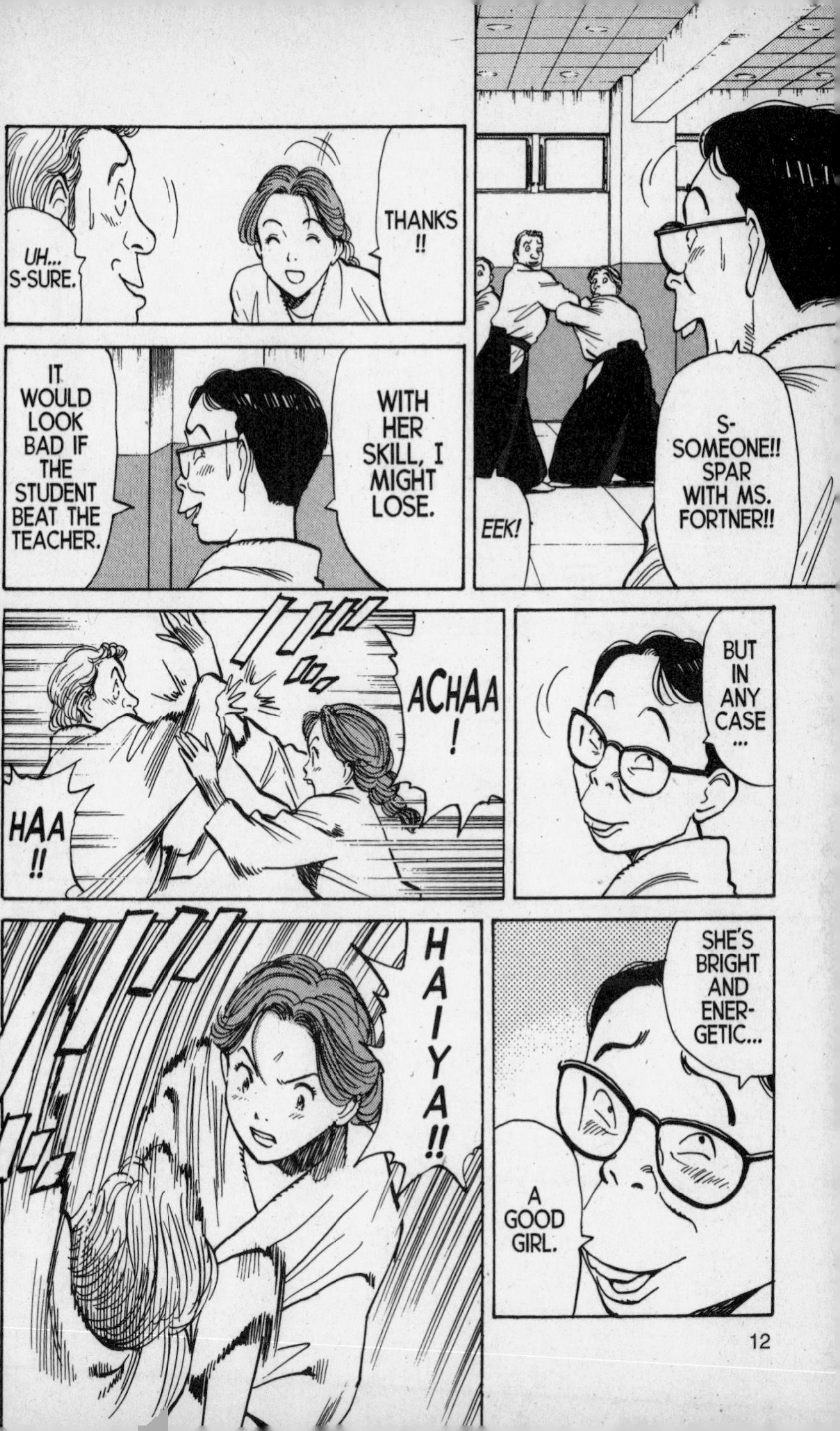
S-
SOMEONE!! SPAR WITH MS. FORTNER!!
EEK!
THANKS!!
UH... S-SURE.
WITH HER SKILL, I MIGHT LOSE.
IT WOULD LOOK BAD IF THE STUDENT BEAT THE TEACHER.
BUT IN ANY CASE...
ACHAA!
HAA!!
SHE'S BRIGHT AND ENER-GETIC...
A GOOD GIRL.
HAIYA!!

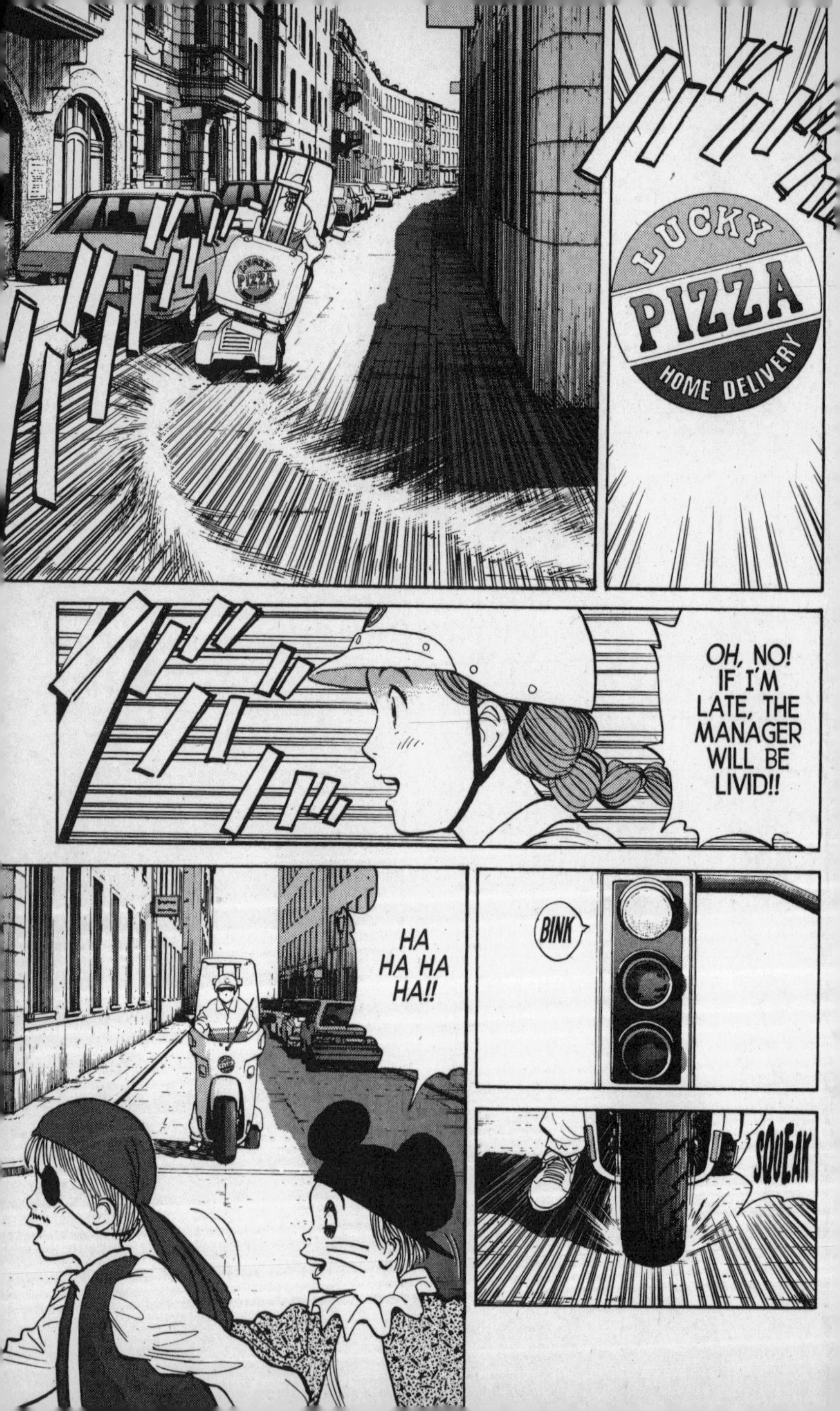
LUCKY
PIZZA
HOME DELIVERY
OH, NO! IF I'M LATE, THE MANAGER WILL BE LIVID!!
BINK
SQUEAK
HA HA HA HA!!

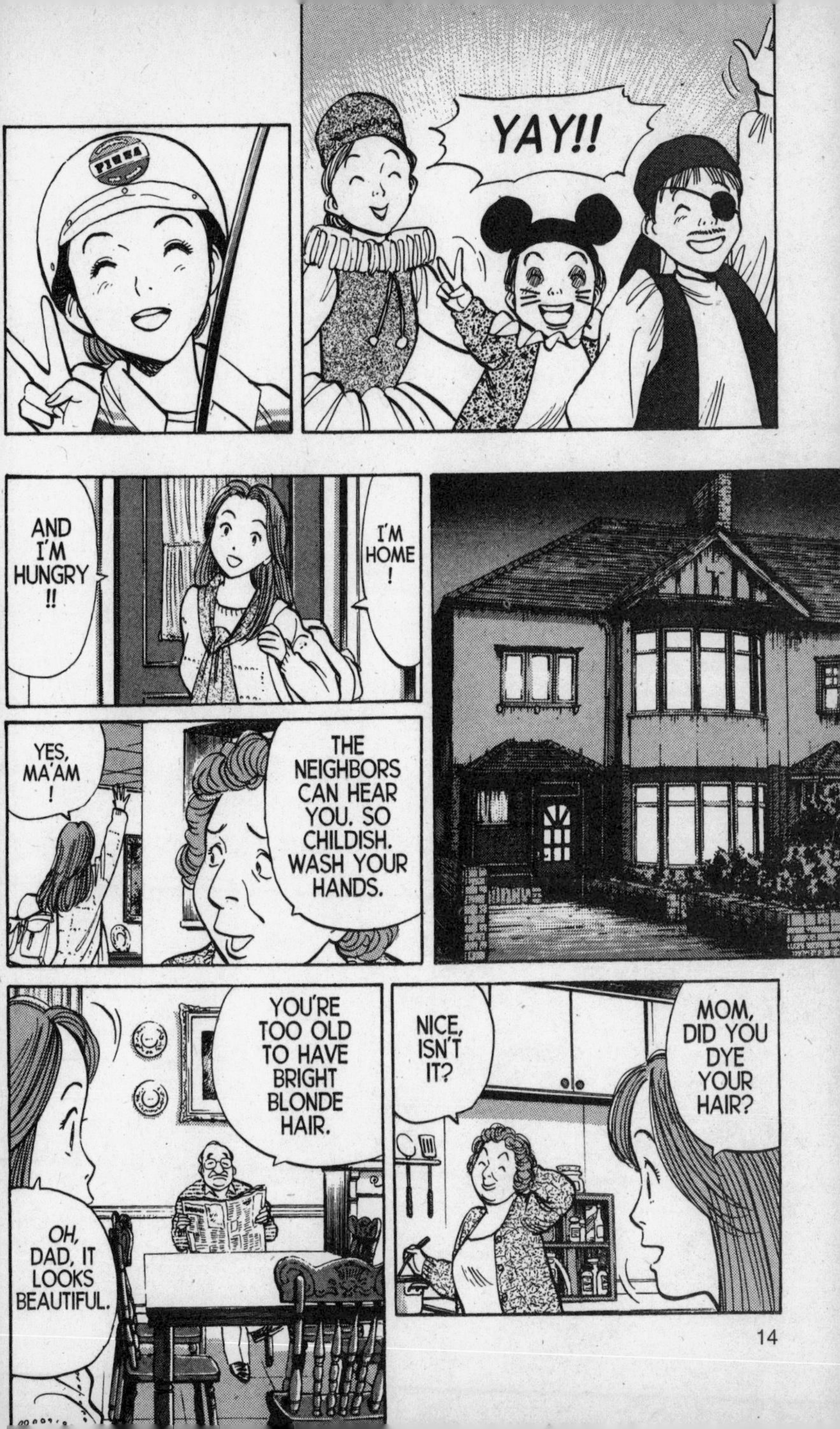
YAY!!
I'M HOME!
AND I'M HUNGRY!!
THE NEIGHBORS CAN HEAR YOU. SO CHILDISH. WASH YOUR HANDS.
YES, MA'AM!
MOM, DID YOU DYE YOUR HAIR?
NICE, ISN'T IT?
YOU'RE TOO OLD TO HAVE BRIGHT BLONDE HAIR.
OH, DAD, IT LOOKS BEAUTIFUL.

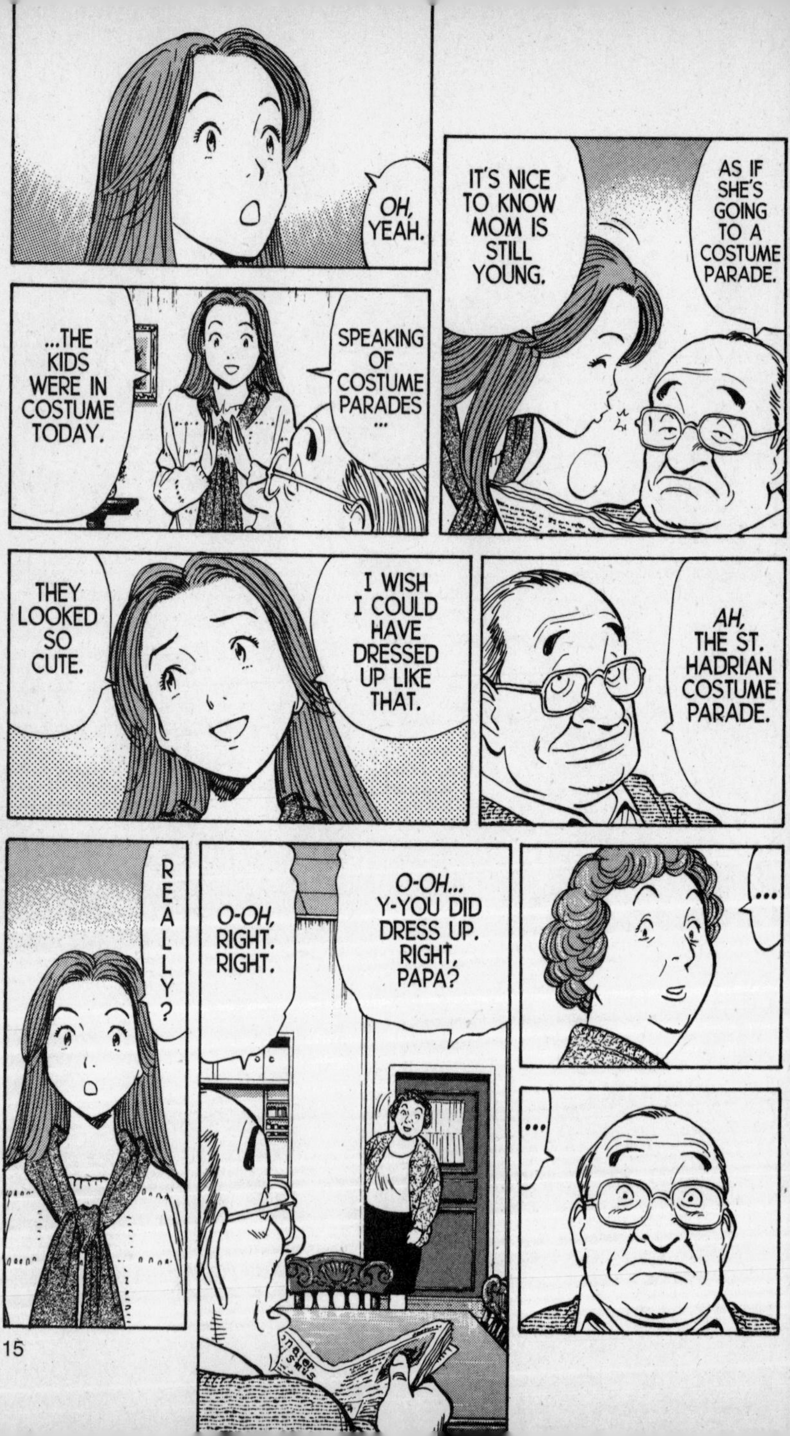
AS IF SHE'S GOING TO A COSTUME PARADE.
IT'S NICE TO KNOW MOM IS STILL YOUNG.
OH, YEAH.
SPEAKING OF COSTUME PARADES ...
...THE KIDS WERE IN COSTUME TODAY.
AH, THE ST. HADRIAN COSTUME PARADE.
I WISH I COULD HAVE DRESSED UP LIKE THAT.
THEY LOOKED SO CUTE.
...
...
O-OH... Y-YOU DID DRESS UP. RIGHT, PAPA?
O-OH, RIGHT. RIGHT.
REALLY?

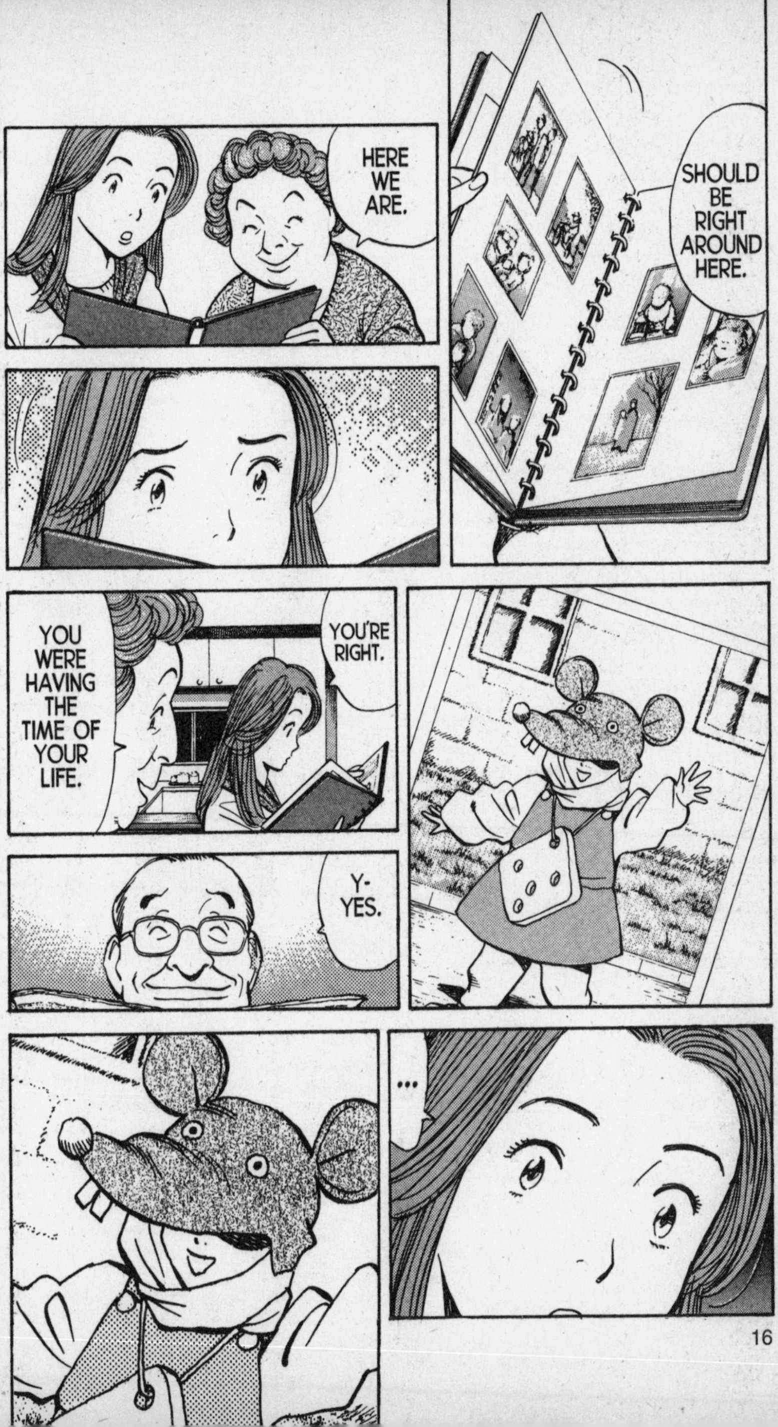
SHOULD BE RIGHT AROUND HERE.
HERE WE ARE.
YOU'RE RIGHT.
YOU WERE HAVING THE TIME OF YOUR LIFE.
Y-YES.
...

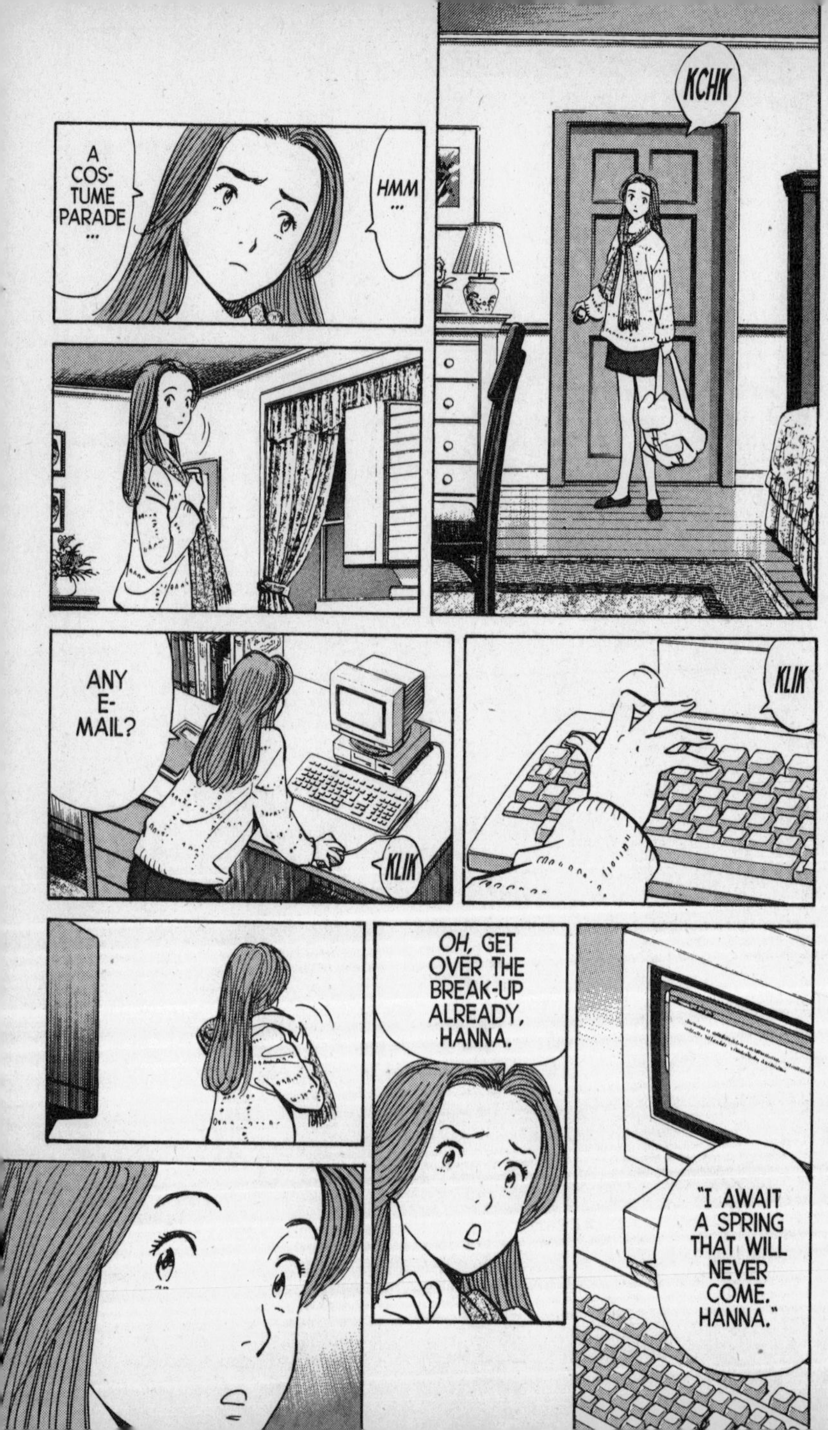
KCHK
HMM...
A COSTUME PARADE...
KLIK
ANY E-MAIL?
KLIK
"I AWAIT A SPRING THAT WILL NEVER COME. HANNA."
OH, GET OVER THE BREAK-UP ALREADY, HANNA.

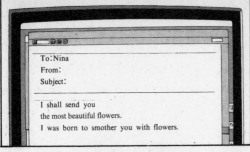

To: Nina
From:
Subject:

I shall send you
the most beautiful flowers.
I was born to smother you with flowers.

"I WAS BORN TO SMOTHER YOU WITH FLOWERS."

"I SHALL SEND YOU THE MOST BEAUTIFUL FLOWERS.

NOT BAD, PETER.

AH-HA!

WOW!

WHO SENT THIS?

HOW HAVE YOU BEEN, NINA?

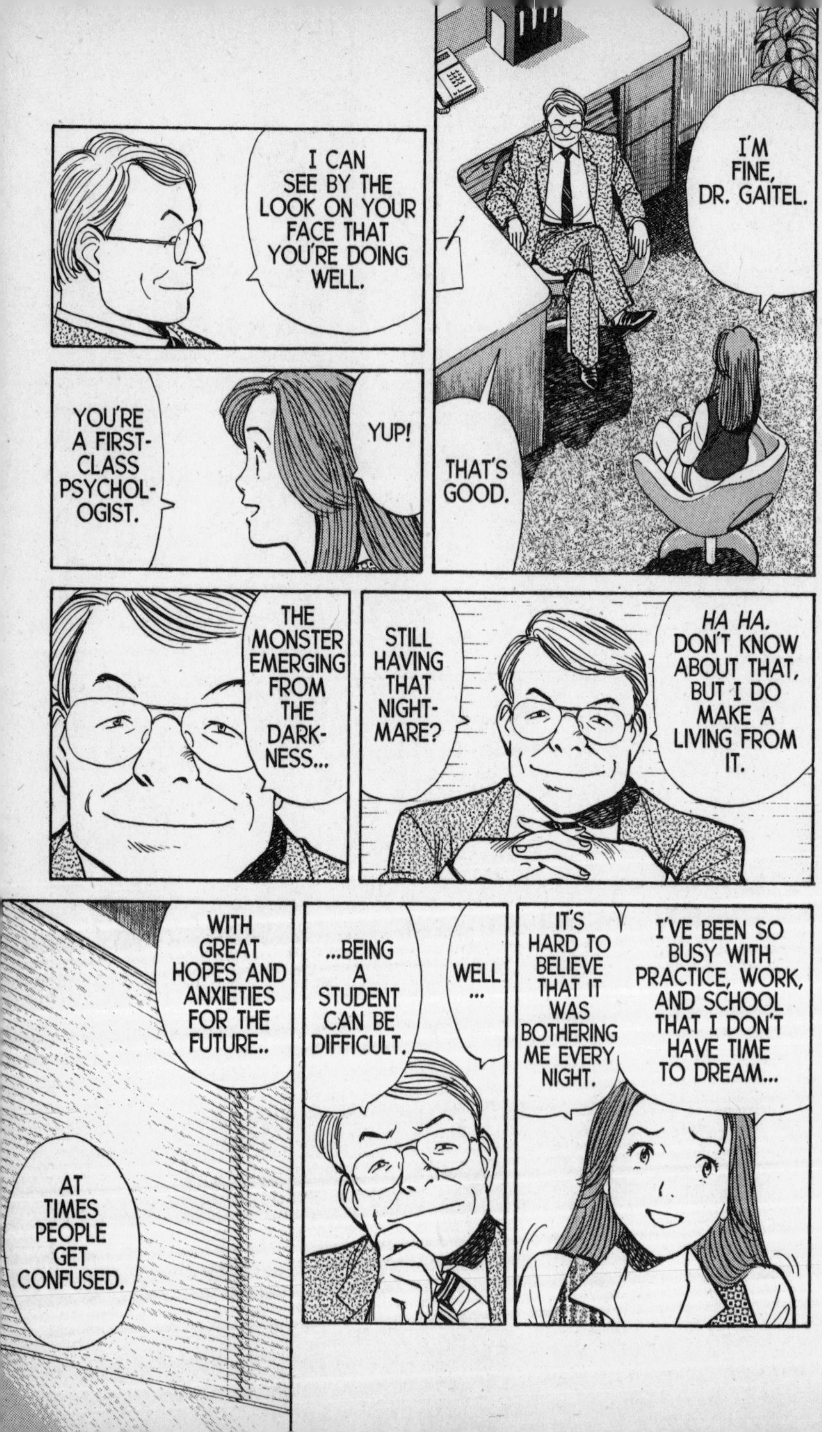
I'M FINE, DR. GAITEL.
THAT'S GOOD.
I CAN SEE BY THE LOOK ON YOUR FACE THAT YOU'RE DOING WELL.
YUP!
YOU'RE A FIRST-CLASS PSYCHOLOGIST.
HA HA. DON'T KNOW ABOUT THAT, BUT I DO MAKE A LIVING FROM IT.
STILL HAVING THAT NIGHTMARE?
THE MONSTER EMERGING FROM THE DARKNESS...
I'VE BEEN SO BUSY WITH PRACTICE, WORK, AND SCHOOL THAT I DON'T HAVE TIME TO DREAM...
IT'S HARD TO BELIEVE THAT IT WAS BOTHERING ME EVERY NIGHT.
WELL ...
...BEING A STUDENT CAN BE DIFFICULT.
WITH GREAT HOPES AND ANXIETIES FOR THE FUTURE..
AT TIMES PEOPLE GET CONFUSED.

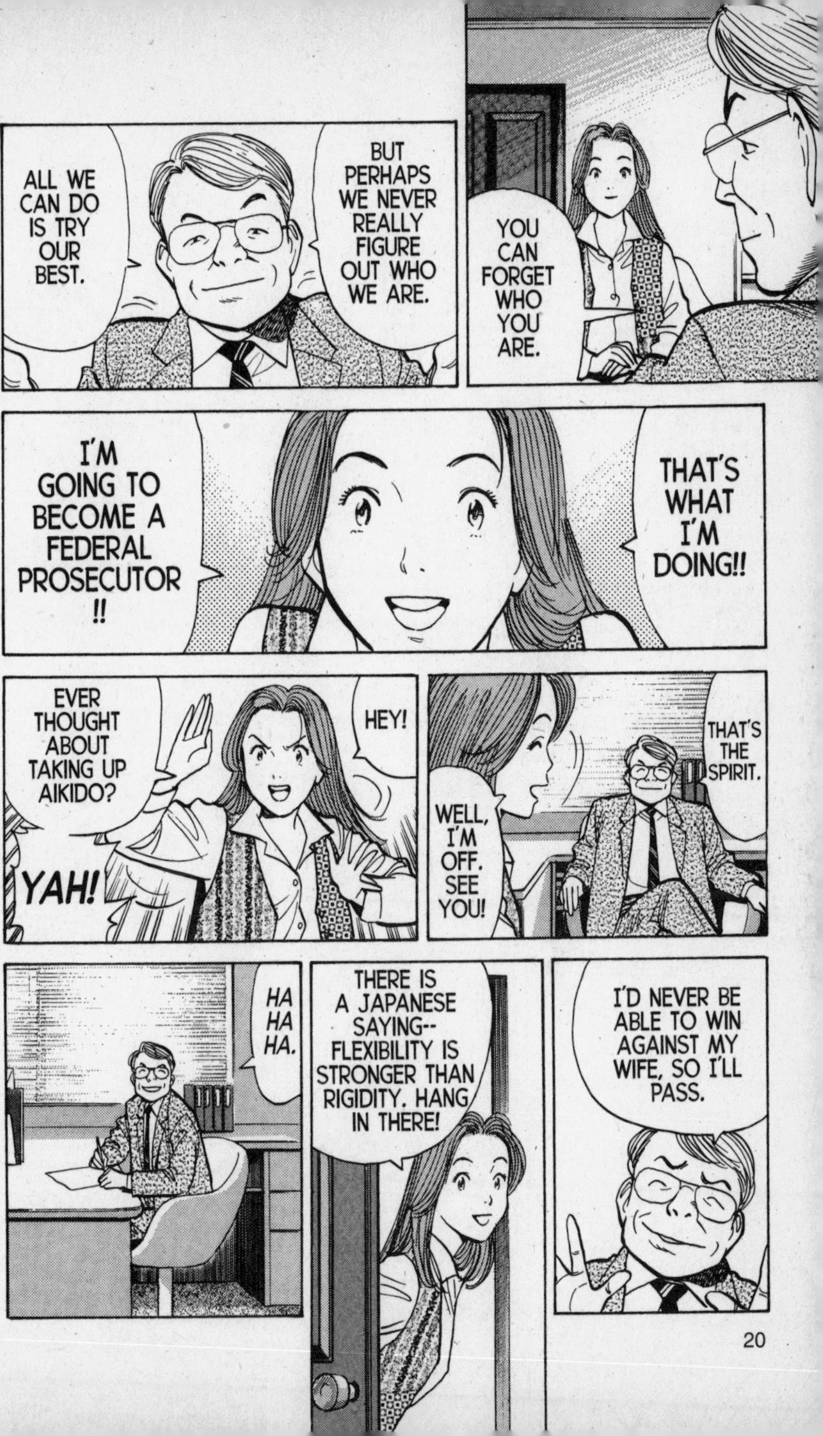
ALL WE CAN DO IS TRY OUR BEST.
BUT PERHAPS WE NEVER REALLY FIGURE OUT WHO WE ARE.
YOU CAN FORGET WHO YOU ARE.
I'M GOING TO BECOME A FEDERAL PROSECUTOR!!
THAT'S WHAT I'M DOING!!
HEY!
EVER THOUGHT ABOUT TAKING UP AIKIDO?
YAH!
THAT'S THE SPIRIT.
WELL, I'M OFF. SEE YOU!
HA HA HA.
THERE IS A JAPANESE SAYING-- FLEXIBILITY IS STRONGER THAN RIGIDITY. HANG IN THERE!
I'D NEVER BE ABLE TO WIN AGAINST MY WIFE, SO I'LL PASS.

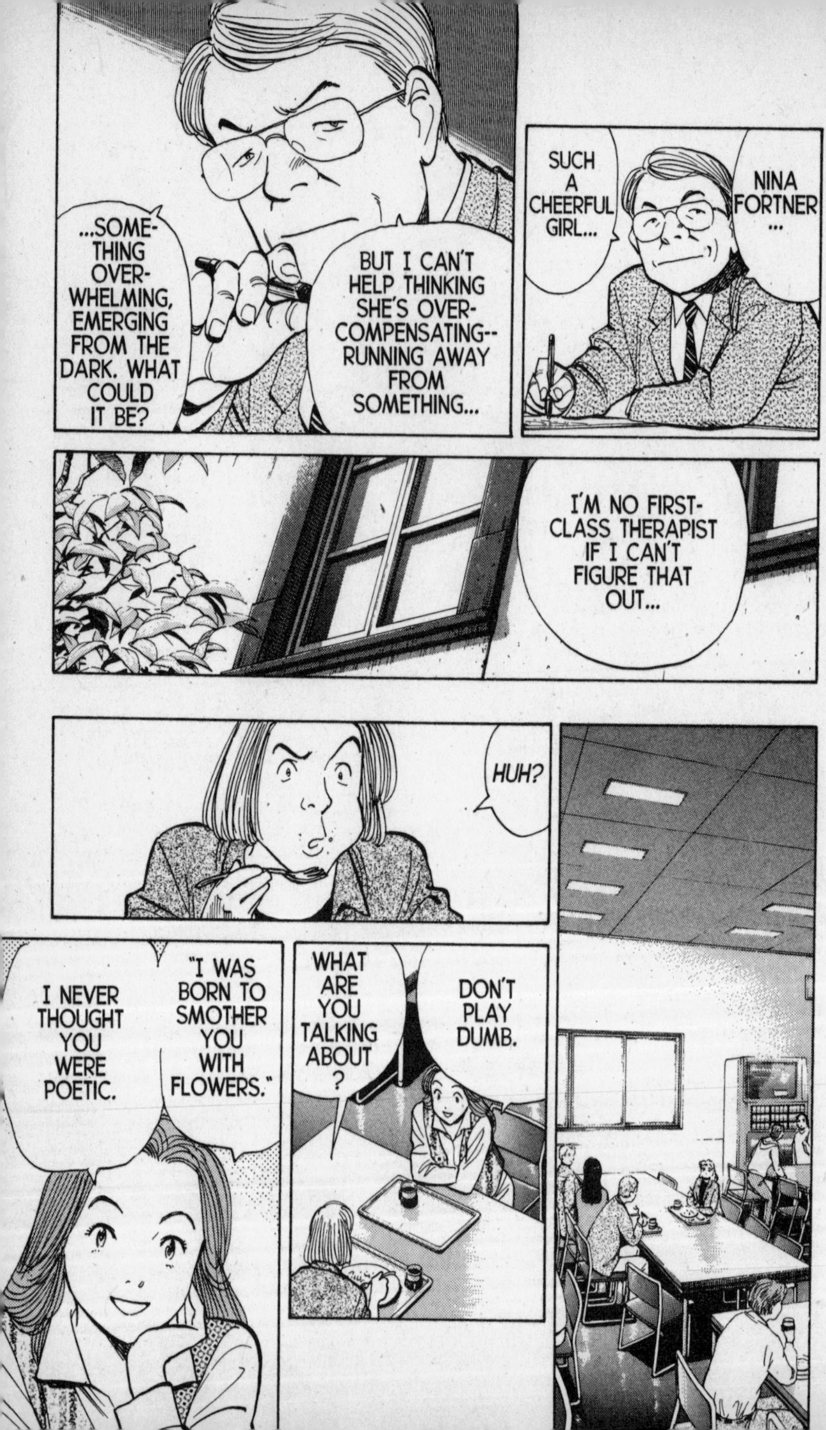
NINA FORTNER...
SUCH A CHEERFUL GIRL...
BUT I CAN'T HELP THINKING SHE'S OVER-COMPENSATING--RUNNING AWAY FROM SOMETHING...
...SOME-THING OVER-WHELMING, EMERGING FROM THE DARK. WHAT COULD IT BE?
I'M NO FIRST-CLASS THERAPIST IF I CAN'T FIGURE THAT OUT...
HUH?
DON'T PLAY DUMB.
WHAT ARE YOU TALKING ABOUT?
"I WAS BORN TO SMOTHER YOU WITH FLOWERS."
I NEVER THOUGHT YOU WERE POETIC.

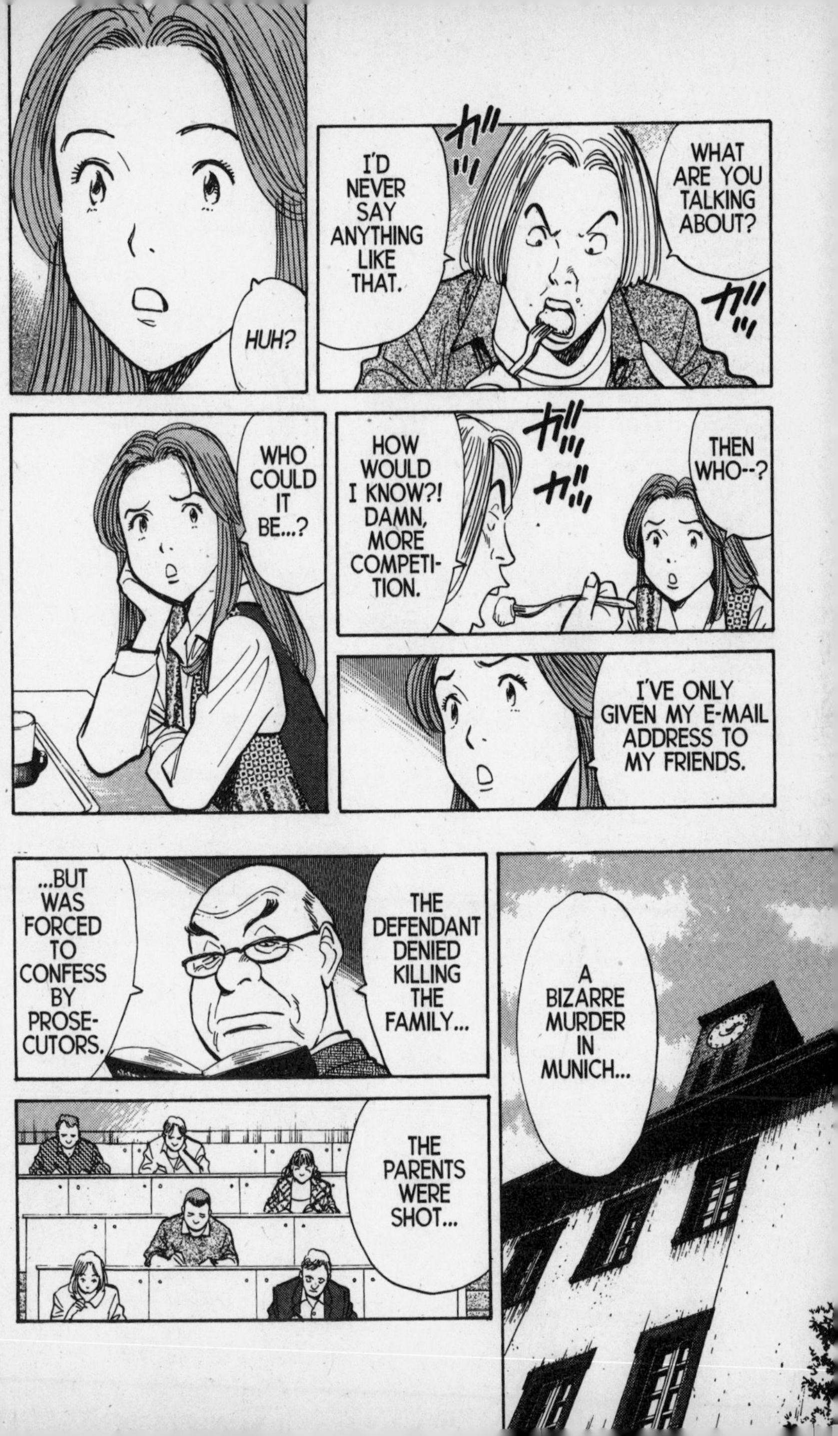
WHAT ARE YOU TALKING ABOUT?
I'D NEVER SAY ANYTHING LIKE THAT.
HUH?
THEN WHO--?
HOW WOULD I KNOW?! DAMN, MORE COMPETITION.
I'VE ONLY GIVEN MY E-MAIL ADDRESS TO MY FRIENDS.
WHO COULD IT BE...?
A BIZARRE MURDER IN MUNICH...
THE DEFENDANT DENIED KILLING THE FAMILY...
...BUT WAS FORCED TO CONFESS BY PROSECUTORS.
THE PARENTS WERE SHOT...

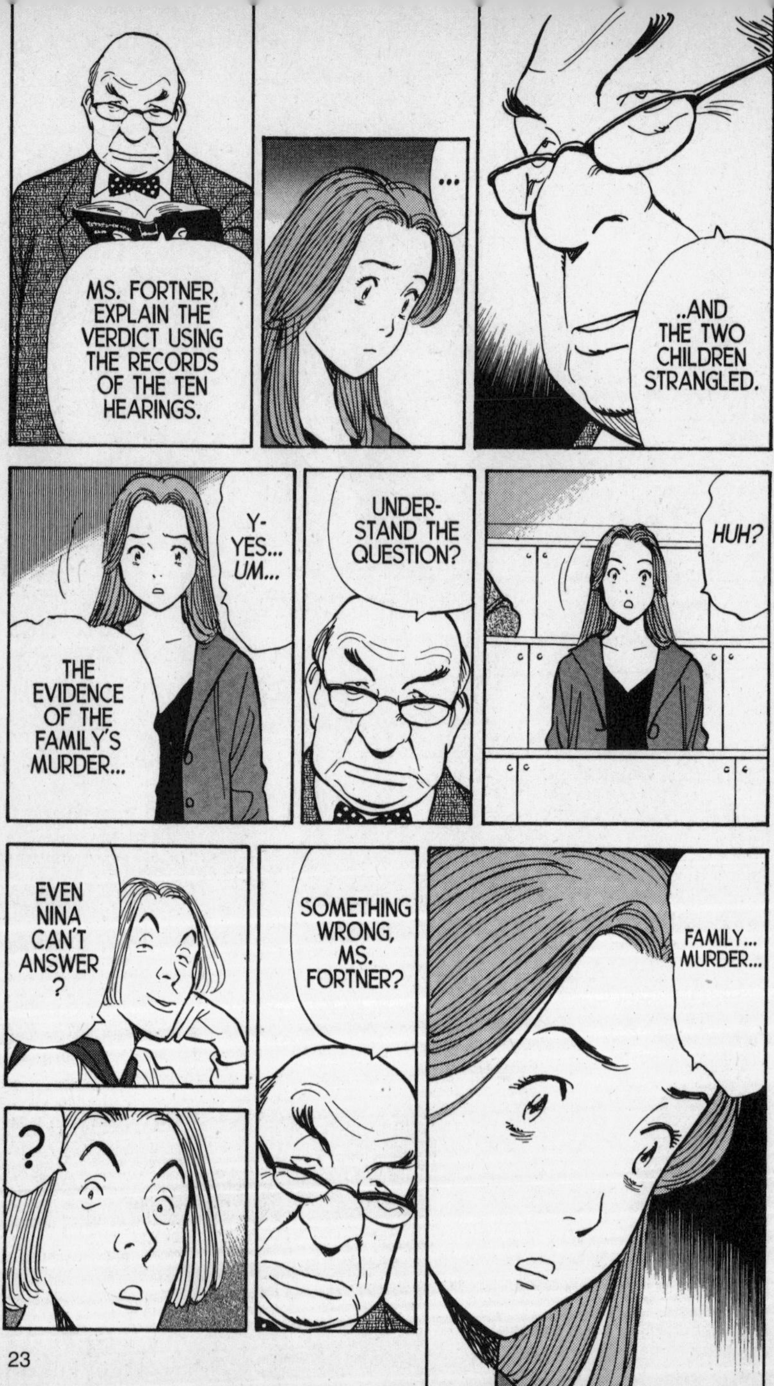
..AND THE TWO CHILDREN STRANGLED.
...
MS. FORTNER, EXPLAIN THE VERDICT USING THE RECORDS OF THE TEN HEARINGS.
HUH?
UNDER-STAND THE QUESTION?
Y-YES... *UM...*
THE EVIDENCE OF THE FAMILY'S MURDER...
FAMILY... MURDER...
SOMETHING WRONG, MS. FORTNER?
EVEN NINA CAN'T ANSWER?
?

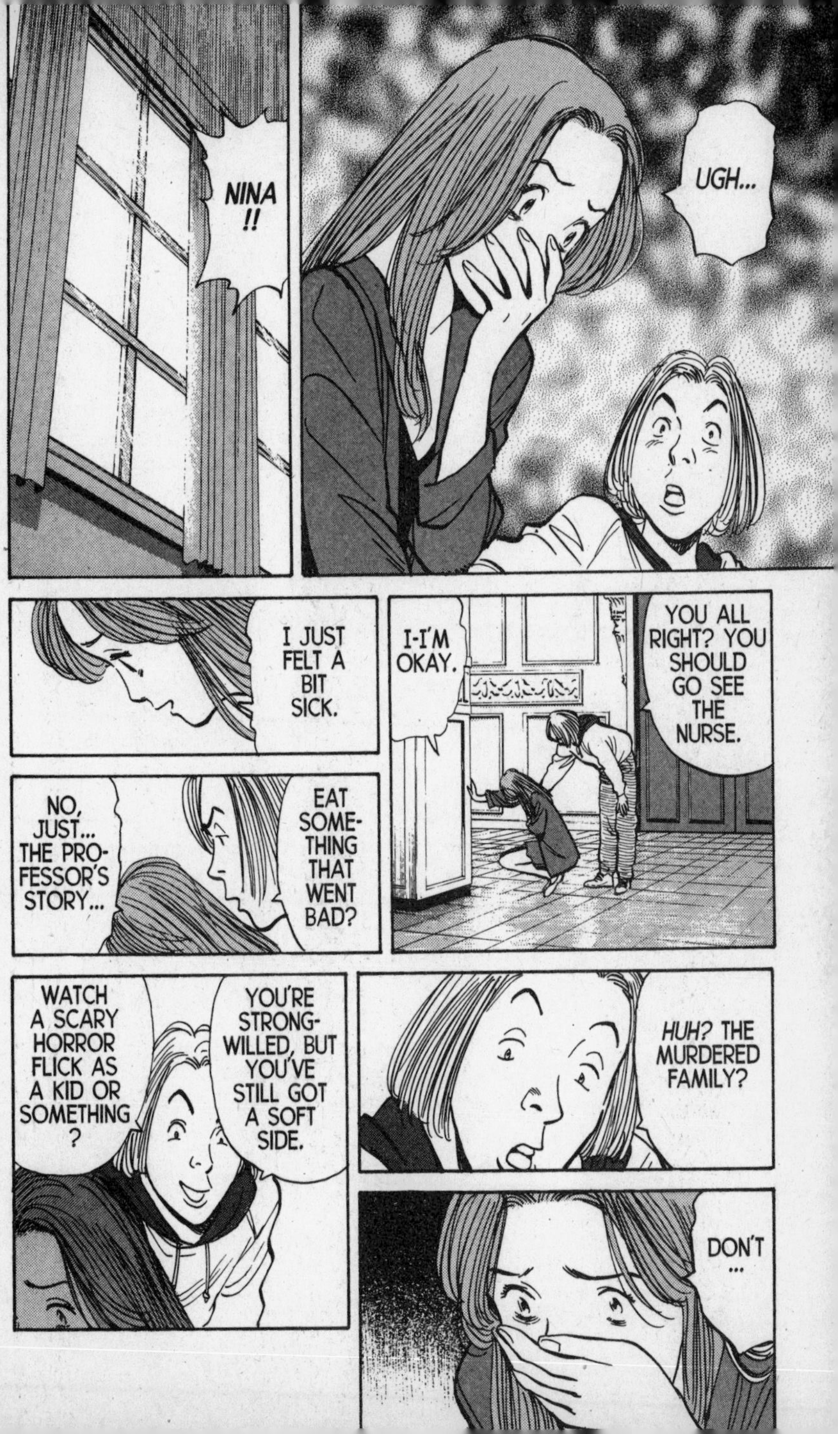
UGH...
NINA !!
YOU ALL RIGHT? YOU SHOULD GO SEE THE NURSE.
I-I'M OKAY.
I JUST FELT A BIT SICK.
EAT SOME-THING THAT WENT BAD?
NO, JUST... THE PRO-FESSOR'S STORY...
YOU'RE STRONG-WILLED, BUT YOU'VE STILL GOT A SOFT SIDE.
WATCH A SCARY HORROR FLICK AS A KID OR SOMETHING ?
HUH? THE MURDERED FAMILY?
DON'T ...

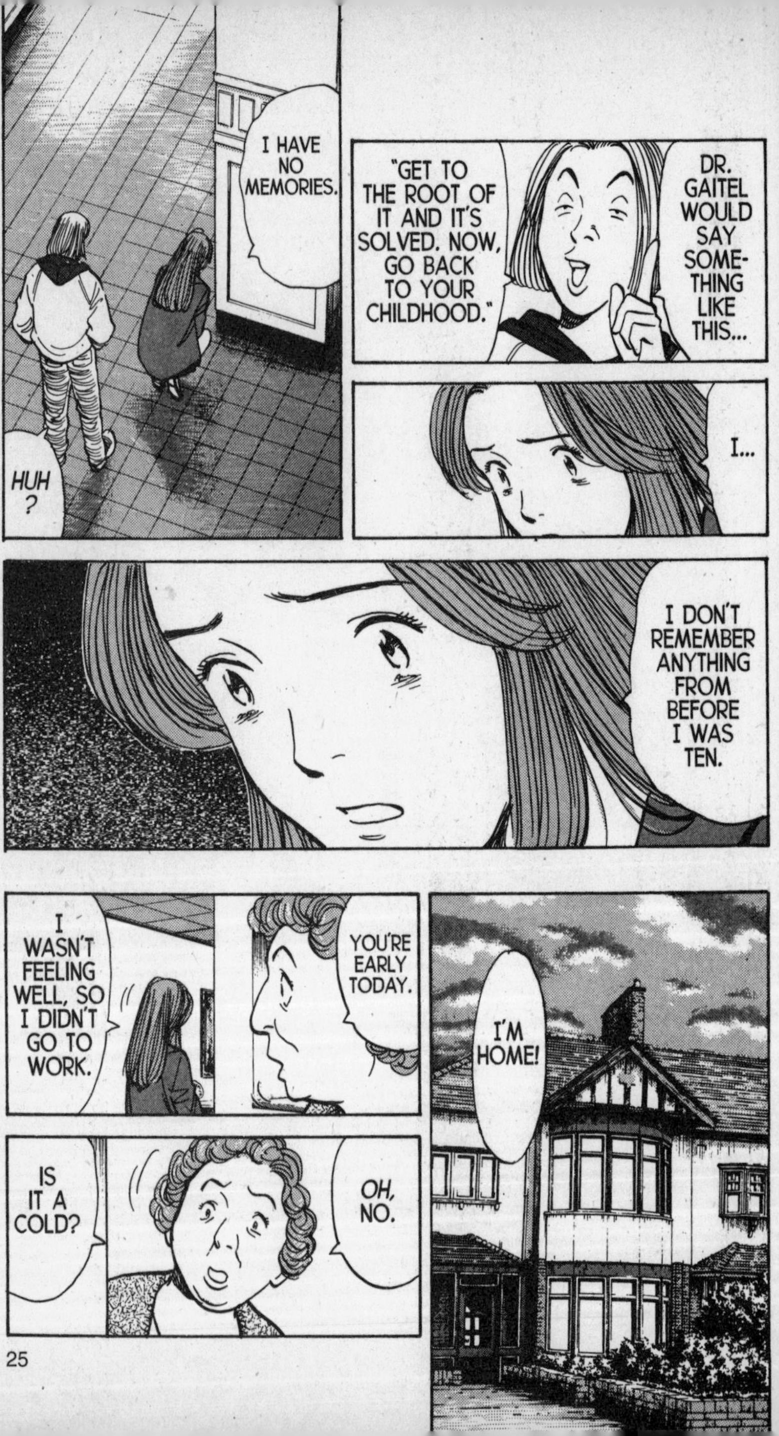
DR. GAITEL WOULD SAY SOME-THING LIKE THIS...
"GET TO THE ROOT OF IT AND IT'S SOLVED. NOW, GO BACK TO YOUR CHILDHOOD."
I...
I HAVE NO MEMORIES.
HUH?
I DON'T REMEMBER ANYTHING FROM BEFORE I WAS TEN.
I'M HOME!
YOU'RE EARLY TODAY.
I WASN'T FEELING WELL, SO I DIDN'T GO TO WORK.
OH, NO.
IS IT A COLD?

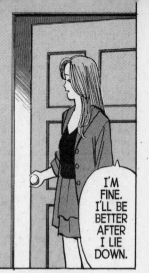

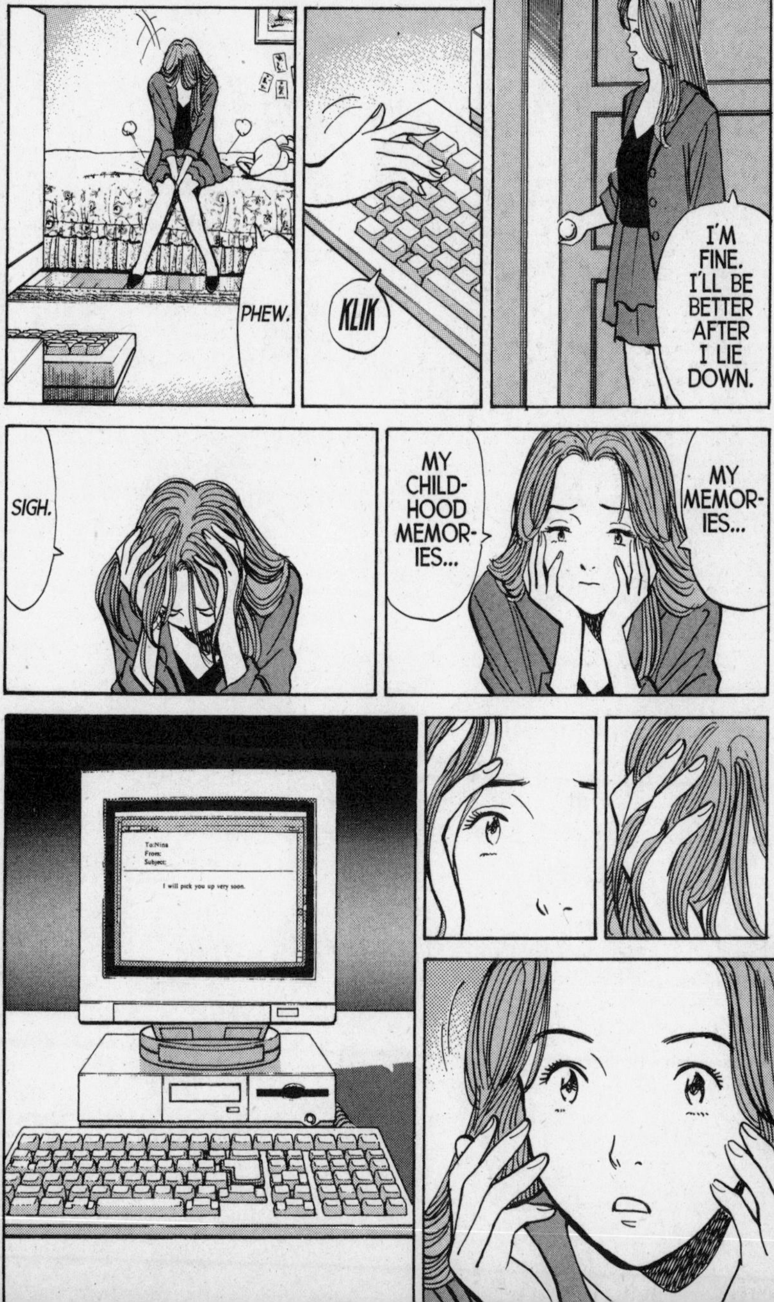
I'M FINE. I'LL BE BETTER AFTER I LIE DOWN.
KLIK
PHEW.
MY MEMORIES...
MY CHILDHOOD MEMORIES...
SIGH.
To:Nina
From:
Subject:
I will pick you up very soon.

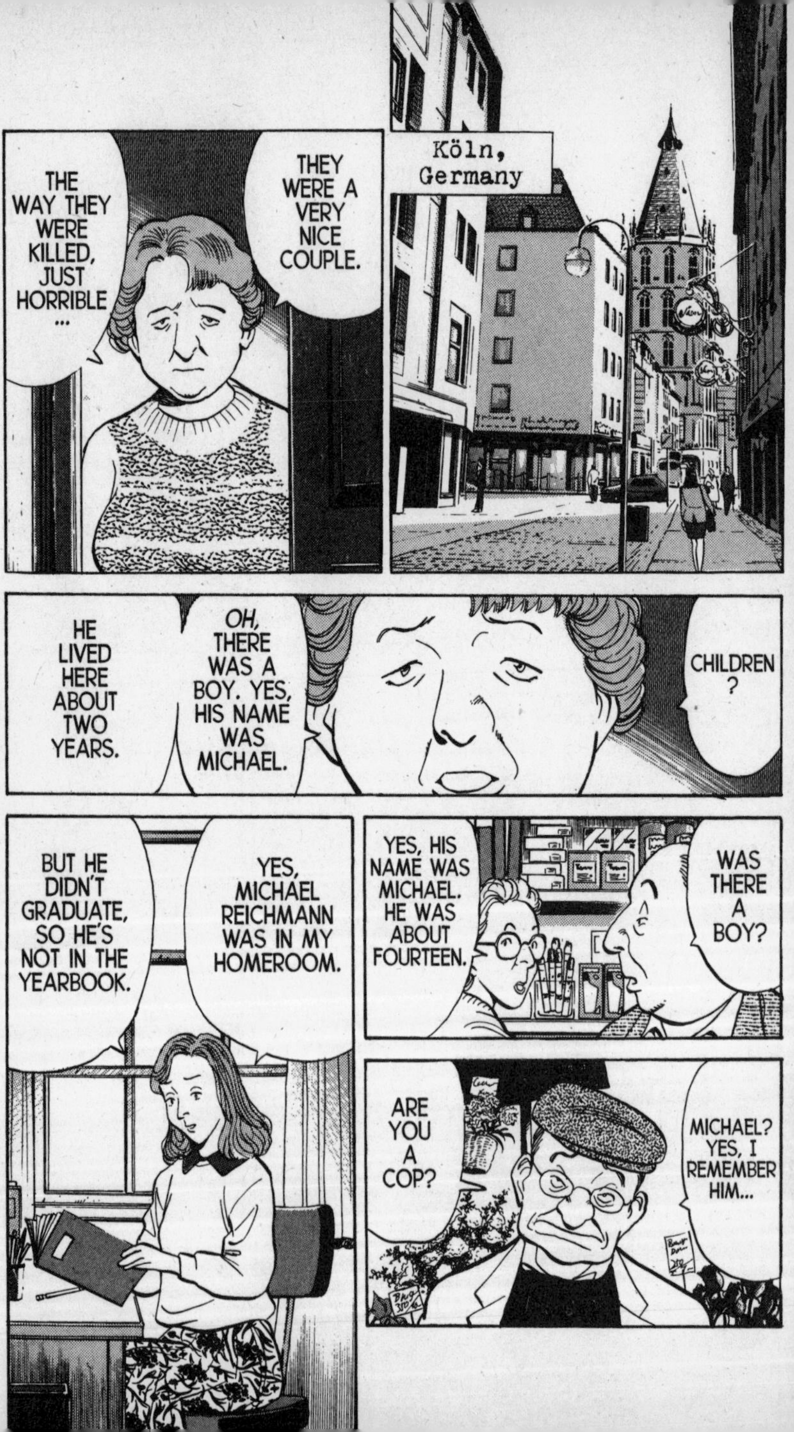
Köln, Germany
THEY WERE A VERY NICE COUPLE.
THE WAY THEY WERE KILLED, JUST HORRIBLE ...
CHILDREN?
OH, THERE WAS A BOY. YES, HIS NAME WAS MICHAEL.
HE LIVED HERE ABOUT TWO YEARS.
WAS THERE A BOY?
YES, HIS NAME WAS MICHAEL. HE WAS ABOUT FOURTEEN.
MICHAEL? YES, I REMEMBER HIM...
ARE YOU A COP?
YES, MICHAEL REICHMANN WAS IN MY HOMEROOM.
BUT HE DIDN'T GRADUATE, SO HE'S NOT IN THE YEARBOOK.

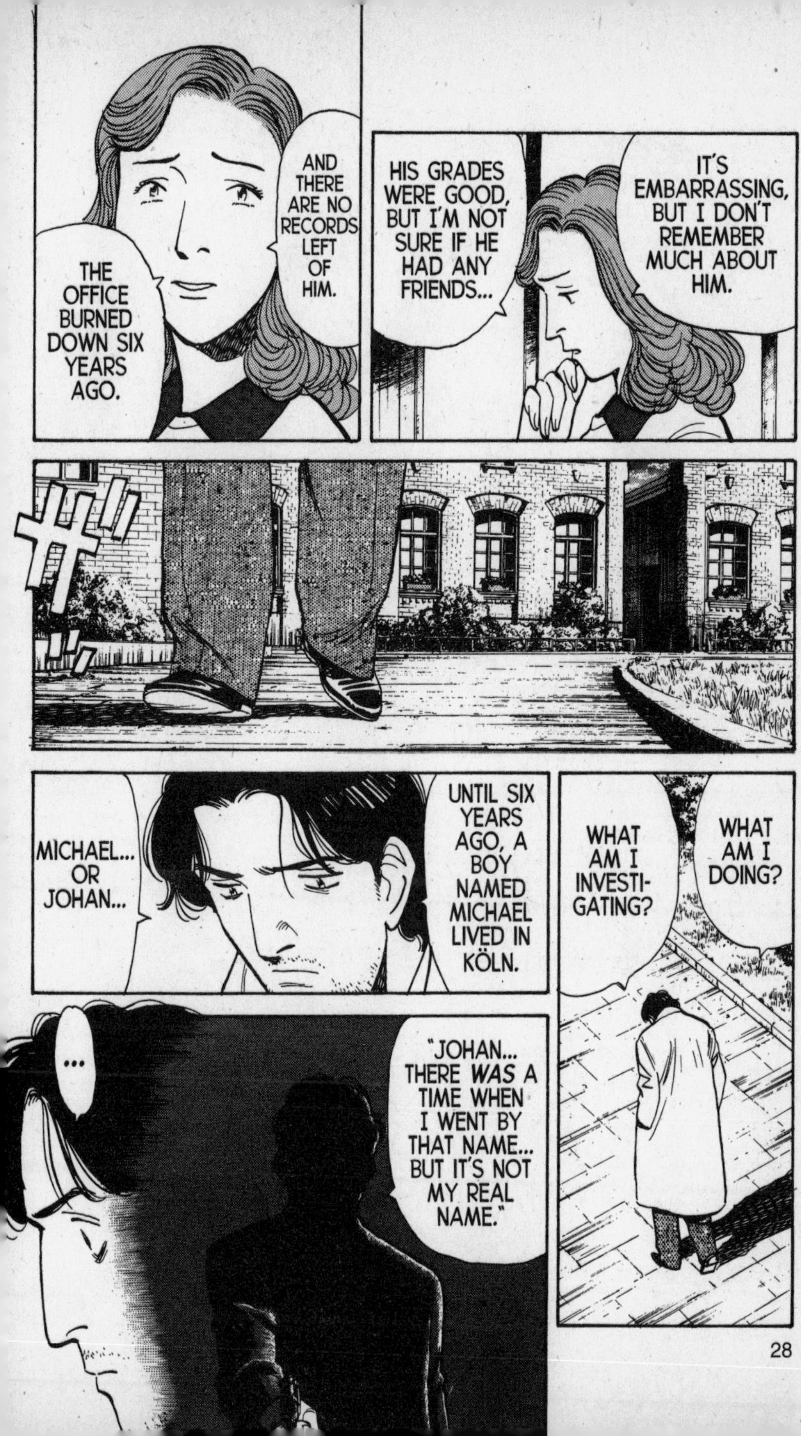
IT'S EMBARRASSING, BUT I DON'T REMEMBER MUCH ABOUT HIM.
HIS GRADES WERE GOOD, BUT I'M NOT SURE IF HE HAD ANY FRIENDS...
AND THERE ARE NO RECORDS LEFT OF HIM.
THE OFFICE BURNED DOWN SIX YEARS AGO.
WHAT AM I DOING?
WHAT AM I INVESTIGATING?
UNTIL SIX YEARS AGO, A BOY NAMED MICHAEL LIVED IN KÖLN.
MICHAEL... OR JOHAN...
"JOHAN... THERE *WAS* A TIME WHEN I WENT BY THAT NAME... BUT IT'S NOT MY REAL NAME."
...

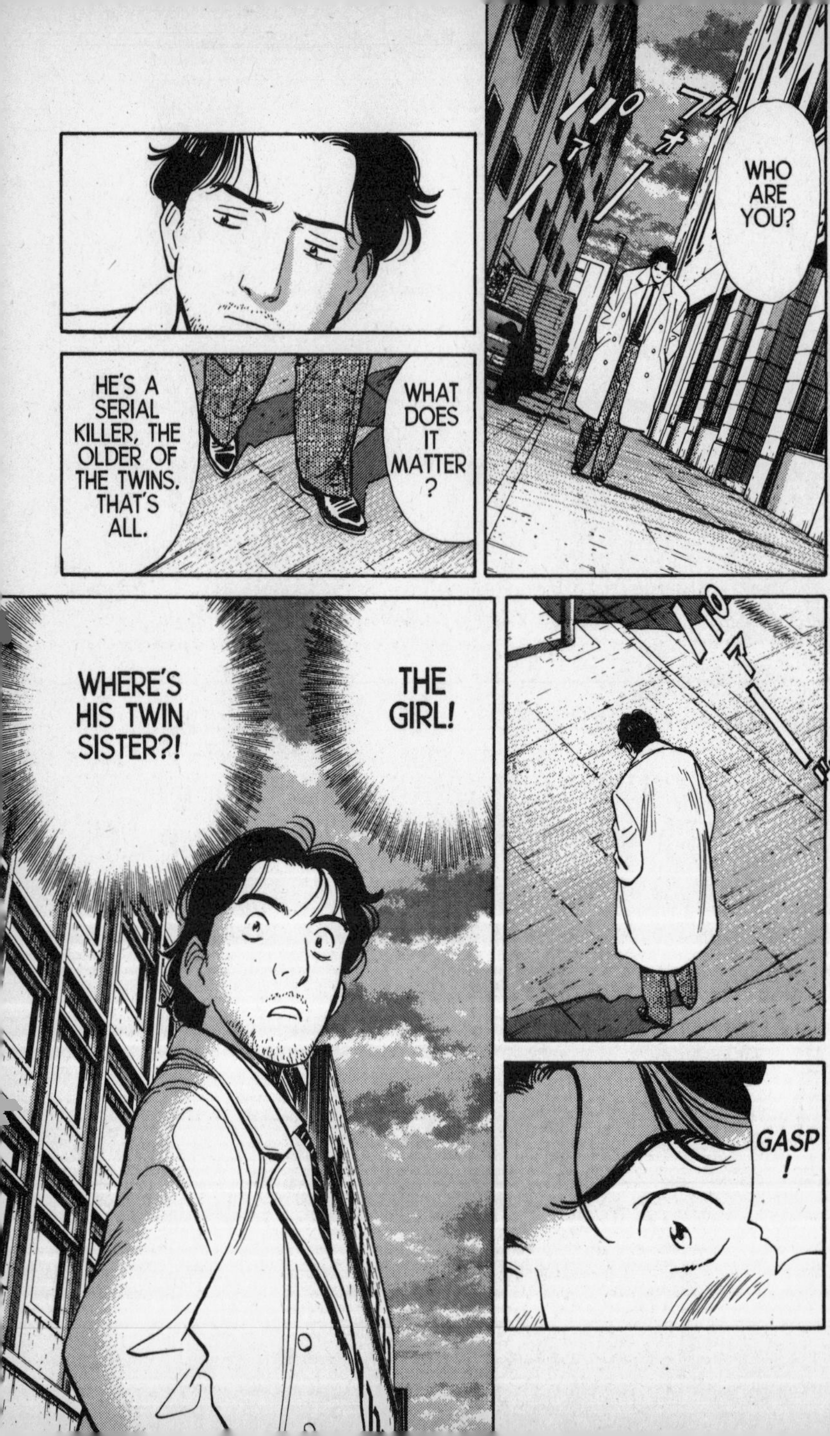
WHO ARE YOU?
WHAT DOES IT MATTER?
HE'S A SERIAL KILLER, THE OLDER OF THE TWINS. THAT'S ALL.
GASP!
THE GIRL!
WHERE'S HIS TWIN SISTER?!

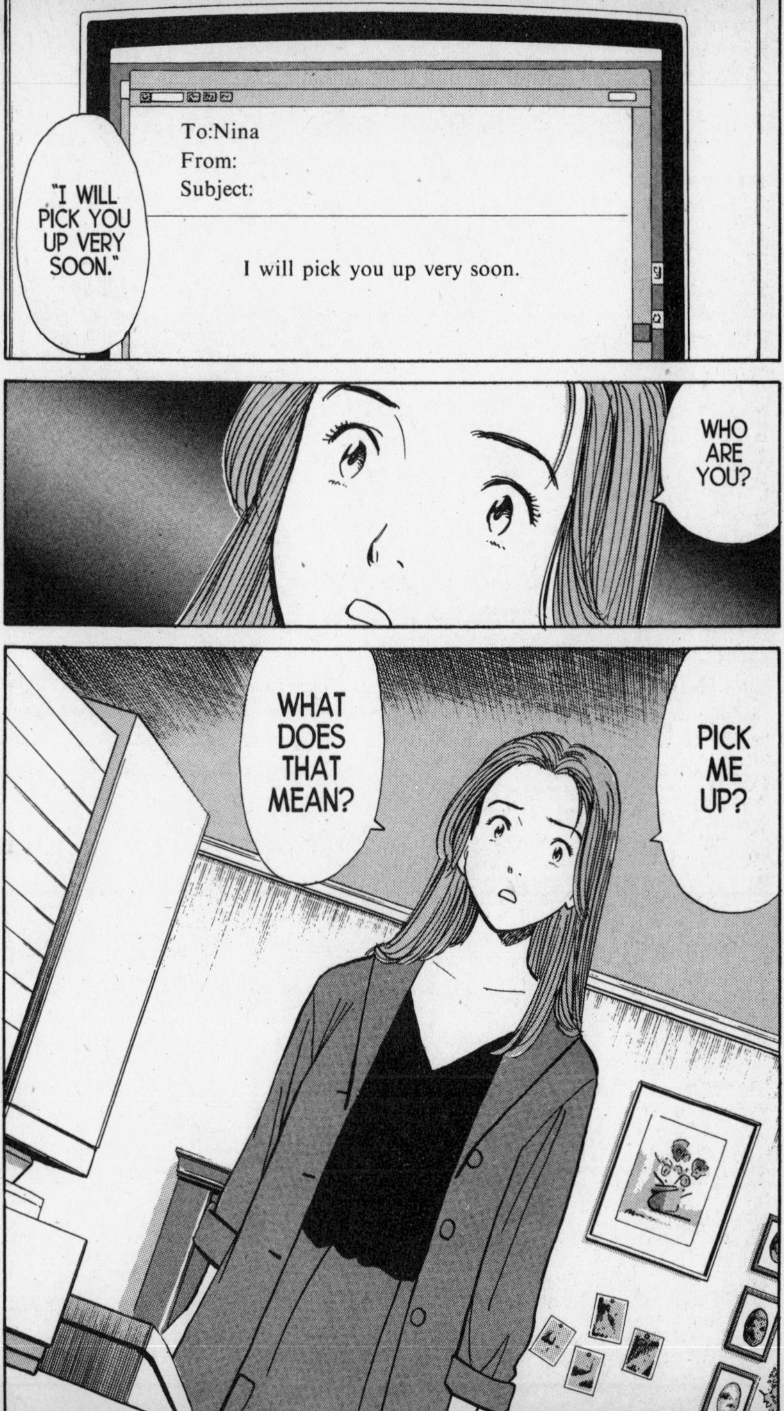
To:Nina
From:
Subject:
I will pick you up very soon.
"I WILL PICK YOU UP VERY SOON."
WHO ARE YOU?
PICK ME UP?
WHAT DOES THAT MEAN?

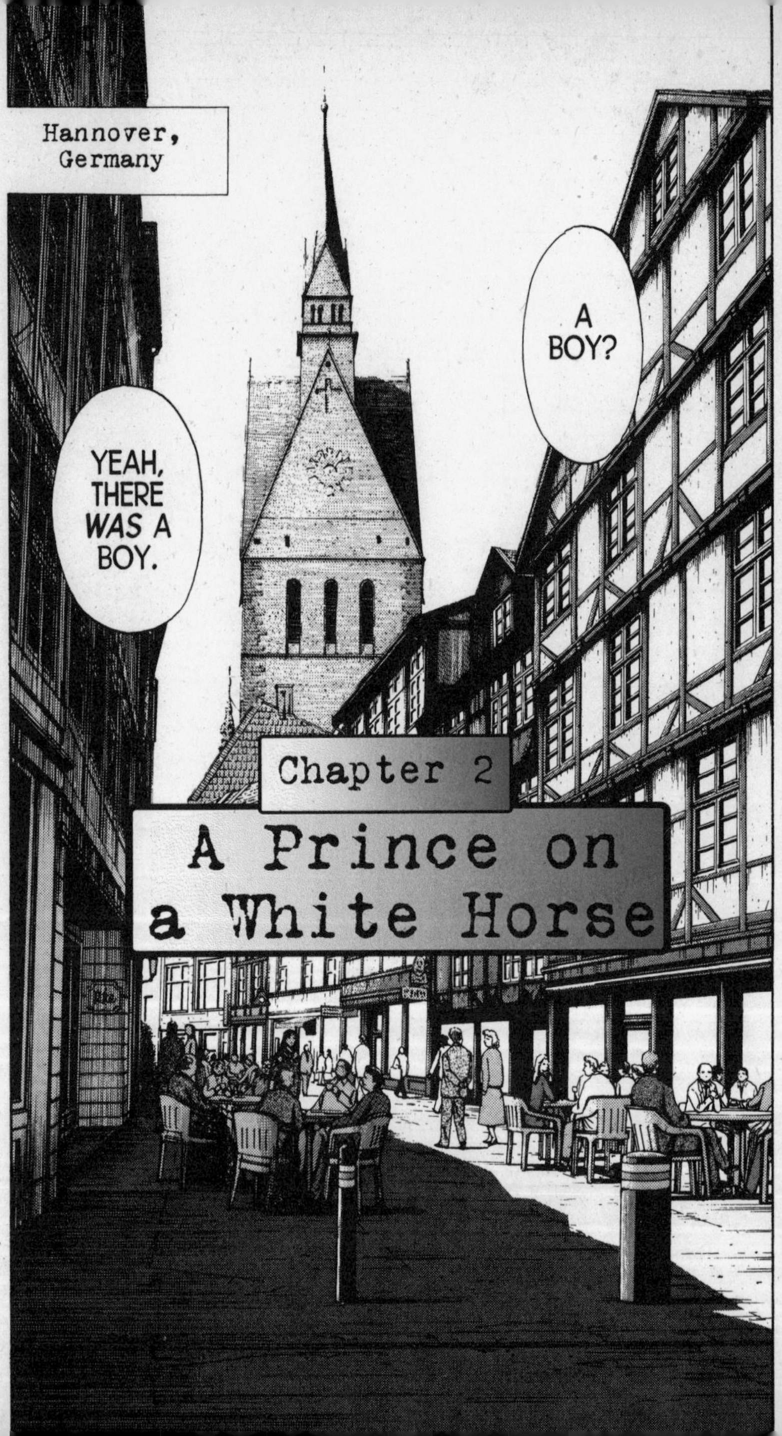
Hannover, Germany
A BOY?
YEAH, THERE WAS A BOY.
Chapter 2
A Prince on a White Horse

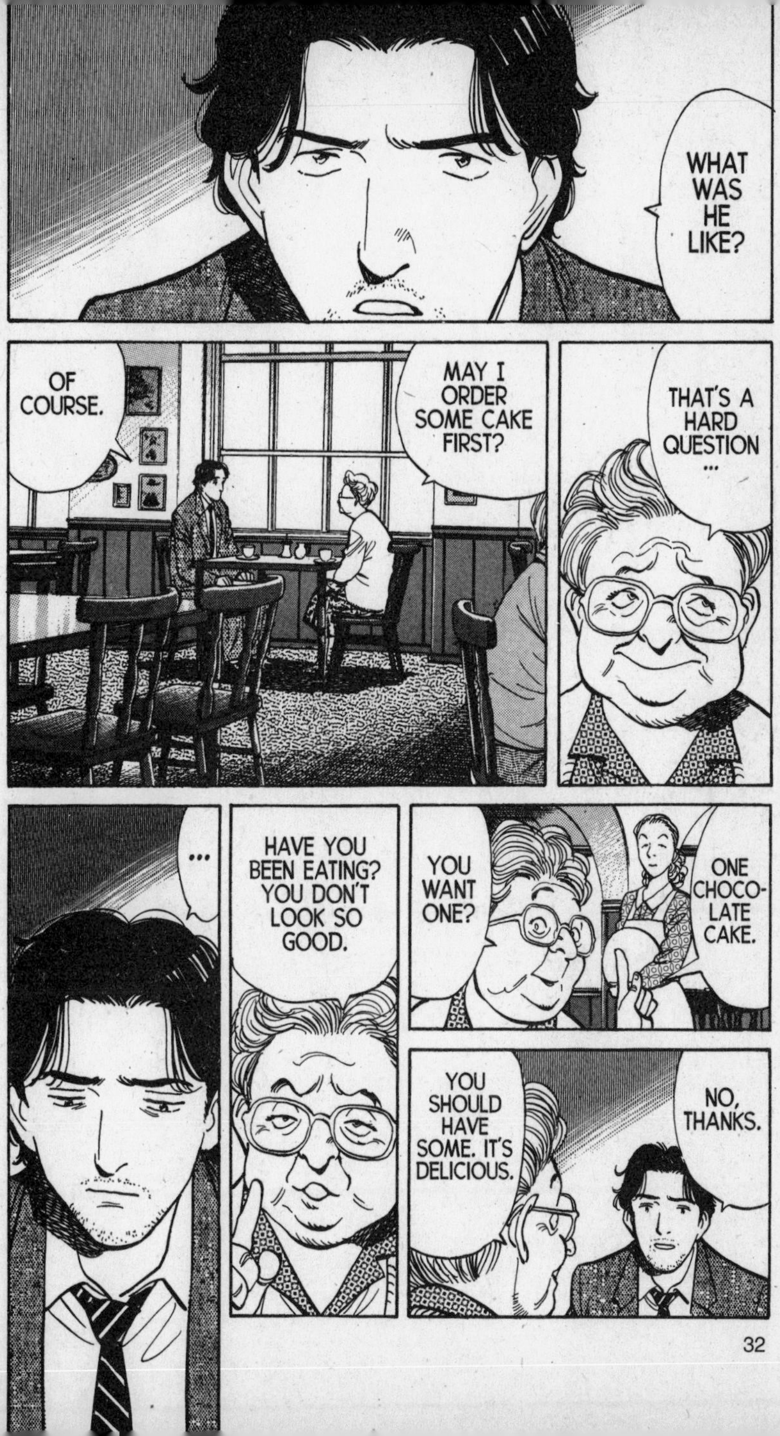
WHAT WAS HE LIKE?
THAT'S A HARD QUESTION ...
MAY I ORDER SOME CAKE FIRST?
OF COURSE.
ONE CHOCO-LATE CAKE.
YOU WANT ONE?
NO, THANKS.
YOU SHOULD HAVE SOME. IT'S DELICIOUS.
HAVE YOU BEEN EATING? YOU DON'T LOOK SO GOOD.
...

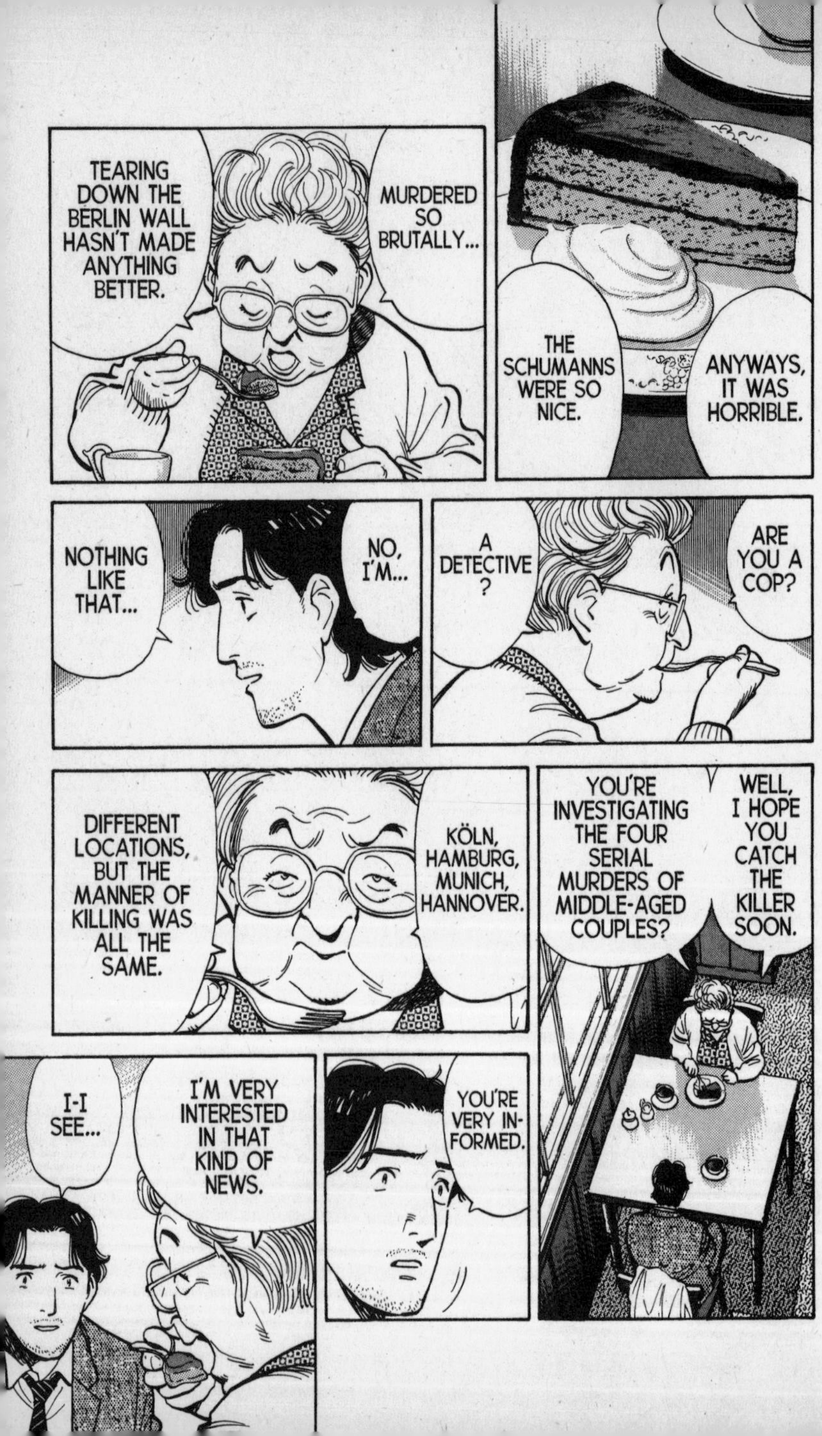
ANYWAYS, IT WAS HORRIBLE.
THE SCHUMANNS WERE SO NICE.
MURDERED SO BRUTALLY...
TEARING DOWN THE BERLIN WALL HASN'T MADE ANYTHING BETTER.
ARE YOU A COP?
A DETECTIVE?
NO, I'M...
NOTHING LIKE THAT...
WELL, I HOPE YOU CATCH THE KILLER SOON.
YOU'RE INVESTIGATING THE FOUR SERIAL MURDERS OF MIDDLE-AGED COUPLES?
KÖLN, HAMBURG, MUNICH, HANNOVER.
DIFFERENT LOCATIONS, BUT THE MANNER OF KILLING WAS ALL THE SAME.
YOU'RE VERY IN-FORMED.
I'M VERY INTERESTED IN THAT KIND OF NEWS.
I-I SEE...

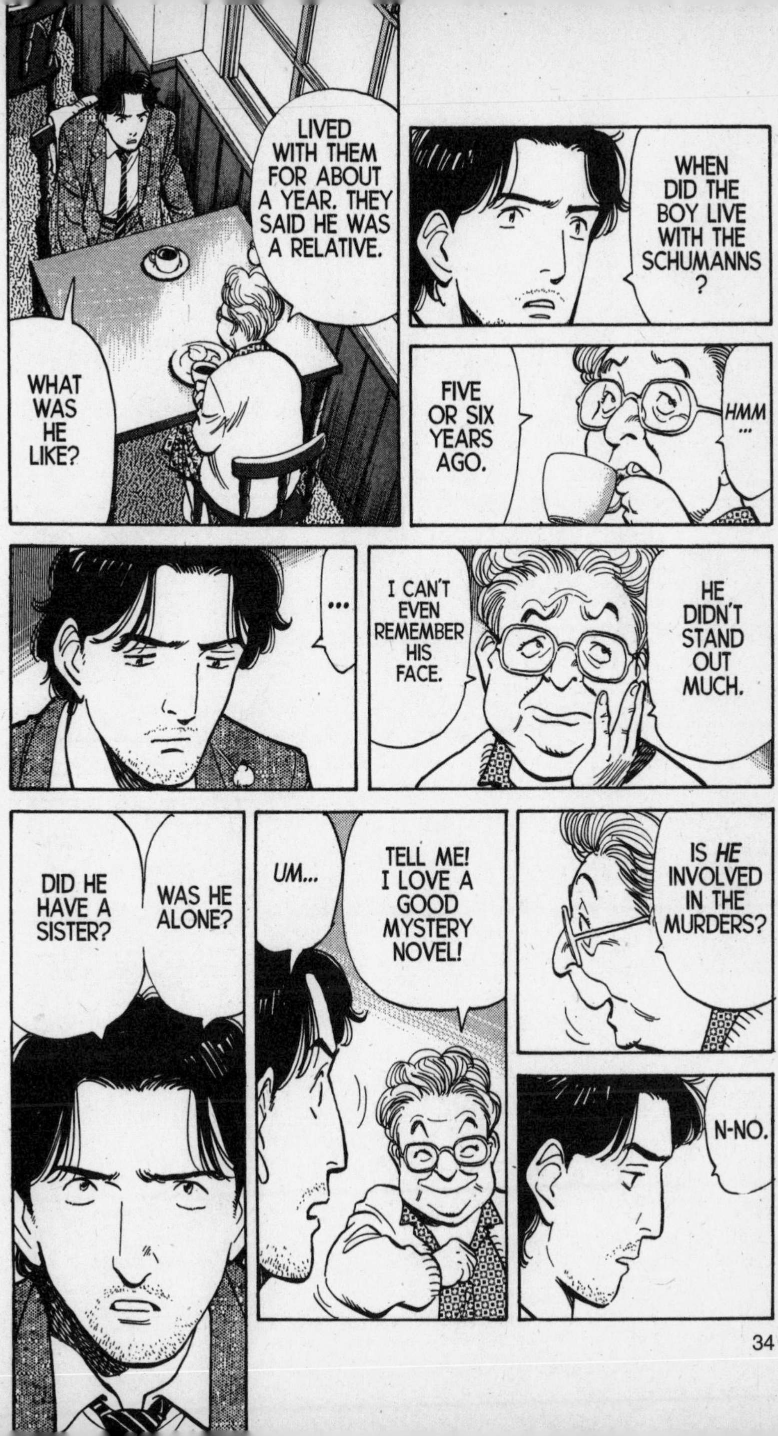
WHEN DID THE BOY LIVE WITH THE SCHUMANNS?
HMM...
FIVE OR SIX YEARS AGO.
LIVED WITH THEM FOR ABOUT A YEAR. THEY SAID HE WAS A RELATIVE.
WHAT WAS HE LIKE?
HE DIDN'T STAND OUT MUCH.
I CAN'T EVEN REMEMBER HIS FACE.
...
IS *HE* INVOLVED IN THE MURDERS?
N-NO.
TELL ME! I LOVE A GOOD MYSTERY NOVEL!
UM...
WAS HE ALONE?
DID HE HAVE A SISTER?

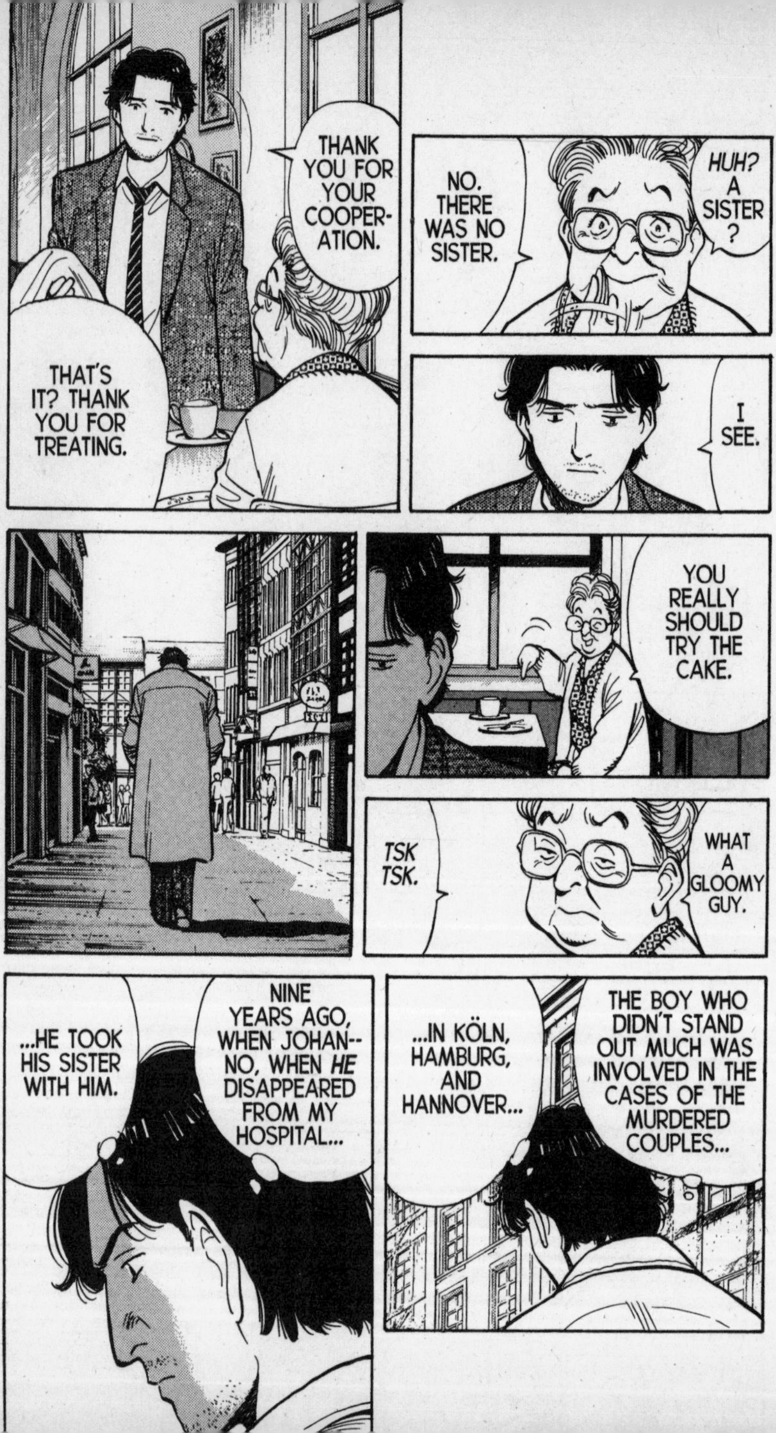
HUH? A SISTER?
NO. THERE WAS NO SISTER.
I SEE.
THANK YOU FOR YOUR COOPERATION.
THAT'S IT? THANK YOU FOR TREATING.
YOU REALLY SHOULD TRY THE CAKE.
WHAT A GLOOMY GUY.
TSK TSK.
THE BOY WHO DIDN'T STAND OUT MUCH WAS INVOLVED IN THE CASES OF THE MURDERED COUPLES...
...IN KÖLN, HAMBURG, AND HANNOVER...
NINE YEARS AGO, WHEN JOHAN-- NO, WHEN *HE* DISAPPEARED FROM MY HOSPITAL...
...HE TOOK HIS SISTER WITH HIM.

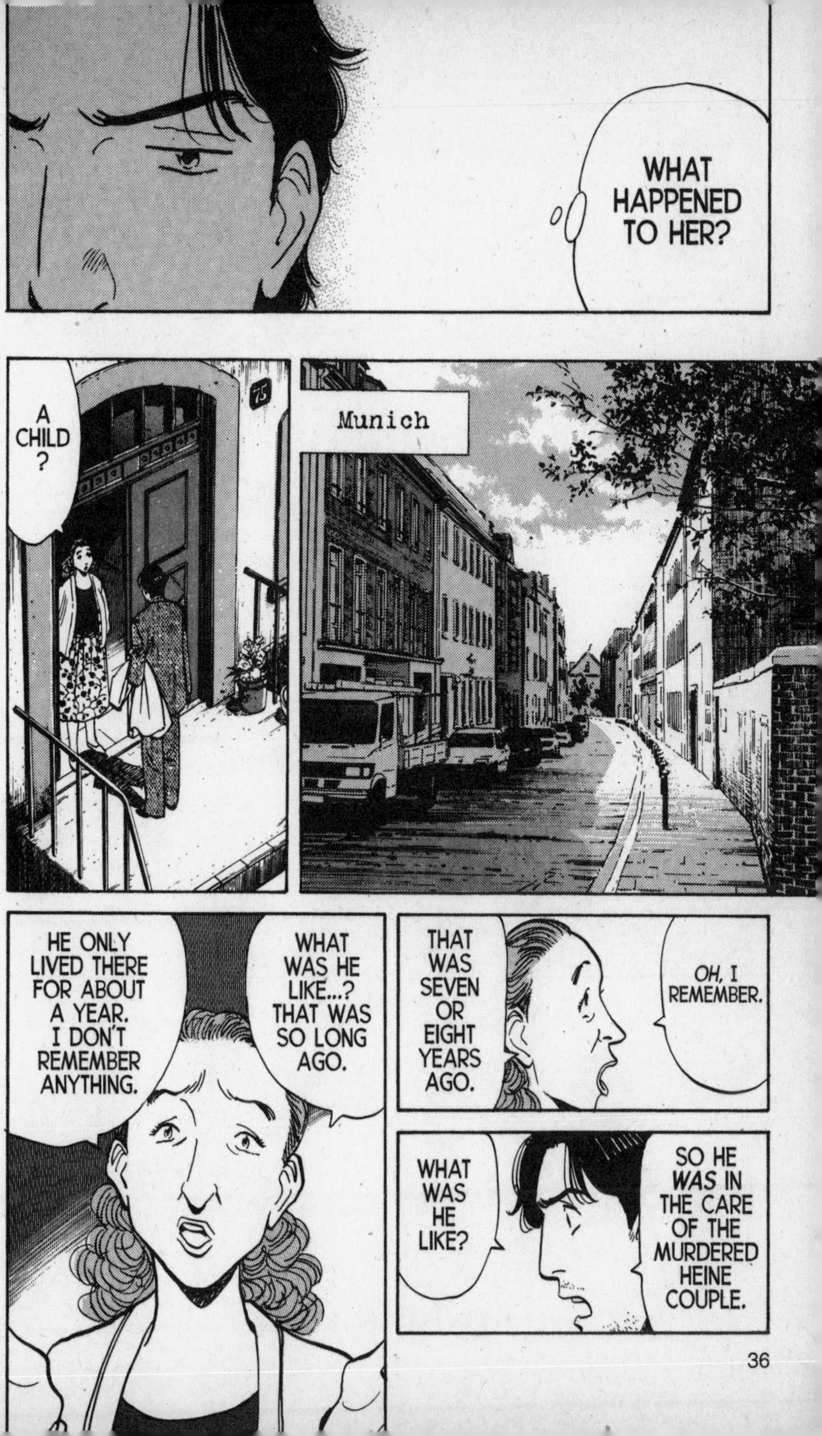
WHAT HAPPENED TO HER?
Munich
A CHILD ?
OH, I REMEMBER.
THAT WAS SEVEN OR EIGHT YEARS AGO.
SO HE *WAS* IN THE CARE OF THE MURDERED HEINE COUPLE.
WHAT WAS HE LIKE?
WHAT WAS HE LIKE...? THAT WAS SO LONG AGO.
HE ONLY LIVED THERE FOR ABOUT A YEAR. I DON'T REMEMBER ANYTHING.

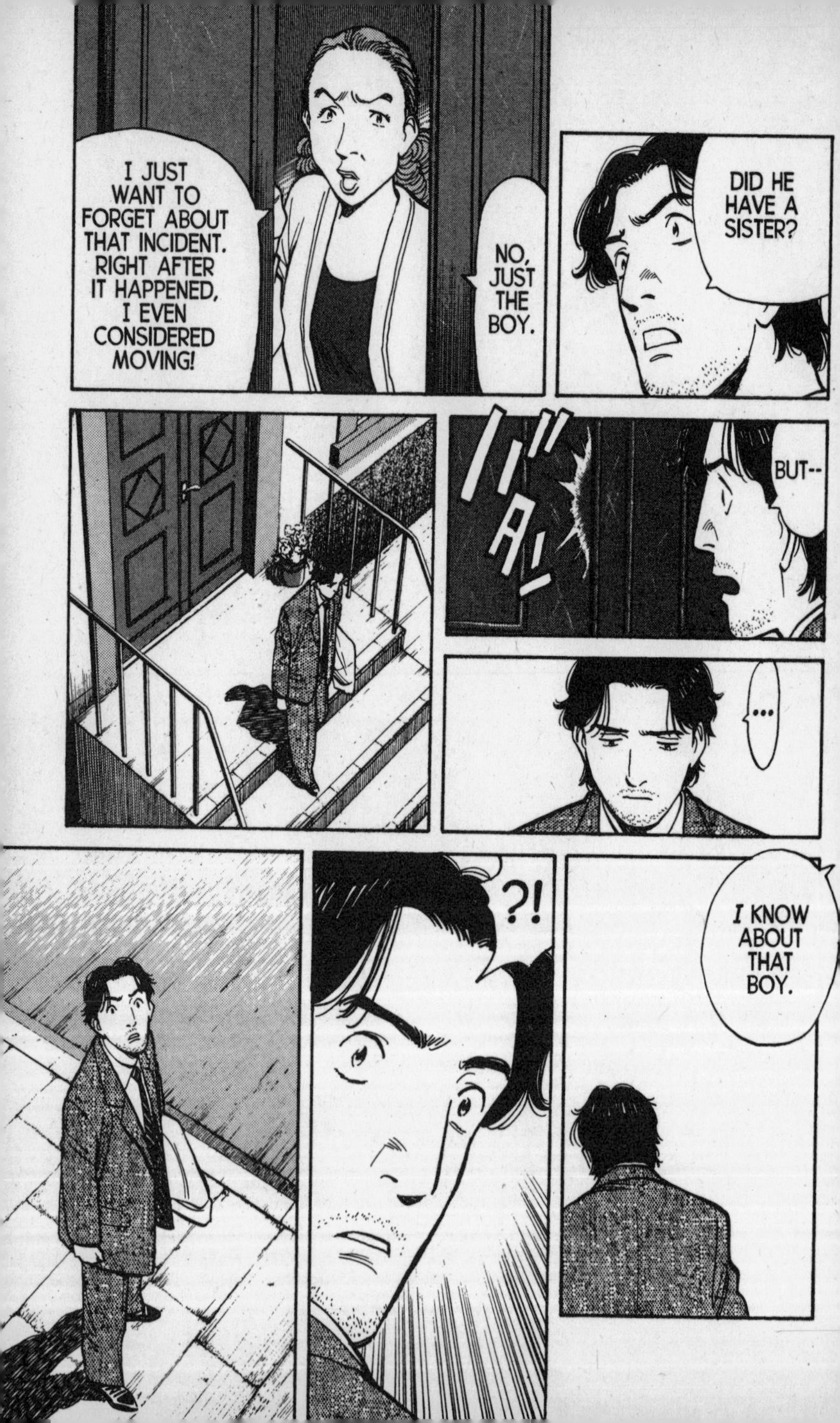
DID HE HAVE A SISTER?
NO, JUST THE BOY.
I JUST WANT TO FORGET ABOUT THAT INCIDENT. RIGHT AFTER IT HAPPENED, I EVEN CONSIDERED MOVING!
BUT--
バタン
...
I KNOW ABOUT THAT BOY.
?!

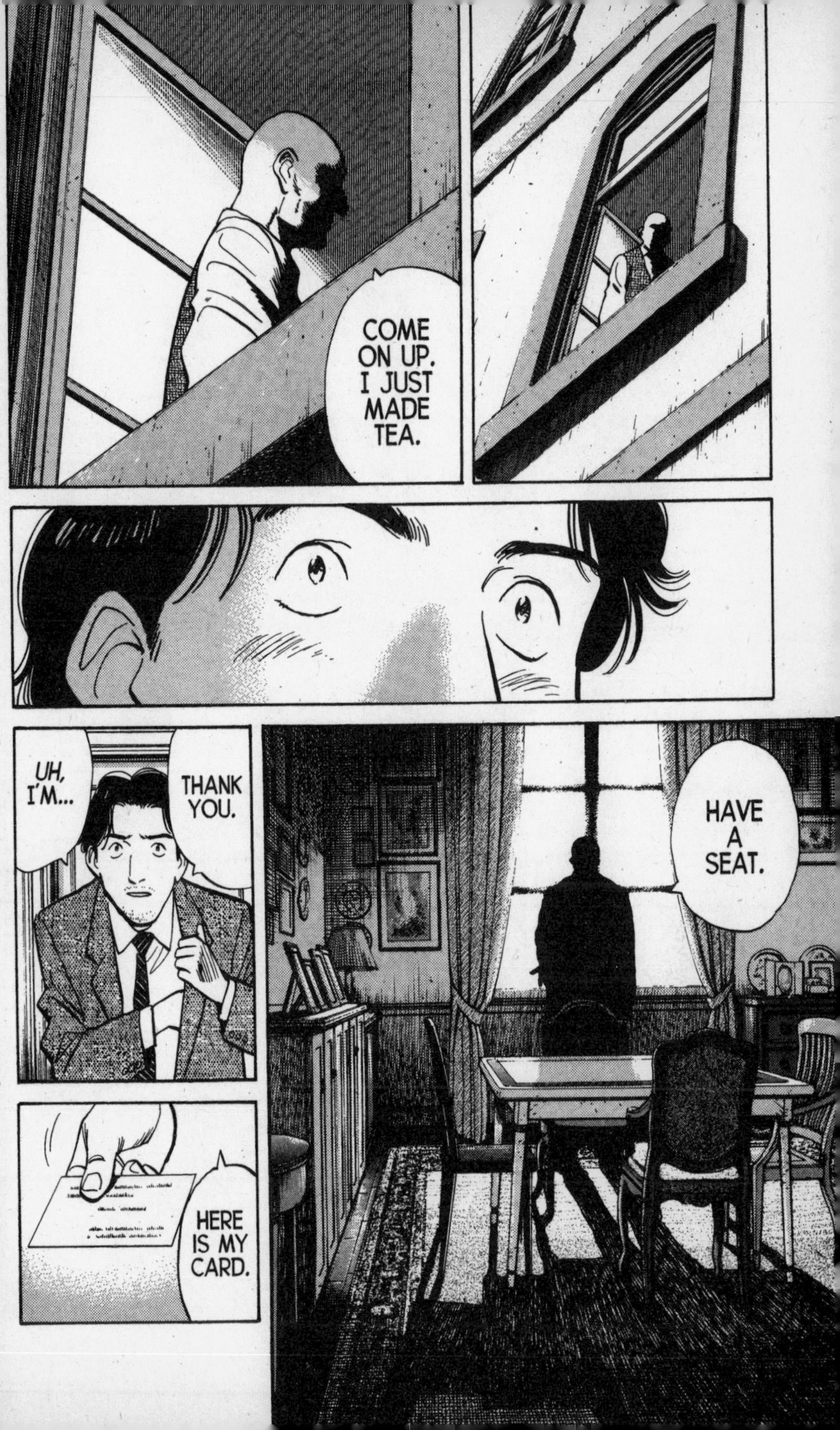
COME ON UP. I JUST MADE TEA.
HAVE A SEAT.
THANK YOU.
UH, I'M...
HERE IS MY CARD.

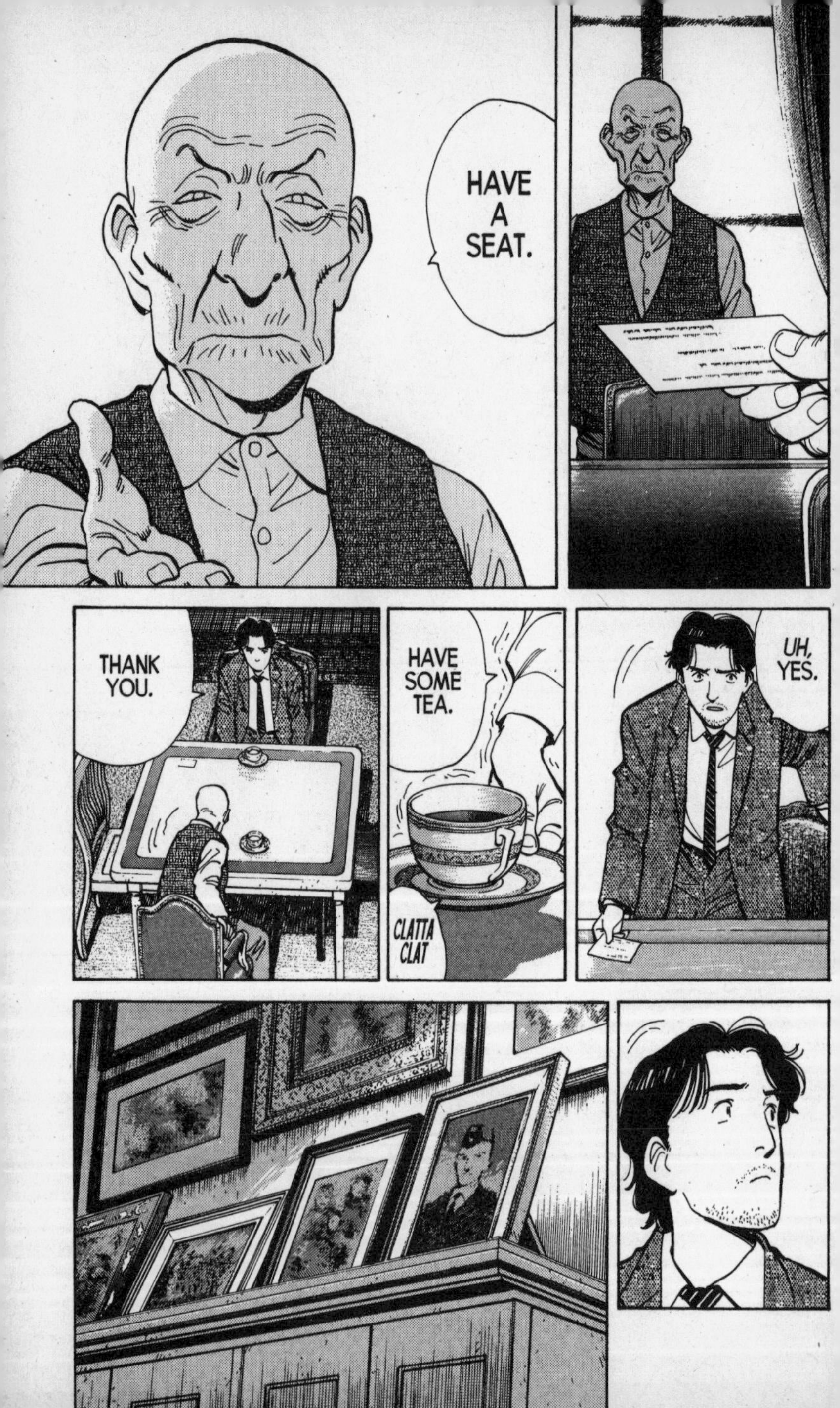
HAVE A SEAT.
THANK YOU.
HAVE SOME TEA.
CLATTA CLAT
UH, YES.

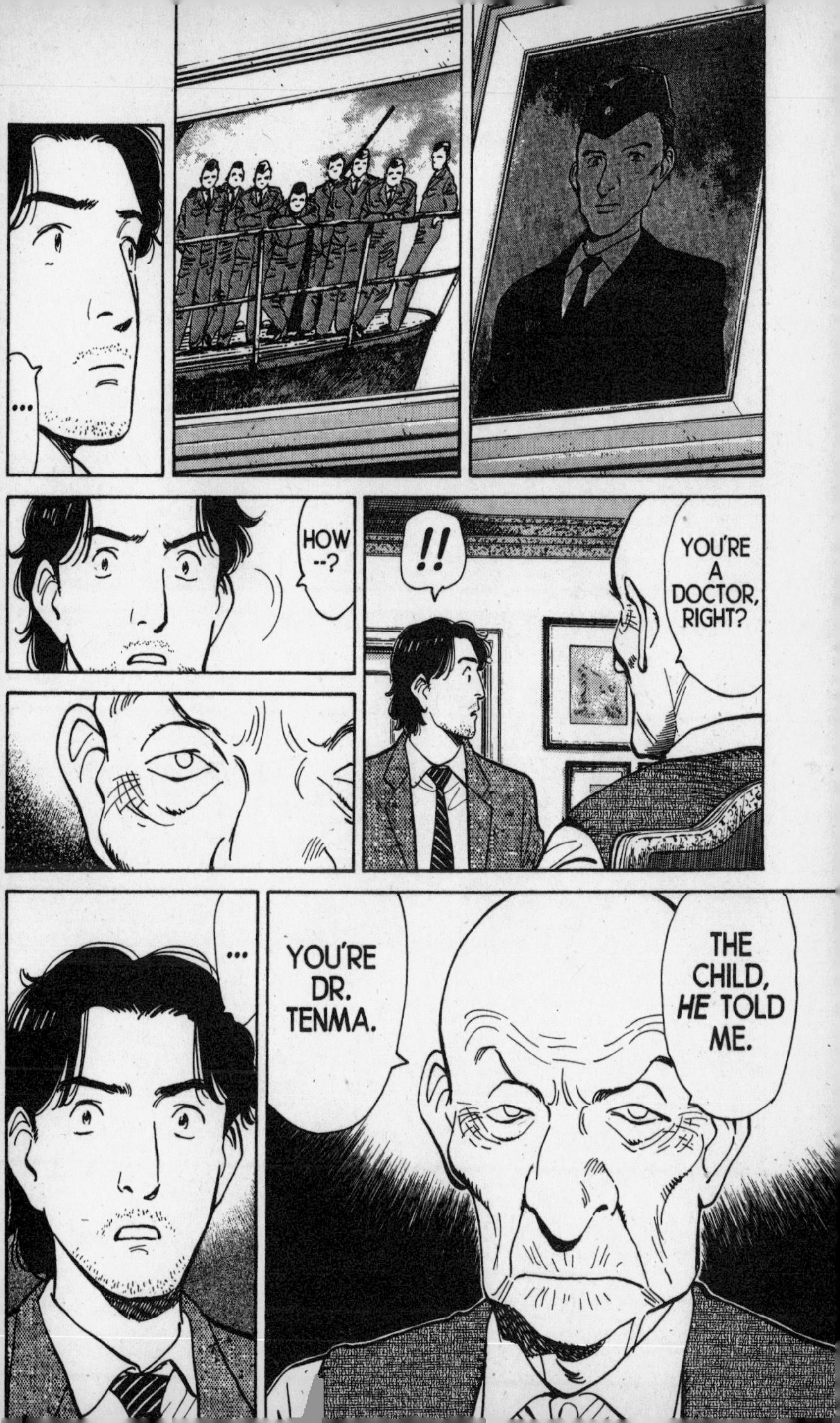
...
YOU'RE A DOCTOR, RIGHT?
!!
HOW --?
THE CHILD, *HE* TOLD ME.
YOU'RE DR. TENMA.
...

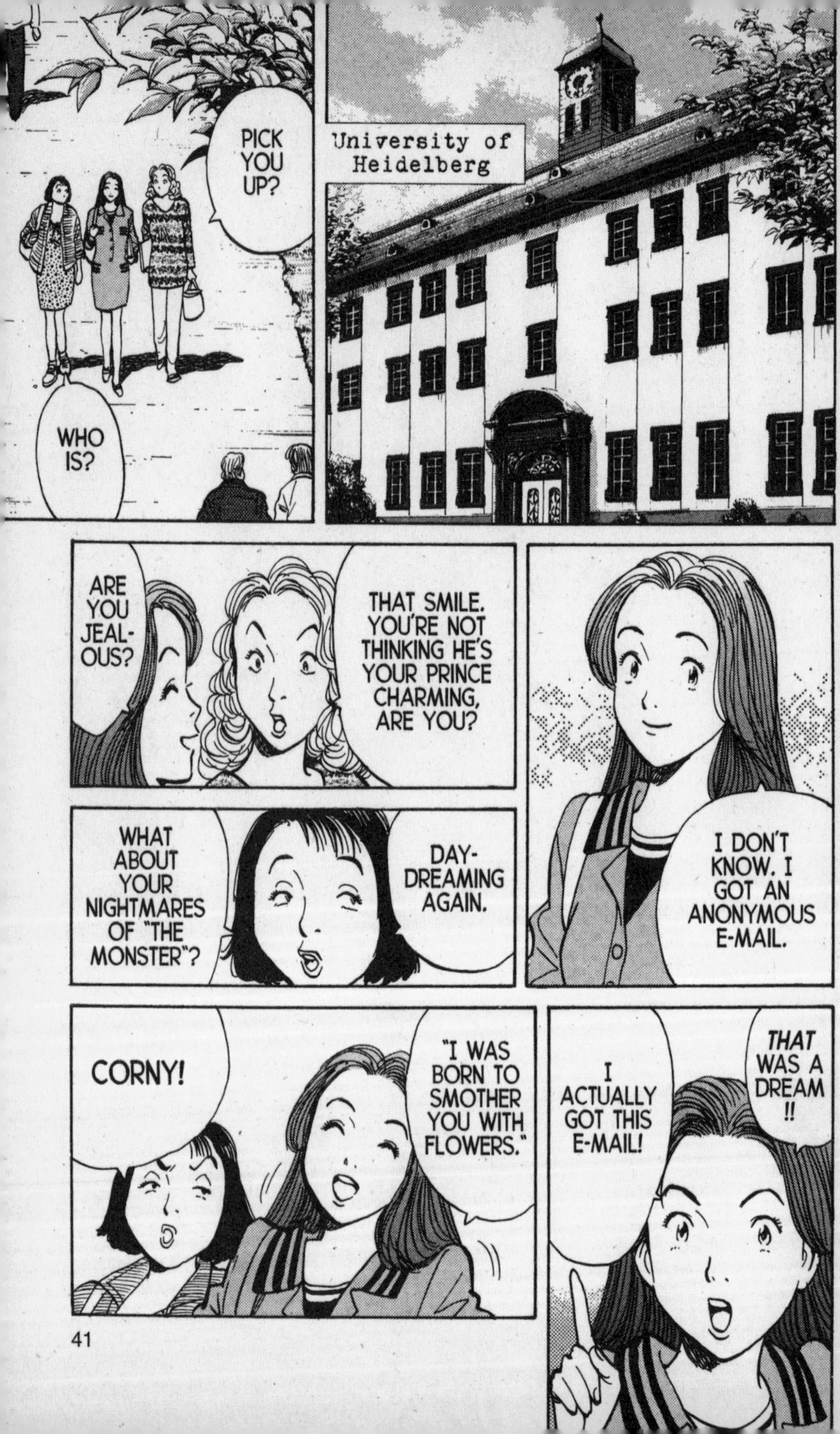
University of Heidelberg
PICK YOU UP?
WHO IS?
I DON'T KNOW. I GOT AN ANONYMOUS E-MAIL.
THAT SMILE. YOU'RE NOT THINKING HE'S YOUR PRINCE CHARMING, ARE YOU?
ARE YOU JEAL-OUS?
DAY-DREAMING AGAIN.
WHAT ABOUT YOUR NIGHTMARES OF "THE MONSTER"?
THAT WAS A DREAM !!
I ACTUALLY GOT THIS E-MAIL!
"I WAS BORN TO SMOTHER YOU WITH FLOWERS."
CORNY!

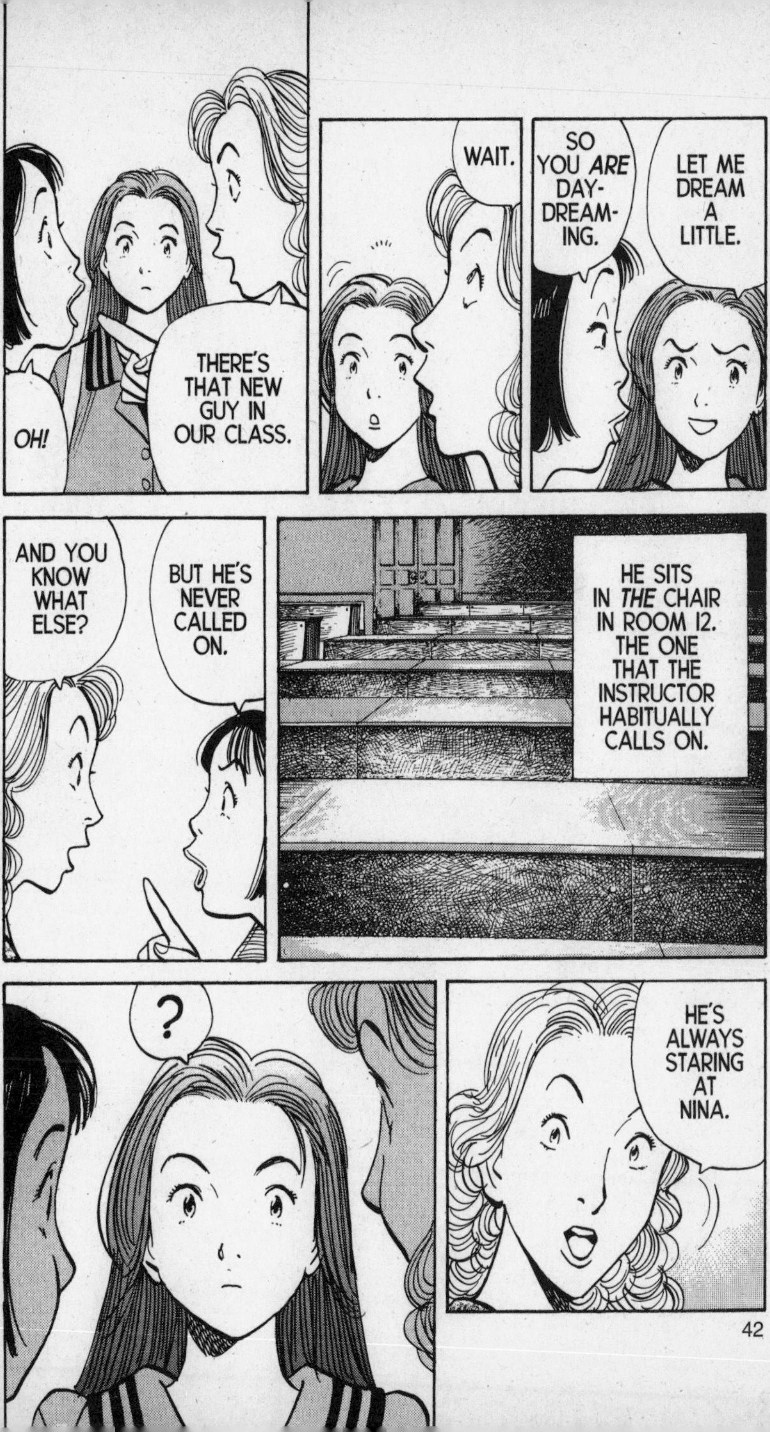
LET ME DREAM A LITTLE.
SO YOU *ARE* DAY-DREAM-ING.
WAIT.
THERE'S THAT NEW GUY IN OUR CLASS.
OH!
HE SITS IN *THE* CHAIR IN ROOM 12. THE ONE THAT THE INSTRUCTOR HABITUALLY CALLS ON.
BUT HE'S NEVER CALLED ON.
AND YOU KNOW WHAT ELSE?
HE'S ALWAYS STARING AT NINA.
?

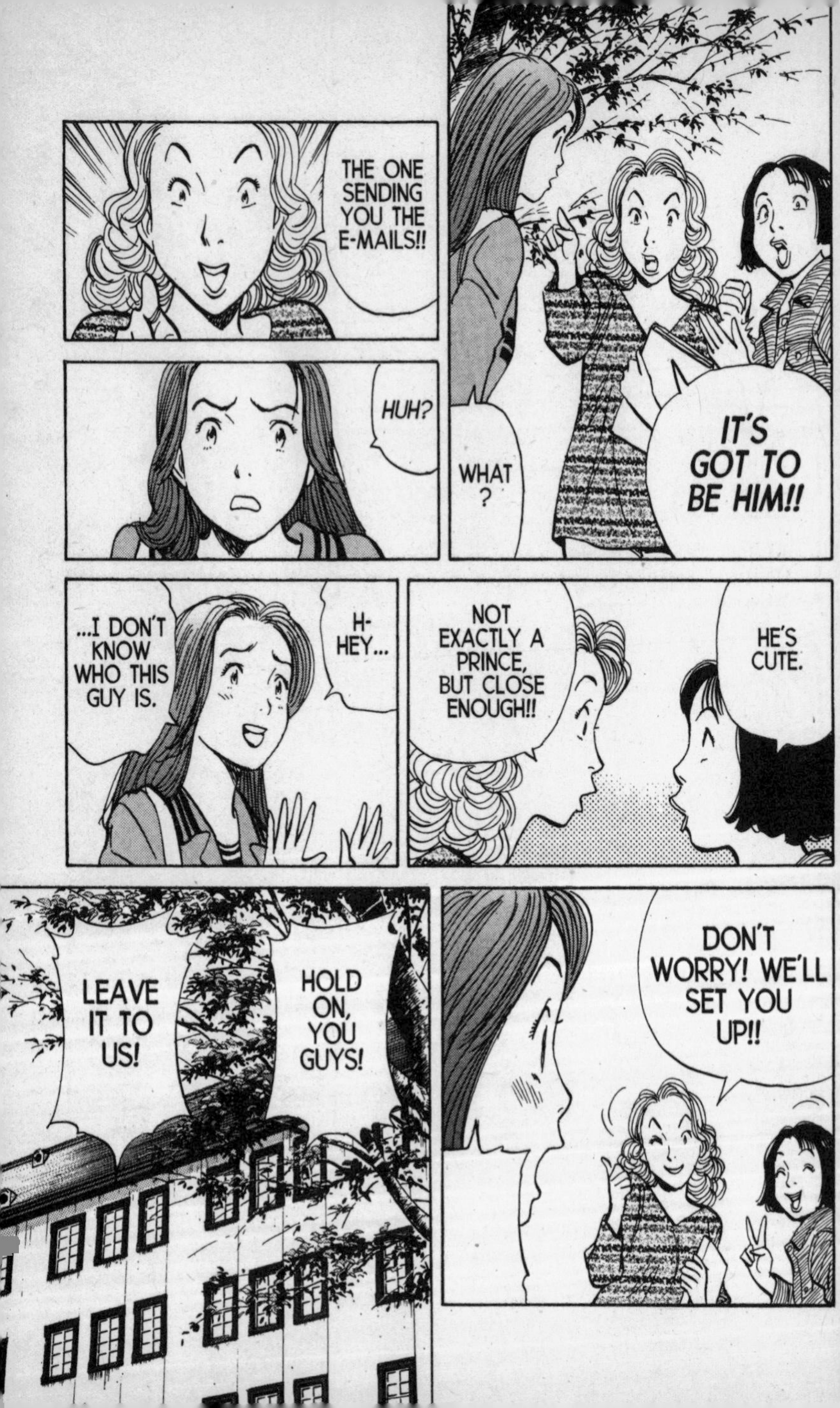
IT'S GOT TO BE HIM!!
WHAT?
THE ONE SENDING YOU THE E-MAILS!!
HUH?
HE'S CUTE.
NOT EXACTLY A PRINCE, BUT CLOSE ENOUGH!!
H-HEY...
...I DON'T KNOW WHO THIS GUY IS.
DON'T WORRY! WE'LL SET YOU UP!!
HOLD ON, YOU GUYS!
LEAVE IT TO US!

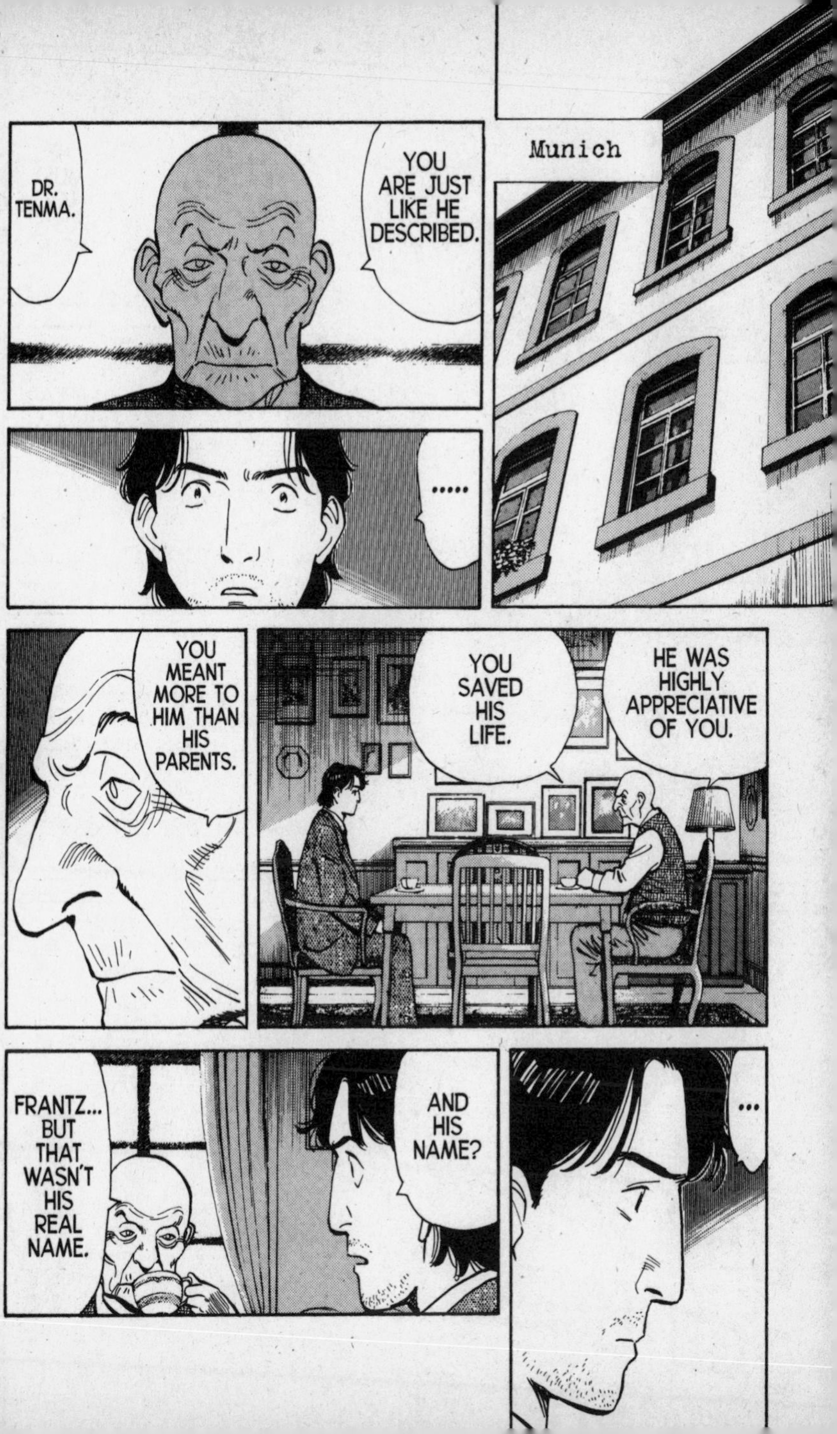
Munich
YOU ARE JUST LIKE HE DESCRIBED.
DR. TENMA.
.....
HE WAS HIGHLY APPRECIATIVE OF YOU.
YOU SAVED HIS LIFE.
YOU MEANT MORE TO HIM THAN HIS PARENTS.
...
AND HIS NAME?
FRANTZ... BUT THAT WASN'T HIS REAL NAME.

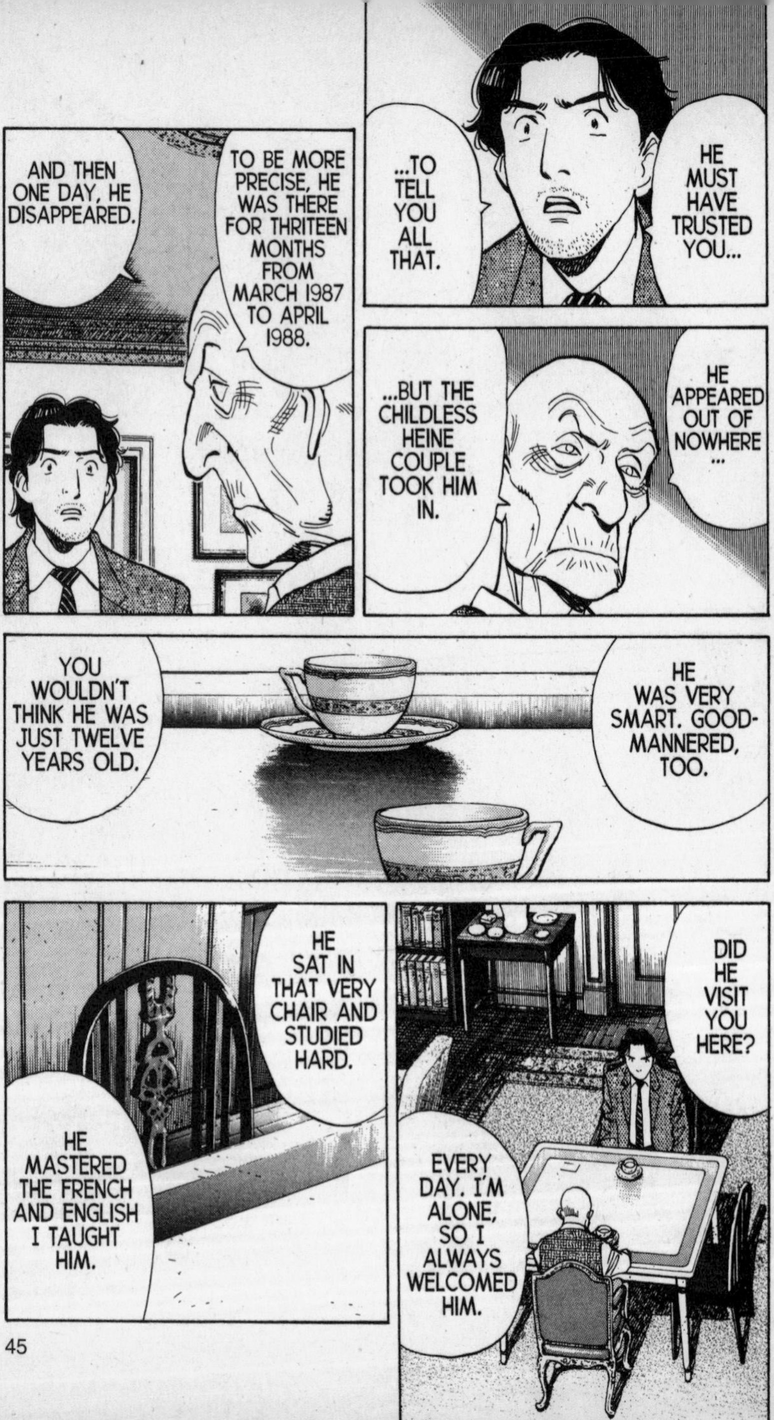
HE MUST HAVE TRUSTED YOU...
...TO TELL YOU ALL THAT.
HE APPEARED OUT OF NOWHERE...
...BUT THE CHILDLESS HEINE COUPLE TOOK HIM IN.
TO BE MORE PRECISE, HE WAS THERE FOR THRITEEN MONTHS FROM MARCH 1987 TO APRIL 1988.
AND THEN ONE DAY, HE DISAPPEARED.
HE WAS VERY SMART. GOOD-MANNERED, TOO.
YOU WOULDN'T THINK HE WAS JUST TWELVE YEARS OLD.
DID HE VISIT YOU HERE?
EVERY DAY. I'M ALONE, SO I ALWAYS WELCOMED HIM.
HE SAT IN THAT VERY CHAIR AND STUDIED HARD.
HE MASTERED THE FRENCH AND ENGLISH I TAUGHT HIM.

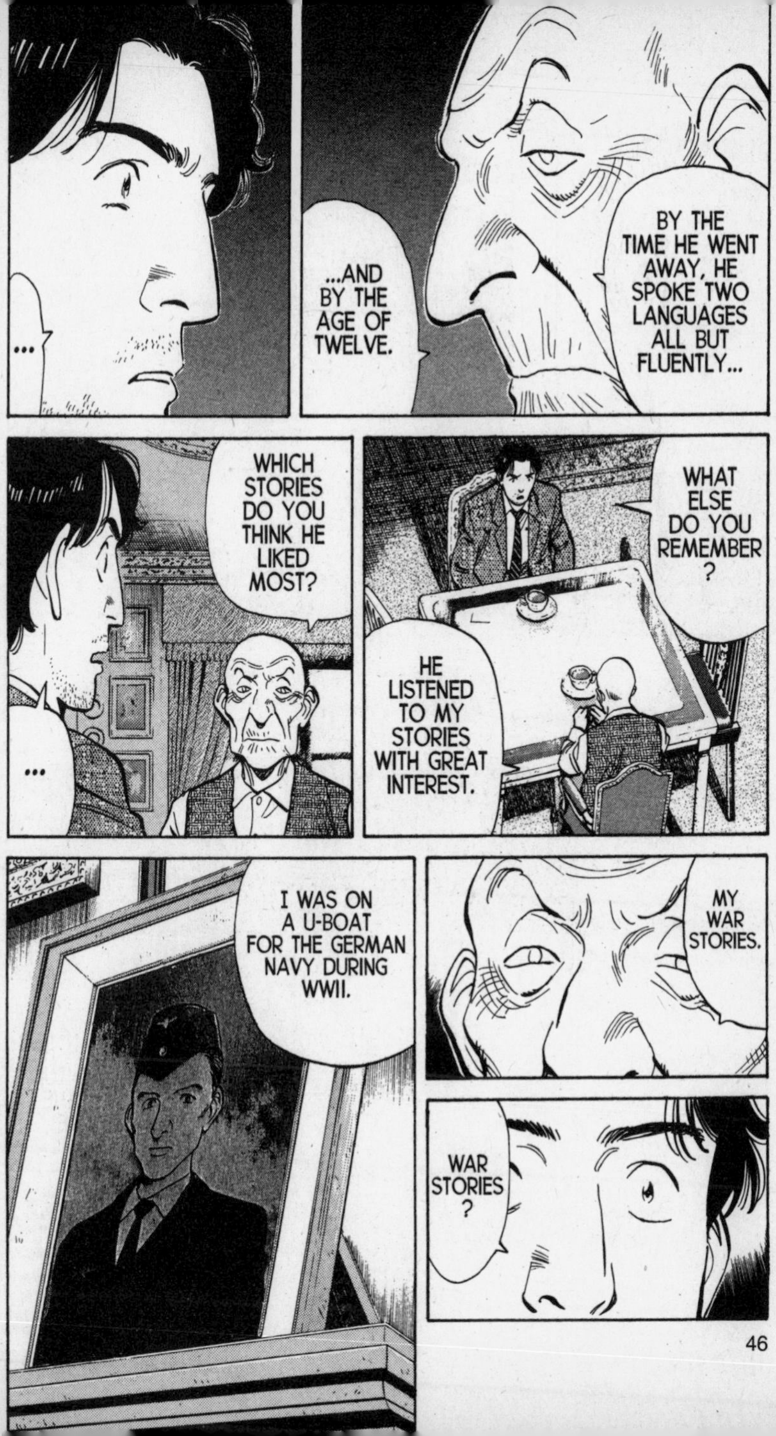
BY THE TIME HE WENT AWAY, HE SPOKE TWO LANGUAGES ALL BUT FLUENTLY...
...AND BY THE AGE OF TWELVE.
...
WHAT ELSE DO YOU REMEMBER?
HE LISTENED TO MY STORIES WITH GREAT INTEREST.
WHICH STORIES DO YOU THINK HE LIKED MOST?
...
MY WAR STORIES.
WAR STORIES?
I WAS ON A U-BOAT FOR THE GERMAN NAVY DURING WWII.

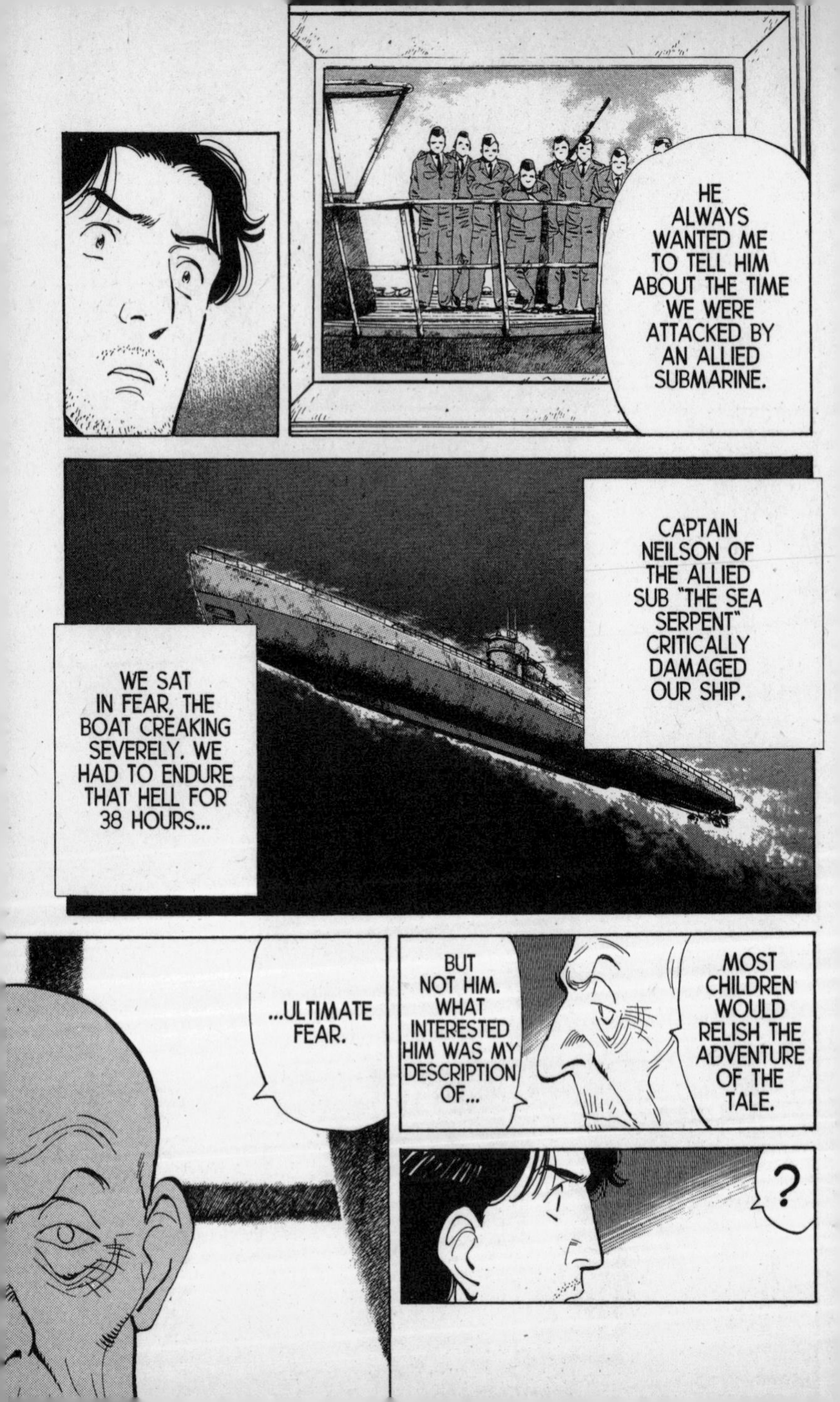
HE ALWAYS WANTED ME TO TELL HIM ABOUT THE TIME WE WERE ATTACKED BY AN ALLIED SUBMARINE.
CAPTAIN NEILSON OF THE ALLIED SUB "THE SEA SERPENT" CRITICALLY DAMAGED OUR SHIP.
WE SAT IN FEAR, THE BOAT CREAKING SEVERELY. WE HAD TO ENDURE THAT HELL FOR 38 HOURS...
MOST CHILDREN WOULD RELISH THE ADVENTURE OF THE TALE.
BUT NOT HIM. WHAT INTERESTED HIM WAS MY DESCRIPTION OF...
?
...ULTIMATE FEAR.

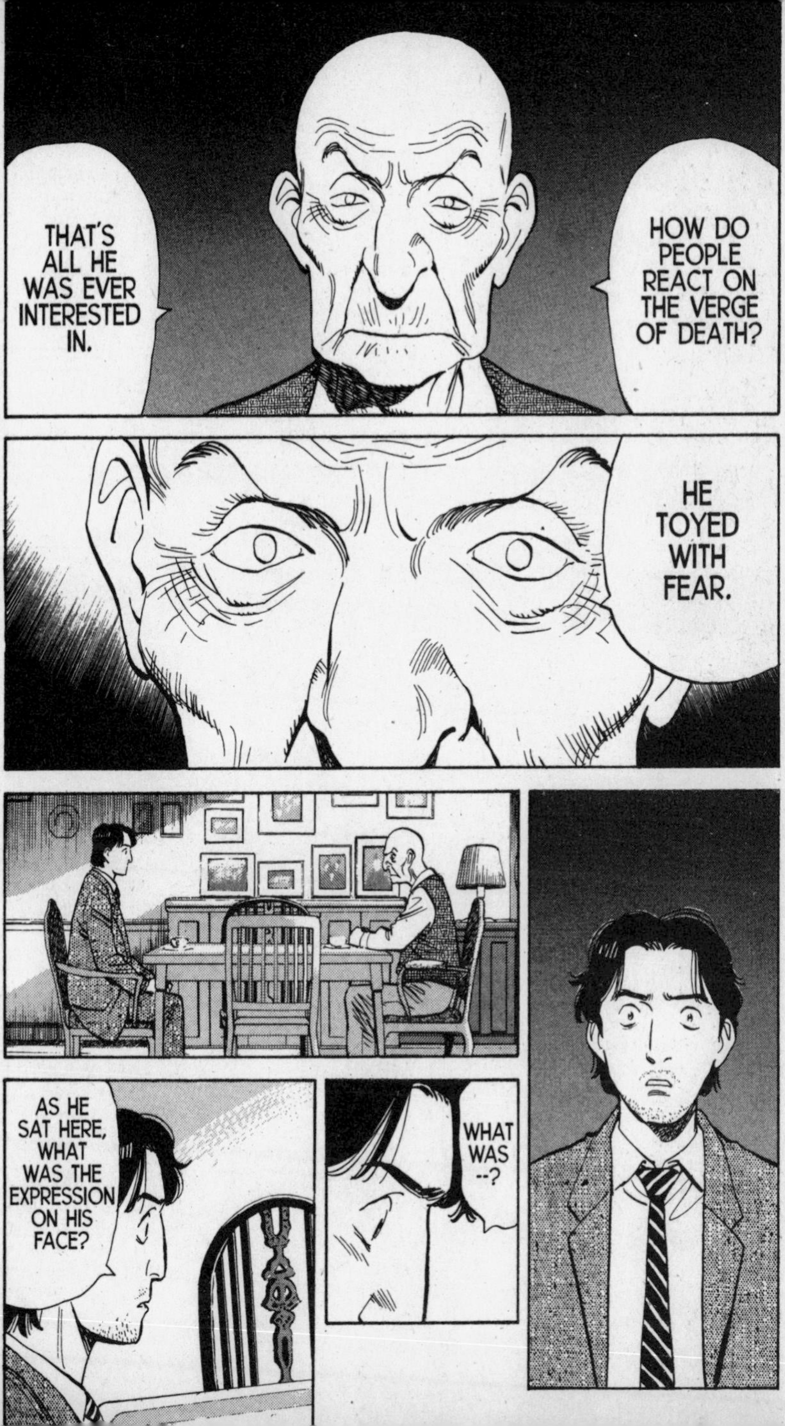
HOW DO PEOPLE REACT ON THE VERGE OF DEATH?
THAT'S ALL HE WAS EVER INTERESTED IN.
HE TOYED WITH FEAR.
WHAT WAS --?
AS HE SAT HERE, WHAT WAS THE EXPRESSION ON HIS FACE?

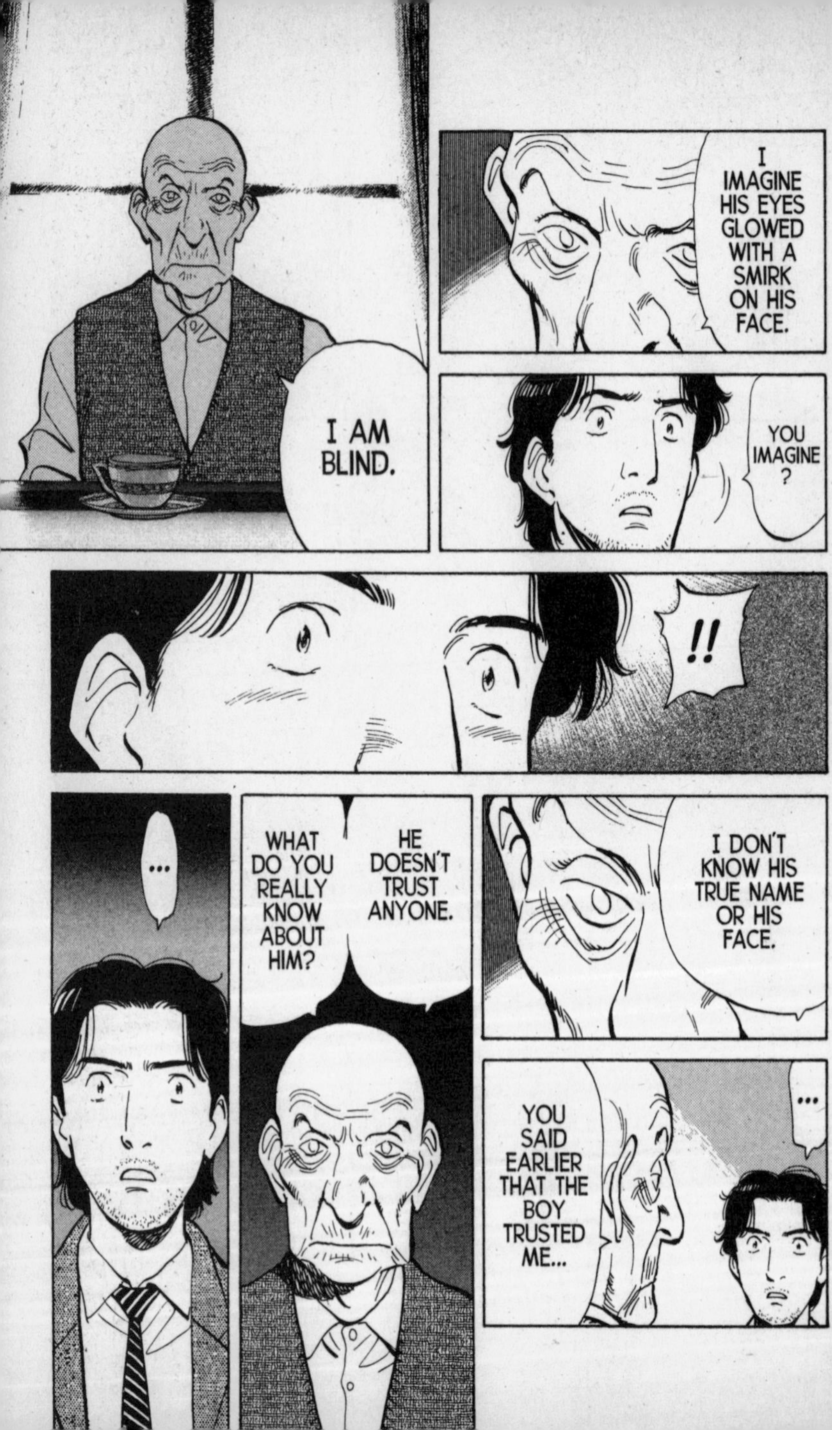
I IMAGINE HIS EYES GLOWED WITH A SMIRK ON HIS FACE.
YOU IMAGINE?
I AM BLIND.
!!
I DON'T KNOW HIS TRUE NAME OR HIS FACE.
...
YOU SAID EARLIER THAT THE BOY TRUSTED ME...
HE DOESN'T TRUST ANYONE.
WHAT DO YOU REALLY KNOW ABOUT HIM?
...

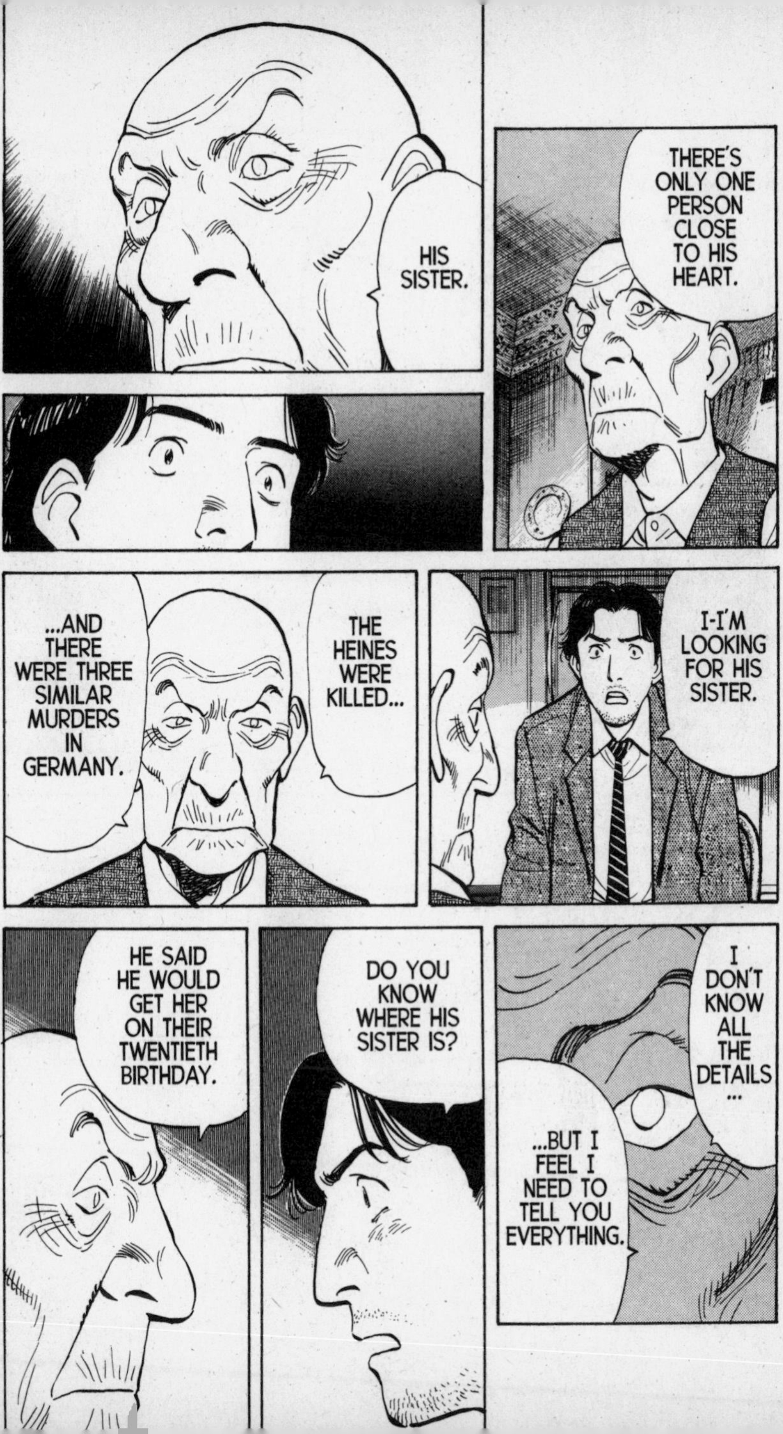
THERE'S ONLY ONE PERSON CLOSE TO HIS HEART.
HIS SISTER.
I-I'M LOOKING FOR HIS SISTER.
THE HEINES WERE KILLED...
...AND THERE WERE THREE SIMILAR MURDERS IN GERMANY.
I DON'T KNOW ALL THE DETAILS...
...BUT I FEEL I NEED TO TELL YOU EVERYTHING.
DO YOU KNOW WHERE HIS SISTER IS?
HE SAID HE WOULD GET HER ON THEIR TWENTIETH BIRTHDAY.

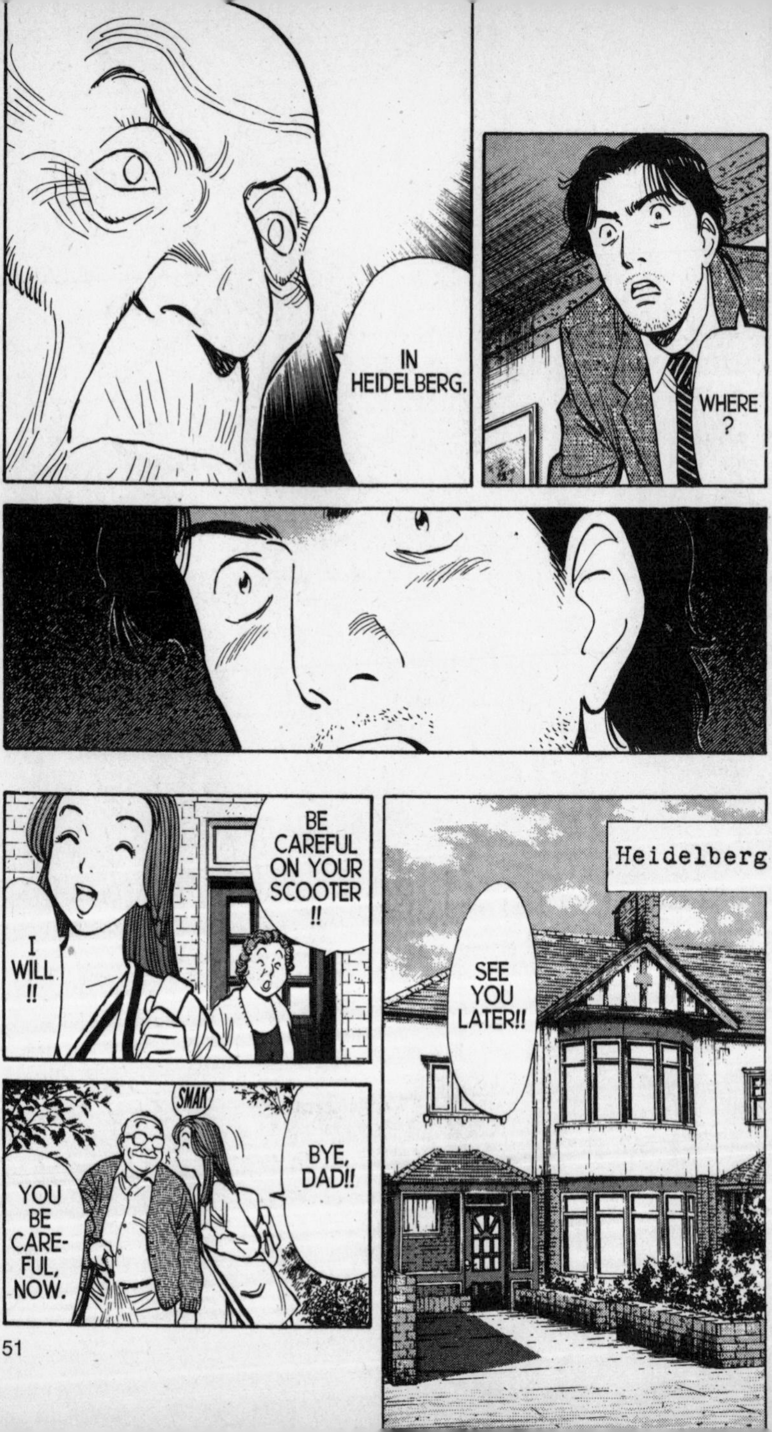
WHERE ?
IN HEIDELBERG.
Heidelberg
SEE YOU LATER!!
BE CAREFUL ON YOUR SCOOTER !!
I WILL !!
SMAK
BYE, DAD!!
YOU BE CARE-FUL, NOW.

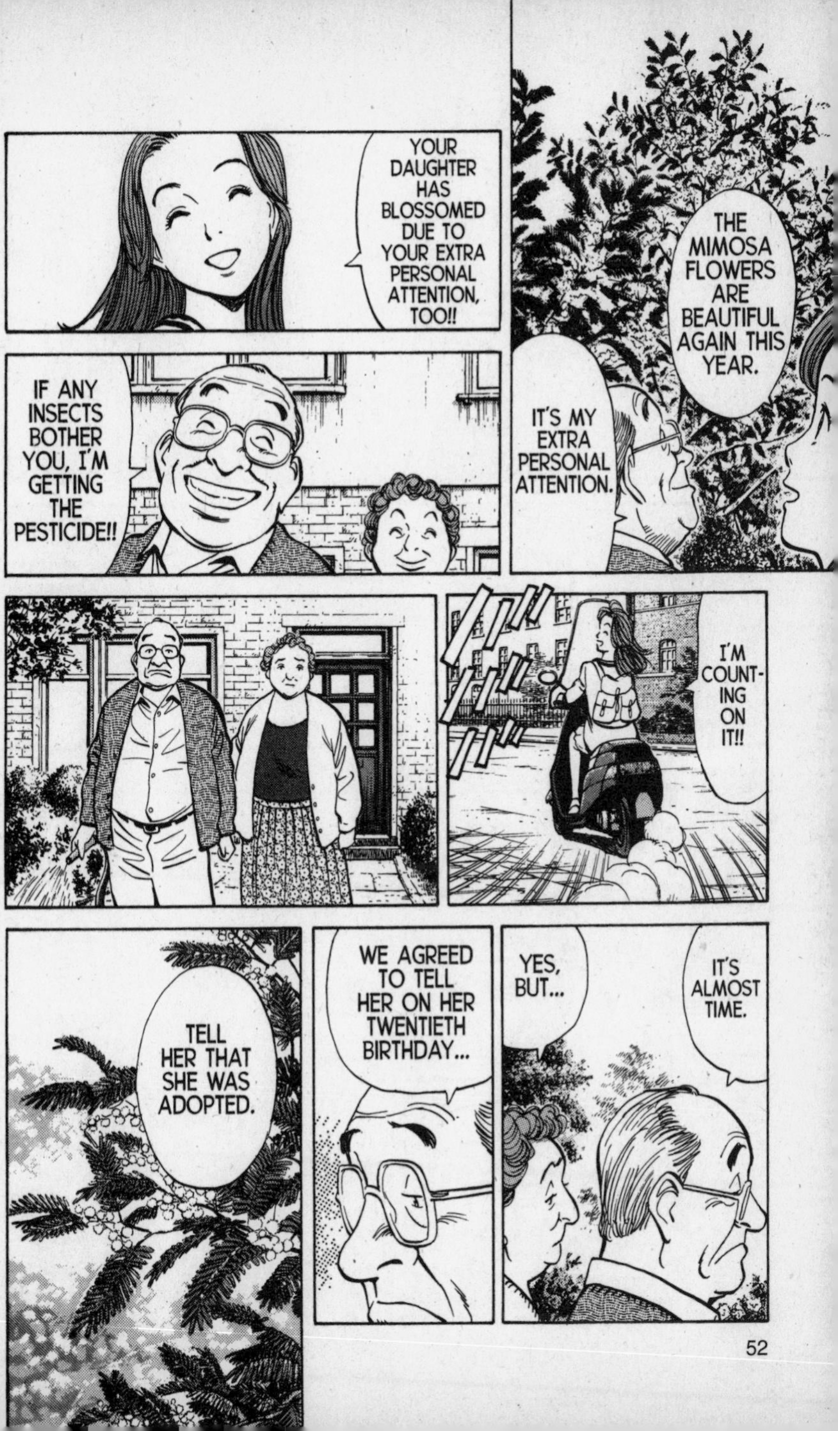
THE MIMOSA FLOWERS ARE BEAUTIFUL AGAIN THIS YEAR.
IT'S MY EXTRA PERSONAL ATTENTION.
YOUR DAUGHTER HAS BLOSSOMED DUE TO YOUR EXTRA PERSONAL ATTENTION, TOO!!
IF ANY INSECTS BOTHER YOU, I'M GETTING THE PESTICIDE!!
I'M COUNTING ON IT!!
IT'S ALMOST TIME.
YES, BUT...
WE AGREED TO TELL HER ON HER TWENTIETH BIRTHDAY...
TELL HER THAT SHE WAS ADOPTED.

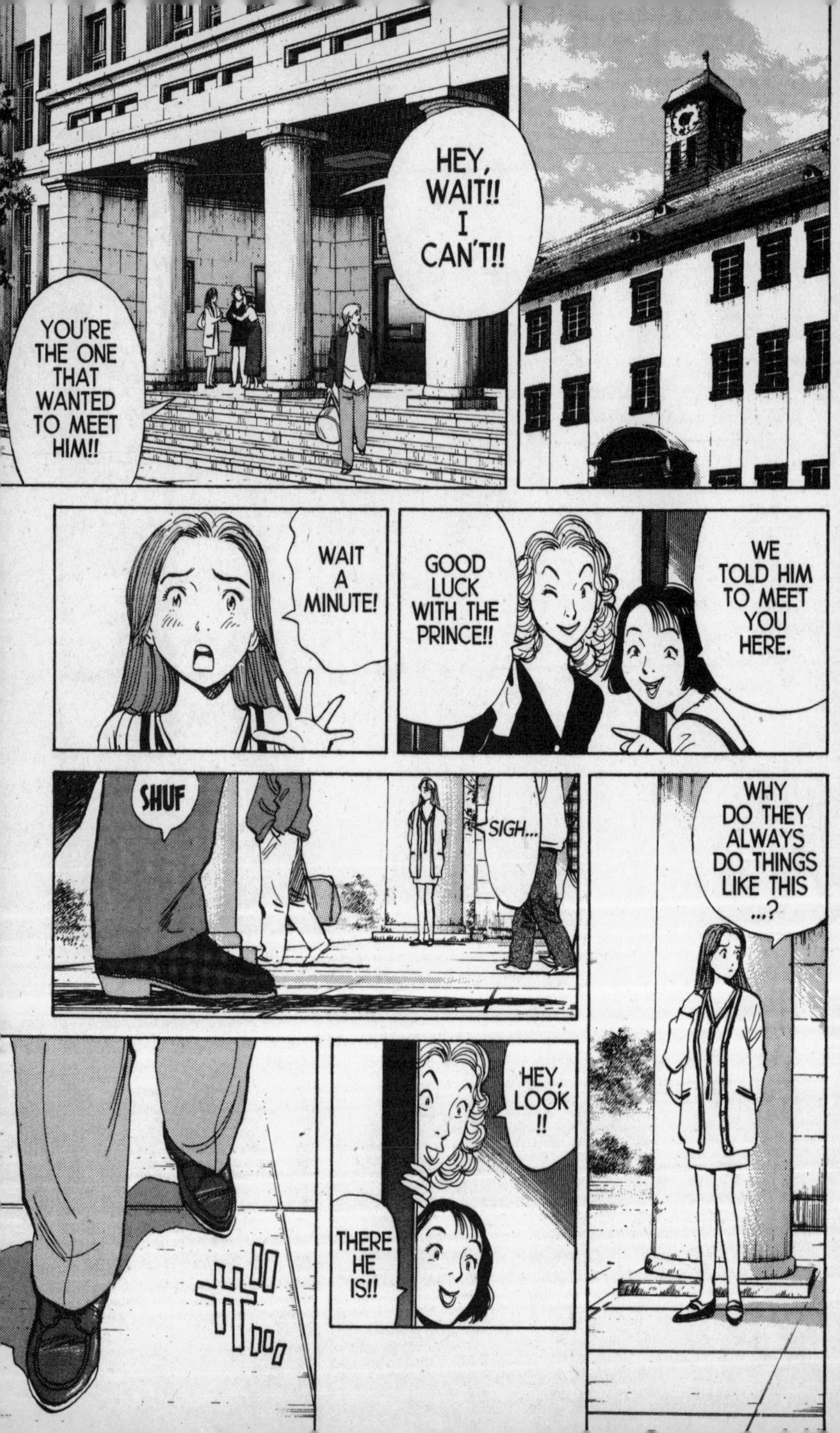
HEY, WAIT!! I CAN'T!!
YOU'RE THE ONE THAT WANTED TO MEET HIM!!
WE TOLD HIM TO MEET YOU HERE.
GOOD LUCK WITH THE PRINCE!!
WAIT A MINUTE!
WHY DO THEY ALWAYS DO THINGS LIKE THIS ...?
SIGH...
SHUF
HEY, LOOK!!
THERE HE IS!!

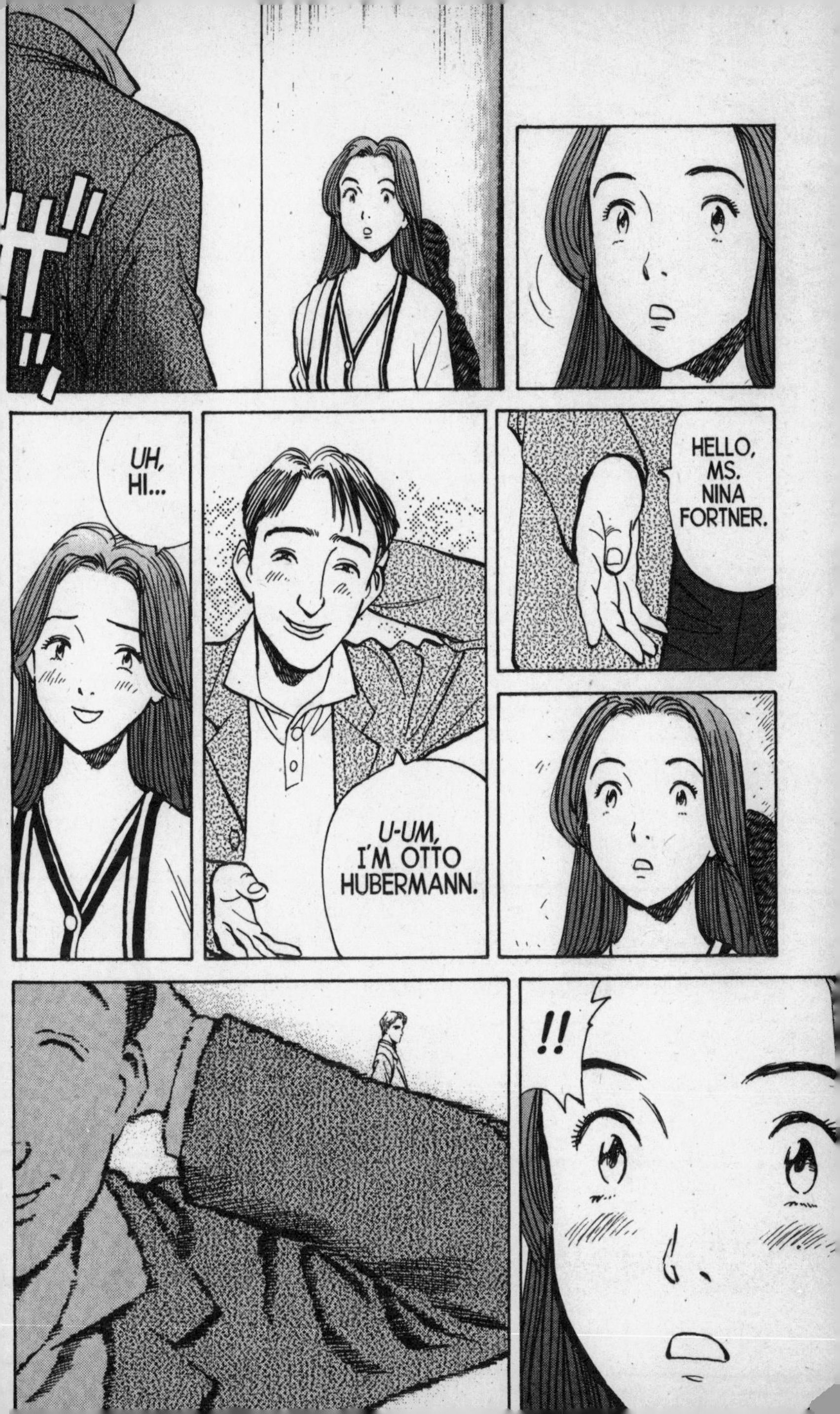
HELLO, MS. NINA FORTNER.
U-UM, I'M OTTO HUBERMANN.
UH, HI...
!!

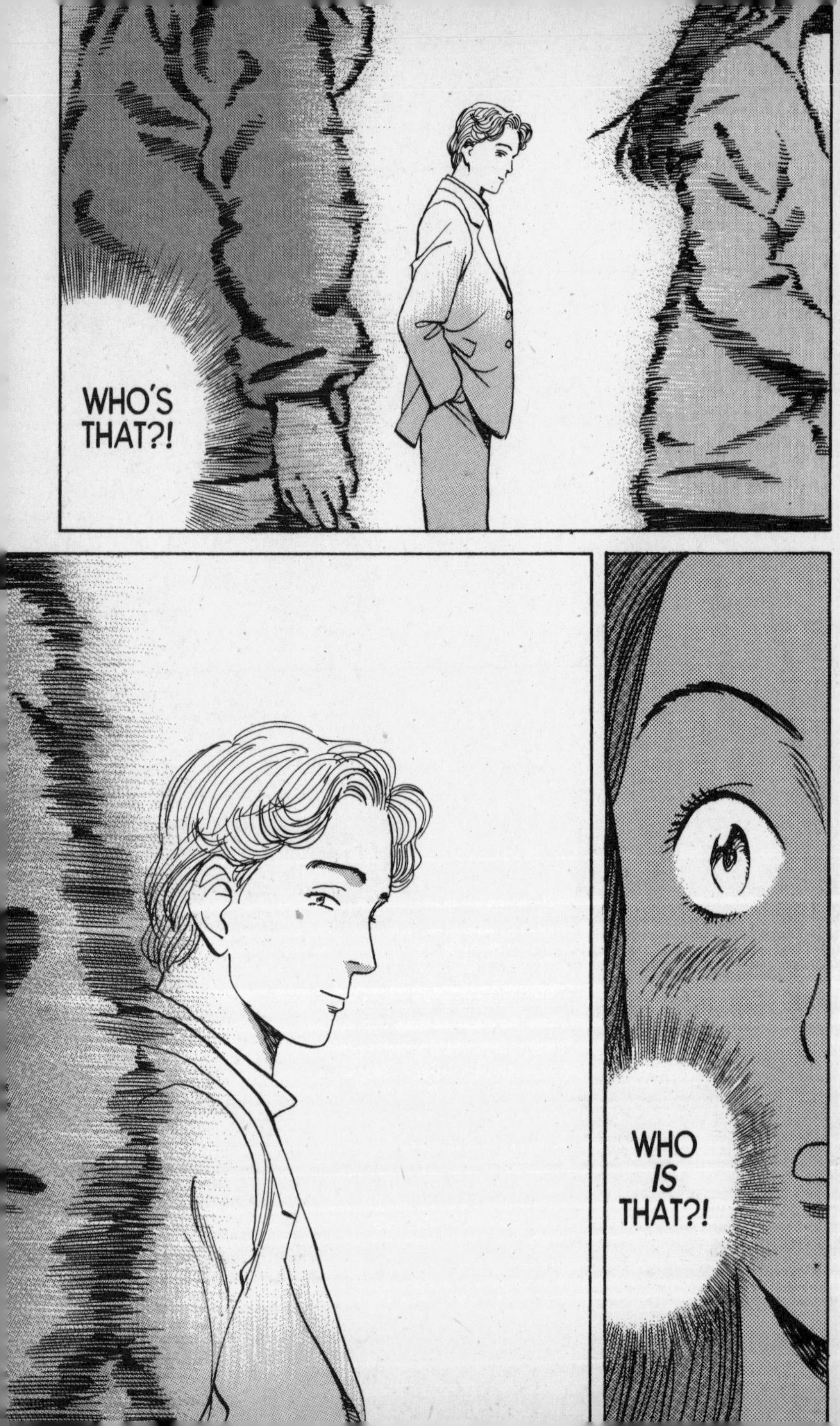
WHO'S THAT?!
WHO *IS* THAT?!

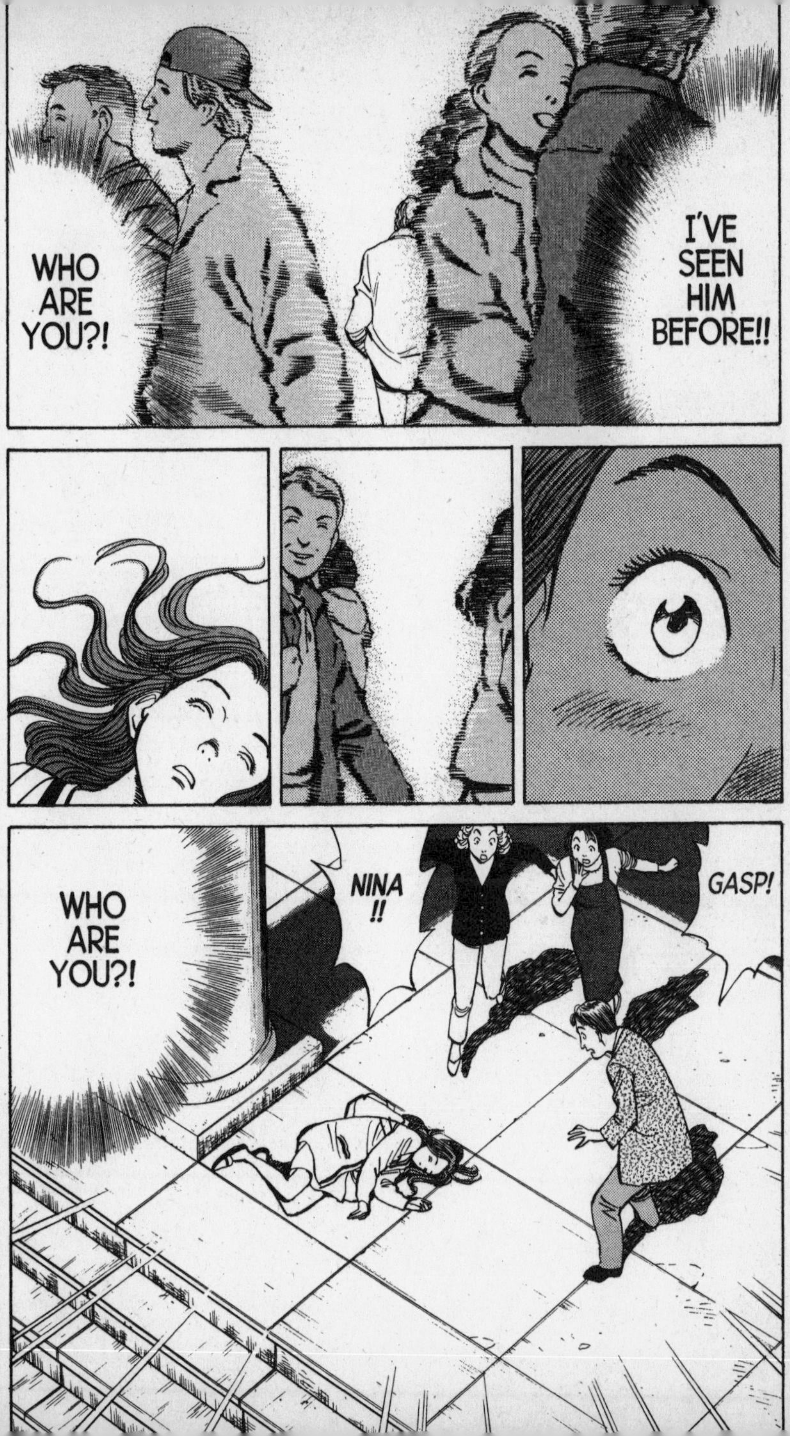
I'VE SEEN HIM BEFORE!!
WHO ARE YOU?!
GASP!
NINA!!
WHO ARE YOU?!

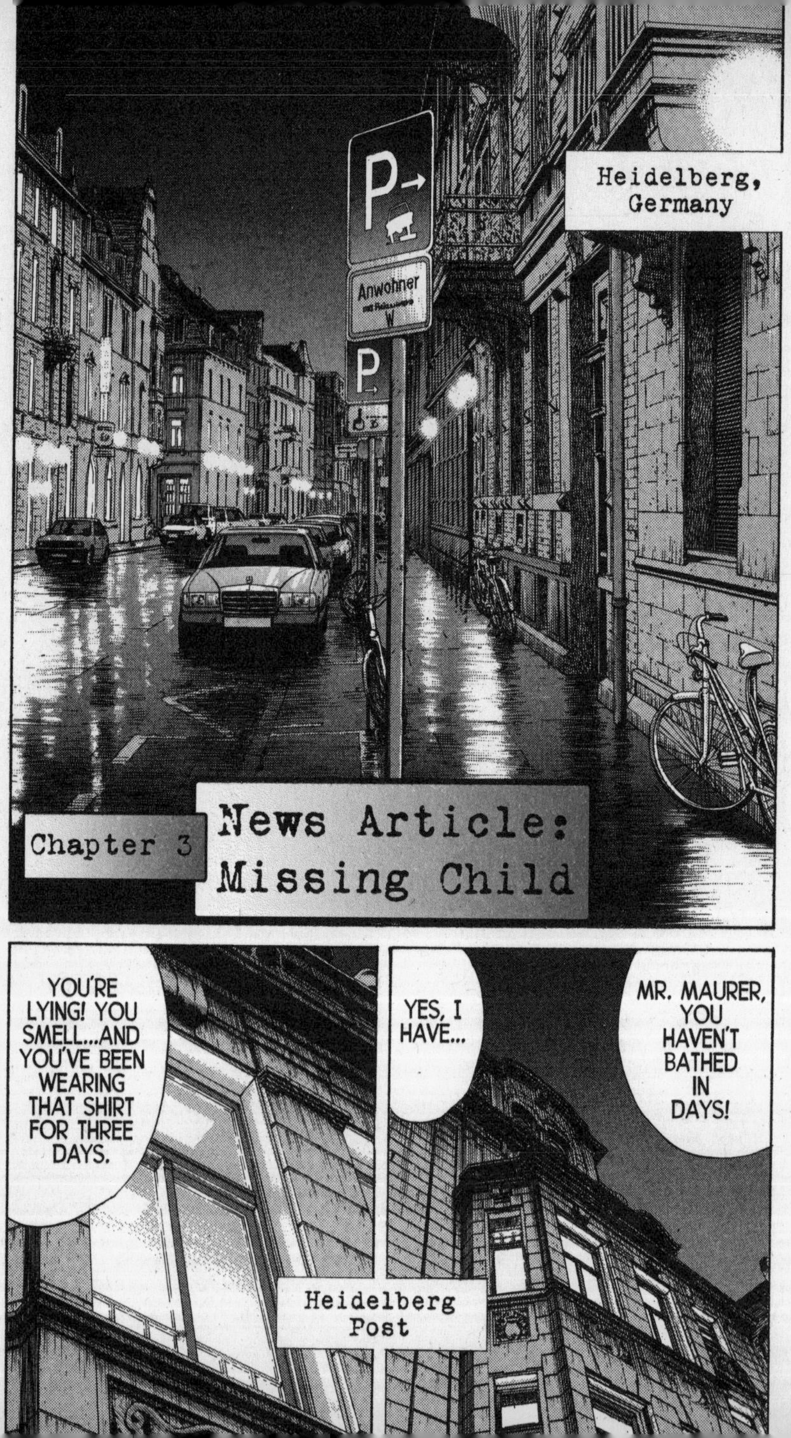
Heidelberg, Germany
Anwohner
Chapter 3
News Article: Missing Child
MR. MAURER, YOU HAVEN'T BATHED IN DAYS!
YES, I HAVE...
Heidelberg Post
YOU'RE LYING! YOU SMELL...AND YOU'VE BEEN WEARING THAT SHIRT FOR THREE DAYS.

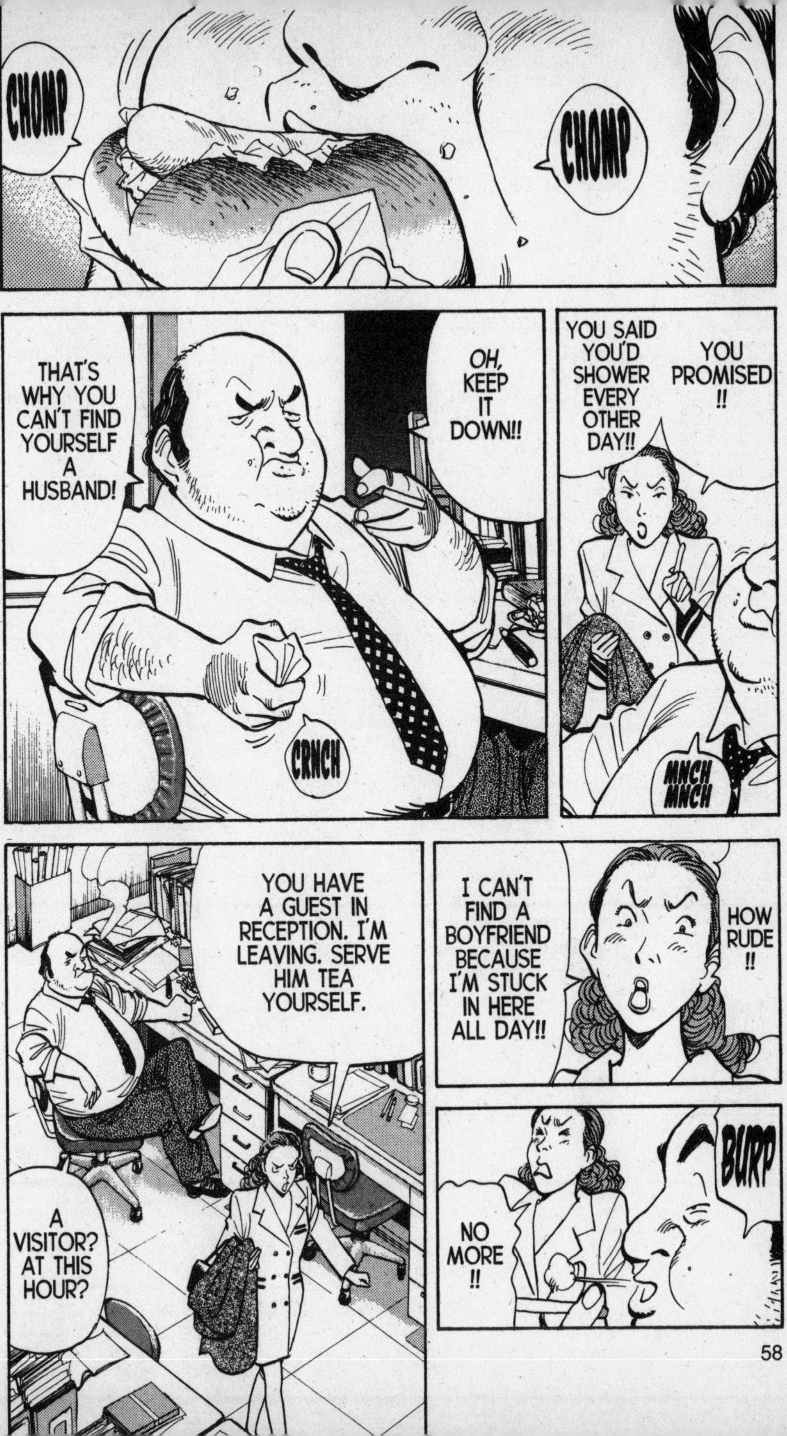
CHOMP
CHOMP
YOU PROMISED!!
YOU SAID YOU'D SHOWER EVERY OTHER DAY!!
MNCH MNCH
OH, KEEP IT DOWN!!
THAT'S WHY YOU CAN'T FIND YOURSELF A HUSBAND!
CRNCH
HOW RUDE!!
I CAN'T FIND A BOYFRIEND BECAUSE I'M STUCK IN HERE ALL DAY!!
BURP
NO MORE!!
YOU HAVE A GUEST IN RECEPTION. I'M LEAVING. SERVE HIM TEA YOURSELF.
A VISITOR? AT THIS HOUR?

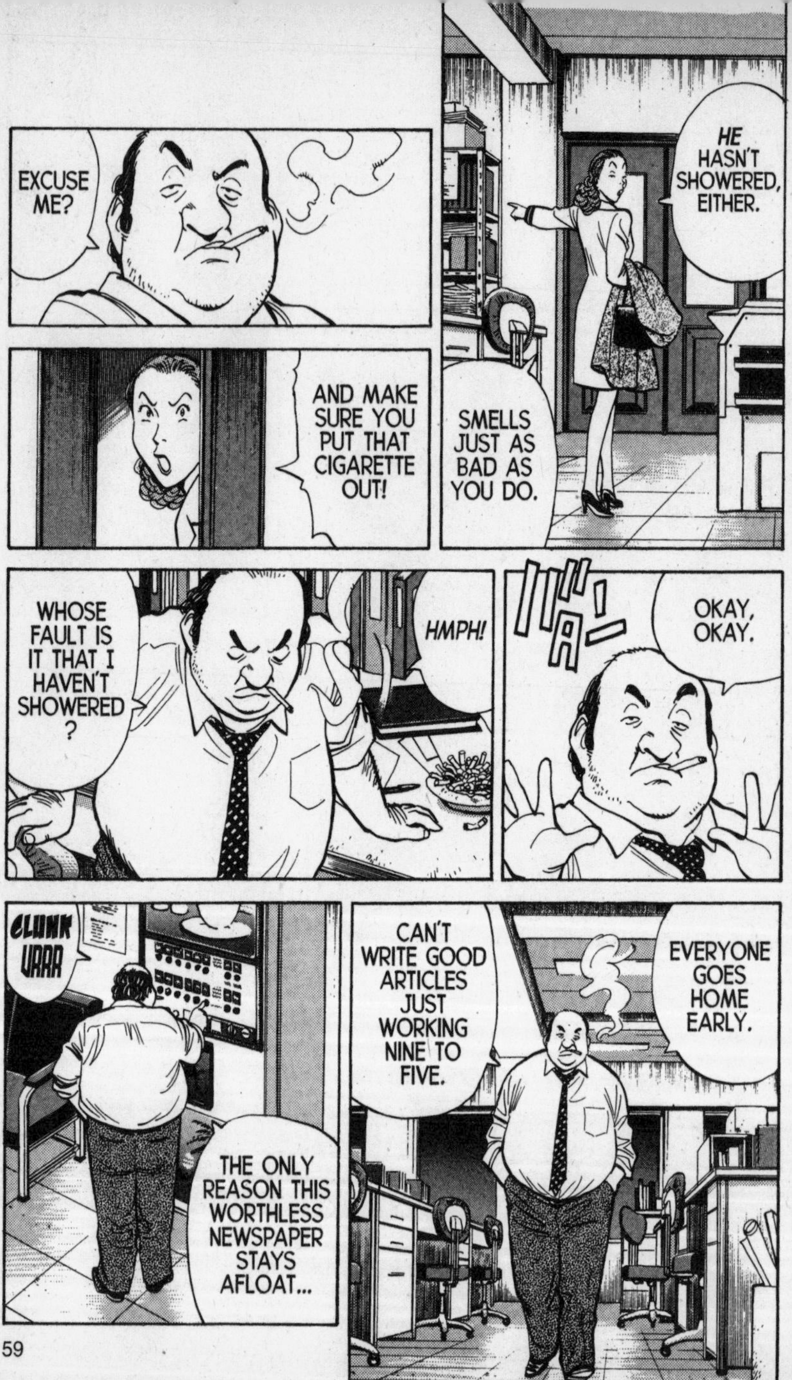
HE HASN'T SHOWERED, EITHER.
SMELLS JUST AS BAD AS YOU DO.
EXCUSE ME?
AND MAKE SURE YOU PUT THAT CIGARETTE OUT!
OKAY, OKAY.
HMPH!
WHOSE FAULT IS IT THAT I HAVEN'T SHOWERED?
EVERYONE GOES HOME EARLY.
CAN'T WRITE GOOD ARTICLES JUST WORKING NINE TO FIVE.
CLUNK
URRR
THE ONLY REASON THIS WORTHLESS NEWSPAPER STAYS AFLOAT...

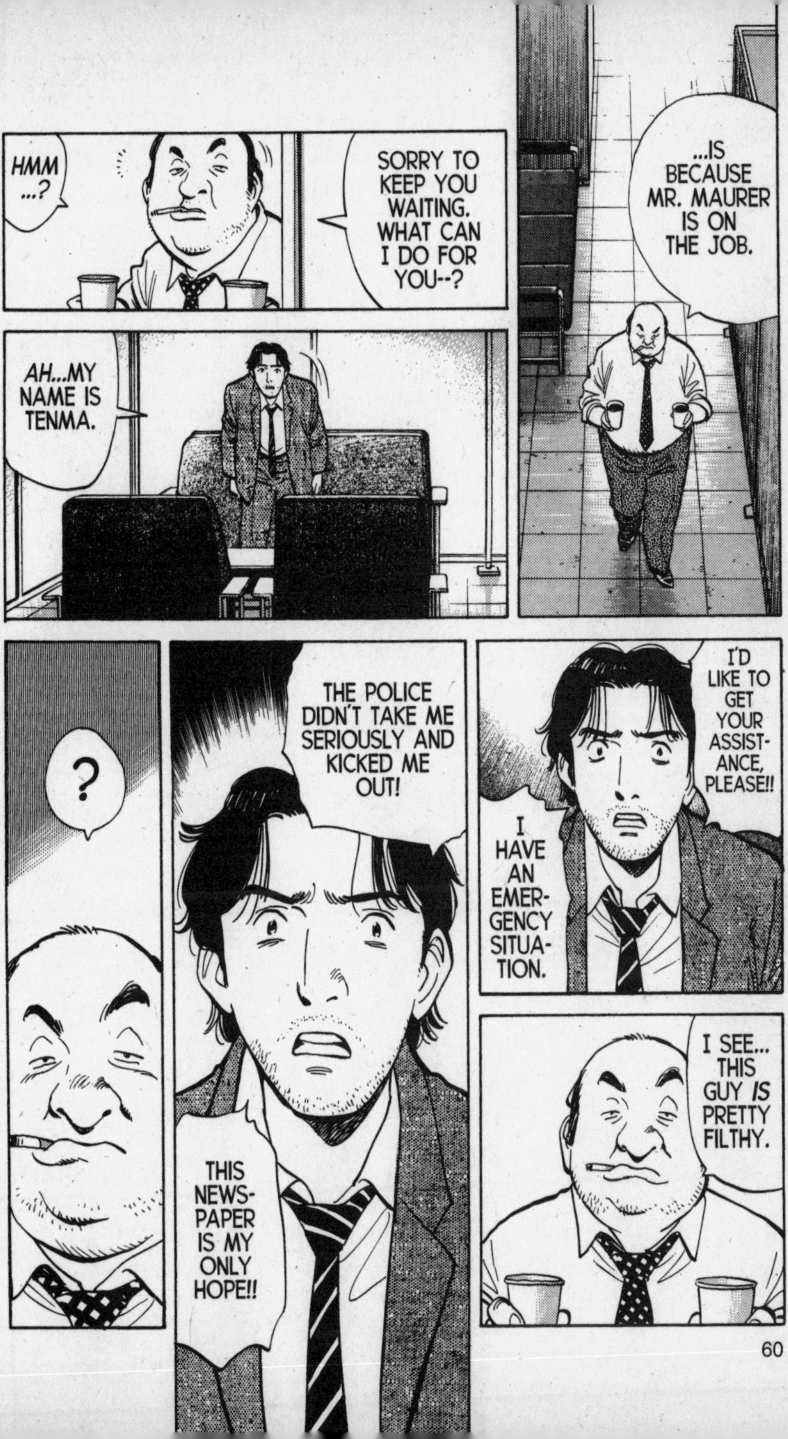
...IS BECAUSE MR. MAURER IS ON THE JOB.
SORRY TO KEEP YOU WAITING. WHAT CAN I DO FOR YOU--?
HMM ...?
AH...MY NAME IS TENMA.
I'D LIKE TO GET YOUR ASSIST-ANCE, PLEASE!!
I HAVE AN EMER-GENCY SITUA-TION.
I SEE... THIS GUY *IS* PRETTY FILTHY.
THE POLICE DIDN'T TAKE ME SERIOUSLY AND KICKED ME OUT!
THIS NEWS-PAPER IS MY ONLY HOPE!!
?

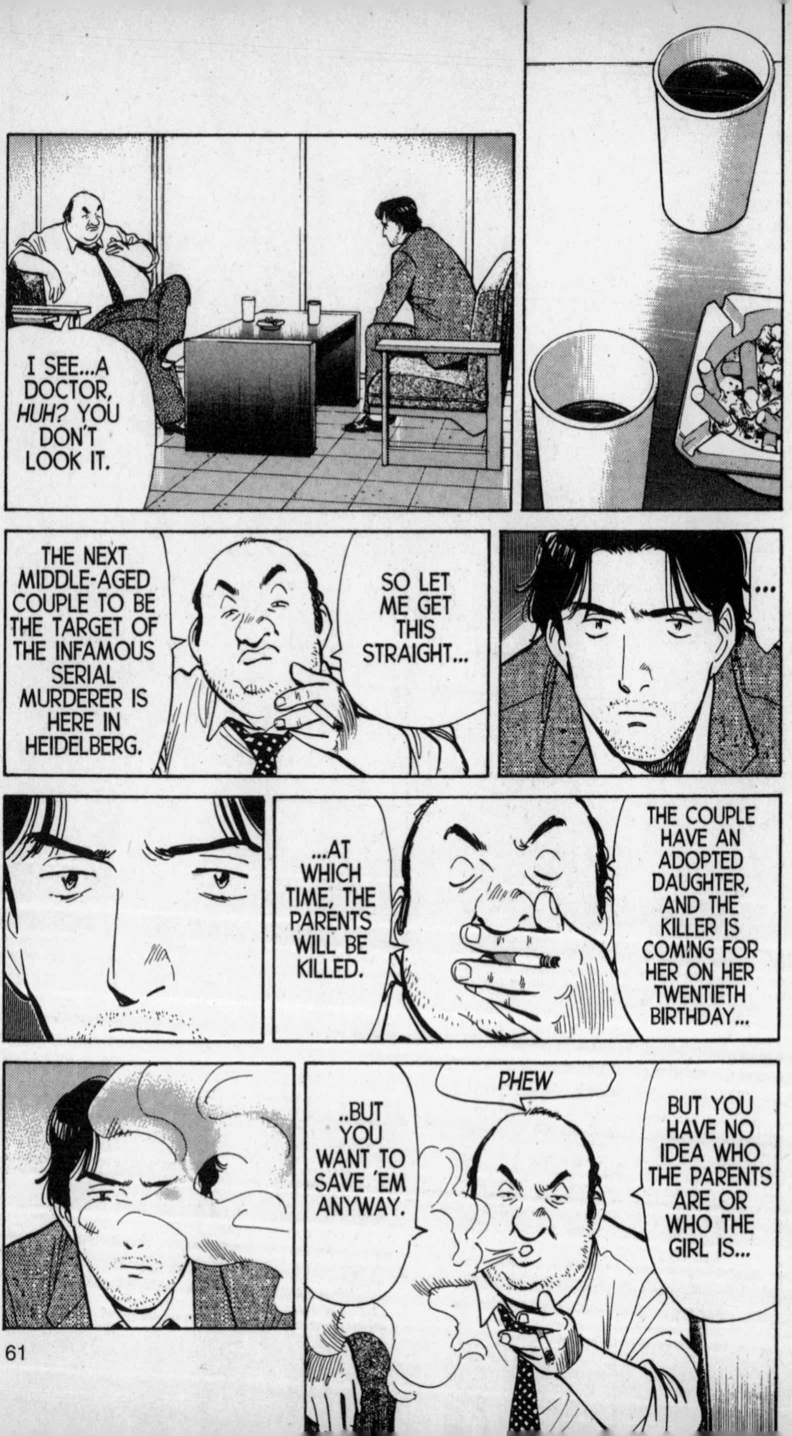
I SEE...A DOCTOR, HUH? YOU DON'T LOOK IT.
...
SO LET ME GET THIS STRAIGHT...
THE NEXT MIDDLE-AGED COUPLE TO BE THE TARGET OF THE INFAMOUS SERIAL MURDERER IS HERE IN HEIDELBERG.
THE COUPLE HAVE AN ADOPTED DAUGHTER, AND THE KILLER IS COMING FOR HER ON HER TWENTIETH BIRTHDAY...
...AT WHICH TIME, THE PARENTS WILL BE KILLED.
PHEW
BUT YOU HAVE NO IDEA WHO THE PARENTS ARE OR WHO THE GIRL IS...
..BUT YOU WANT TO SAVE 'EM ANYWAY.

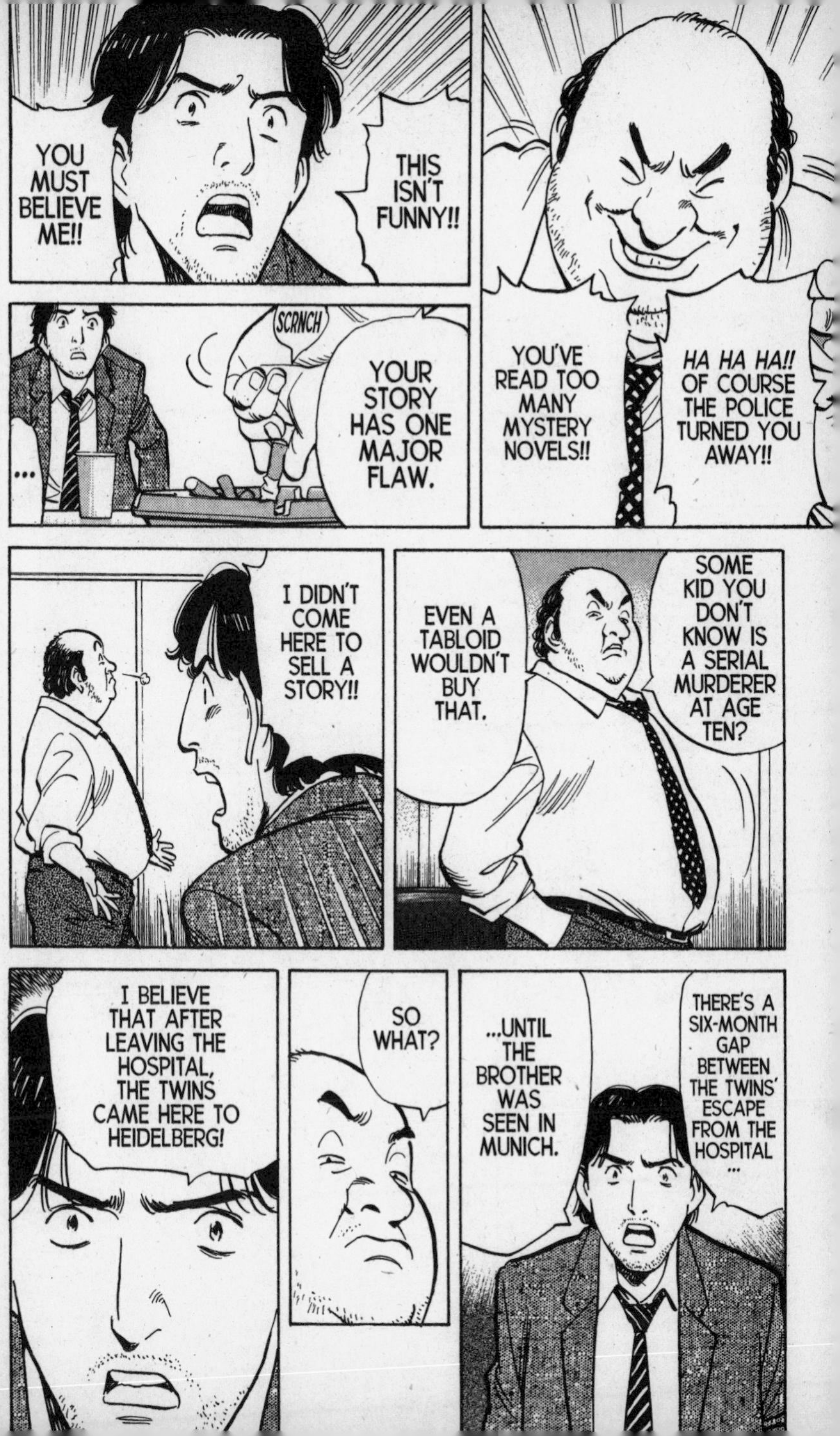
HA HA HA!! OF COURSE THE POLICE TURNED YOU AWAY!!
YOU'VE READ TOO MANY MYSTERY NOVELS!!
THIS ISN'T FUNNY!!
YOU MUST BELIEVE ME!!
YOUR STORY HAS ONE MAJOR FLAW.
SCRNCH
...
SOME KID YOU DON'T KNOW IS A SERIAL MURDERER AT AGE TEN?
EVEN A TABLOID WOULDN'T BUY THAT.
I DIDN'T COME HERE TO SELL A STORY!!
THERE'S A SIX-MONTH GAP BETWEEN THE TWINS' ESCAPE FROM THE HOSPITAL ...
...UNTIL THE BROTHER WAS SEEN IN MUNICH.
SO WHAT?
I BELIEVE THAT AFTER LEAVING THE HOSPITAL, THE TWINS CAME HERE TO HEIDELBERG!

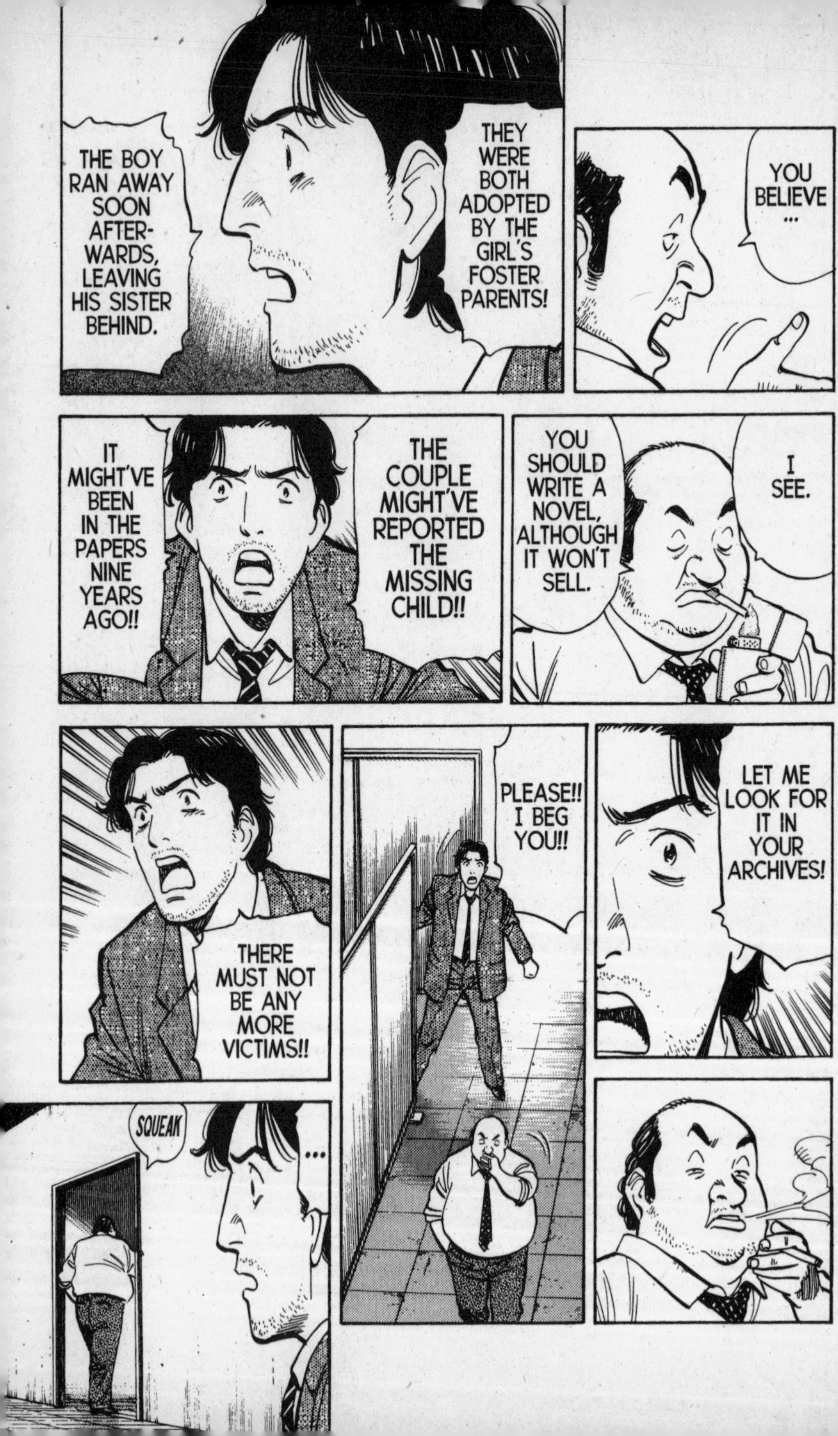
YOU BELIEVE ...
THEY WERE BOTH ADOPTED BY THE GIRL'S FOSTER PARENTS!
THE BOY RAN AWAY SOON AFTER-WARDS, LEAVING HIS SISTER BEHIND.
I SEE.
YOU SHOULD WRITE A NOVEL, ALTHOUGH IT WON'T SELL.
THE COUPLE MIGHT'VE REPORTED THE MISSING CHILD!!
IT MIGHT'VE BEEN IN THE PAPERS NINE YEARS AGO!!
LET ME LOOK FOR IT IN YOUR ARCHIVES!
PLEASE!! I BEG YOU!!
THERE MUST NOT BE ANY MORE VICTIMS!!
...
SQUEAK

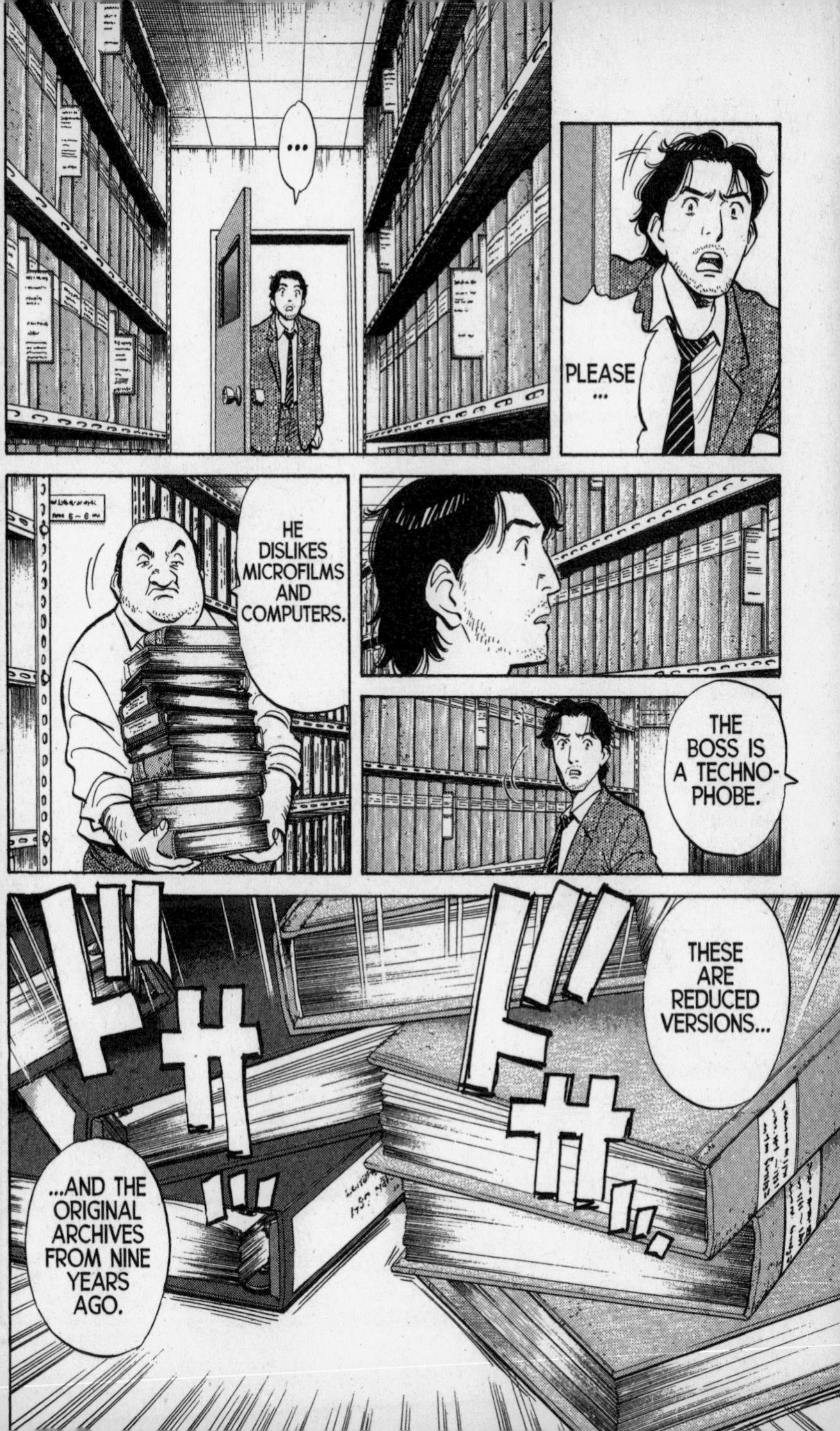
PLEASE ...
...
THE BOSS IS A TECHNO-PHOBE.
HE DISLIKES MICROFILMS AND COMPUTERS.
THESE ARE REDUCED VERSIONS...
...AND THE ORIGINAL ARCHIVES FROM NINE YEARS AGO.

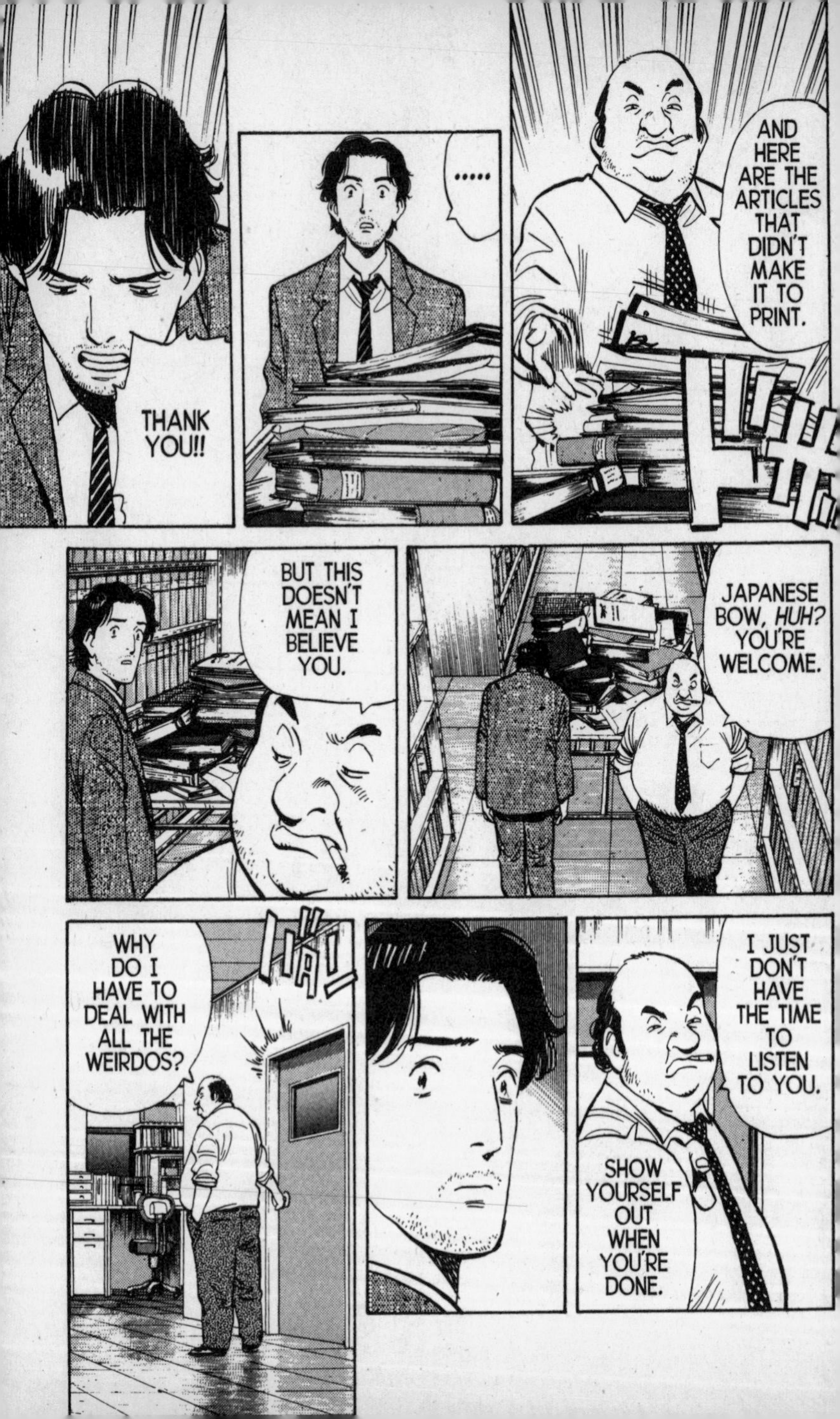
AND HERE ARE THE ARTICLES THAT DIDN'T MAKE IT TO PRINT.
.....
THANK YOU!!
JAPANESE BOW, *HUH?* YOU'RE WELCOME.
BUT THIS DOESN'T MEAN I BELIEVE YOU.
I JUST DON'T HAVE THE TIME TO LISTEN TO YOU.
SHOW YOURSELF OUT WHEN YOU'RE DONE.
WHY DO I HAVE TO DEAL WITH ALL THE WEIRDOS?

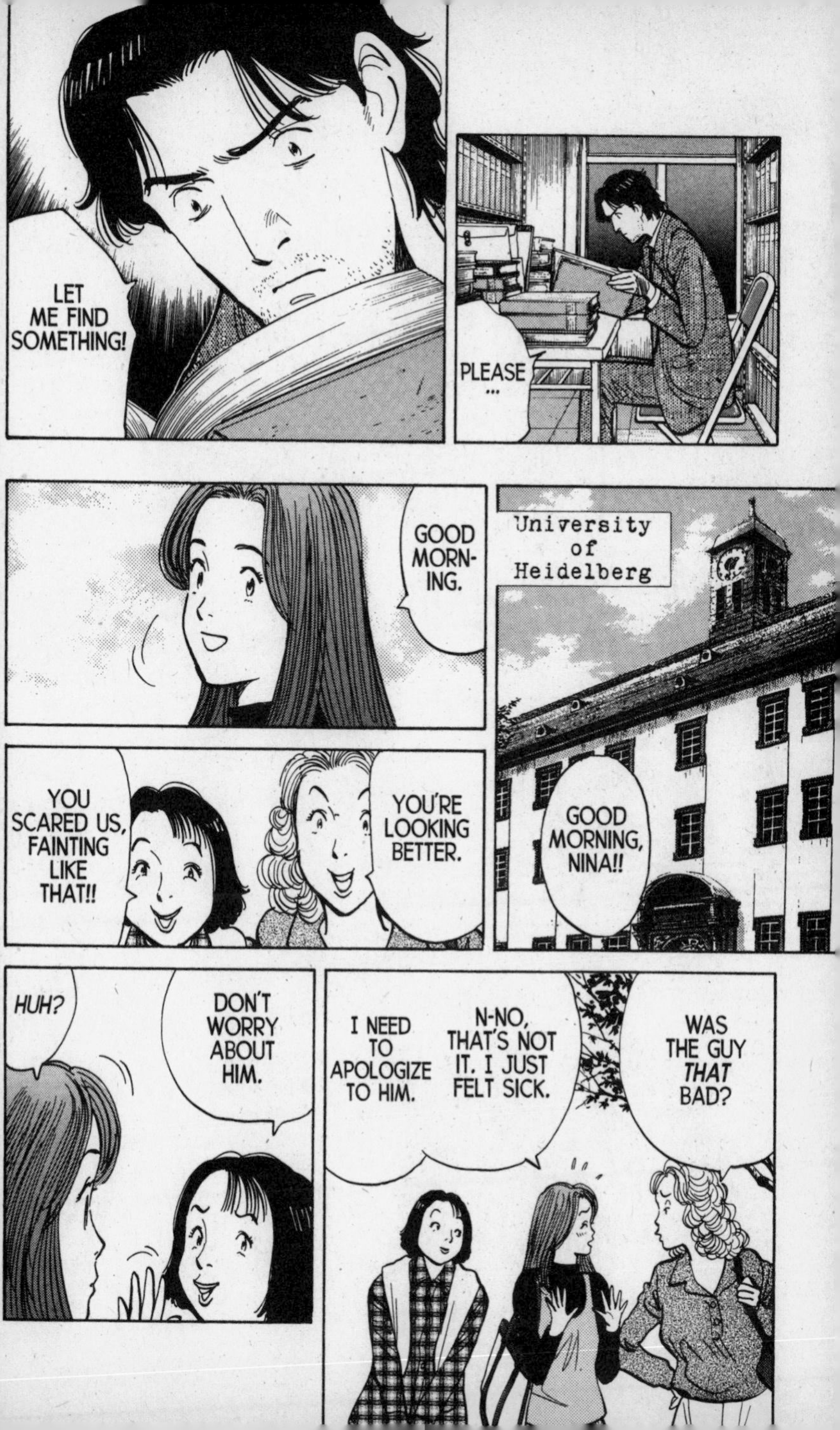
PLEASE ...
LET ME FIND SOMETHING!
University of Heidelberg
GOOD MORNING, NINA!!
GOOD MORNING.
YOU'RE LOOKING BETTER.
YOU SCARED US, FAINTING LIKE THAT!!
WAS THE GUY *THAT* BAD?
N-NO, THAT'S NOT IT. I JUST FELT SICK.
I NEED TO APOLOGIZE TO HIM.
DON'T WORRY ABOUT HIM.
HUH?

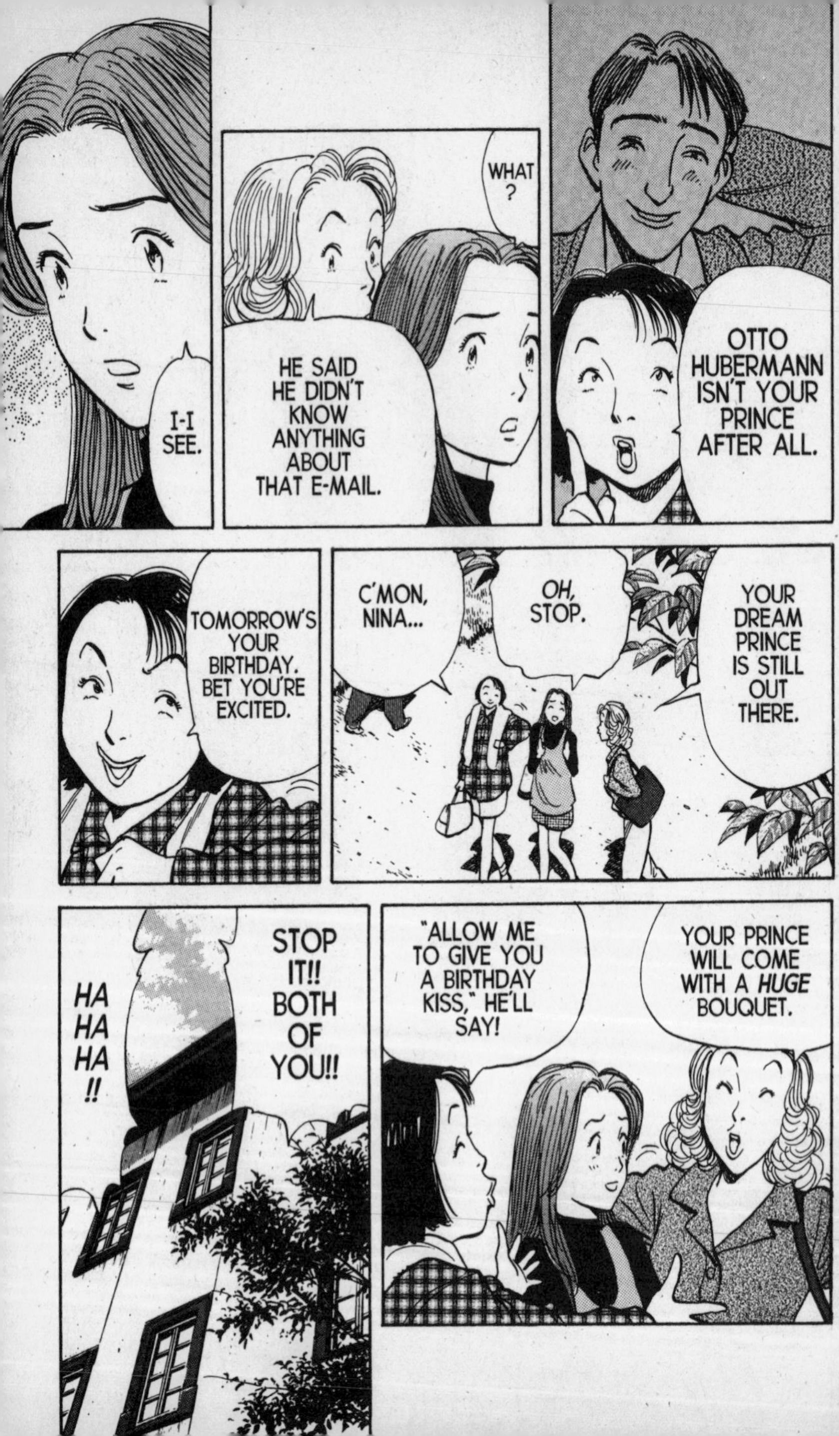
OTTO HUBERMANN ISN'T YOUR PRINCE AFTER ALL.
WHAT?
HE SAID HE DIDN'T KNOW ANYTHING ABOUT THAT E-MAIL.
I-I SEE.
YOUR DREAM PRINCE IS STILL OUT THERE.
OH, STOP.
C'MON, NINA...
TOMORROW'S YOUR BIRTHDAY. BET YOU'RE EXCITED.
YOUR PRINCE WILL COME WITH A *HUGE* BOUQUET.
"ALLOW ME TO GIVE YOU A BIRTHDAY KISS," HE'LL SAY!
STOP IT!! BOTH OF YOU!!
HA HA HA!!

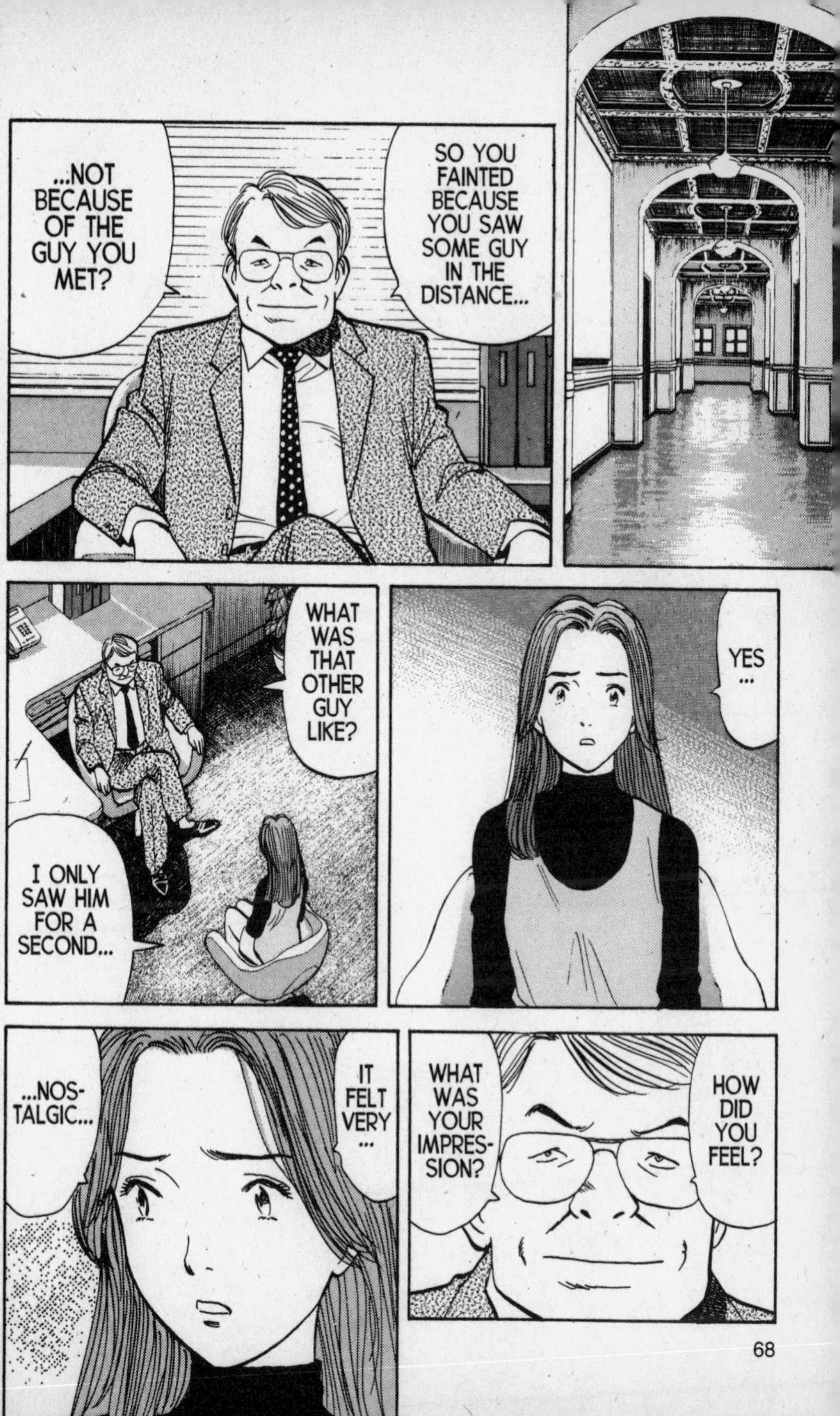
SO YOU FAINTED BECAUSE YOU SAW SOME GUY IN THE DISTANCE...
...NOT BECAUSE OF THE GUY YOU MET?
YES ...
WHAT WAS THAT OTHER GUY LIKE?
I ONLY SAW HIM FOR A SECOND...
HOW DID YOU FEEL?
WHAT WAS YOUR IMPRES-SION?
IT FELT VERY ...
...NOS-TALGIC...

I CAN'T REALLY EXPLAIN IT, BUT...

BUT... MAYBE NOT...

HMM...

BUT?

?

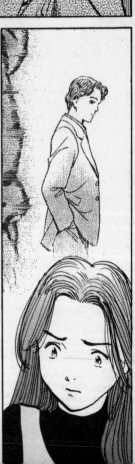

SHIVER SHIVER

SHIVER SHIVER

69

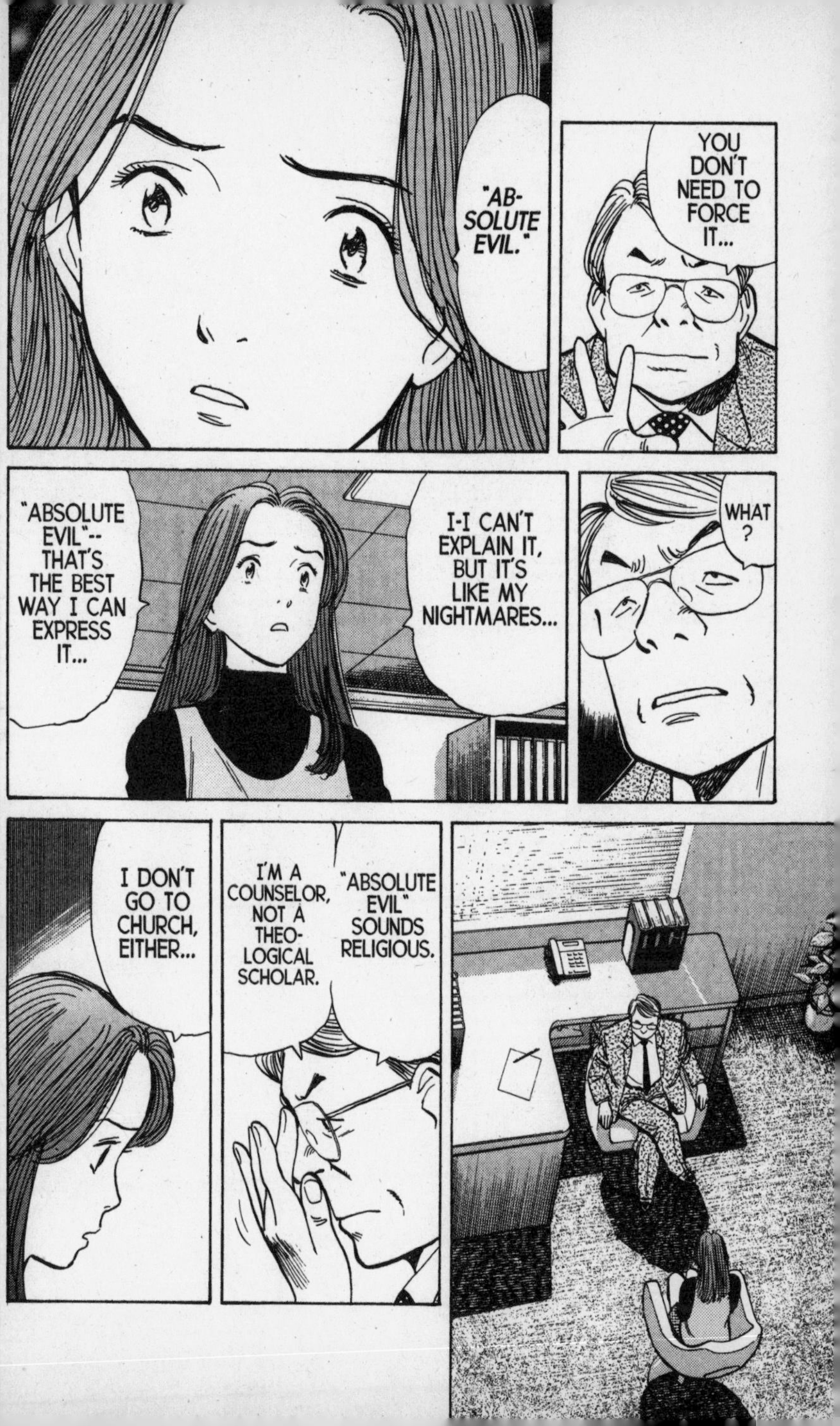
YOU DON'T NEED TO FORCE IT...
"AB-SOLUTE EVIL."
WHAT?
I-I CAN'T EXPLAIN IT, BUT IT'S LIKE MY NIGHTMARES...
"ABSOLUTE EVIL"-- THAT'S THE BEST WAY I CAN EXPRESS IT...
"ABSOLUTE EVIL" SOUNDS RELIGIOUS.
I'M A COUNSELOR, NOT A THEO-LOGICAL SCHOLAR.
I DON'T GO TO CHURCH, EITHER...

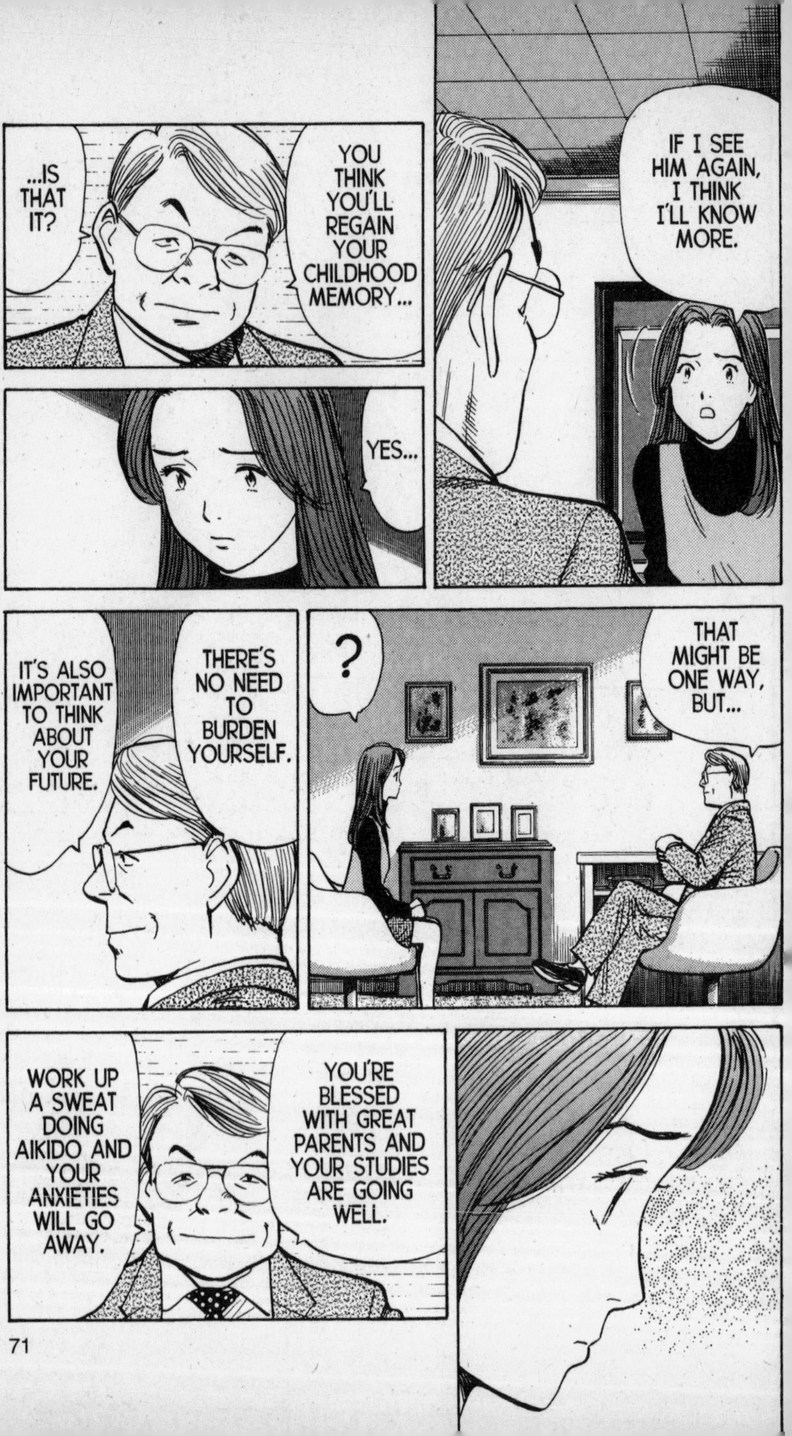
IF I SEE HIM AGAIN, I THINK I'LL KNOW MORE.
YOU THINK YOU'LL REGAIN YOUR CHILDHOOD MEMORY...
...IS THAT IT?
YES...
THAT MIGHT BE ONE WAY, BUT...
?
THERE'S NO NEED TO BURDEN YOURSELF.
IT'S ALSO IMPORTANT TO THINK ABOUT YOUR FUTURE.
YOU'RE BLESSED WITH GREAT PARENTS AND YOUR STUDIES ARE GOING WELL.
WORK UP A SWEAT DOING AIKIDO AND YOUR ANXIETIES WILL GO AWAY.

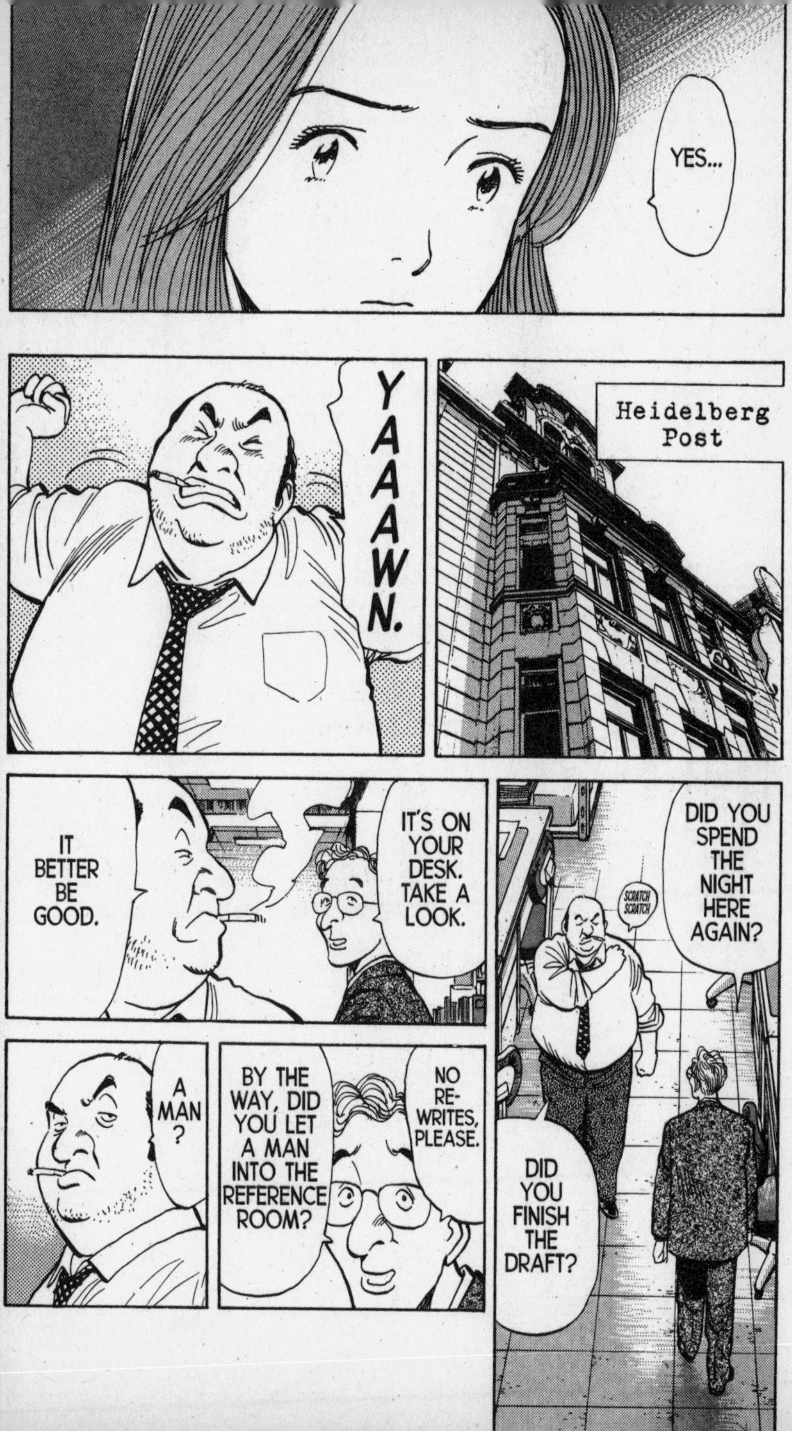
YES...
Heidelberg Post
YAAAWN.
DID YOU SPEND THE NIGHT HERE AGAIN?
SCRATCH SCRATCH
DID YOU FINISH THE DRAFT?
IT'S ON YOUR DESK. TAKE A LOOK.
IT BETTER BE GOOD.
NO RE-WRITES, PLEASE.
BY THE WAY, DID YOU LET A MAN INTO THE REFERENCE ROOM?
A MAN?

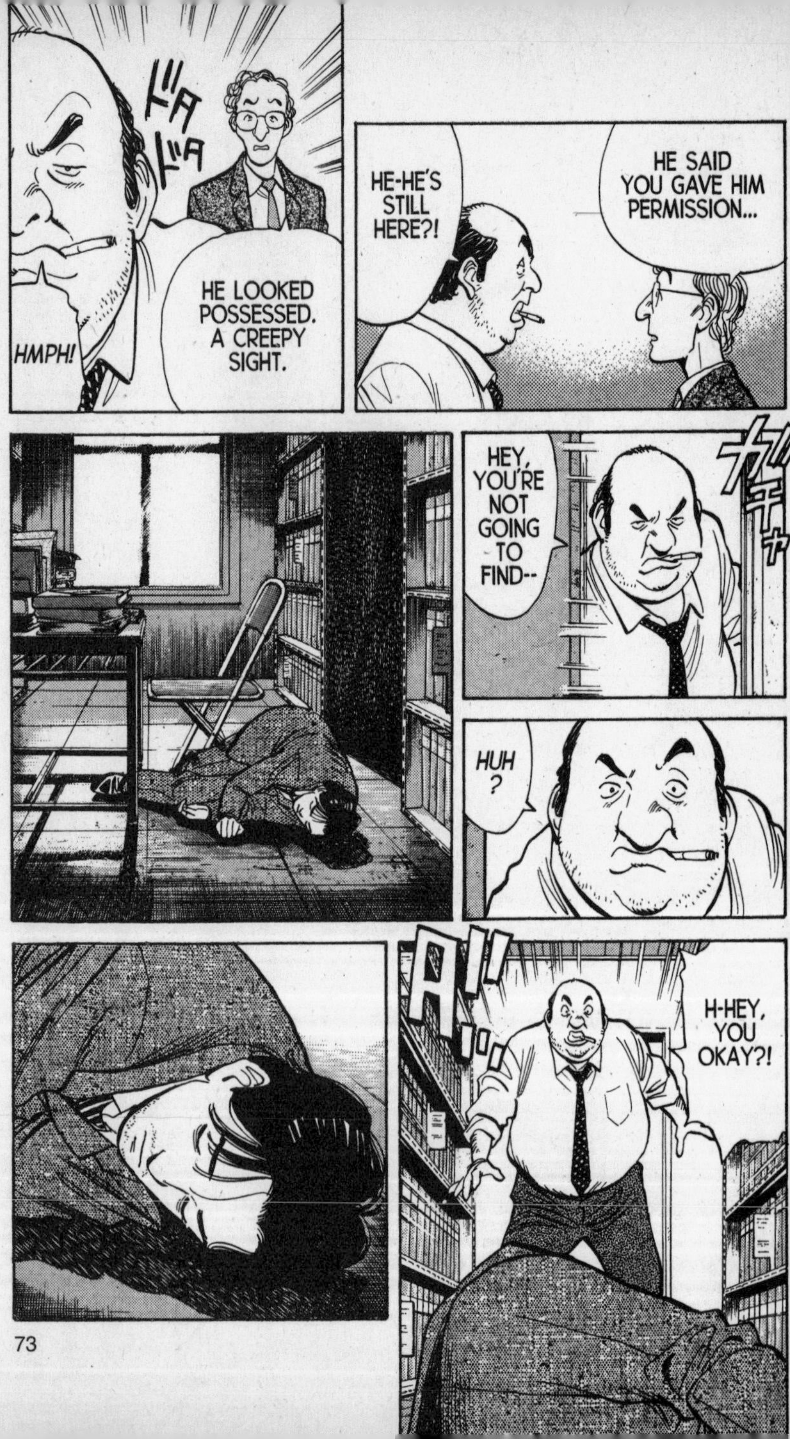
HE SAID YOU GAVE HIM PERMISSION...
HE-HE'S STILL HERE?!
HE LOOKED POSSESSED. A CREEPY SIGHT.
HMPH!
HEY, YOU'RE NOT GOING TO FIND--
HUH?
H-HEY, YOU OKAY?!

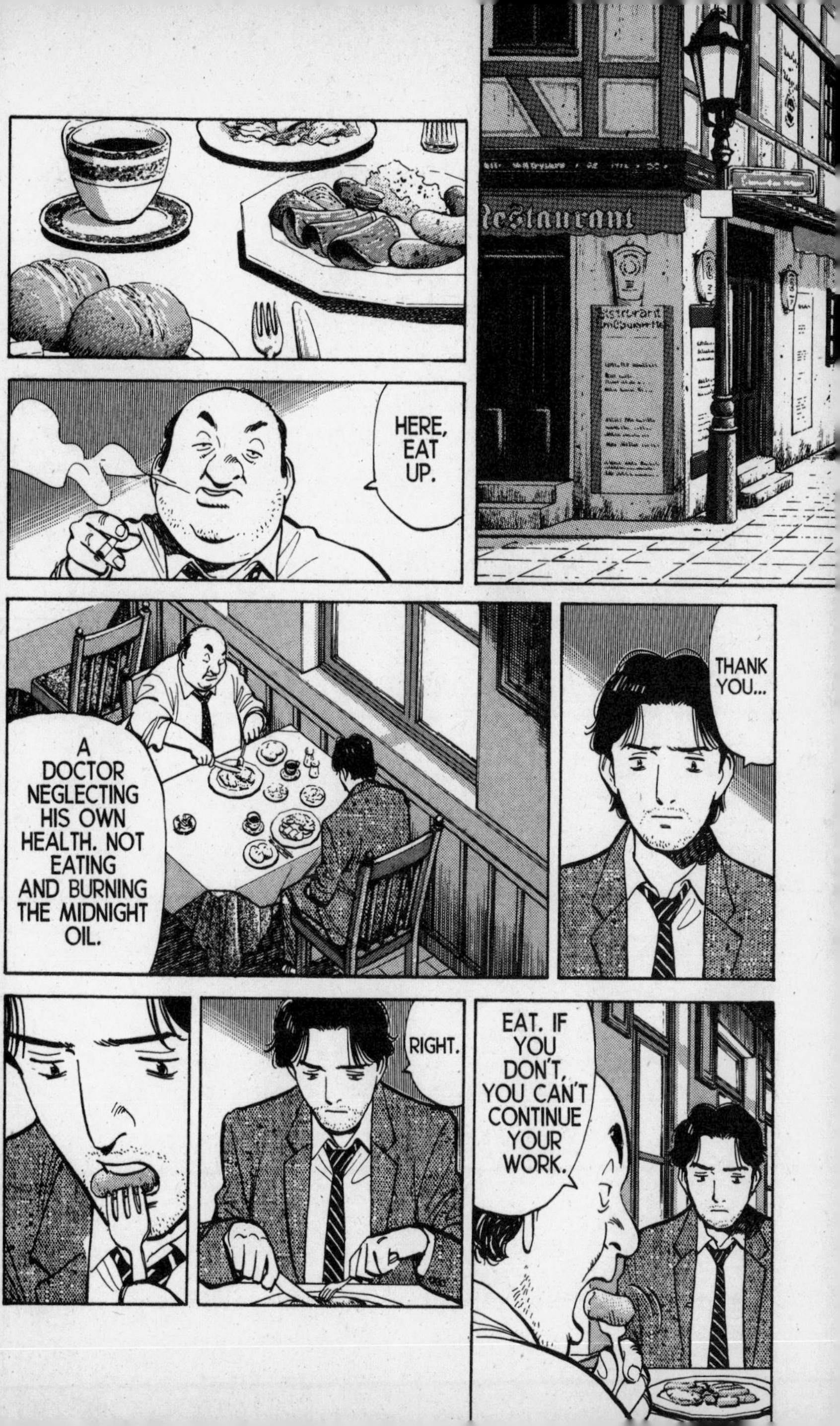
Restaurant
HERE, EAT UP.
THANK YOU...
A DOCTOR NEGLECTING HIS OWN HEALTH. NOT EATING AND BURNING THE MIDNIGHT OIL.
EAT. IF YOU DON'T, YOU CAN'T CONTINUE YOUR WORK.
RIGHT.

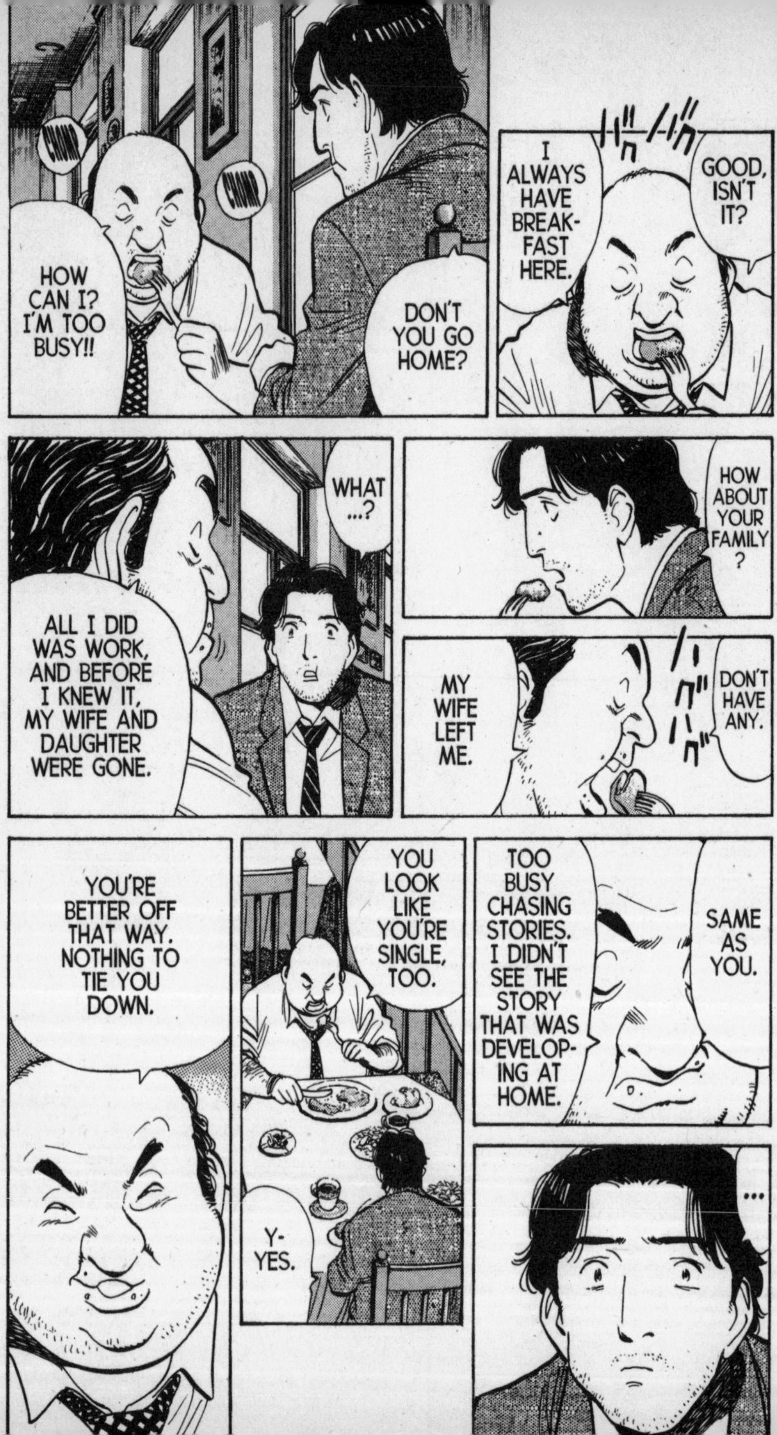
GOOD, ISN'T IT?
I ALWAYS HAVE BREAK-FAST HERE.
CHOMP
CHOMP
DON'T YOU GO HOME?
HOW CAN I? I'M TOO BUSY!!
HOW ABOUT YOUR FAMILY?
DON'T HAVE ANY.
MY WIFE LEFT ME.
WHAT ...?
ALL I DID WAS WORK, AND BEFORE I KNEW IT, MY WIFE AND DAUGHTER WERE GONE.
SAME AS YOU.
TOO BUSY CHASING STORIES. I DIDN'T SEE THE STORY THAT WAS DEVELOP-ING AT HOME.
...
YOU LOOK LIKE YOU'RE SINGLE, TOO.
Y-YES.
YOU'RE BETTER OFF THAT WAY. NOTHING TO TIE YOU DOWN.

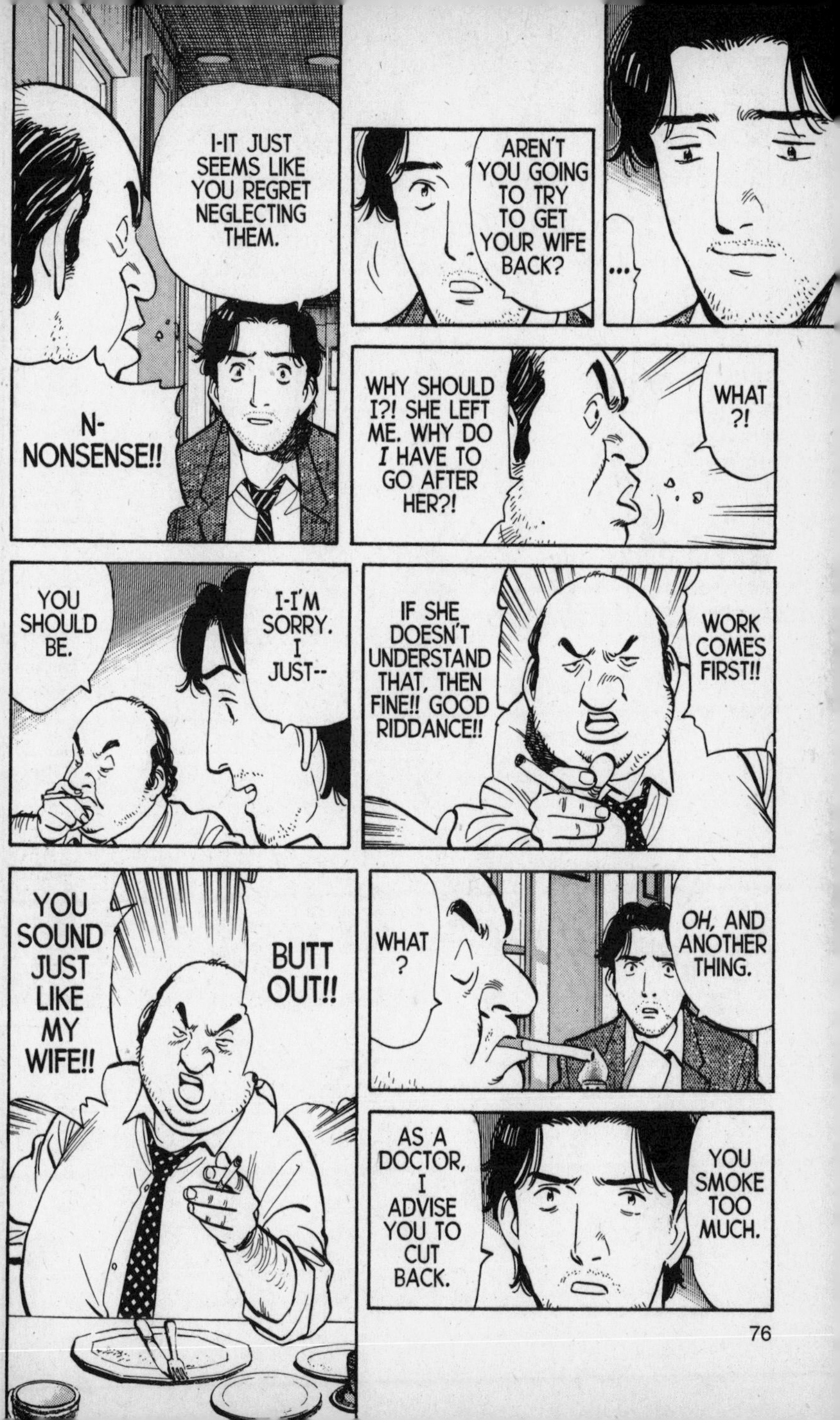
I-IT JUST SEEMS LIKE YOU REGRET NEGLECTING THEM.
N-NONSENSE!!
...
AREN'T YOU GOING TO TRY TO GET YOUR WIFE BACK?
WHAT ?!
WHY SHOULD I?! SHE LEFT ME. WHY DO *I* HAVE TO GO AFTER HER?!
WORK COMES FIRST!!
IF SHE DOESN'T UNDERSTAND THAT, THEN FINE!! GOOD RIDDANCE!!
YOU SOUND JUST LIKE MY WIFE!!
BUTT OUT!!
I-I'M SORRY. I JUST--
YOU SHOULD BE.
OH, AND ANOTHER THING.
WHAT ?
YOU SMOKE TOO MUCH.
AS A DOCTOR, I ADVISE YOU TO CUT BACK.

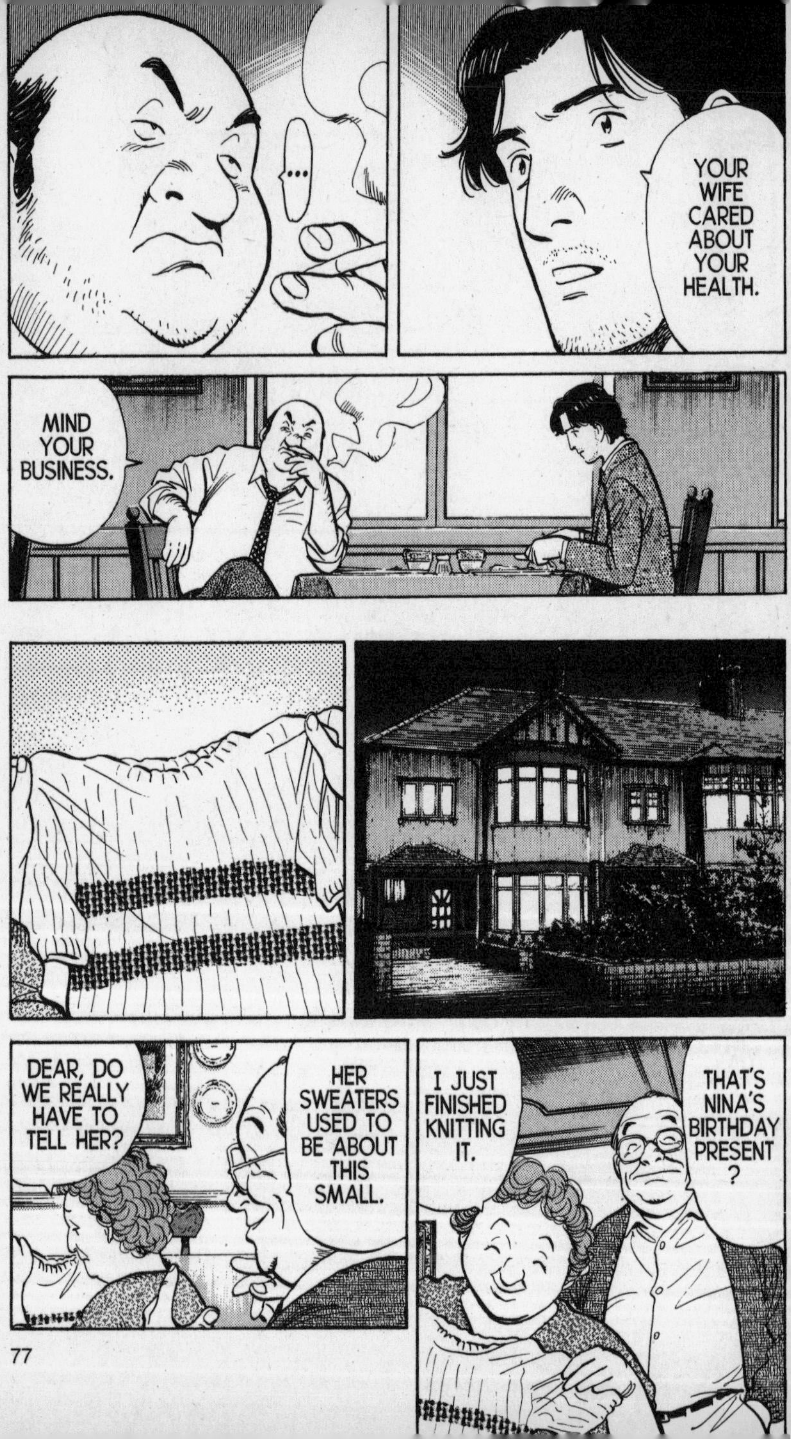
YOUR WIFE CARED ABOUT YOUR HEALTH.
...
MIND YOUR BUSINESS.
THAT'S NINA'S BIRTHDAY PRESENT?
I JUST FINISHED KNITTING IT.
HER SWEATERS USED TO BE ABOUT THIS SMALL.
DEAR, DO WE REALLY HAVE TO TELL HER?

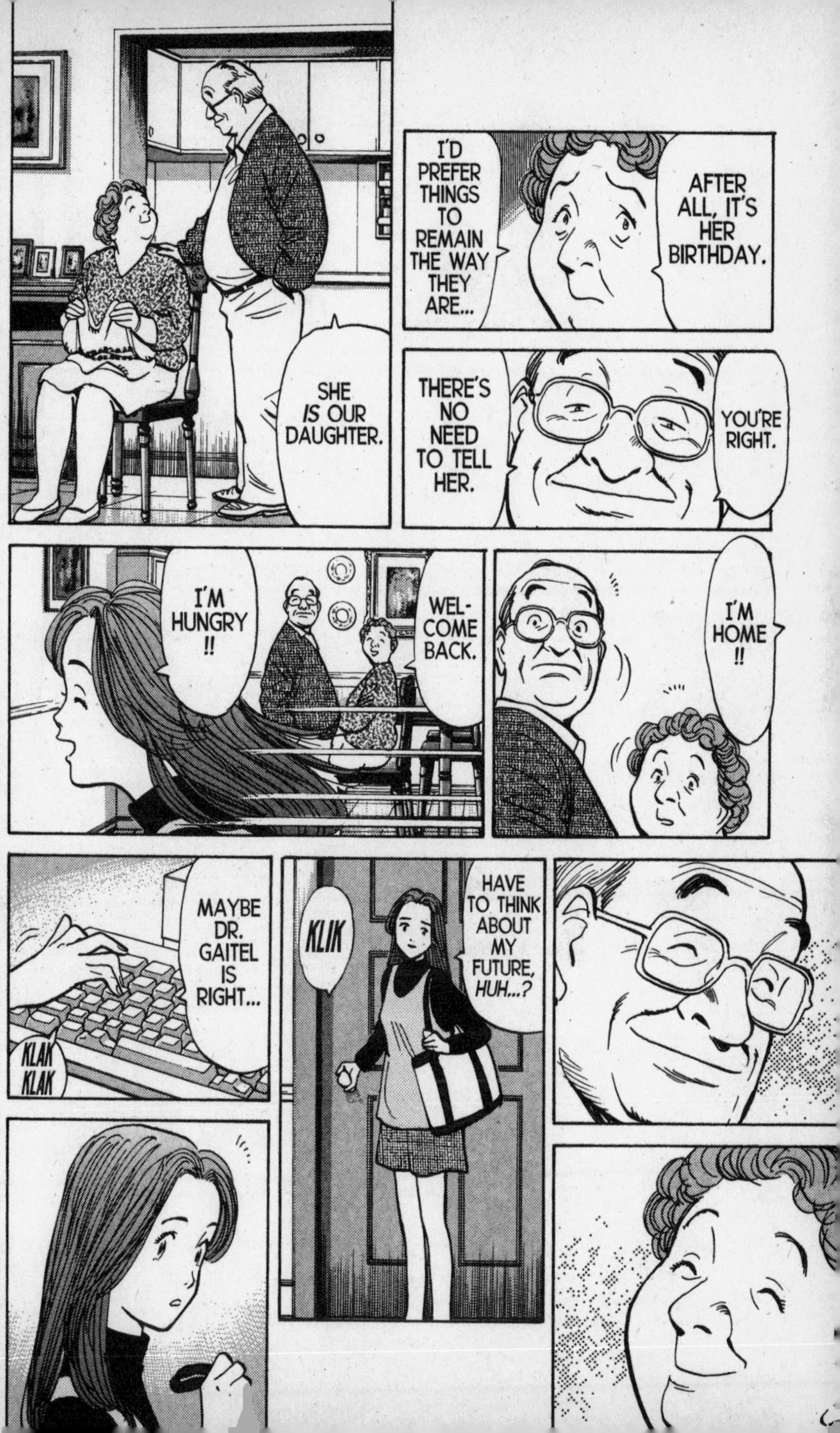
AFTER ALL, IT'S HER BIRTHDAY.
I'D PREFER THINGS TO REMAIN THE WAY THEY ARE...
YOU'RE RIGHT.
THERE'S NO NEED TO TELL HER.
SHE *IS* OUR DAUGHTER.
I'M HOME!!
WEL-COME BACK.
I'M HUNGRY!!
HAVE TO THINK ABOUT MY FUTURE, *HUH...?*
KLIK
MAYBE DR. GAITEL IS RIGHT...
KLAK KLAK

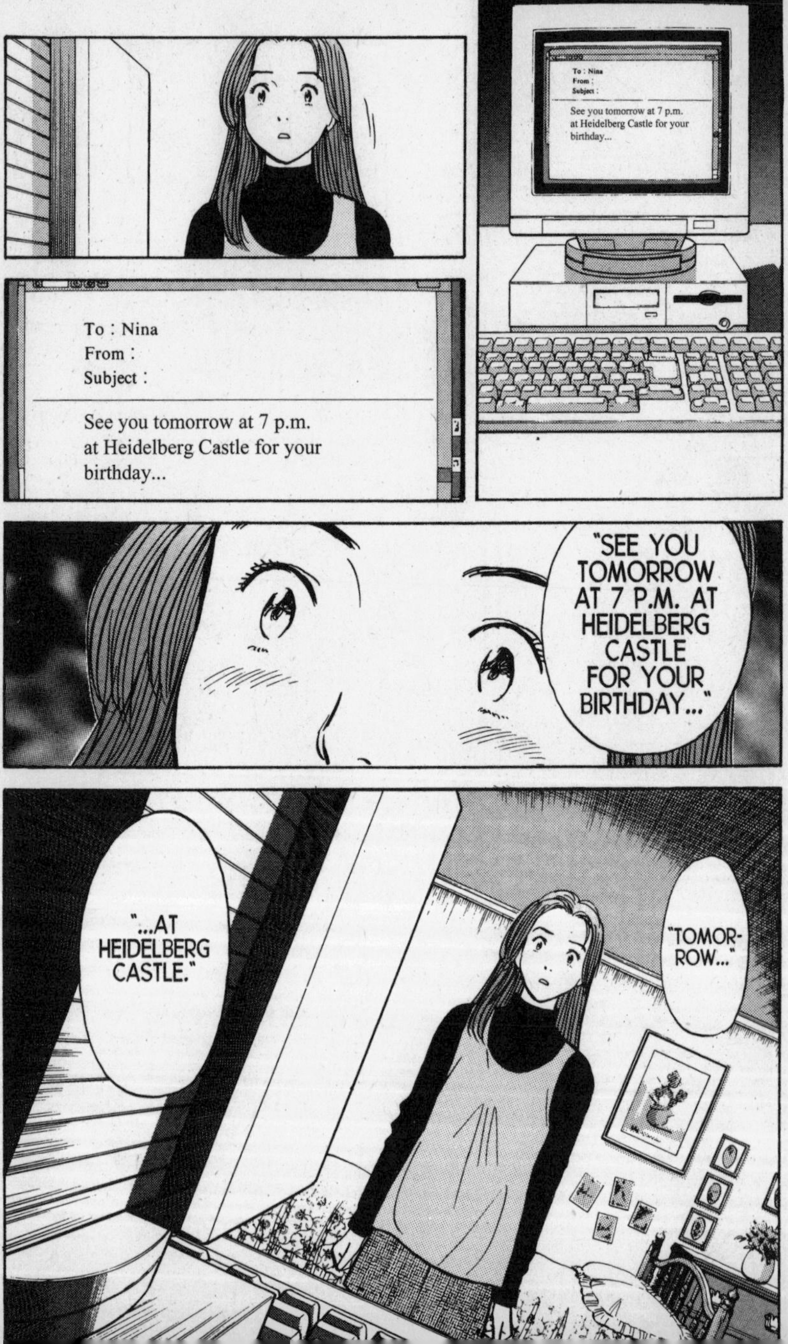
To : Nina
From :
Subject :
See you tomorrow at 7 p.m. at Heidelberg Castle for your birthday...
To : Nina
From :
Subject :
See you tomorrow at 7 p.m. at Heidelberg Castle for your birthday...
"SEE YOU TOMORROW AT 7 P.M. AT HEIDELBERG CASTLE FOR YOUR BIRTHDAY..."
"TOMOR-ROW..."
"...AT HEIDELBERG CASTLE."

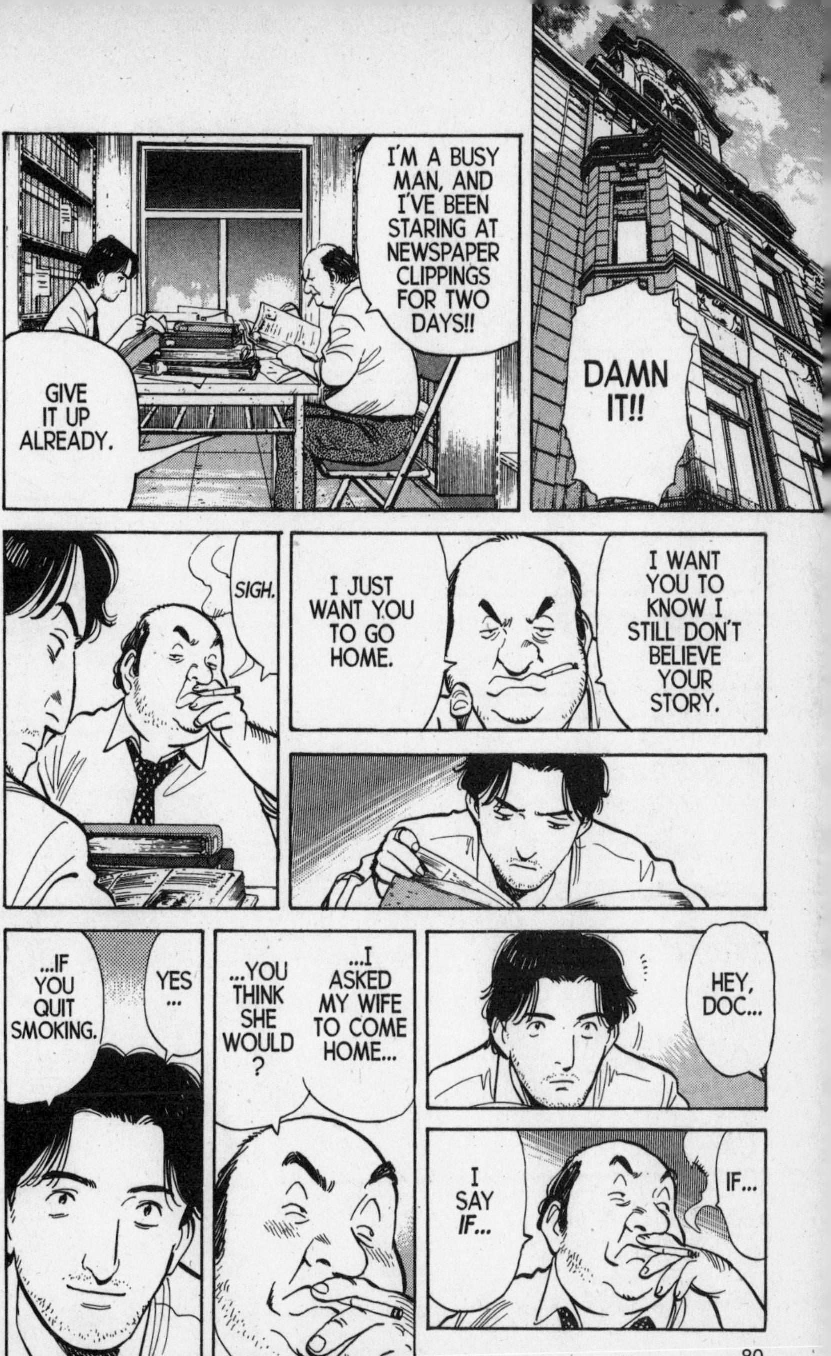
DAMN IT!!
I'M A BUSY MAN, AND I'VE BEEN STARING AT NEWSPAPER CLIPPINGS FOR TWO DAYS!!
GIVE IT UP ALREADY.
I WANT YOU TO KNOW I STILL DON'T BELIEVE YOUR STORY.
I JUST WANT YOU TO GO HOME.
SIGH.
HEY, DOC...
IF...
I SAY IF...
...I ASKED MY WIFE TO COME HOME...
...YOU THINK SHE WOULD?
YES...
...IF YOU QUIT SMOKING.

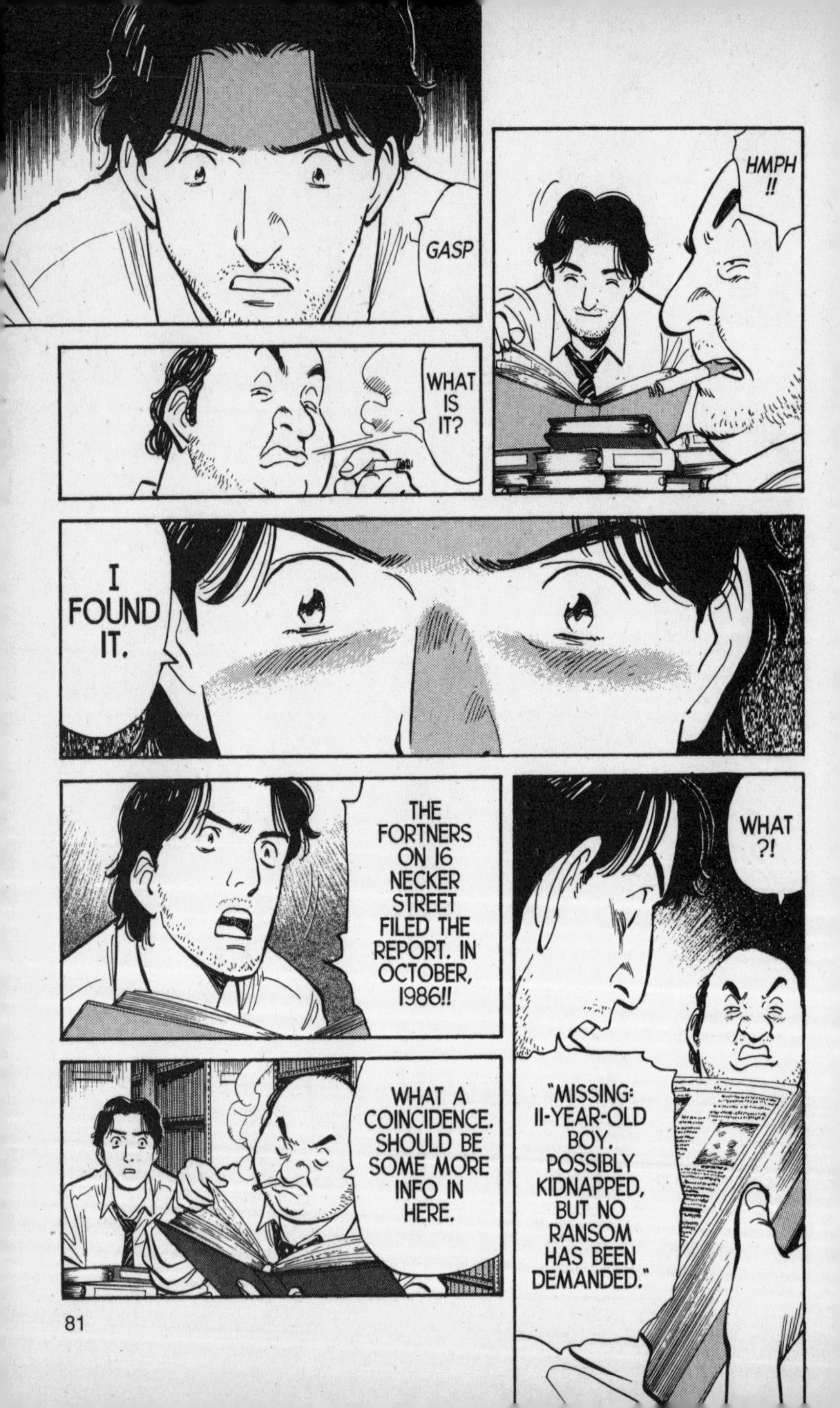
GASP
WHAT IS IT?
HMPH!!
I FOUND IT.
THE FORTNERS ON 16 NECKER STREET FILED THE REPORT. IN OCTOBER, 1986!!
WHAT?!
WHAT A COINCIDENCE. SHOULD BE SOME MORE INFO IN HERE.
"MISSING: 11-YEAR-OLD BOY. POSSIBLY KIDNAPPED, BUT NO RANSOM HAS BEEN DEMANDED."

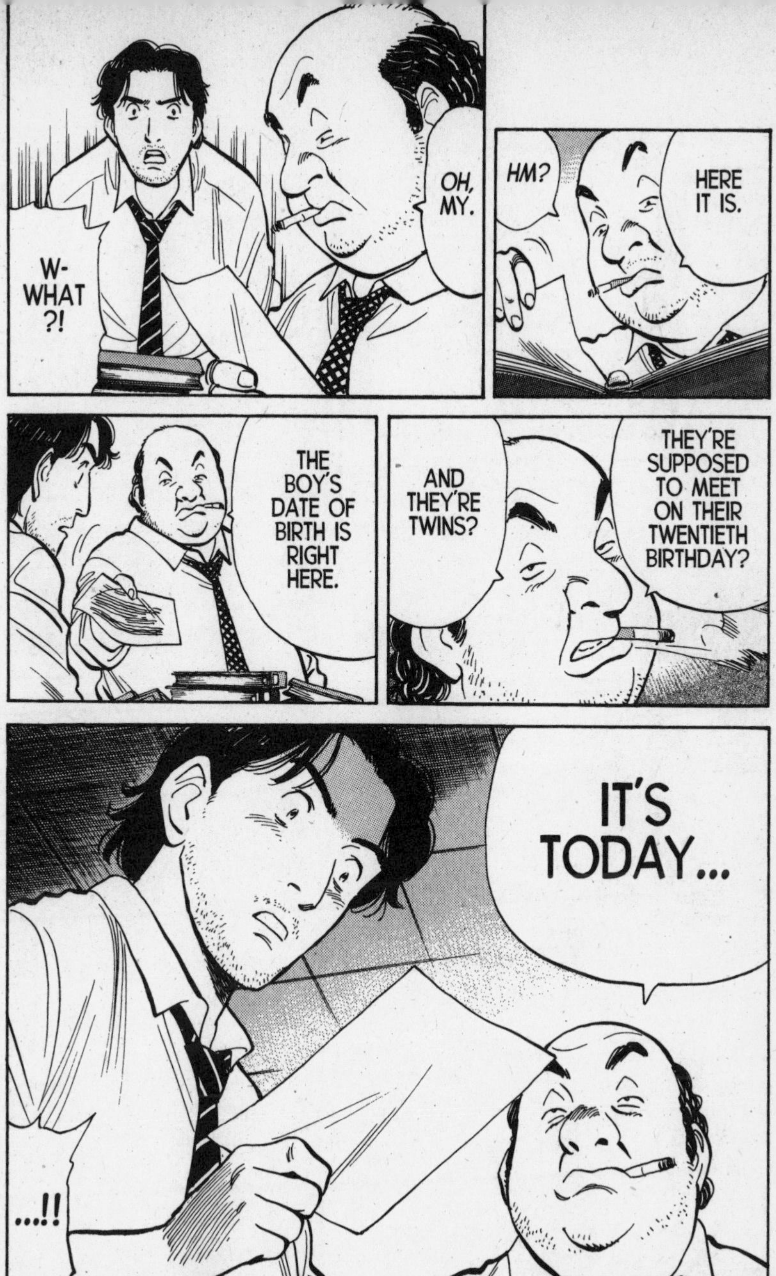
W-WHAT?!
OH, MY.
HM?
HERE IT IS.
THE BOY'S DATE OF BIRTH IS RIGHT HERE.
AND THEY'RE TWINS?
THEY'RE SUPPOSED TO MEET ON THEIR TWENTIETH BIRTHDAY?
...!!
IT'S TODAY...

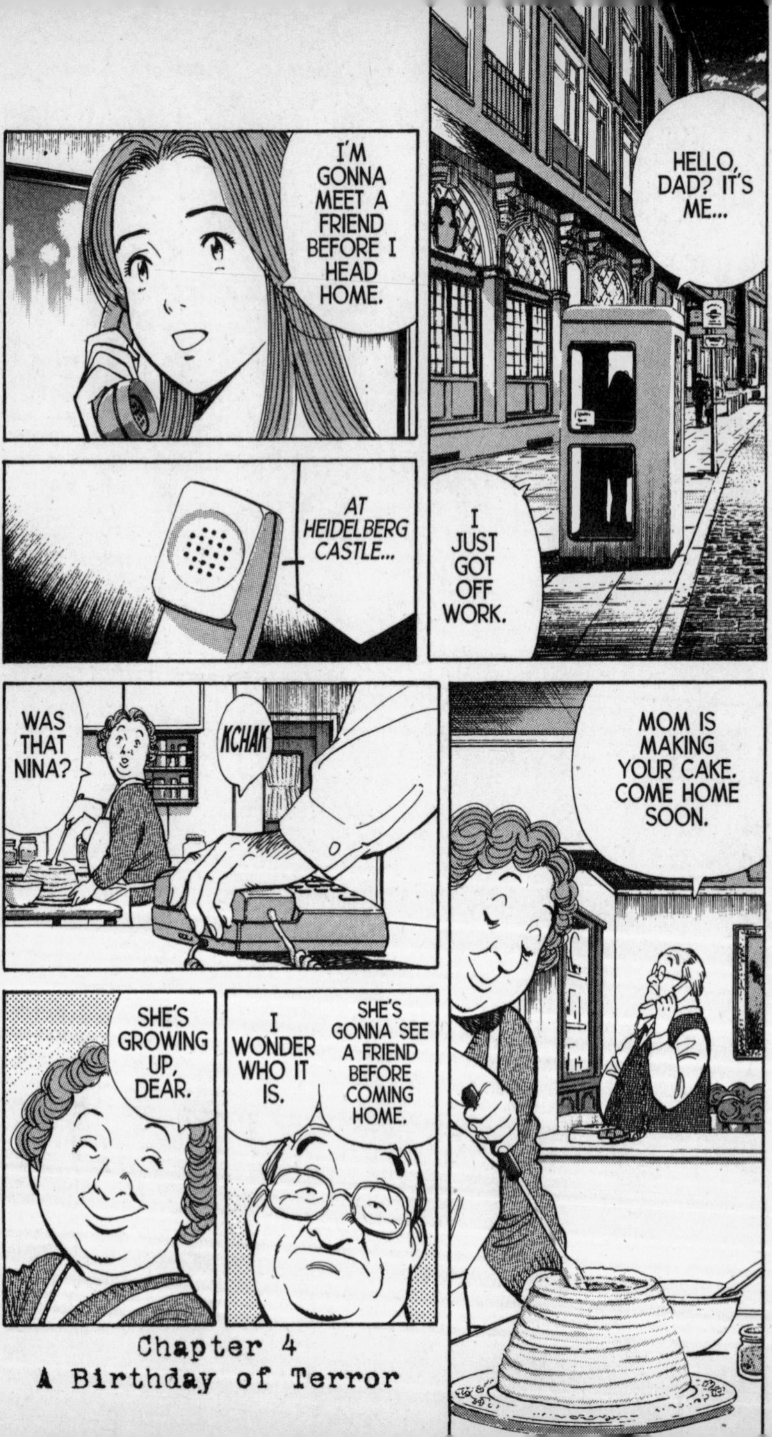
HELLO, DAD? IT'S ME...
I JUST GOT OFF WORK.
I'M GONNA MEET A FRIEND BEFORE I HEAD HOME.
AT HEIDELBERG CASTLE...
MOM IS MAKING YOUR CAKE. COME HOME SOON.
KCHAK
WAS THAT NINA?
SHE'S GONNA SEE A FRIEND BEFORE COMING HOME.
I WONDER WHO IT IS.
SHE'S GROWING UP, DEAR.

Chapter 4
A Birthday of Terror

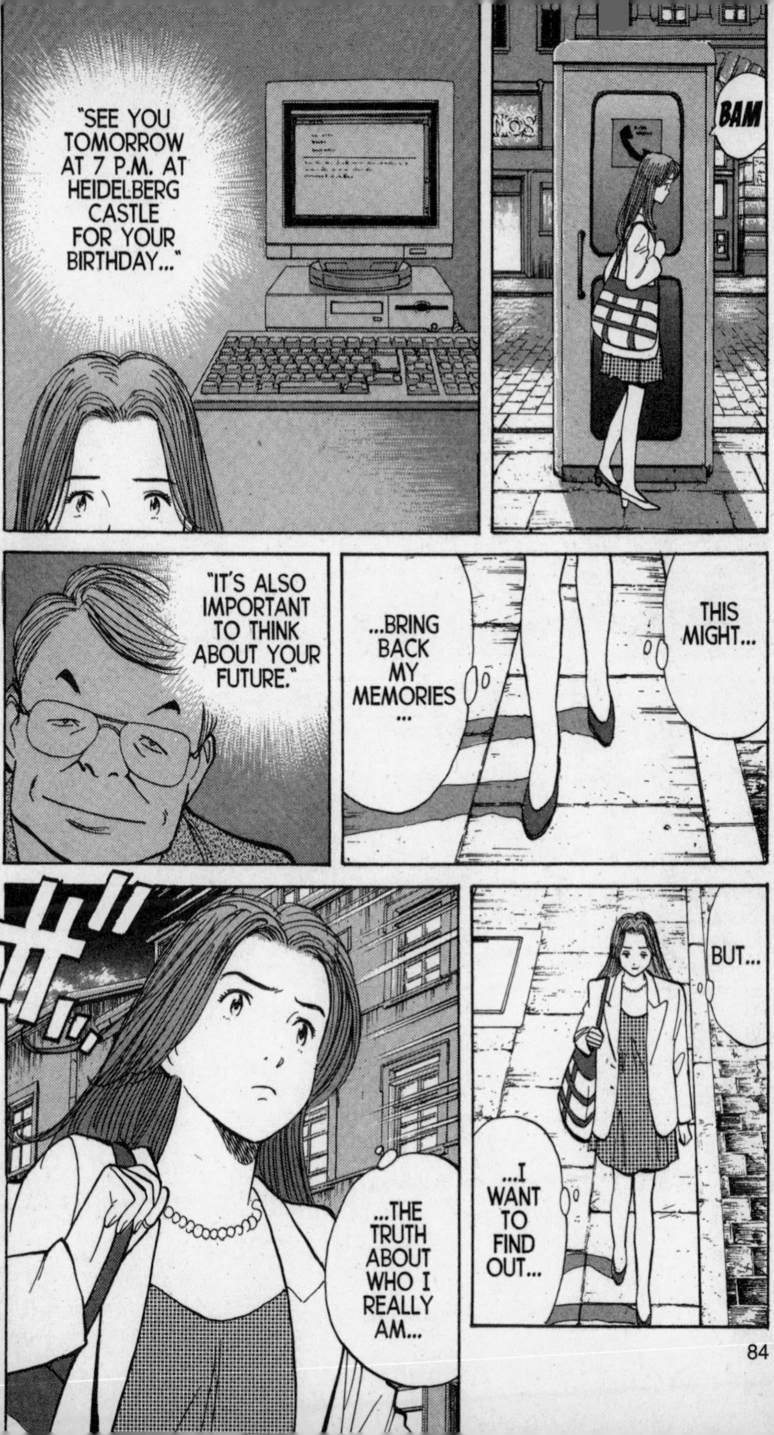
BAM
"SEE YOU TOMORROW AT 7 P.M. AT HEIDELBERG CASTLE FOR YOUR BIRTHDAY..."
THIS MIGHT...
...BRING BACK MY MEMORIES...
"IT'S ALSO IMPORTANT TO THINK ABOUT YOUR FUTURE."
BUT...
...I WANT TO FIND OUT...
...THE TRUTH ABOUT WHO I REALLY AM...

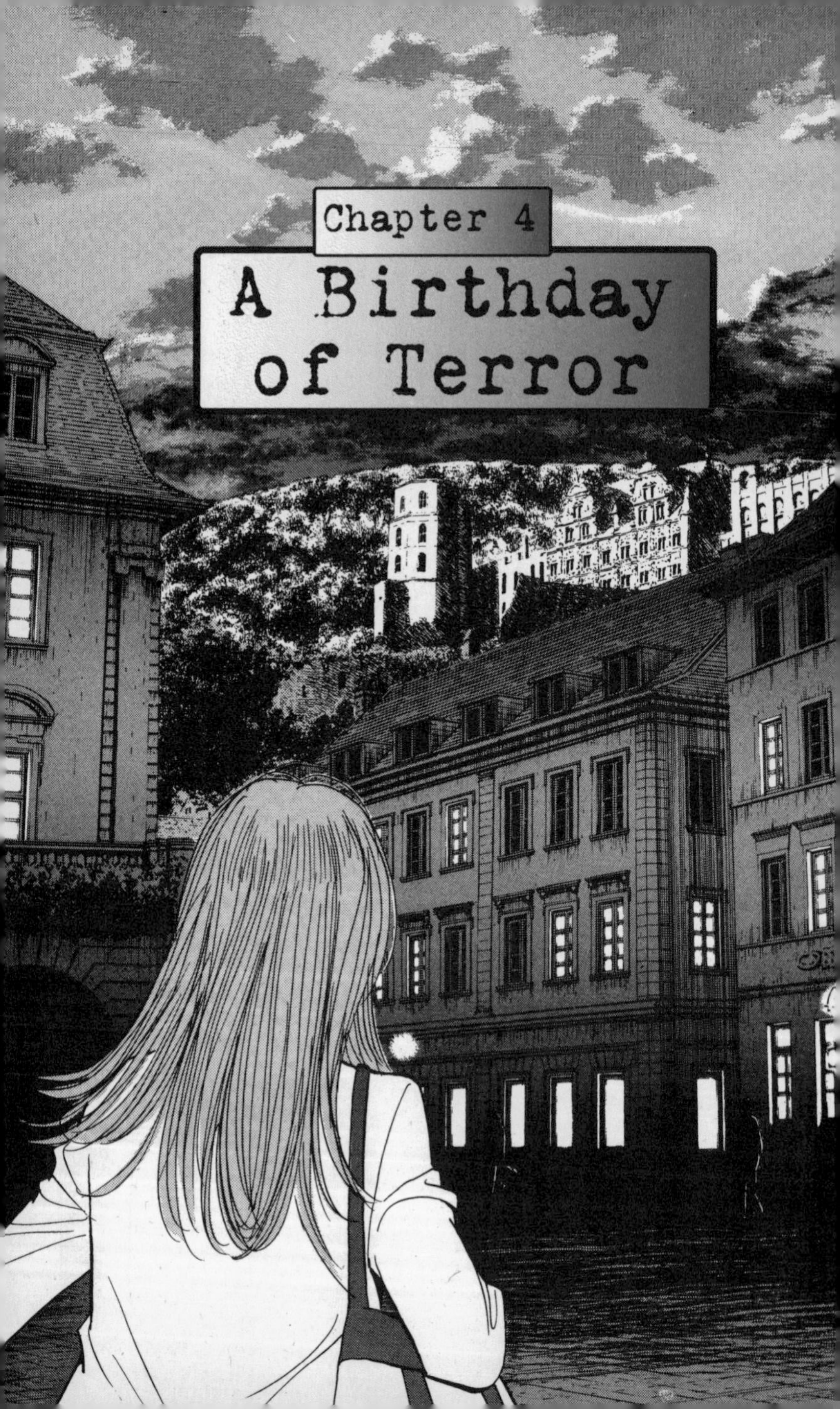
Chapter 4
A Birthday of Terror

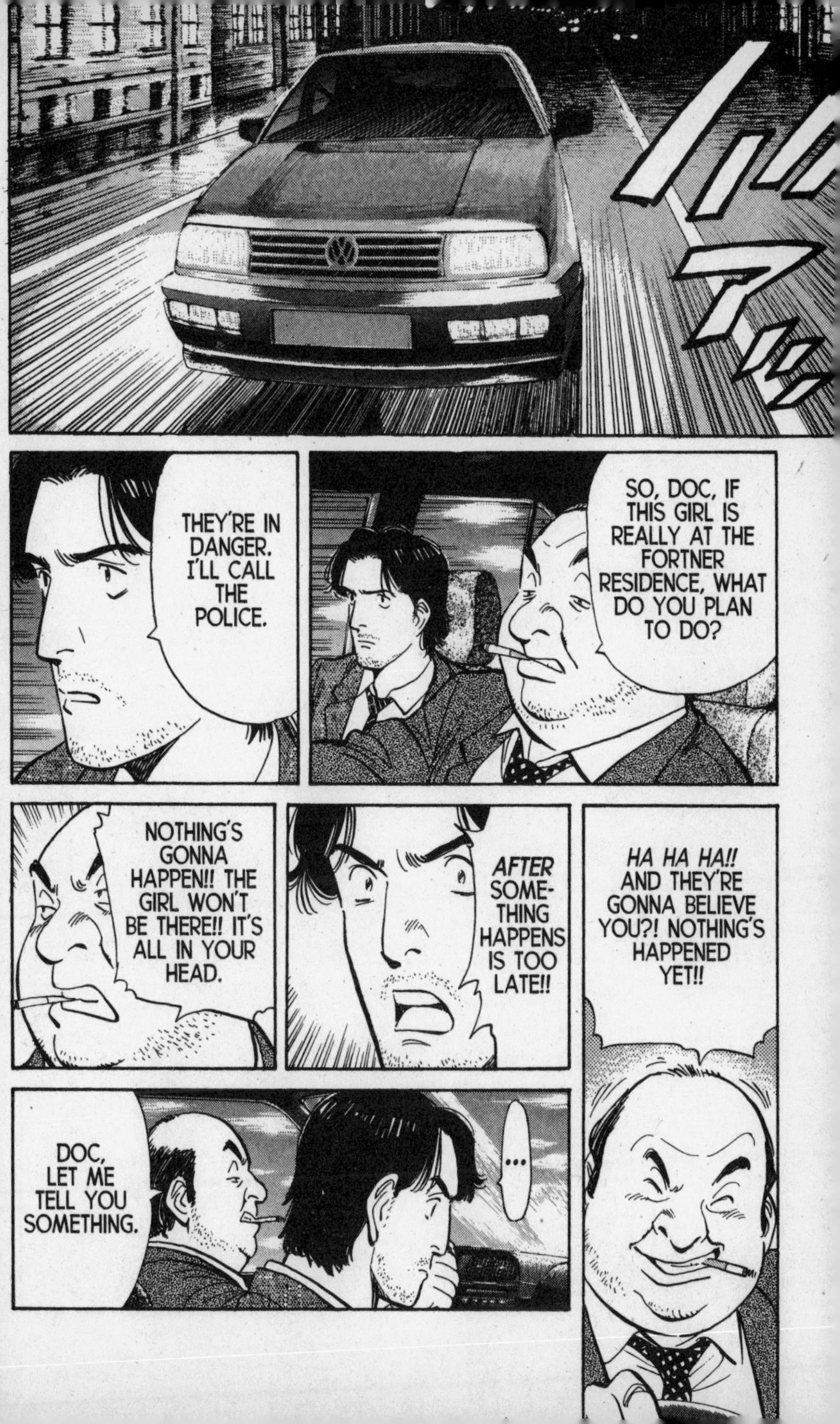

SO, DOC, IF THIS GIRL IS REALLY AT THE FORTNER RESIDENCE, WHAT DO YOU PLAN TO DO?
THEY'RE IN DANGER. I'LL CALL THE POLICE.
HA HA HA!! AND THEY'RE GONNA BELIEVE YOU?! NOTHING'S HAPPENED YET!!
AFTER SOME-THING HAPPENS IS TOO LATE!!
NOTHING'S GONNA HAPPEN!! THE GIRL WON'T BE THERE!! IT'S ALL IN YOUR HEAD.
...
DOC, LET ME TELL YOU SOMETHING.

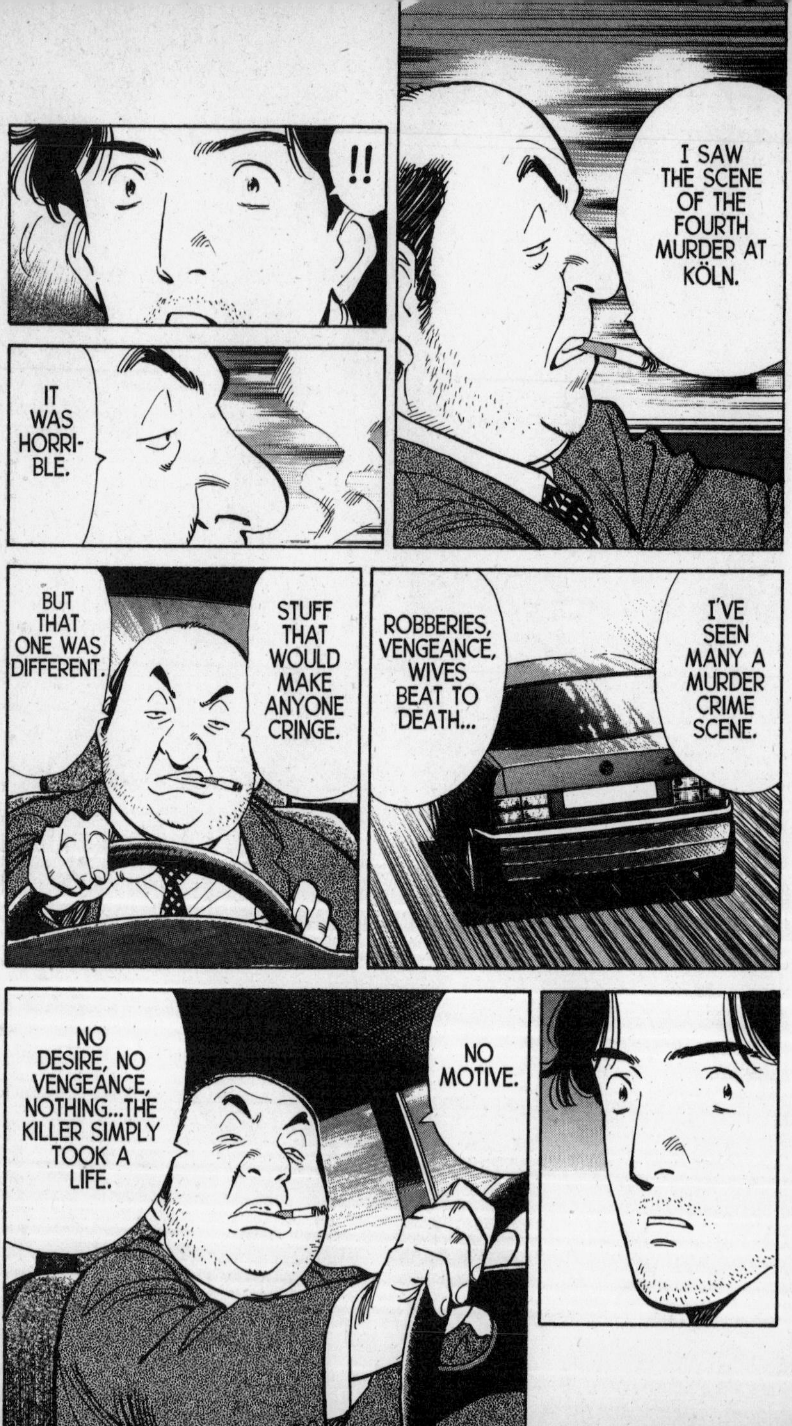
I SAW THE SCENE OF THE FOURTH MURDER AT KÖLN.
!!
IT WAS HORRI-BLE.
I'VE SEEN MANY A MURDER CRIME SCENE.
ROBBERIES, VENGEANCE, WIVES BEAT TO DEATH...
STUFF THAT WOULD MAKE ANYONE CRINGE.
BUT THAT ONE WAS DIFFERENT.
NO MOTIVE.
NO DESIRE, NO VENGEANCE, NOTHING...THE KILLER SIMPLY TOOK A LIFE.

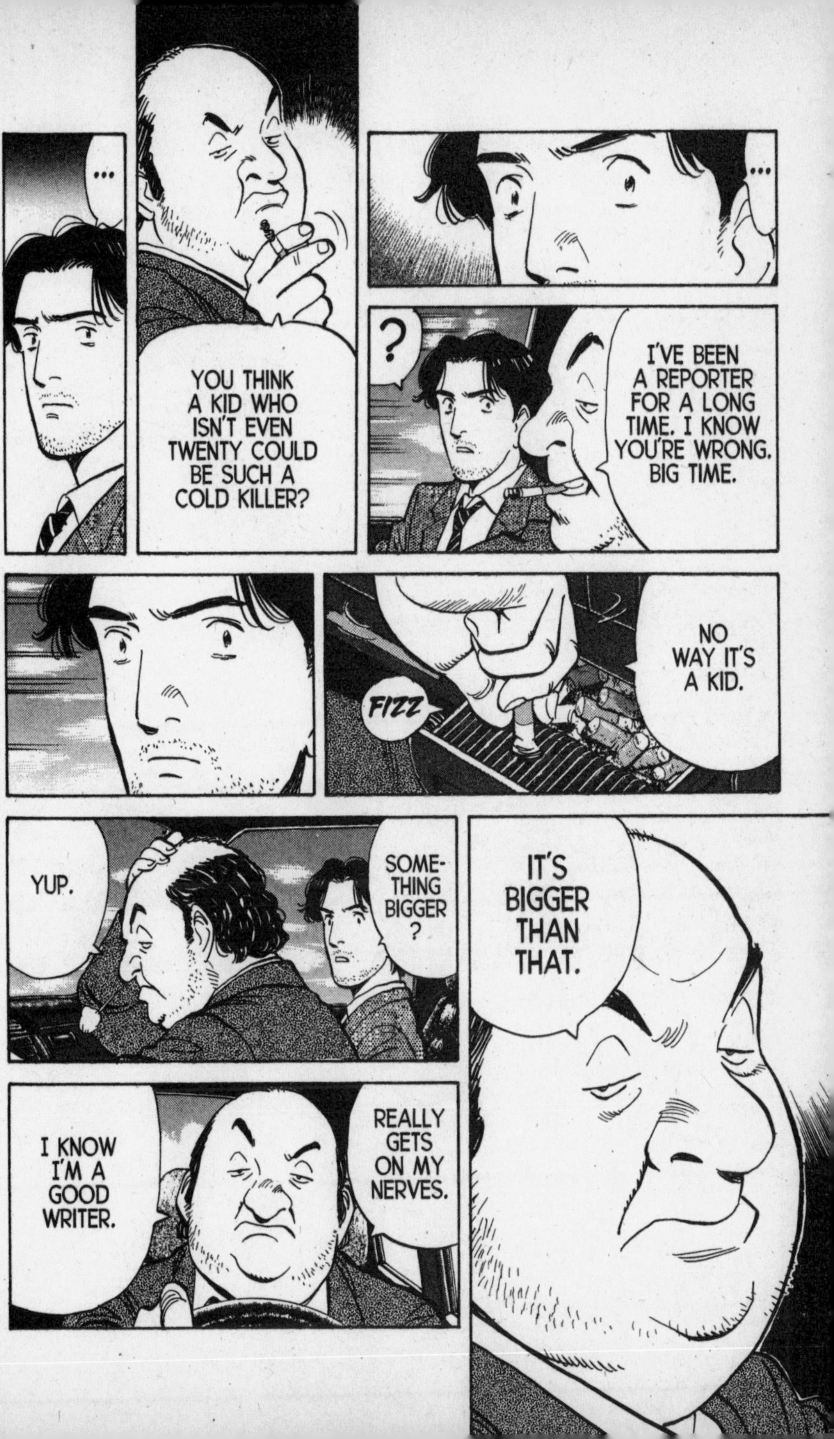
...
?
I'VE BEEN A REPORTER FOR A LONG TIME. I KNOW YOU'RE WRONG. BIG TIME.
YOU THINK A KID WHO ISN'T EVEN TWENTY COULD BE SUCH A COLD KILLER?
...
NO WAY IT'S A KID.
FIZZ
IT'S BIGGER THAN THAT.
SOME-THING BIGGER?
YUP.
REALLY GETS ON MY NERVES.
I KNOW I'M A GOOD WRITER.

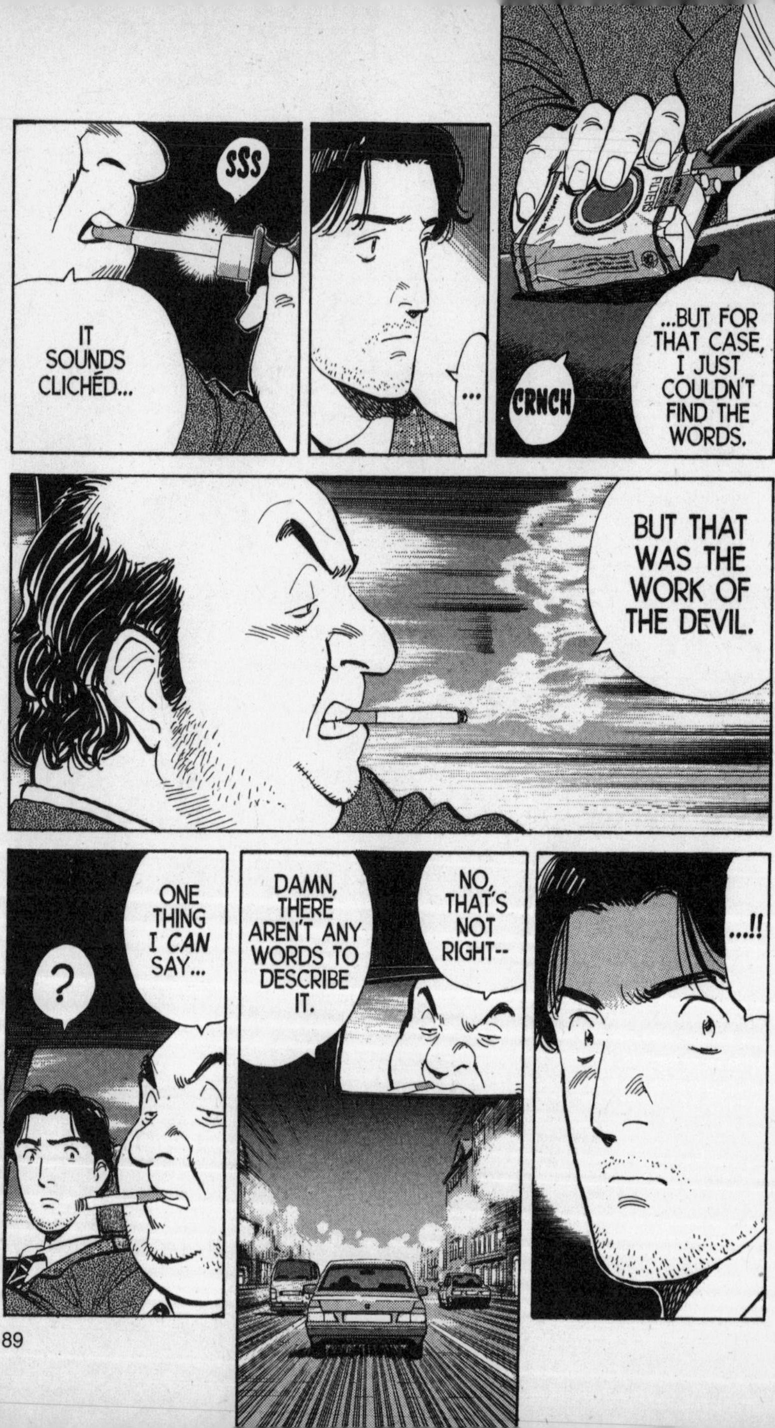
SSS
IT SOUNDS CLICHÉD...
...
CRNCH
...BUT FOR THAT CASE, I JUST COULDN'T FIND THE WORDS.
BUT THAT WAS THE WORK OF THE DEVIL.
?
ONE THING I *CAN* SAY...
DAMN, THERE AREN'T ANY WORDS TO DESCRIBE IT.
NO, THAT'S NOT RIGHT--
...!!

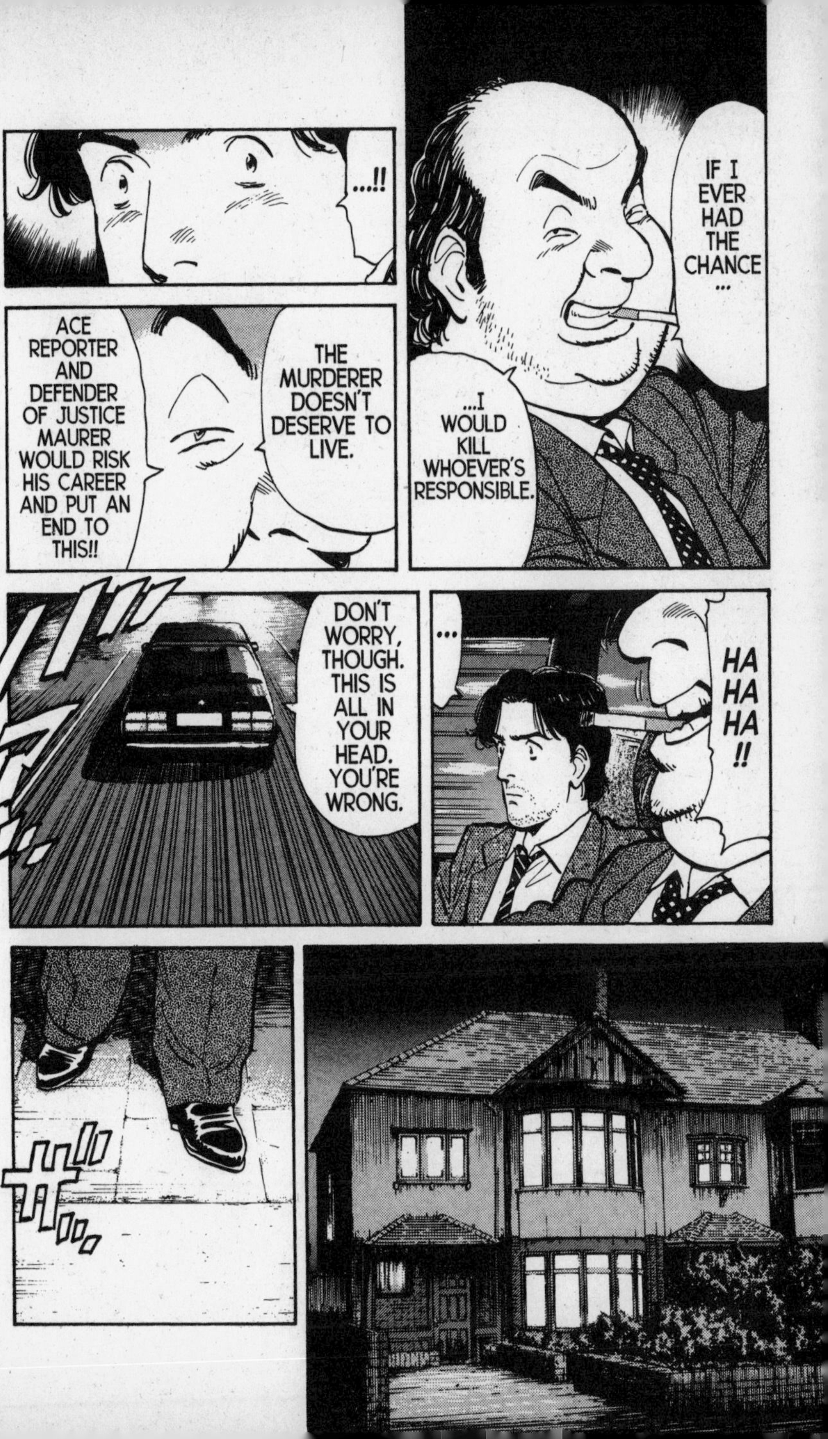
IF I EVER HAD THE CHANCE...
...I WOULD KILL WHOEVER'S RESPONSIBLE.
...!!
THE MURDERER DOESN'T DESERVE TO LIVE.
ACE REPORTER AND DEFENDER OF JUSTICE MAURER WOULD RISK HIS CAREER AND PUT AN END TO THIS!!
HA HA HA!!
...
DON'T WORRY, THOUGH. THIS IS ALL IN YOUR HEAD. YOU'RE WRONG.

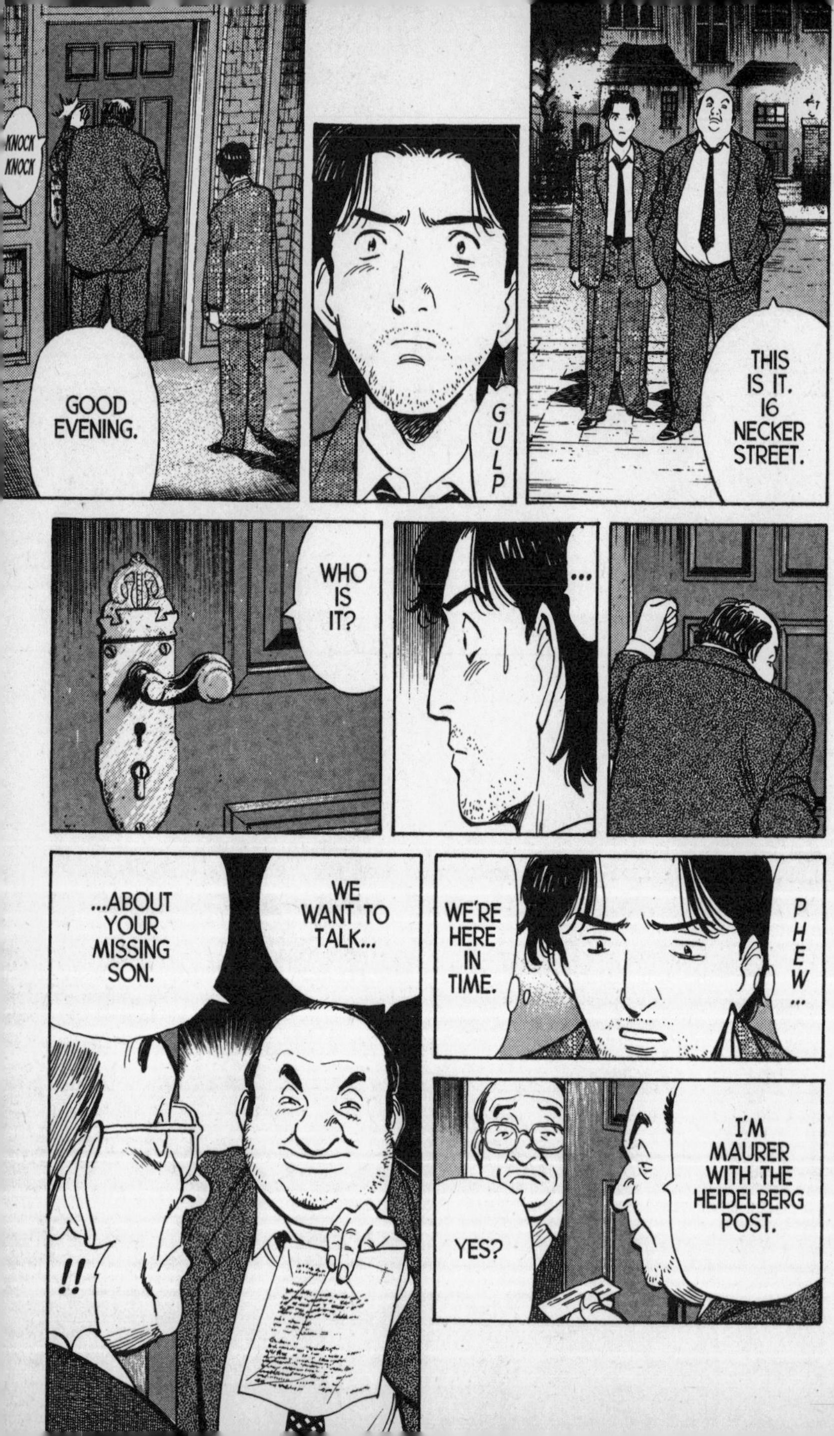
THIS IS IT. 16 NECKER STREET.
GULP
KNOCK KNOCK
GOOD EVENING.
...
WHO IS IT?
PHEW...
WE'RE HERE IN TIME.
I'M MAURER WITH THE HEIDELBERG POST.
YES?
WE WANT TO TALK...
...ABOUT YOUR MISSING SON.
!!

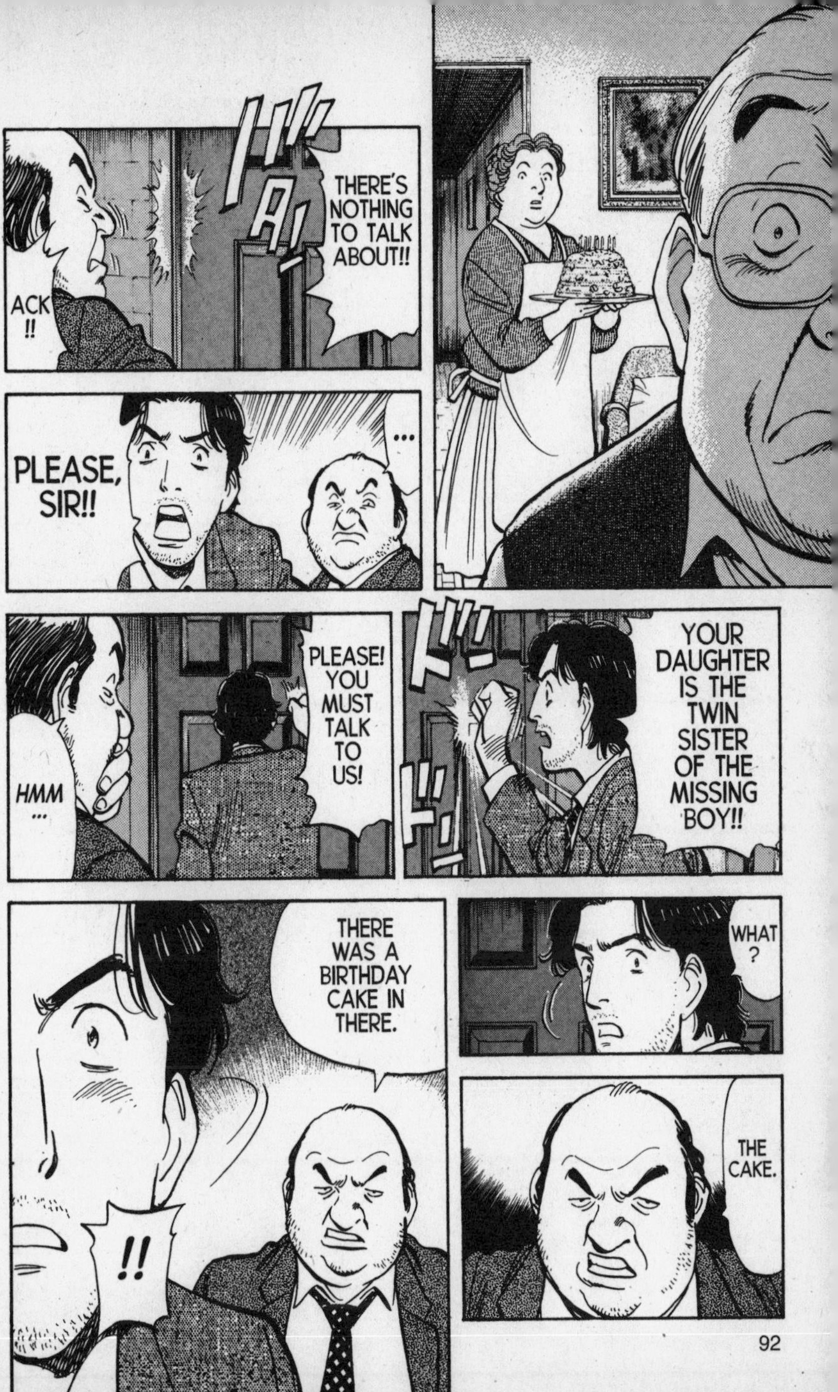
THERE'S NOTHING TO TALK ABOUT!!
ACK !!
...
PLEASE, SIR!!
YOUR DAUGHTER IS THE TWIN SISTER OF THE MISSING BOY!!
PLEASE! YOU MUST TALK TO US!
HMM ...
WHAT ?
THE CAKE.
THERE WAS A BIRTHDAY CAKE IN THERE.
!!

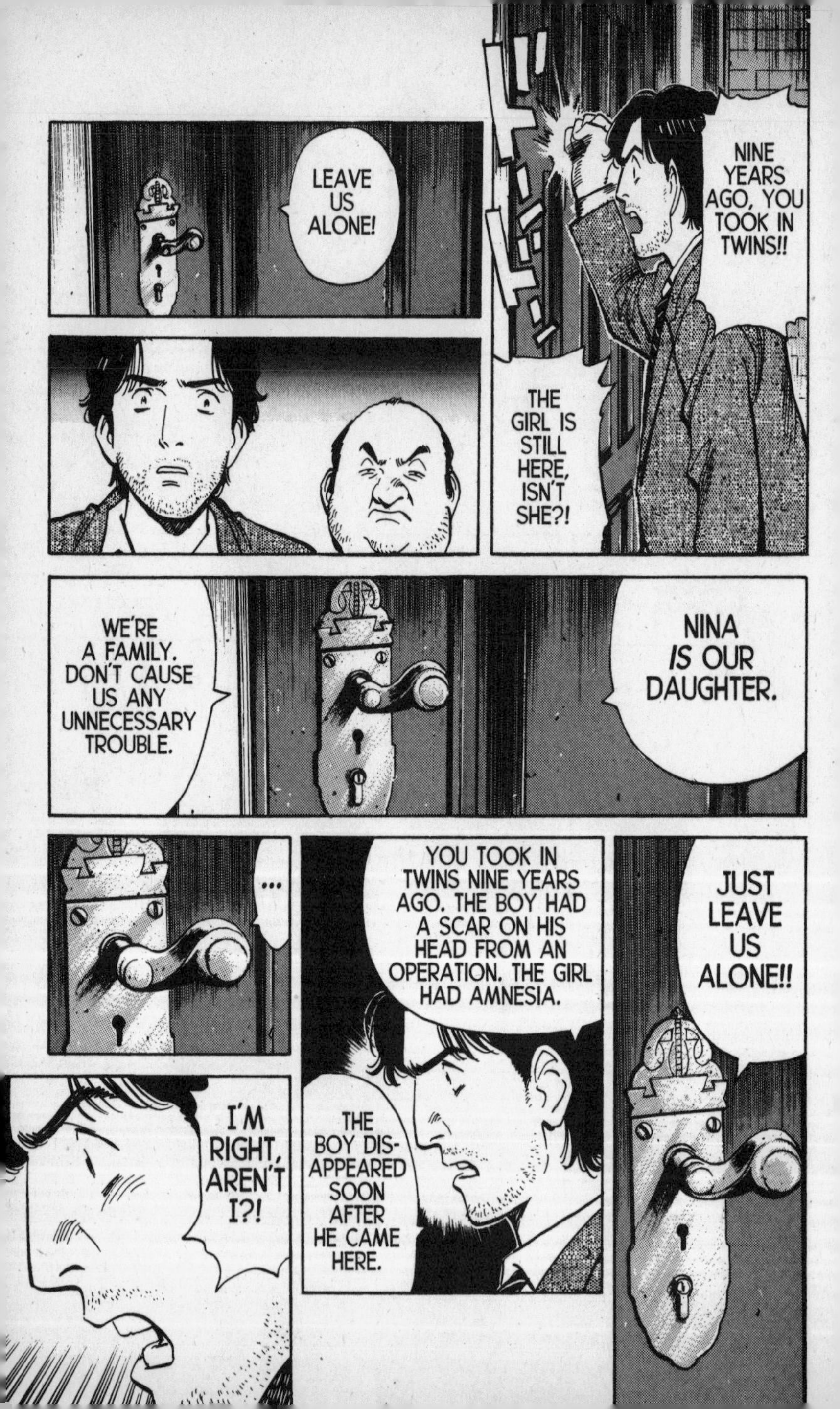
NINE YEARS AGO, YOU TOOK IN TWINS!!
THE GIRL IS STILL HERE, ISN'T SHE?!
LEAVE US ALONE!
NINA *IS* OUR DAUGHTER.
WE'RE A FAMILY. DON'T CAUSE US ANY UNNECESSARY TROUBLE.
JUST LEAVE US ALONE!!
YOU TOOK IN TWINS NINE YEARS AGO. THE BOY HAD A SCAR ON HIS HEAD FROM AN OPERATION. THE GIRL HAD AMNESIA.
THE BOY DIS-APPEARED SOON AFTER HE CAME HERE.
...
I'M RIGHT, AREN'T I?!

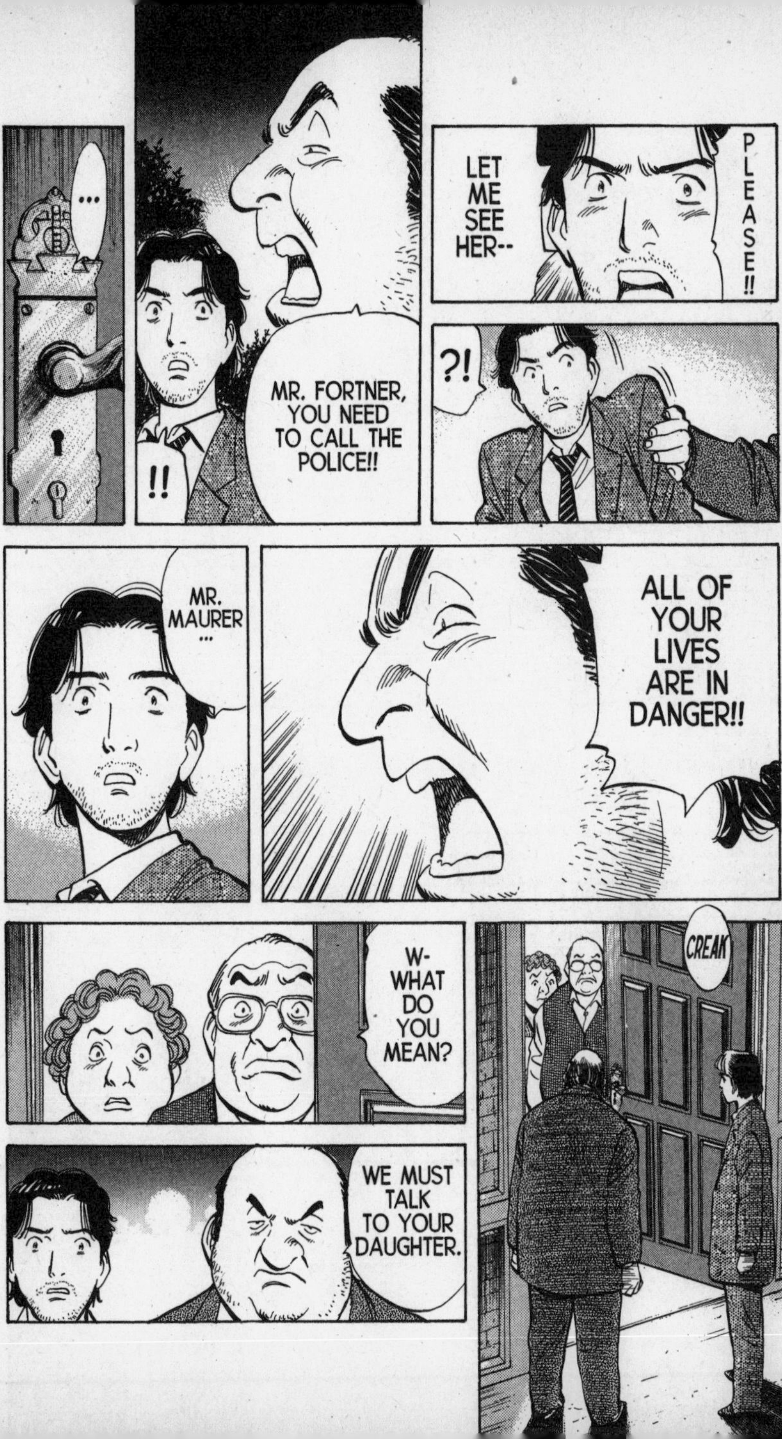
LET ME SEE HER--
PLEASE!!
?!
MR. FORTNER, YOU NEED TO CALL THE POLICE!!
!!
...
ALL OF YOUR LIVES ARE IN DANGER!!
MR. MAURER ...
CREAK
W-WHAT DO YOU MEAN?
WE MUST TALK TO YOUR DAUGHTER.

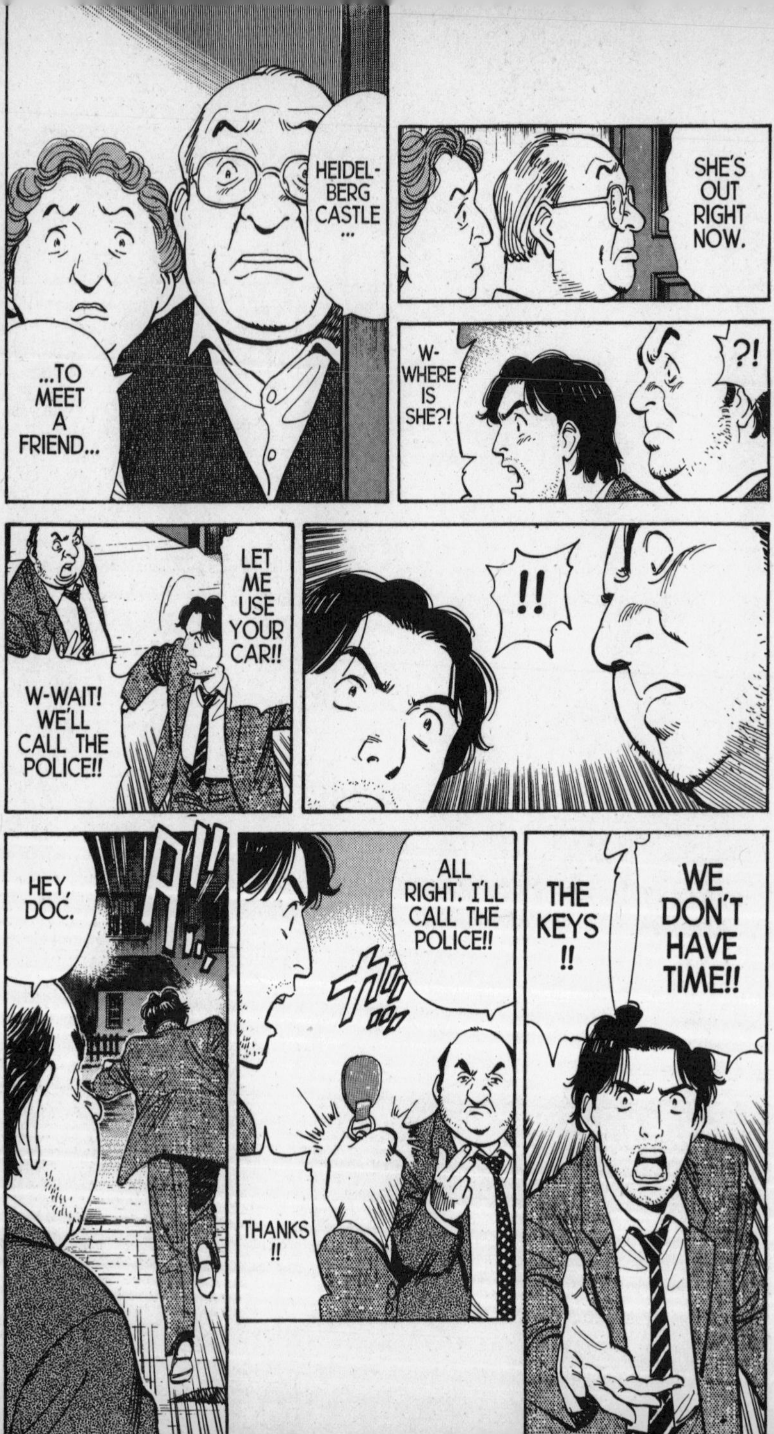
SHE'S OUT RIGHT NOW.
W-WHERE IS SHE?!
?!
HEIDEL-BERG CASTLE ...
...TO MEET A FRIEND...
!!
LET ME USE YOUR CAR!!
W-WAIT! WE'LL CALL THE POLICE!!
WE DON'T HAVE TIME!!
THE KEYS !!
ALL RIGHT. I'LL CALL THE POLICE!!
THANKS !!
HEY, DOC.

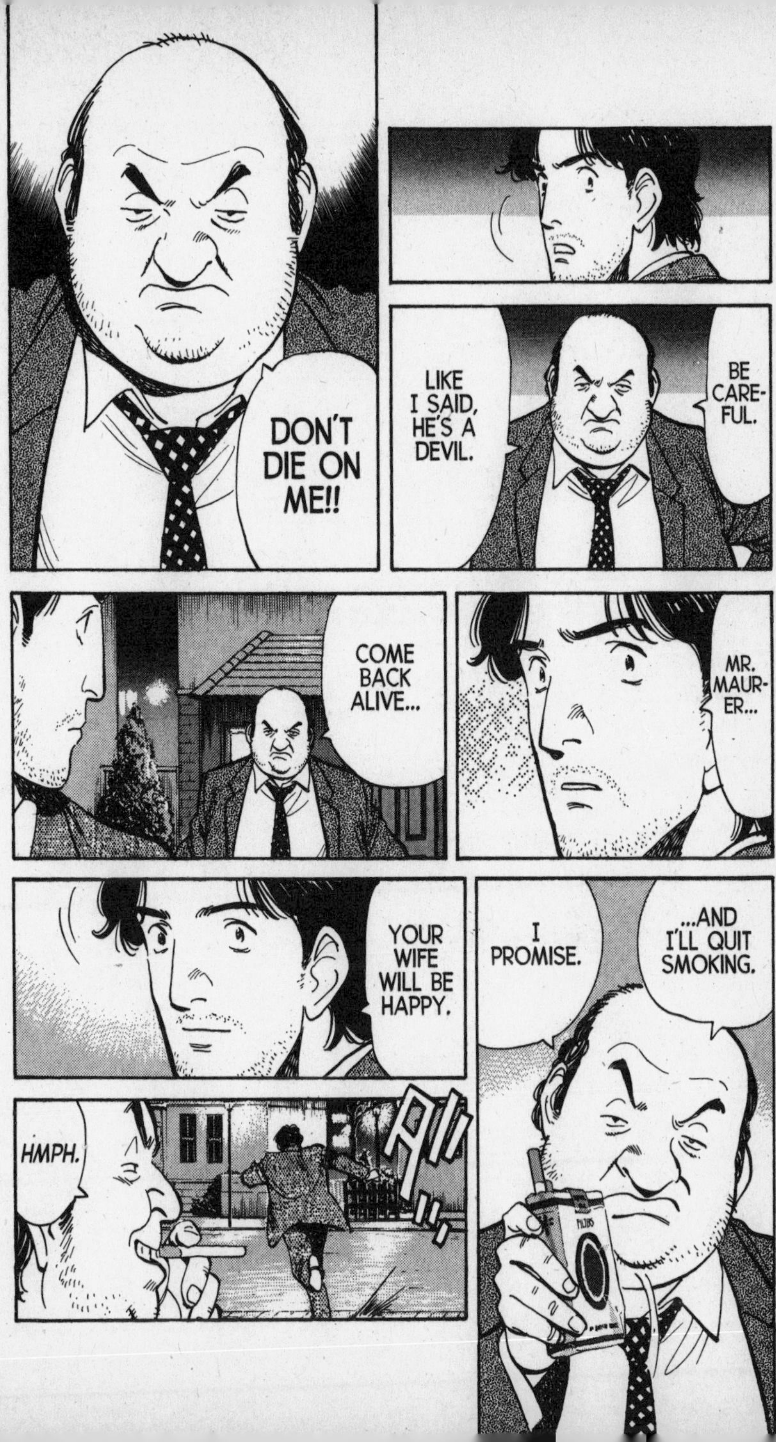
BE CARE-FUL.
LIKE I SAID, HE'S A DEVIL.
DON'T DIE ON ME!!
MR. MAUR-ER...
COME BACK ALIVE...
...AND I'LL QUIT SMOKING.
I PROMISE.
YOUR WIFE WILL BE HAPPY.
HMPH.

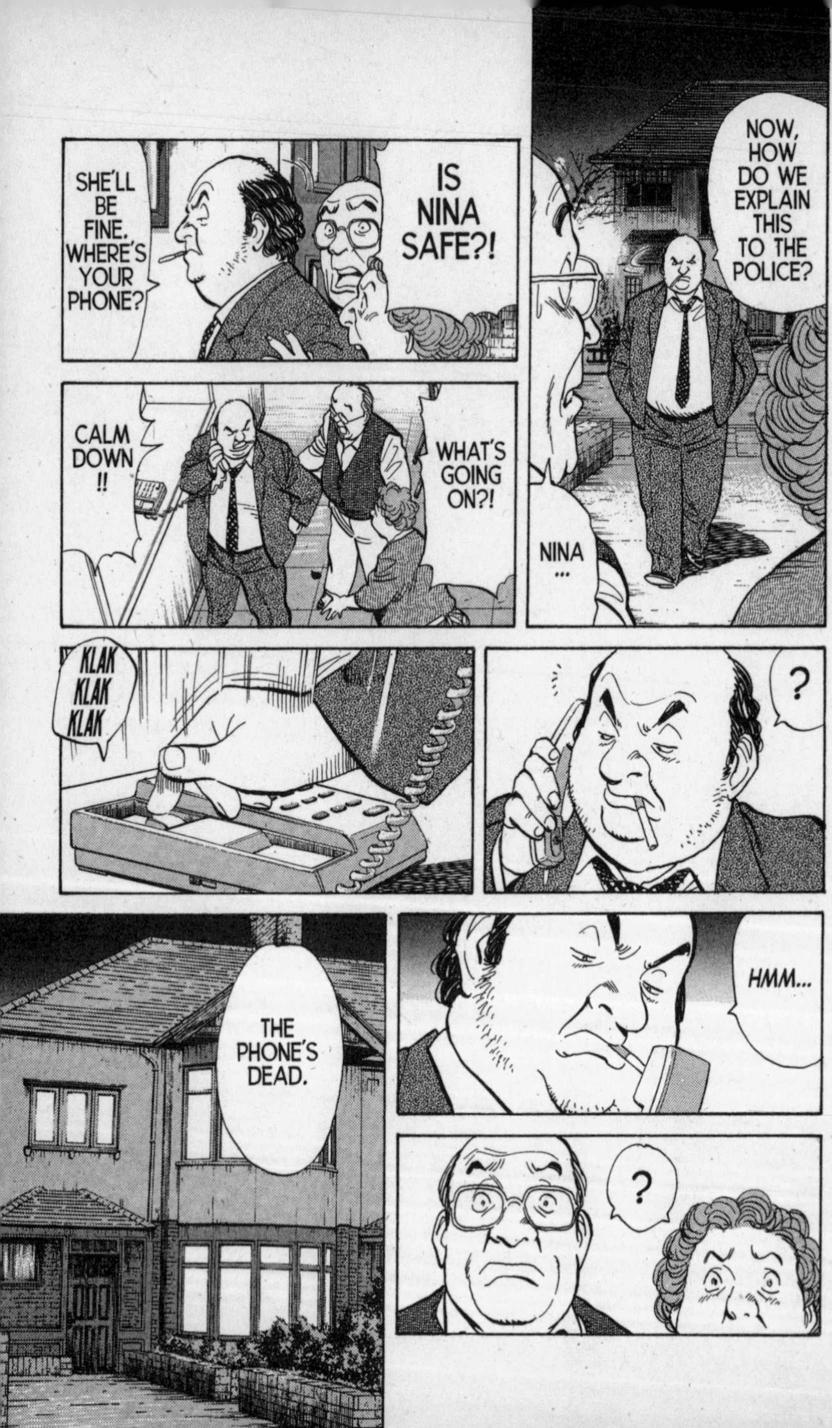
NOW, HOW DO WE EXPLAIN THIS TO THE POLICE?
NINA...
IS NINA SAFE?!
SHE'LL BE FINE. WHERE'S YOUR PHONE?
WHAT'S GOING ON?!
CALM DOWN!!
?
KLAK KLAK KLAK
HMM...
?
THE PHONE'S DEAD.

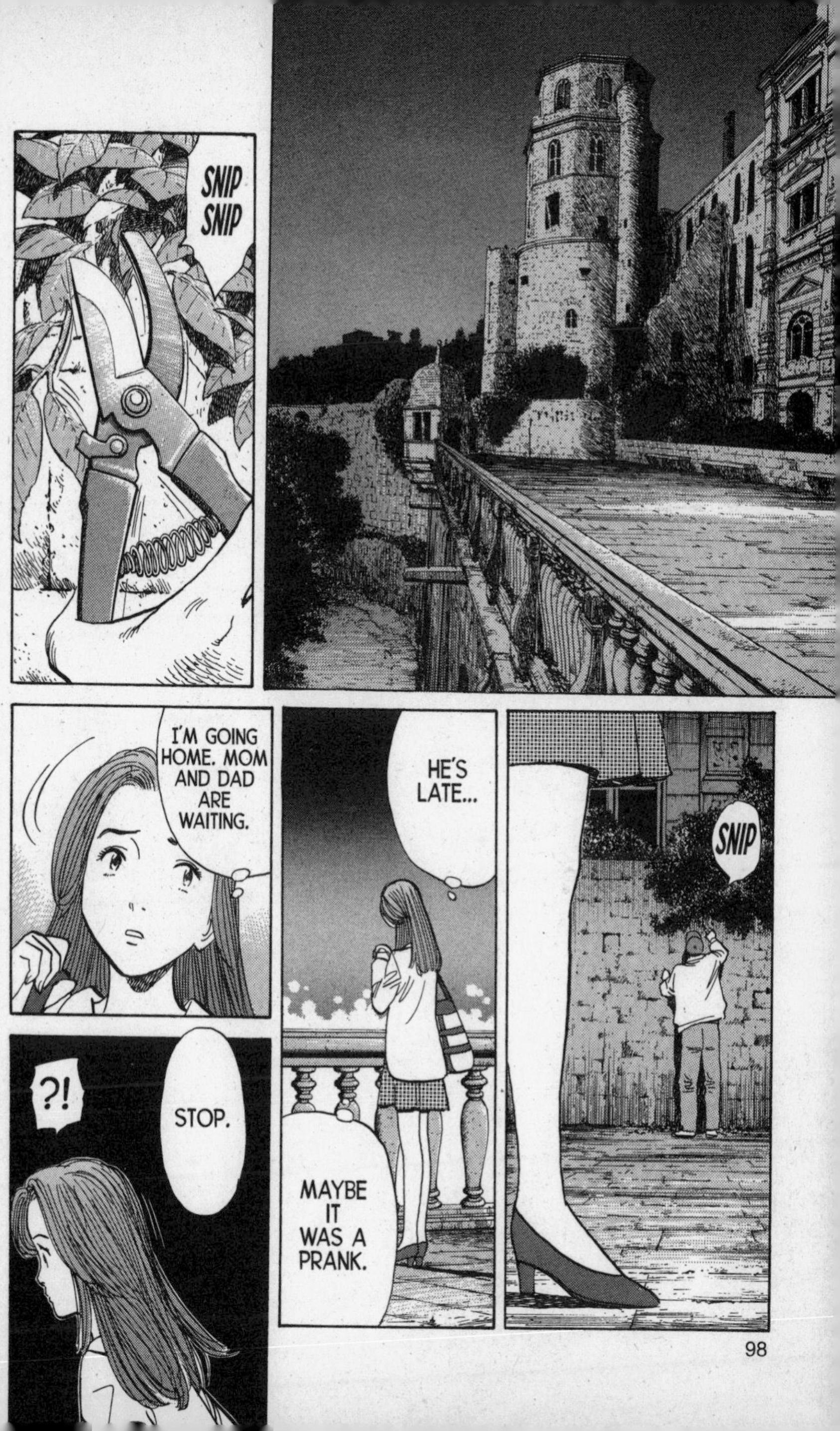
SNIP SNIP
SNIP
HE'S LATE...
MAYBE IT WAS A PRANK.
I'M GOING HOME. MOM AND DAD ARE WAITING.
?!
STOP.

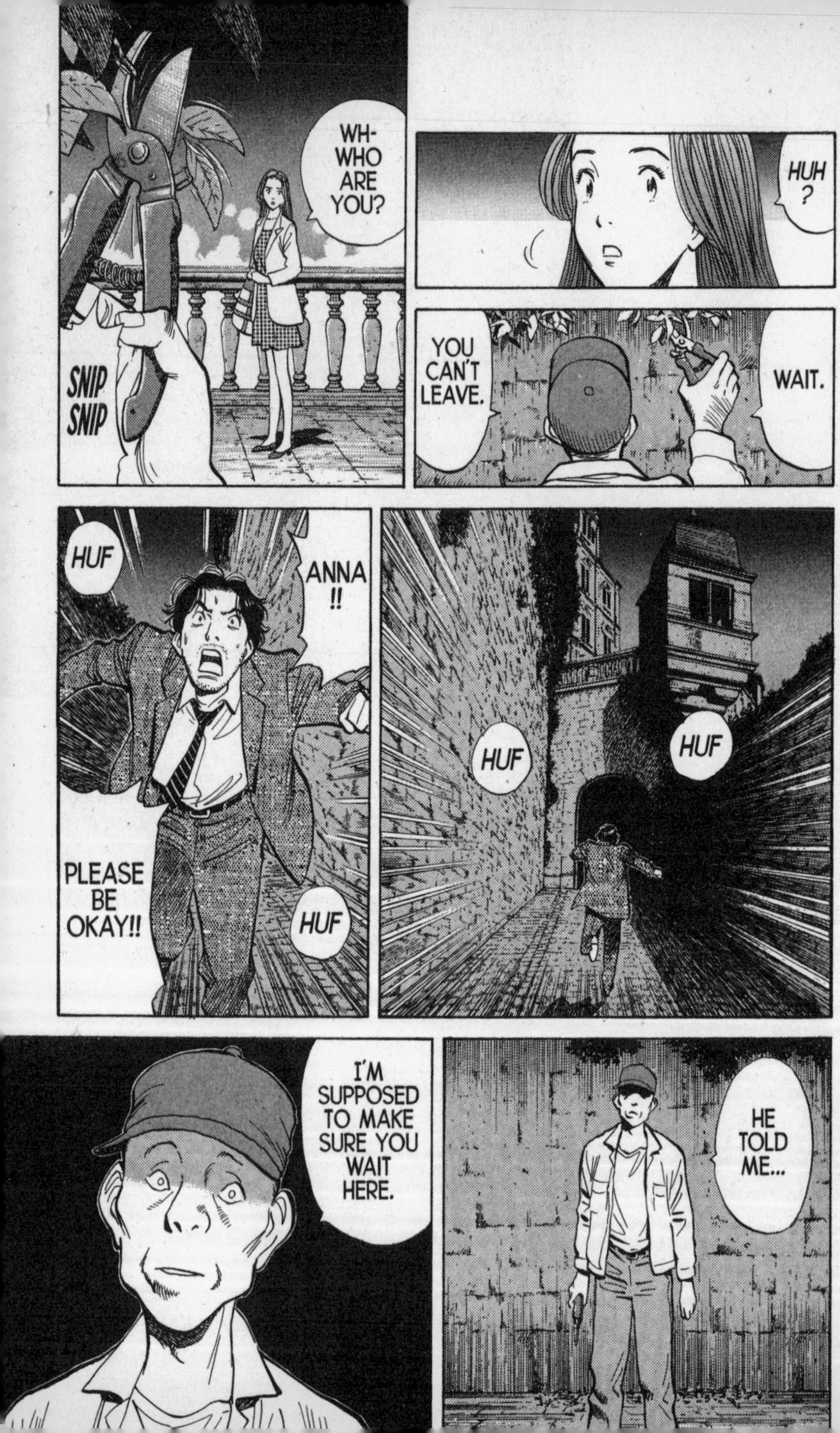
HUH ?
WAIT.
YOU CAN'T LEAVE.
WH- WHO ARE YOU?
SNIP SNIP
HUF
HUF
HUF
ANNA !!
PLEASE BE OKAY!!
HUF
HE TOLD ME...
I'M SUPPOSED TO MAKE SURE YOU WAIT HERE.

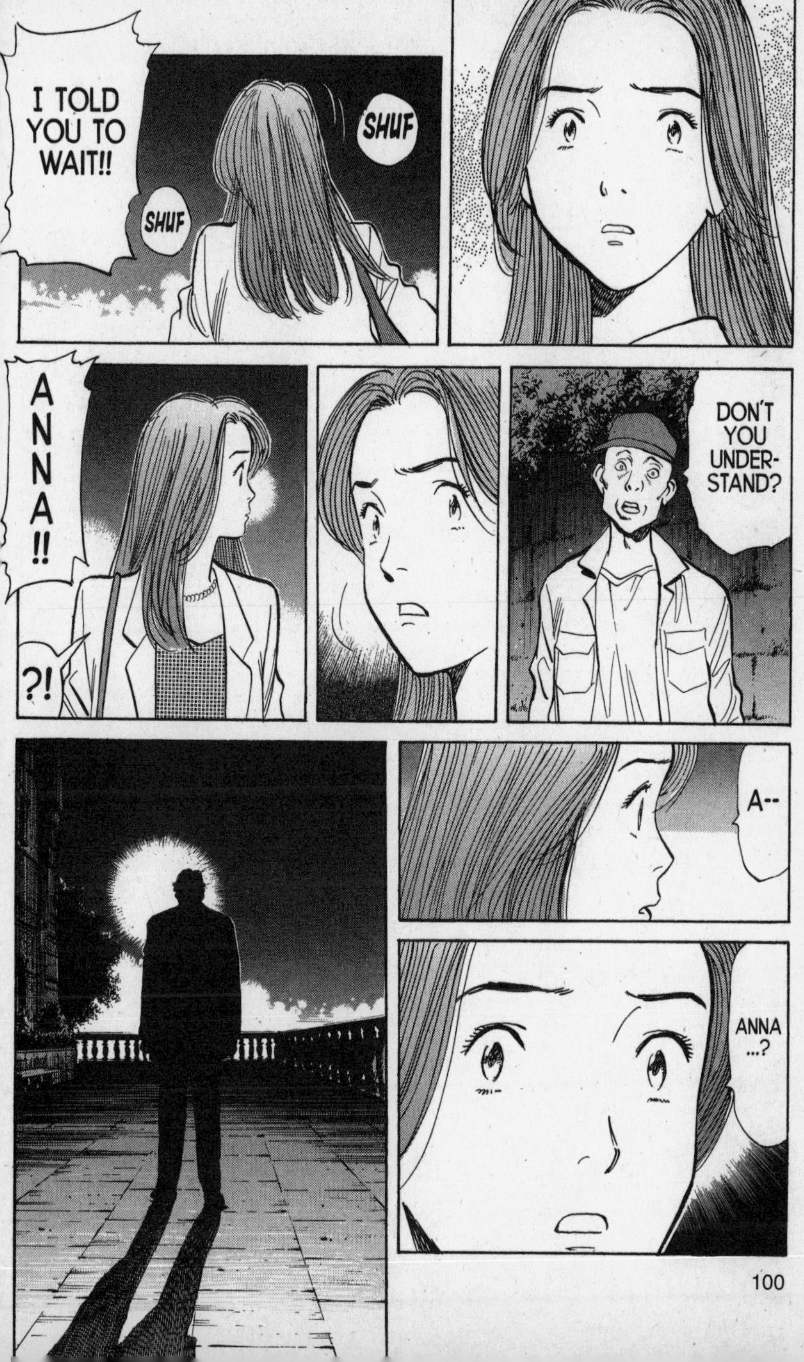
I TOLD YOU TO WAIT!!
SHUF
SHUF
DON'T YOU UNDER-STAND?
ANNA!!
?!
A--
ANNA ...?

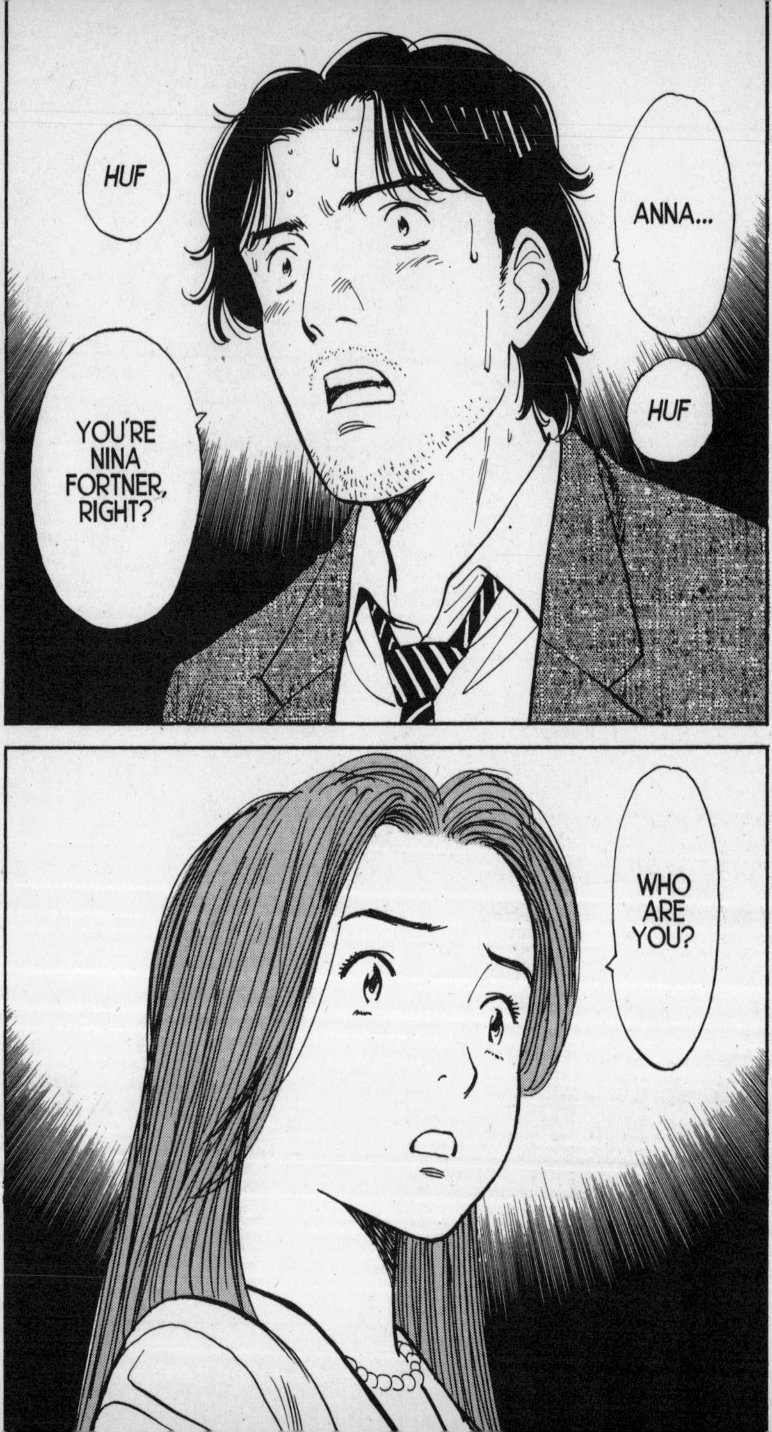
ANNA...
HUF
HUF
YOU'RE NINA FORTNER, RIGHT?
WHO ARE YOU?

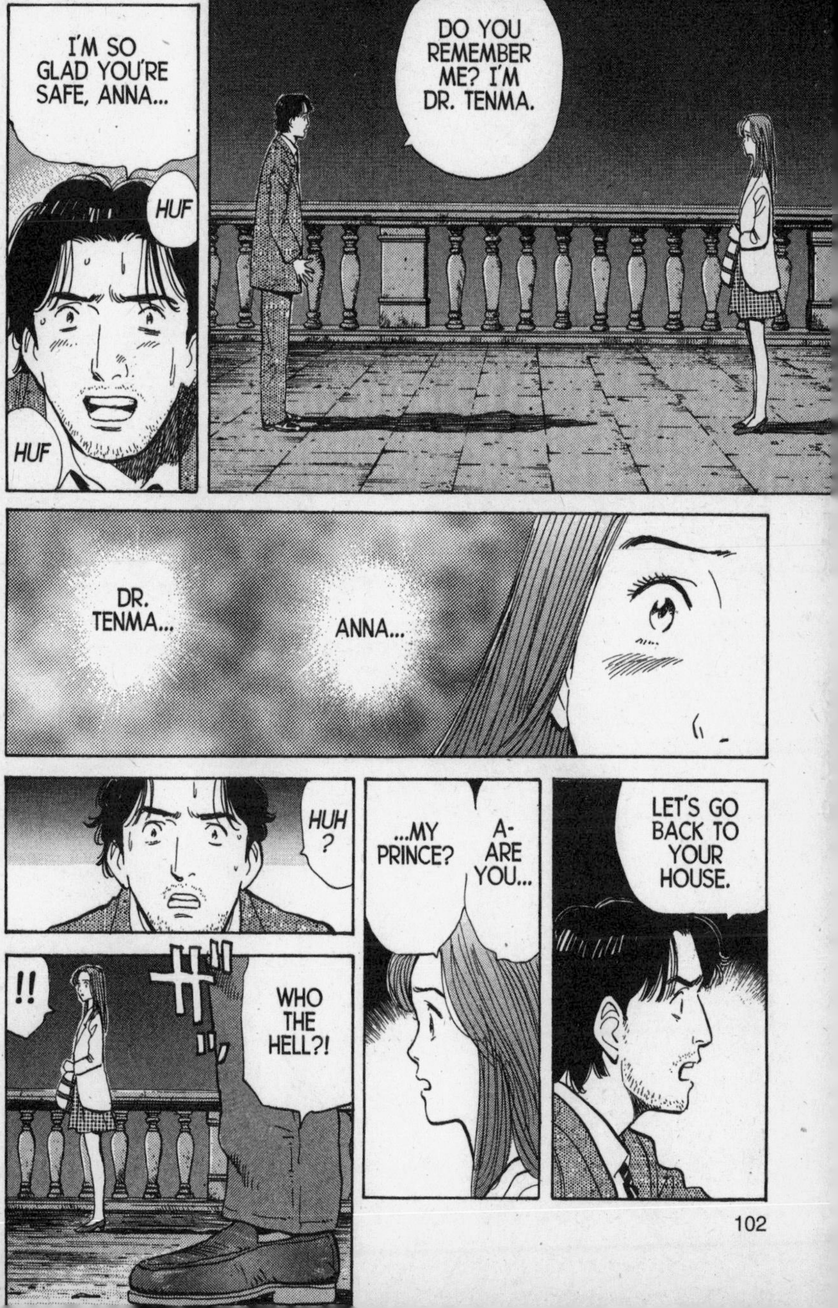
DO YOU REMEMBER ME? I'M DR. TENMA.
I'M SO GLAD YOU'RE SAFE, ANNA...
HUF
HUF
ANNA...
DR. TENMA...
LET'S GO BACK TO YOUR HOUSE.
A- ARE YOU...
...MY PRINCE?
HUH ?
WHO THE HELL?!
!!

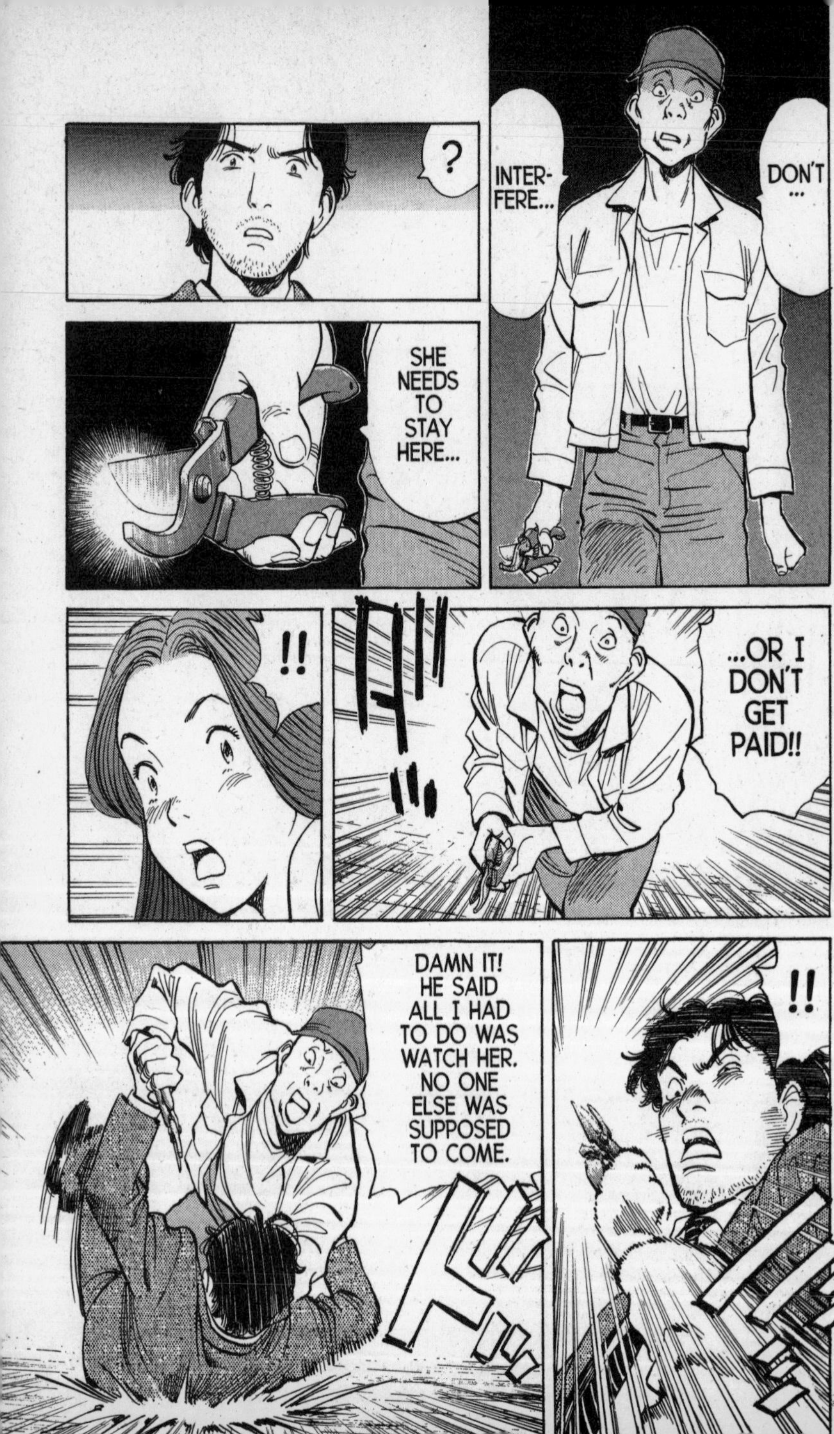

DON'T...
INTER-FERE...
?
SHE NEEDS TO STAY HERE...
...OR I DON'T GET PAID!!
!!
!!
DAMN IT! HE SAID ALL I HAD TO DO WAS WATCH HER. NO ONE ELSE WAS SUPPOSED TO COME.

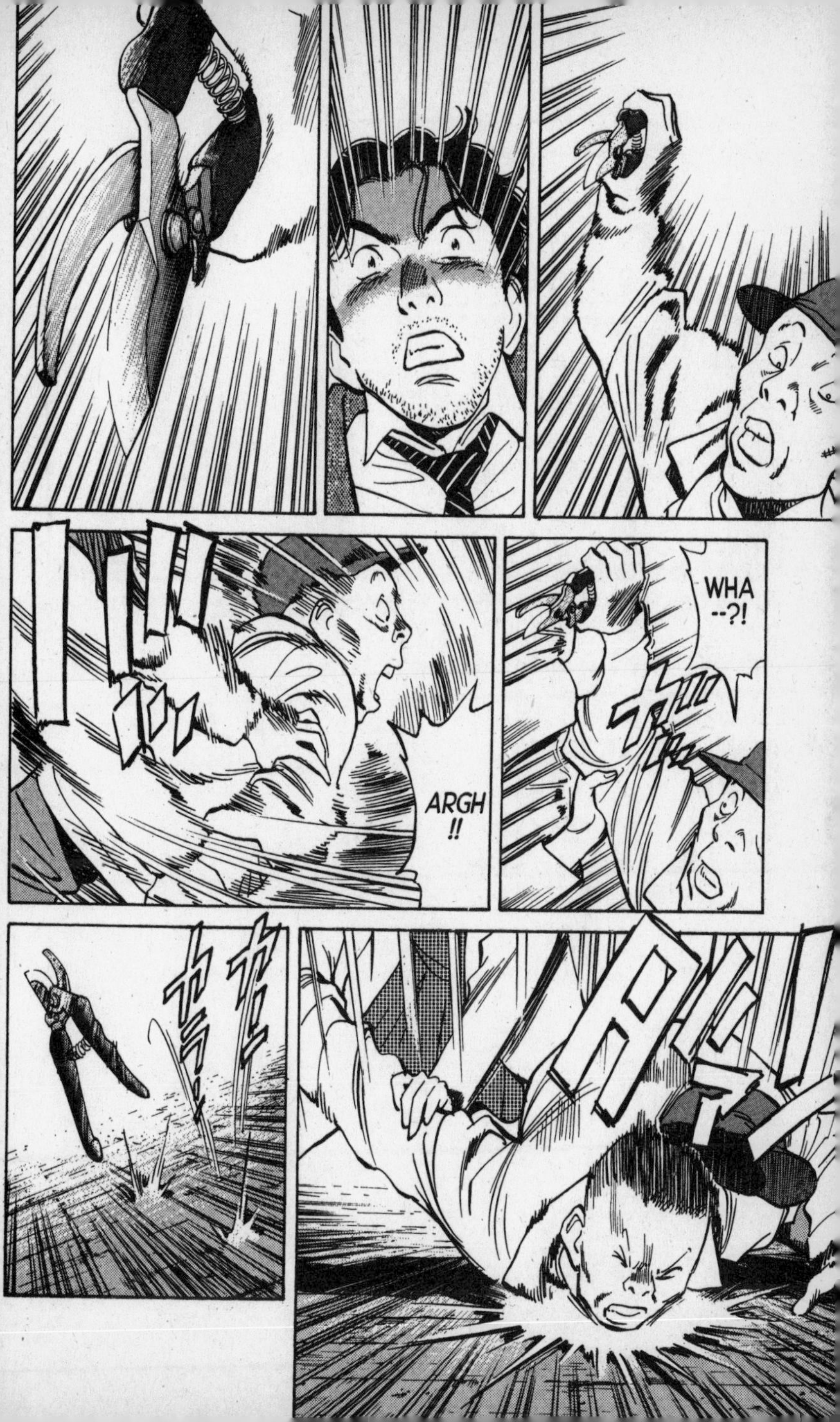
WHA --?!
ARGH !!

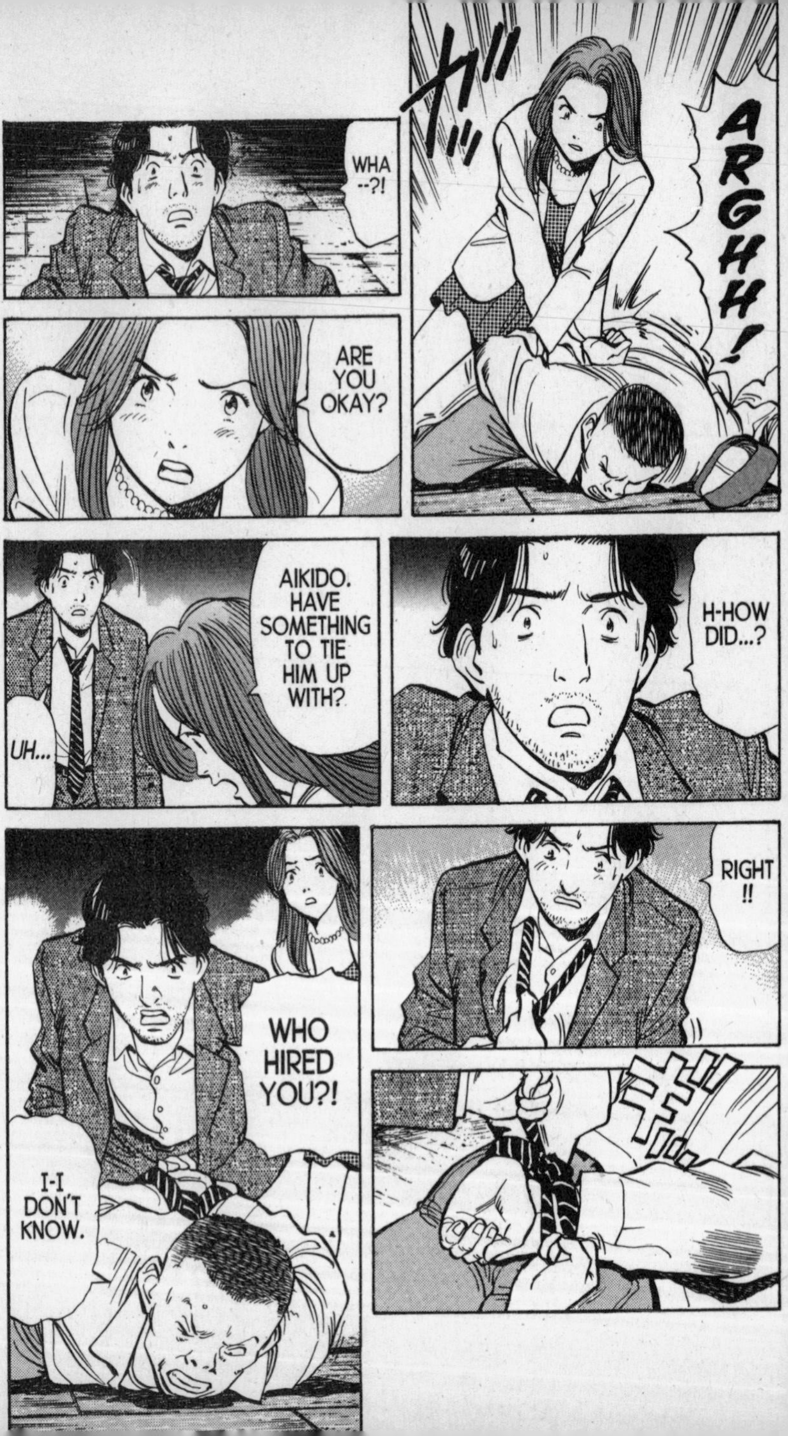
ARGHH!
WHA --?!
ARE YOU OKAY?
H-HOW DID...?
AIKIDO. HAVE SOMETHING TO TIE HIM UP WITH?
UH...
RIGHT !!
WHO HIRED YOU?!
I-I DON'T KNOW.

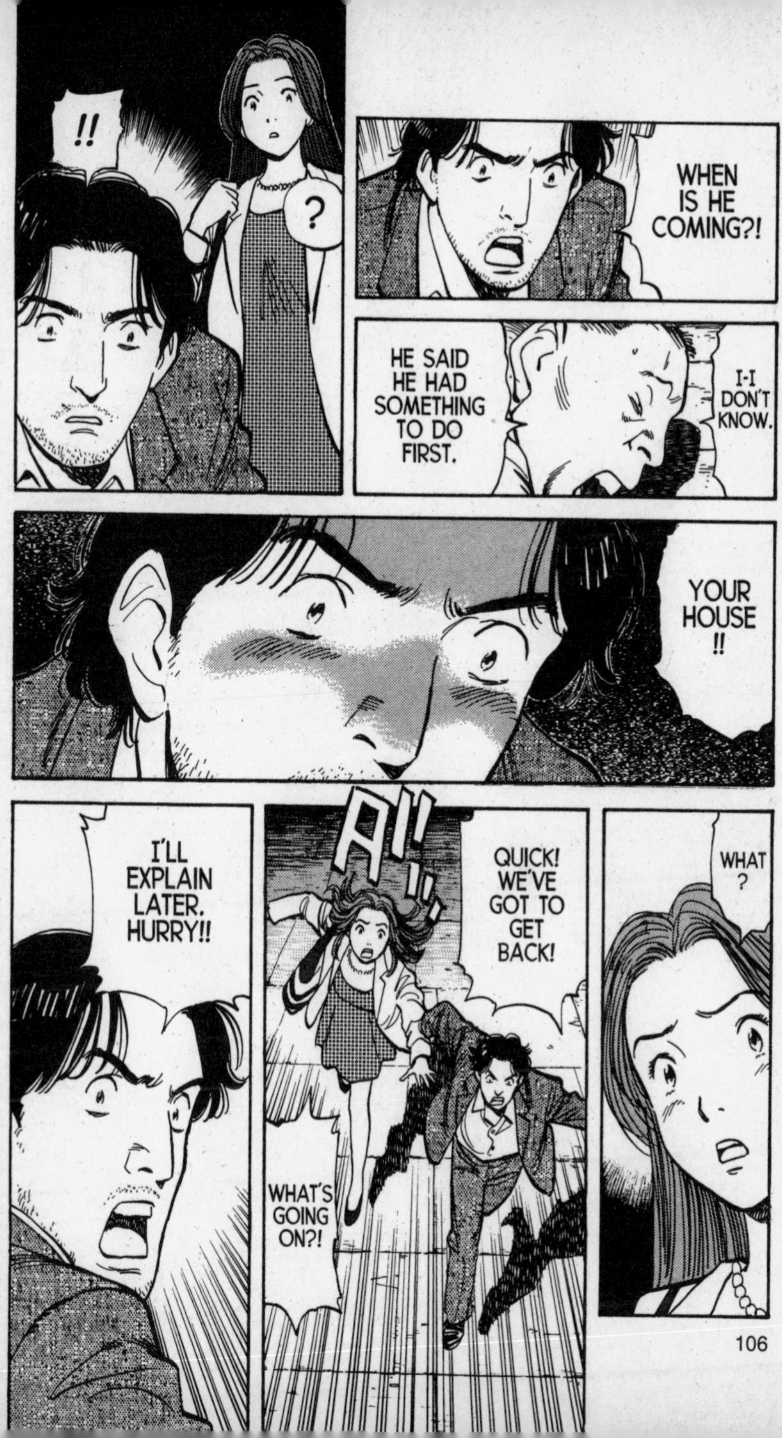
WHEN IS HE COMING?!
I-I DON'T KNOW.
HE SAID HE HAD SOMETHING TO DO FIRST.
!!
?
YOUR HOUSE !!
WHAT ?
A!!
QUICK! WE'VE GOT TO GET BACK!
WHAT'S GOING ON?!
I'LL EXPLAIN LATER. HURRY!!

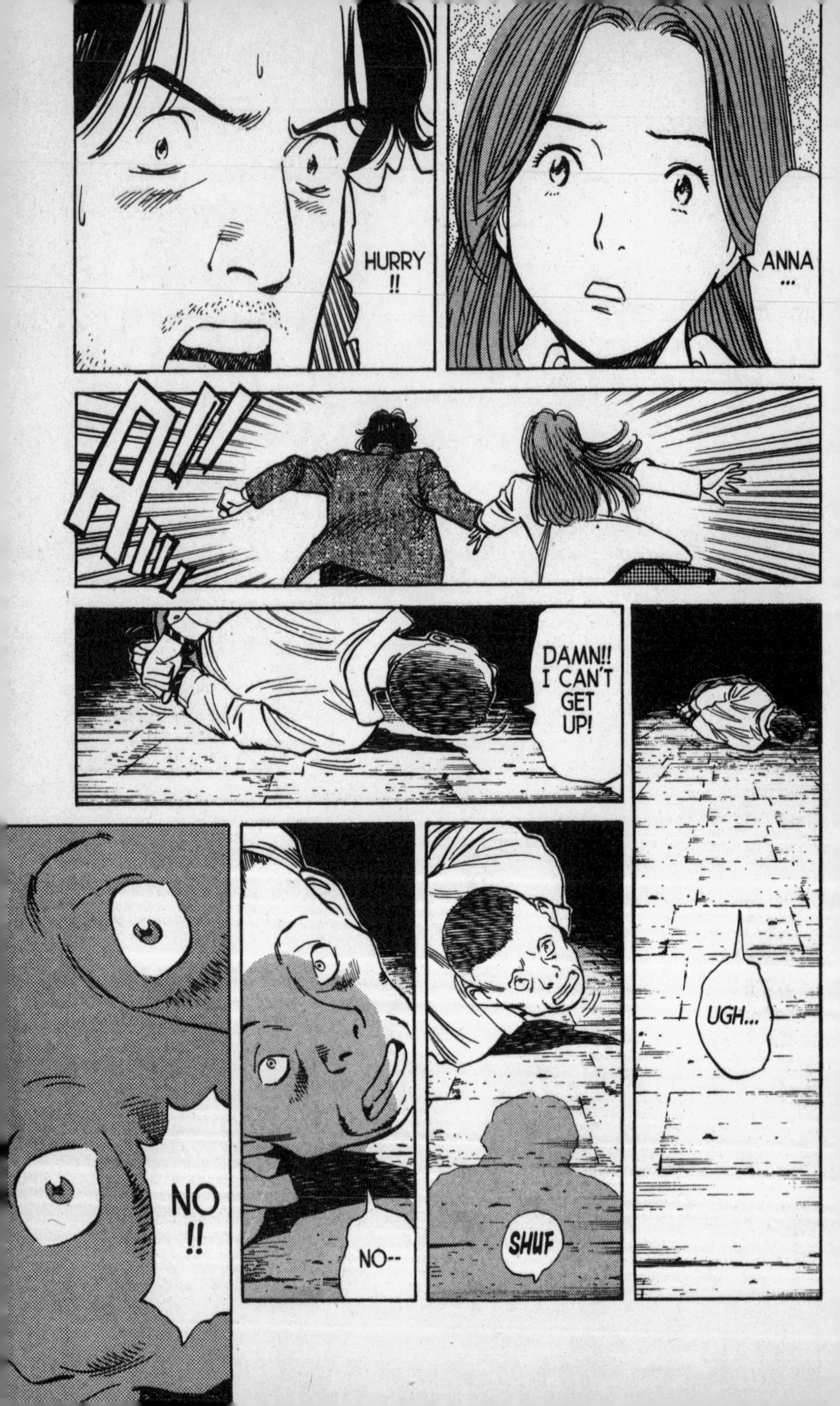
ANNA...
HURRY!!
UGH...
DAMN!! I CAN'T GET UP!
SHUF
NO--
NO!!

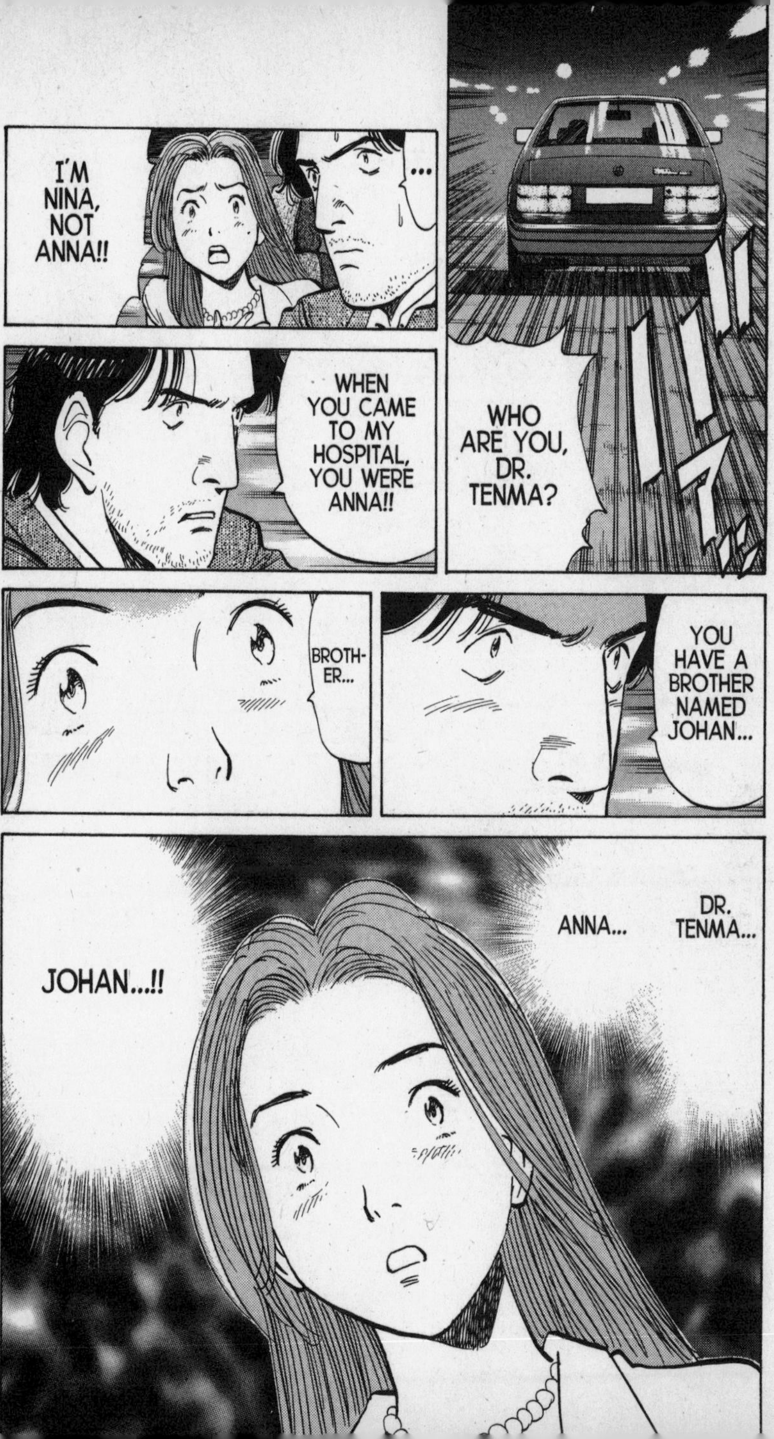
WHO ARE YOU, DR. TENMA?
...
I'M NINA, NOT ANNA!!
WHEN YOU CAME TO MY HOSPITAL, YOU WERE ANNA!!
YOU HAVE A BROTHER NAMED JOHAN...
BROTH-ER...
DR. TENMA...
ANNA...
JOHAN...!!

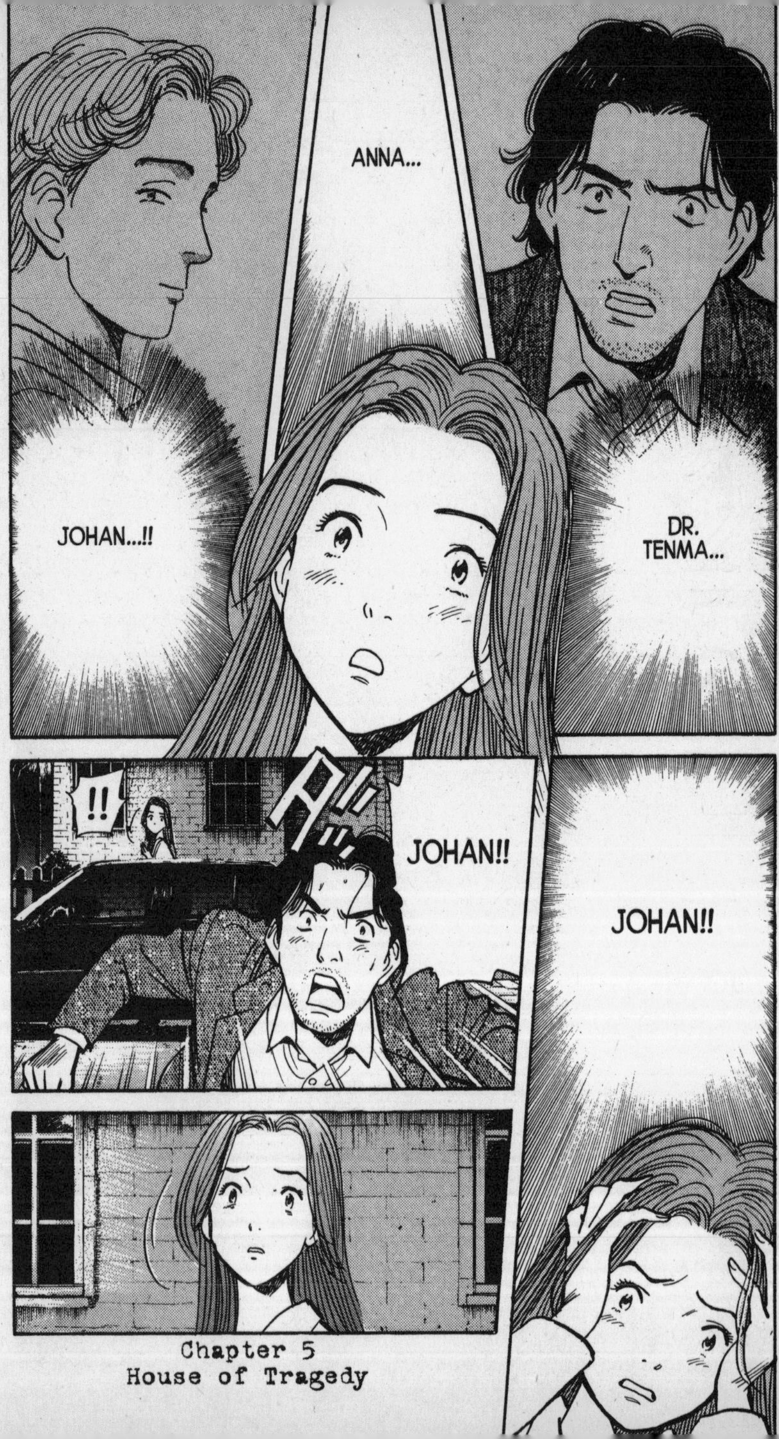
DR.
TENMA...
ANNA...
JOHAN...!!
JOHAN!!
JOHAN!!
!!

Chapter 5
House of Tragedy

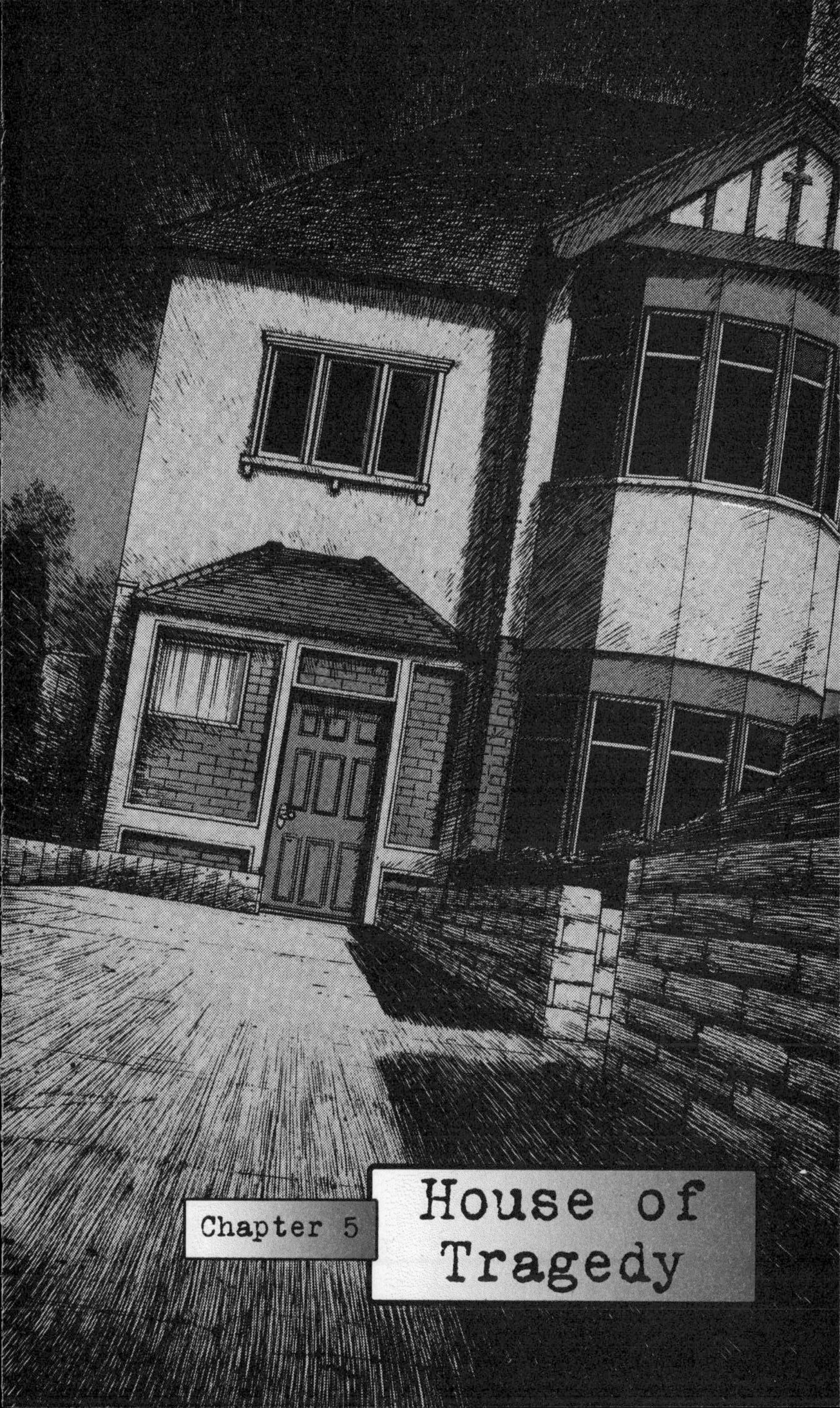
Chapter 5
House of Tragedy

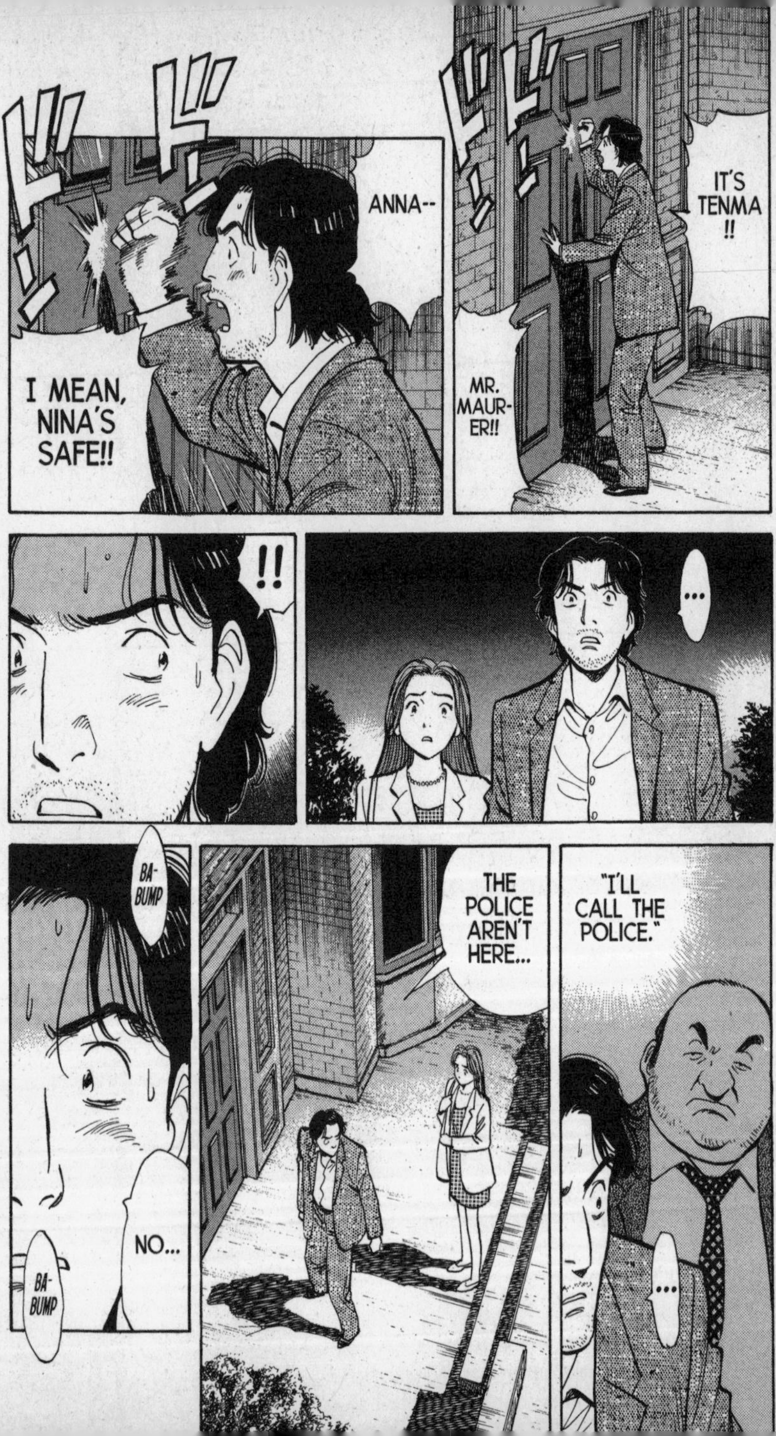
IT'S TENMA!!
MR. MAURER!!
ANNA--
I MEAN, NINA'S SAFE!!
...
!!
"I'LL CALL THE POLICE."
...
THE POLICE AREN'T HERE...
BA-BUMP
NO...
BA-BUMP

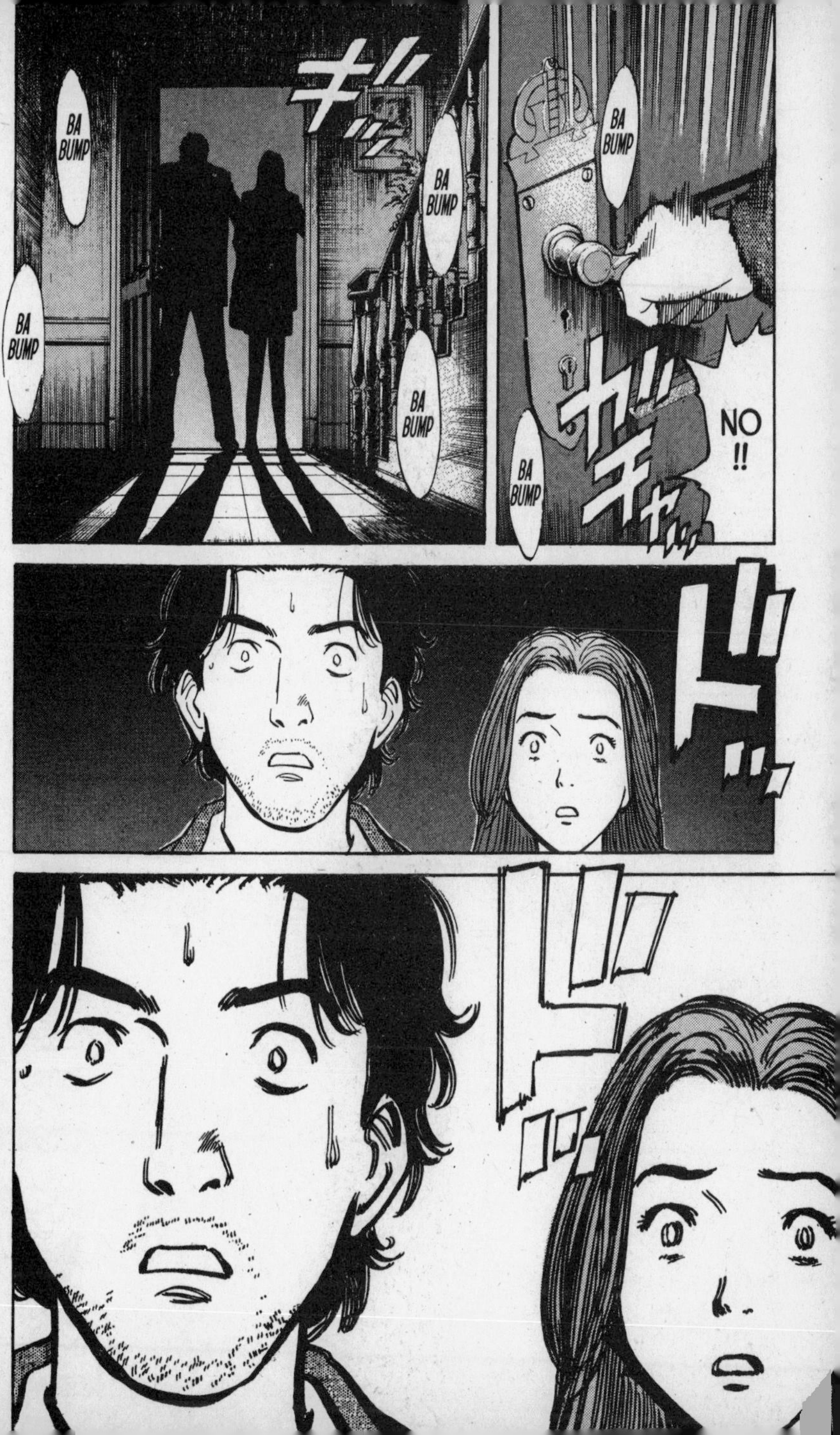
BA BUMP
BA BUMP
NO !!
BA BUMP
BA BUMP
BA BUMP
BA BUMP

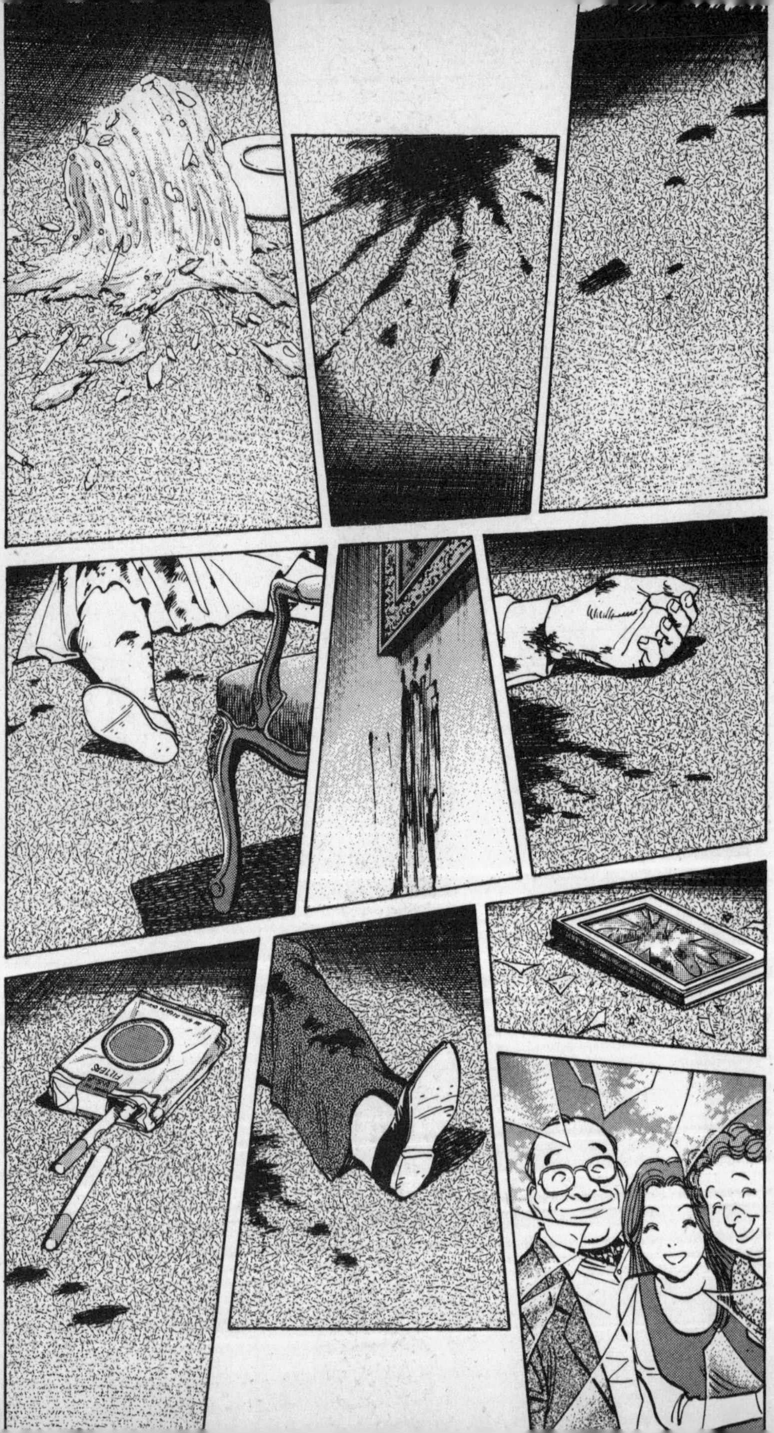
FILTERS

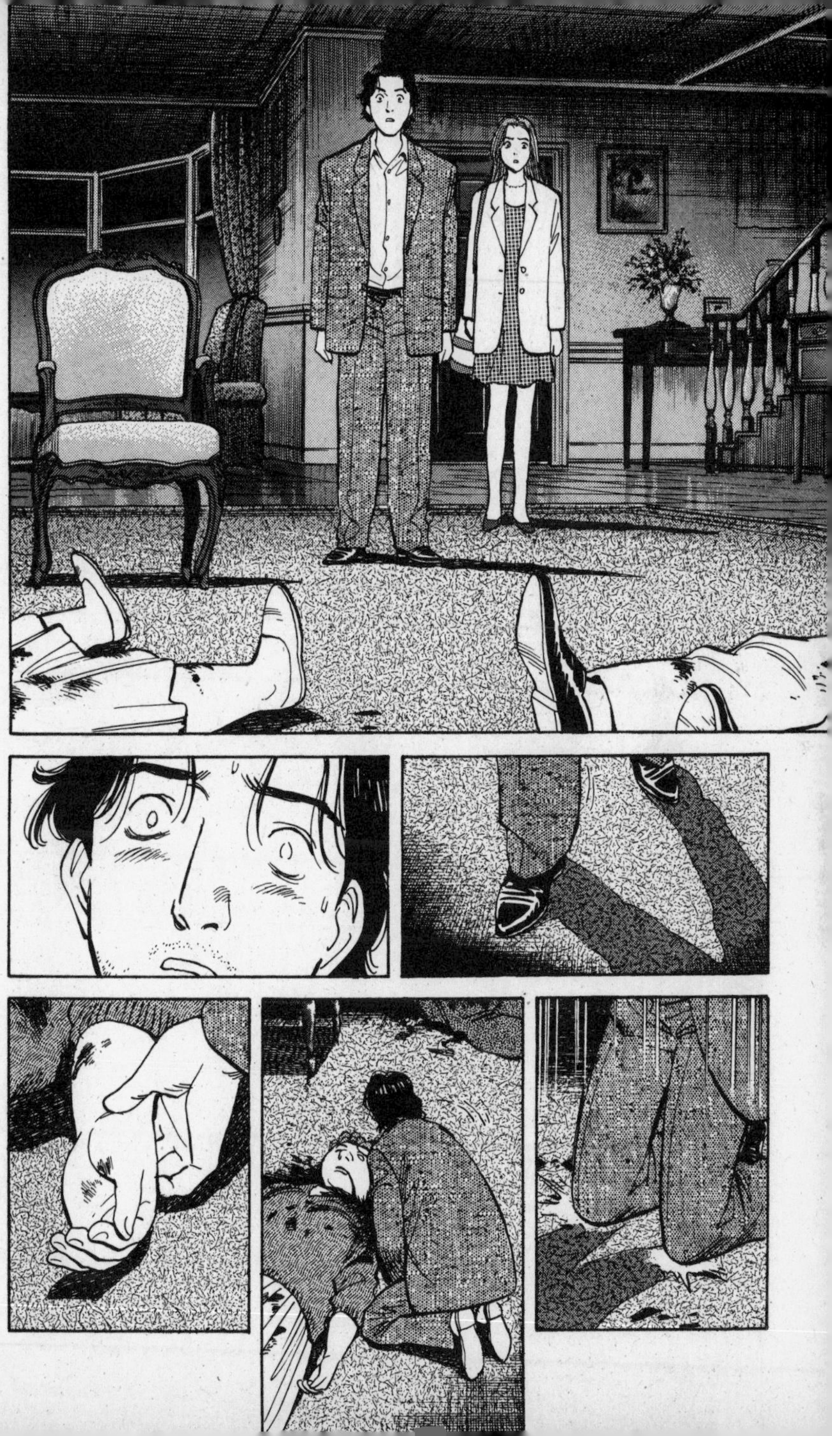

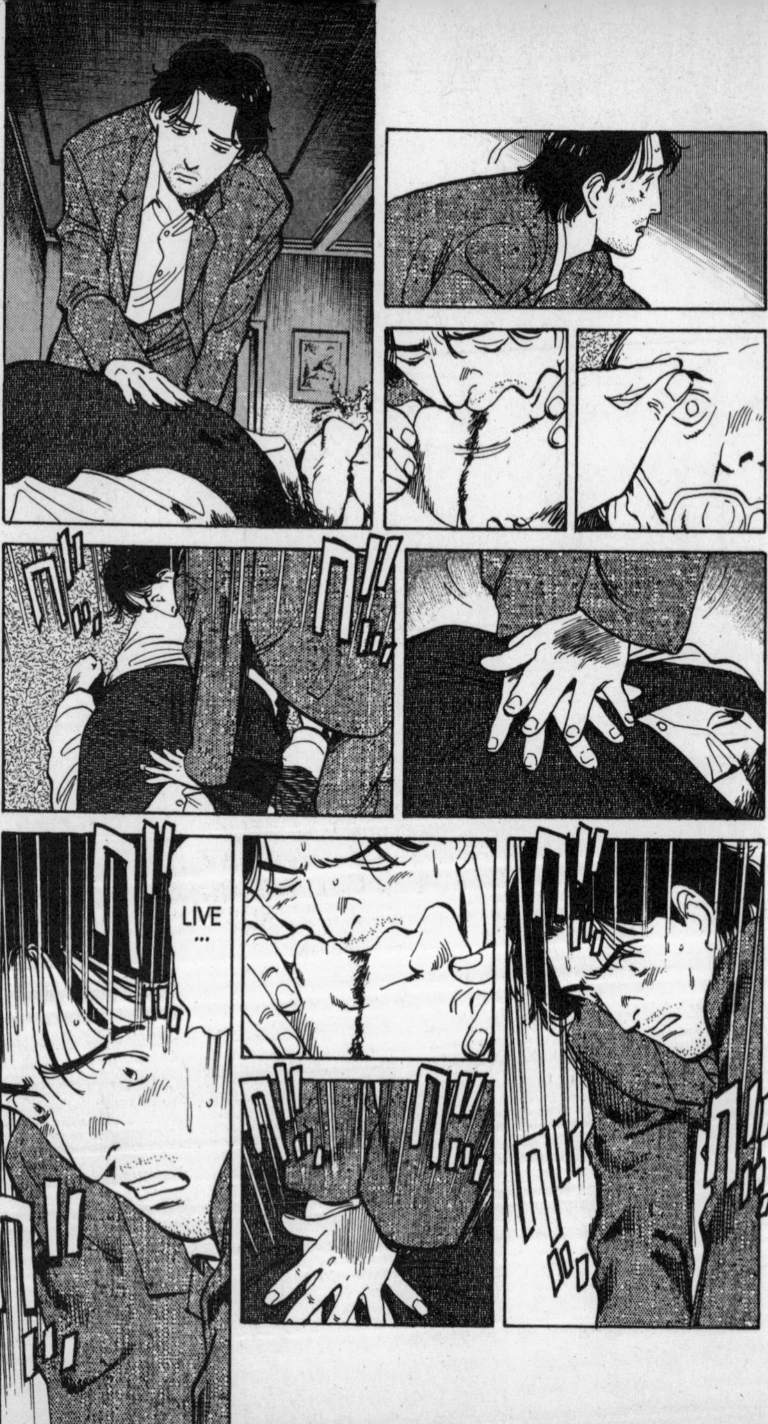
LIVE
...

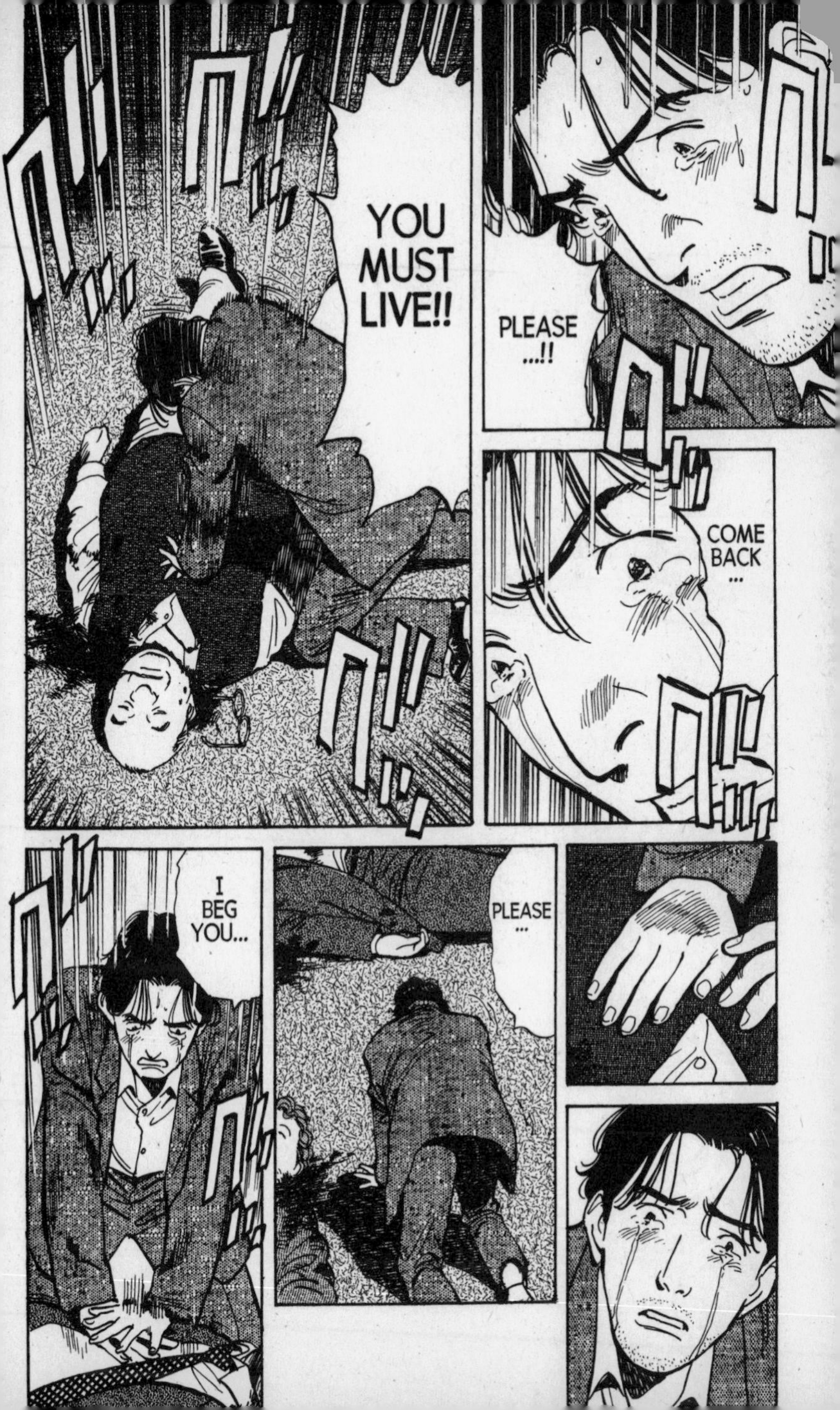
PLEASE ...!!
COME BACK ...
YOU MUST LIVE!!
PLEASE ...
I BEG YOU...

PLEASE
...

YOU
DON'T
HAVE TO
QUIT
SMOKING...

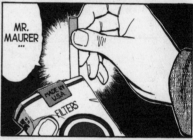

MR.
MAURER
...

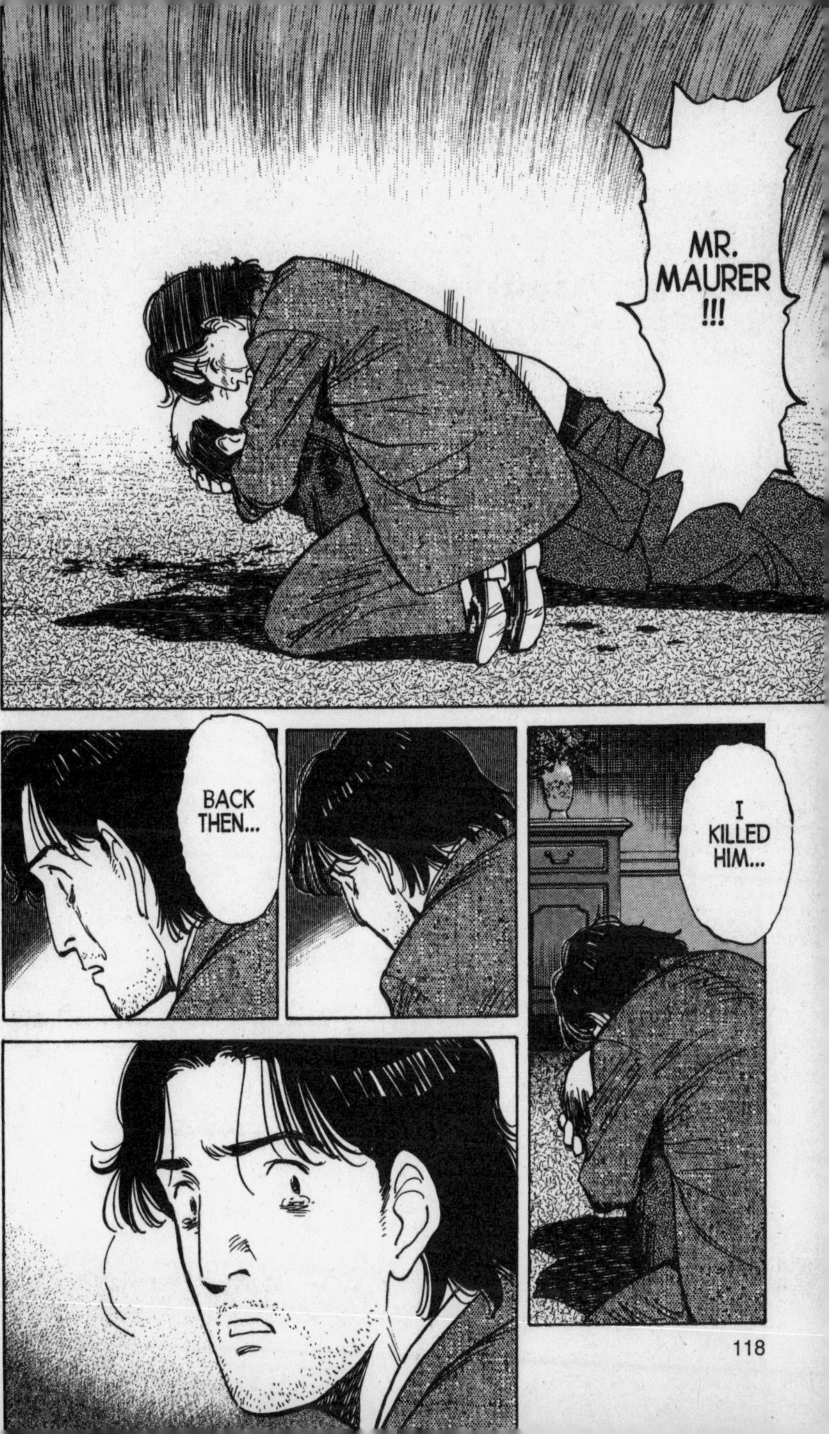
MR. MAURER !!!
BACK THEN...
I KILLED HIM...

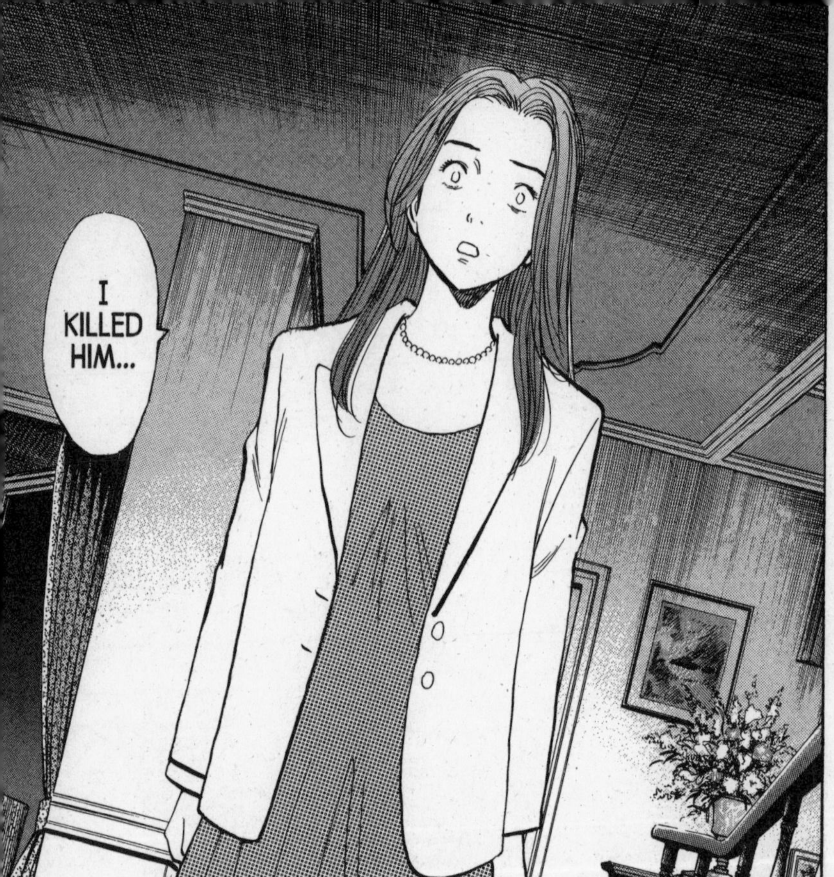
I KILLED HIM...
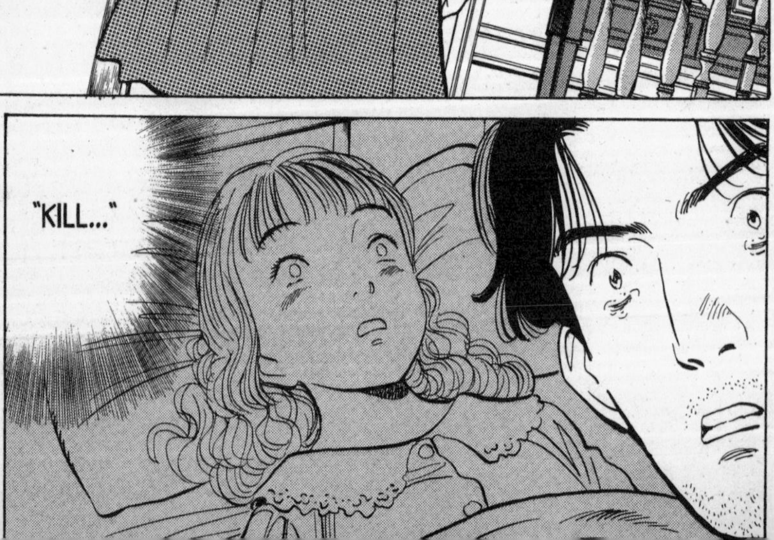
"KILL..."

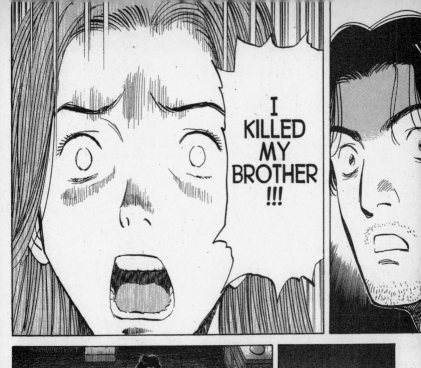

I
KILLED
MY
BROTHER
!!!

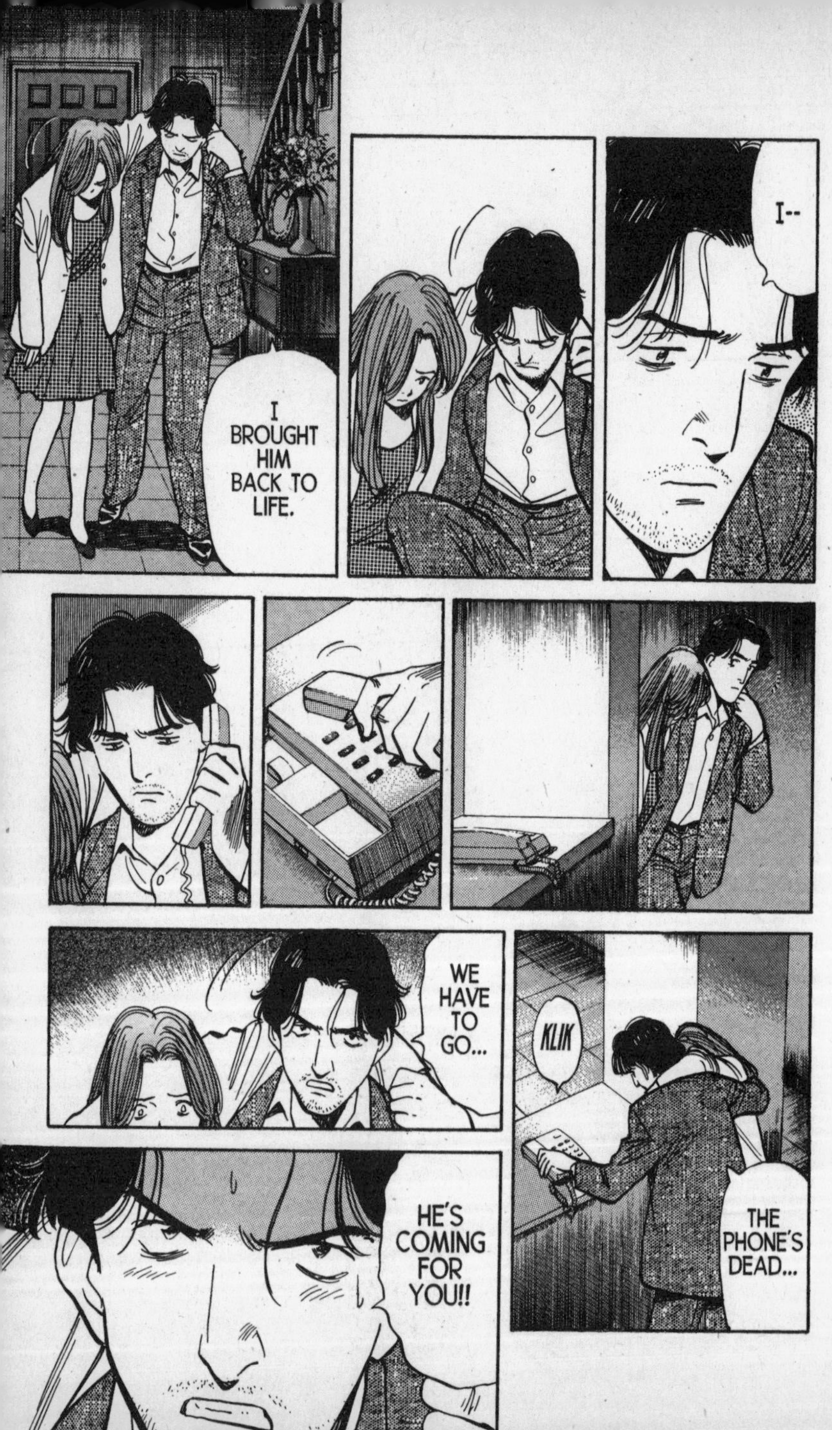
I BROUGHT HIM BACK TO LIFE.
I--
WE HAVE TO GO...
HE'S COMING FOR YOU!!
KLIK
THE PHONE'S DEAD...

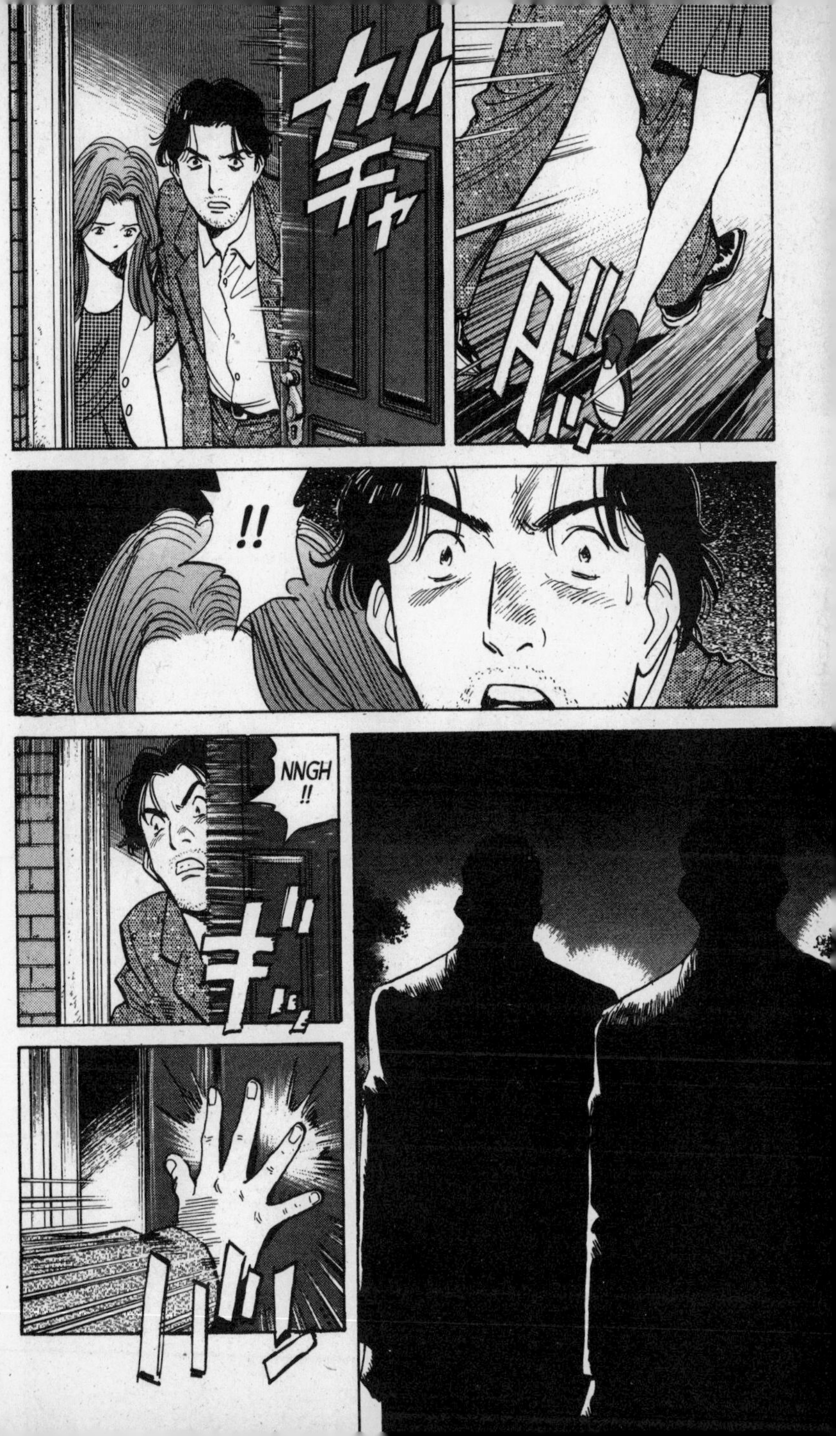
ダッ
カチャ
!!
NNGH
!!
ギリッ
バッ

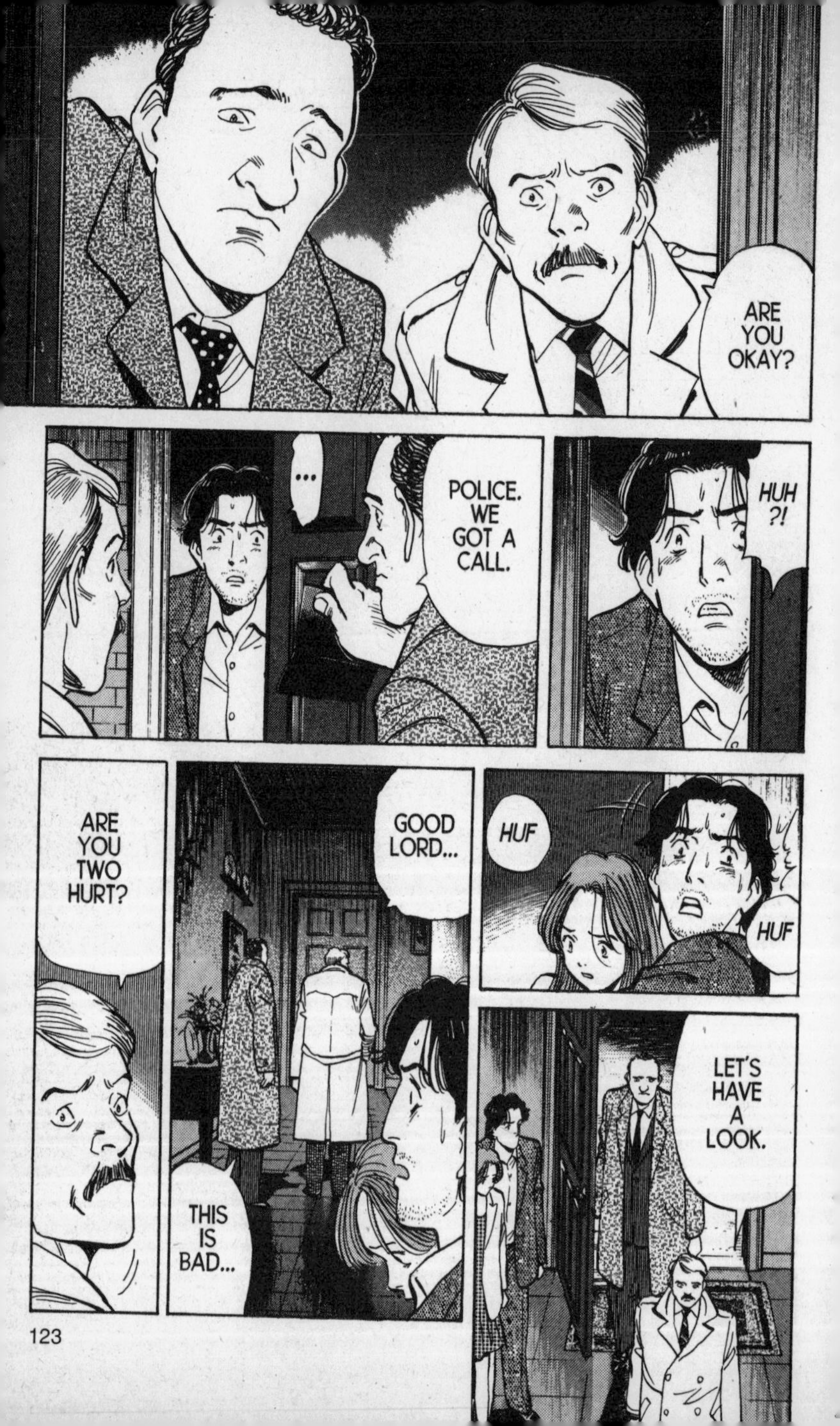
ARE YOU OKAY?
POLICE. WE GOT A CALL.
...
HUH ?!
ARE YOU TWO HURT?
GOOD LORD...
THIS IS BAD...
HUF
HUF
LET'S HAVE A LOOK.

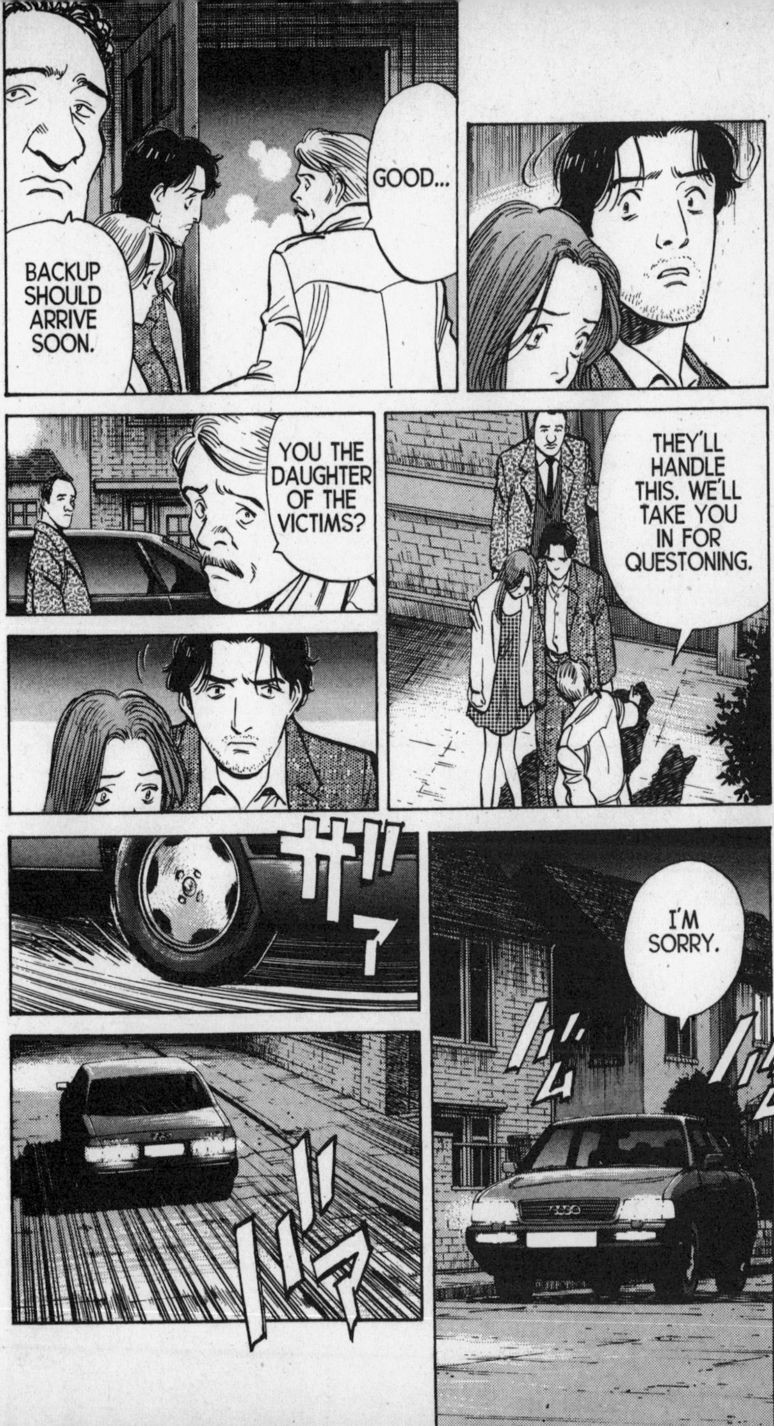
BACKUP SHOULD ARRIVE SOON.
GOOD...
YOU THE DAUGHTER OF THE VICTIMS?
THEY'LL HANDLE THIS. WE'LL TAKE YOU IN FOR QUESTONING.
ザァ
I'M SORRY.

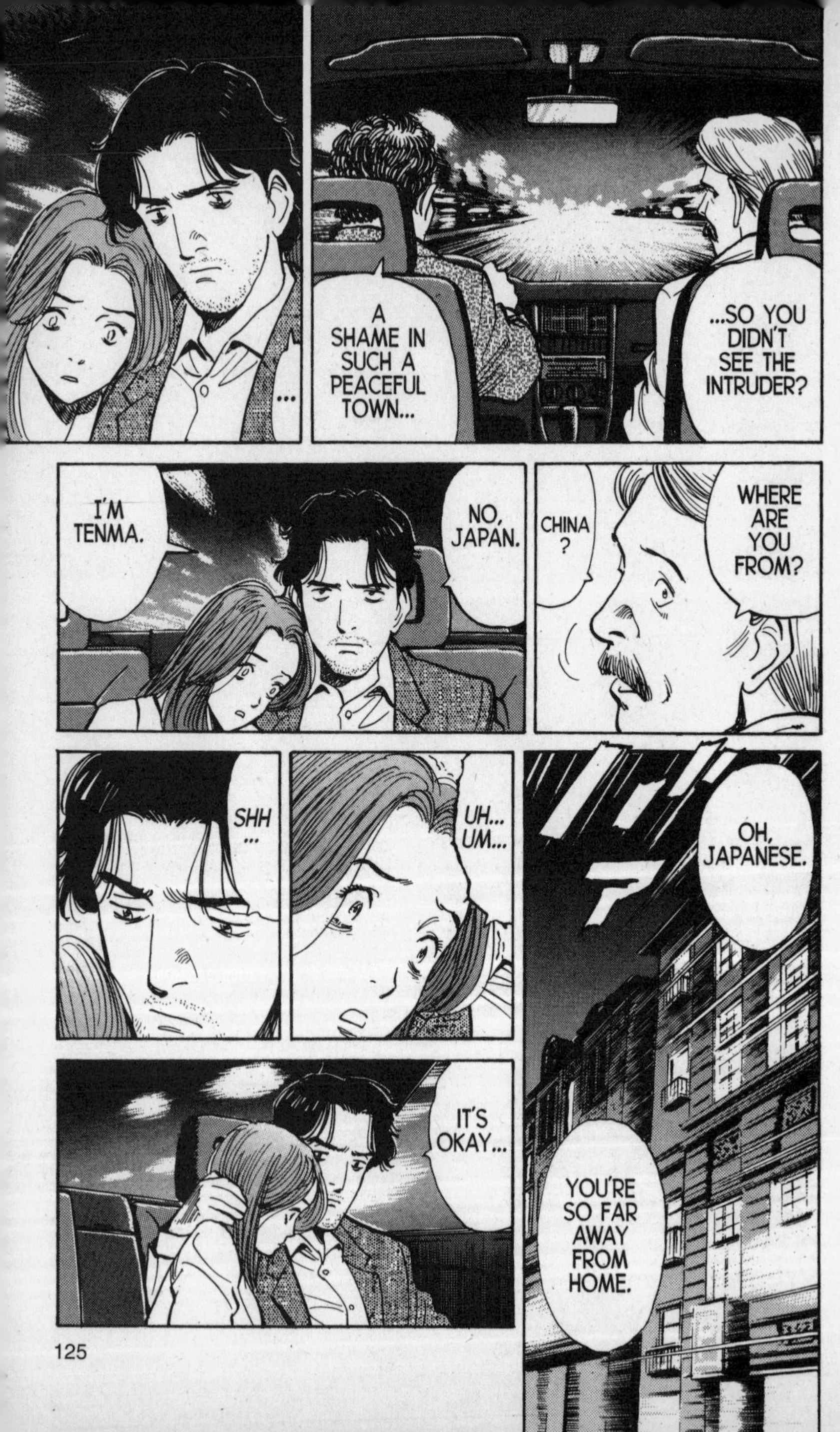
...SO YOU DIDN'T SEE THE INTRUDER?
A SHAME IN SUCH A PEACEFUL TOWN...
...
WHERE ARE YOU FROM?
CHINA ?
NO, JAPAN.
I'M TENMA.
OH, JAPANESE.
YOU'RE SO FAR AWAY FROM HOME.
UH... UM...
SHH ...
IT'S OKAY...

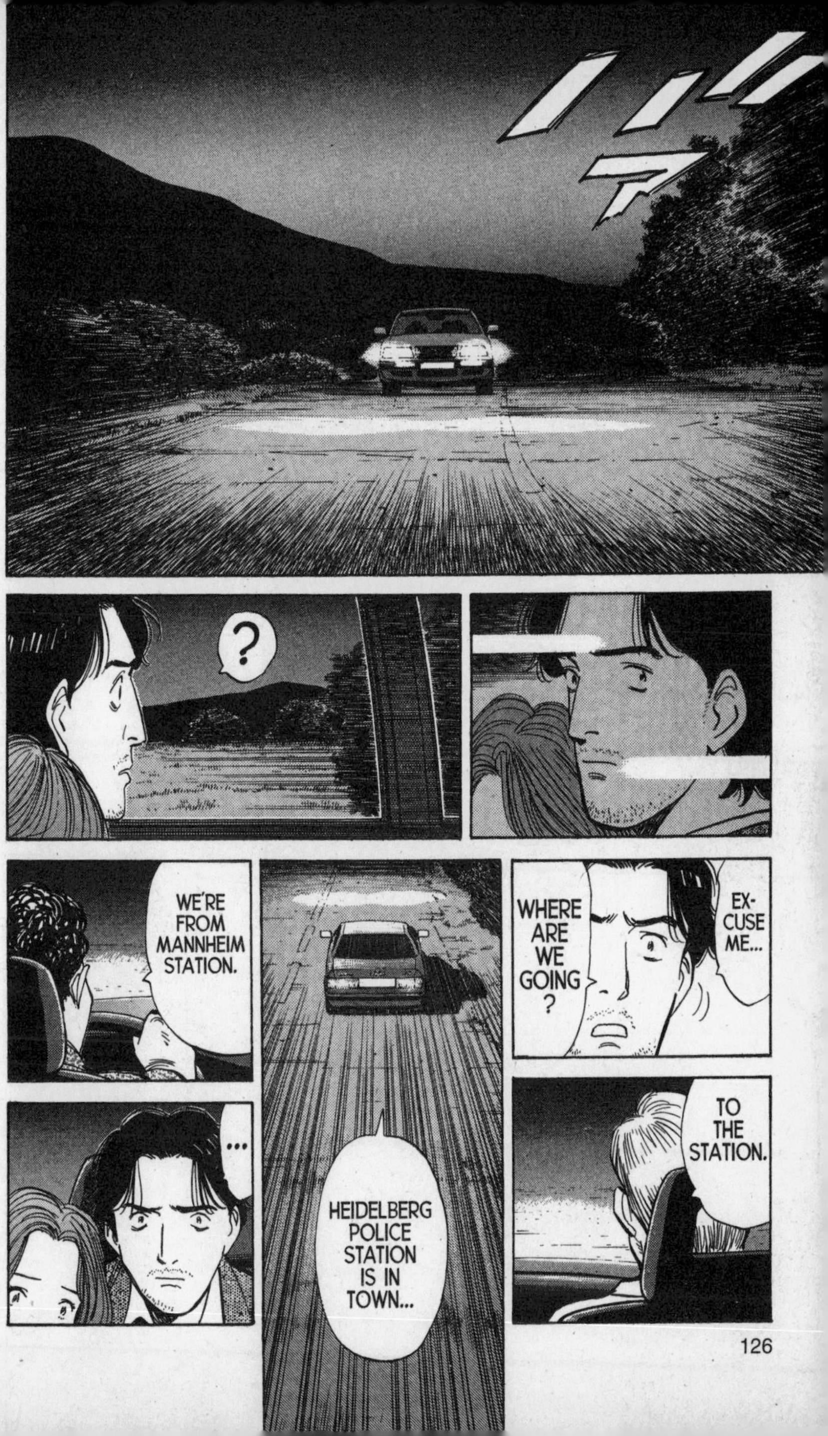
?
EX-CUSE ME...
WHERE ARE WE GOING?
TO THE STATION.
HEIDELBERG POLICE STATION IS IN TOWN...
WE'RE FROM MANNHEIM STATION.
...

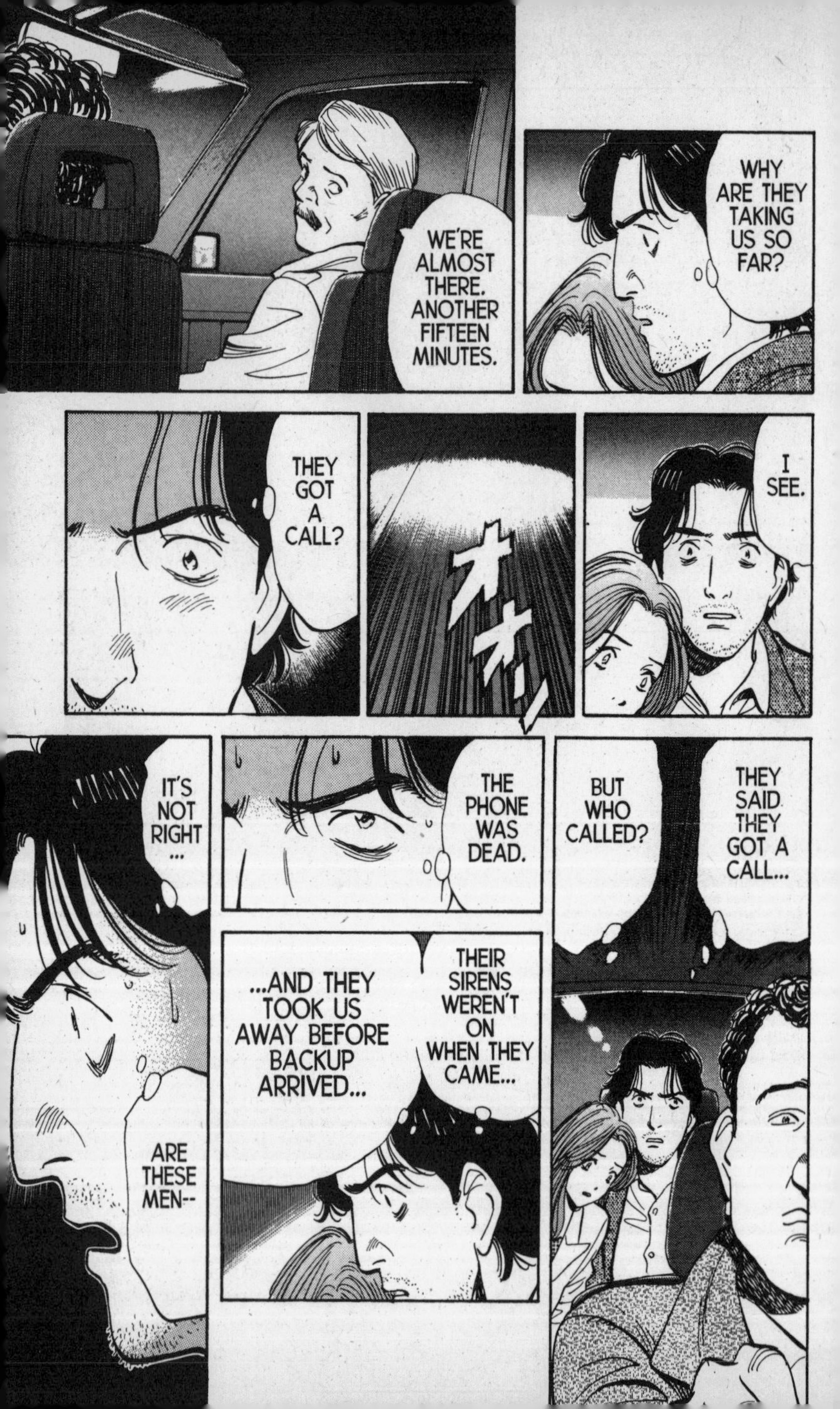
WHY ARE THEY TAKING US SO FAR?
WE'RE ALMOST THERE. ANOTHER FIFTEEN MINUTES.
I SEE.
オオ
THEY GOT A CALL?
THEY SAID THEY GOT A CALL...
BUT WHO CALLED?
THE PHONE WAS DEAD.
THEIR SIRENS WEREN'T ON WHEN THEY CAME...
...AND THEY TOOK US AWAY BEFORE BACKUP ARRIVED...
IT'S NOT RIGHT...
ARE THESE MEN--

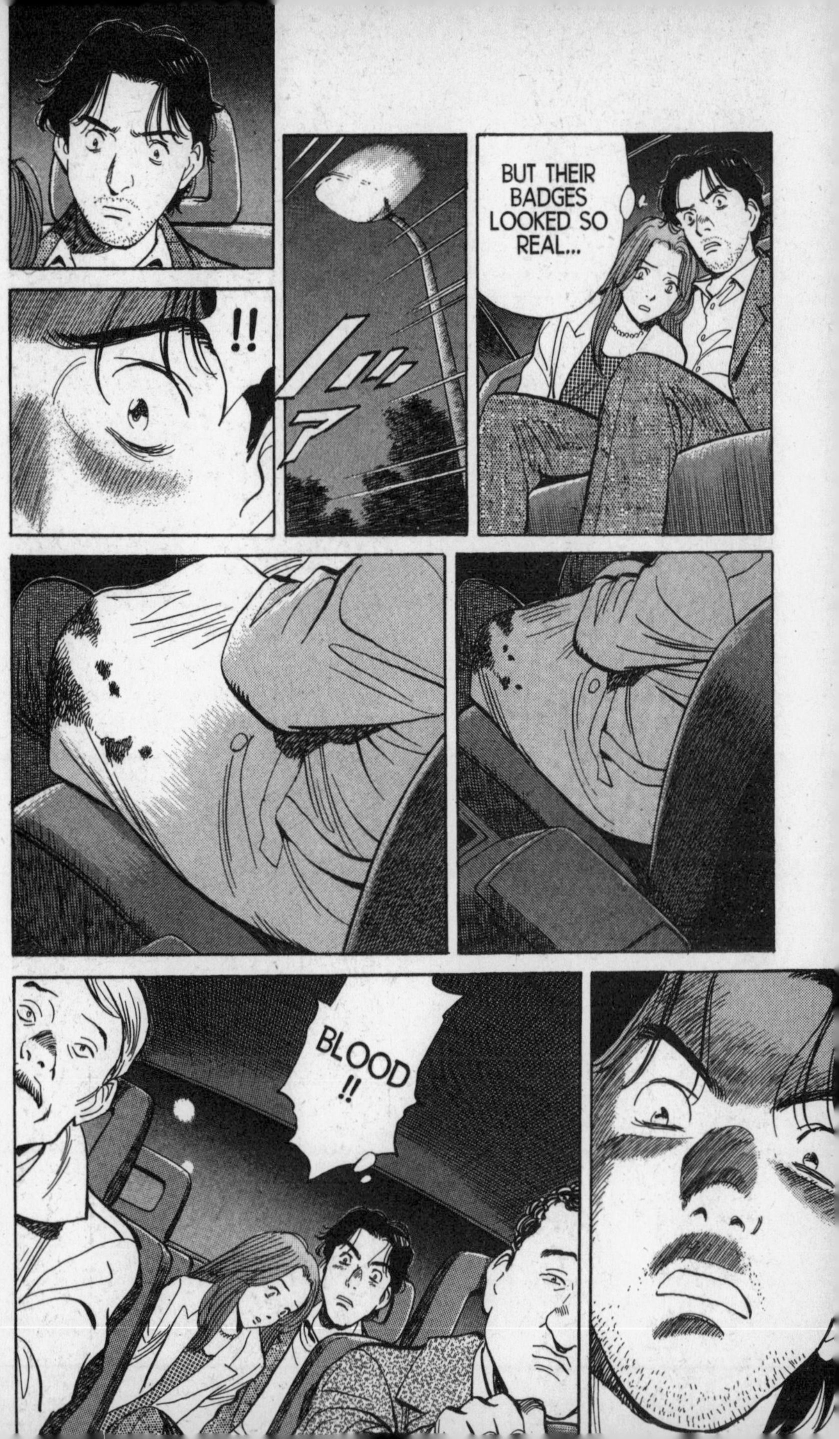
BUT THEIR BADGES LOOKED SO REAL...
!!
BLOOD !!

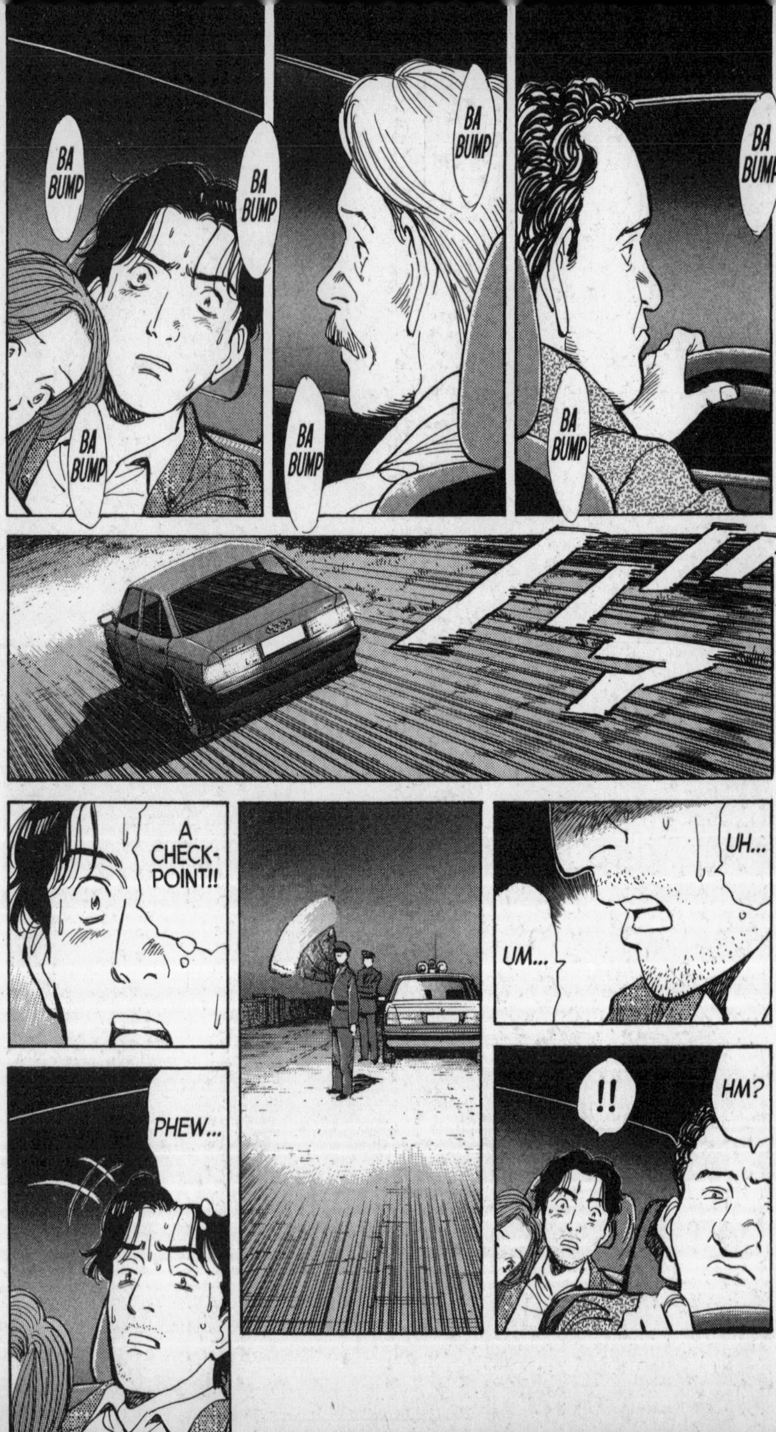
BA BUMP
BA BUMP
BA BUMP
BA BUMP
BA BUMP
BA BUMP
UH...
UM...
HM?
!!
A CHECKPOINT!!
PHEW...

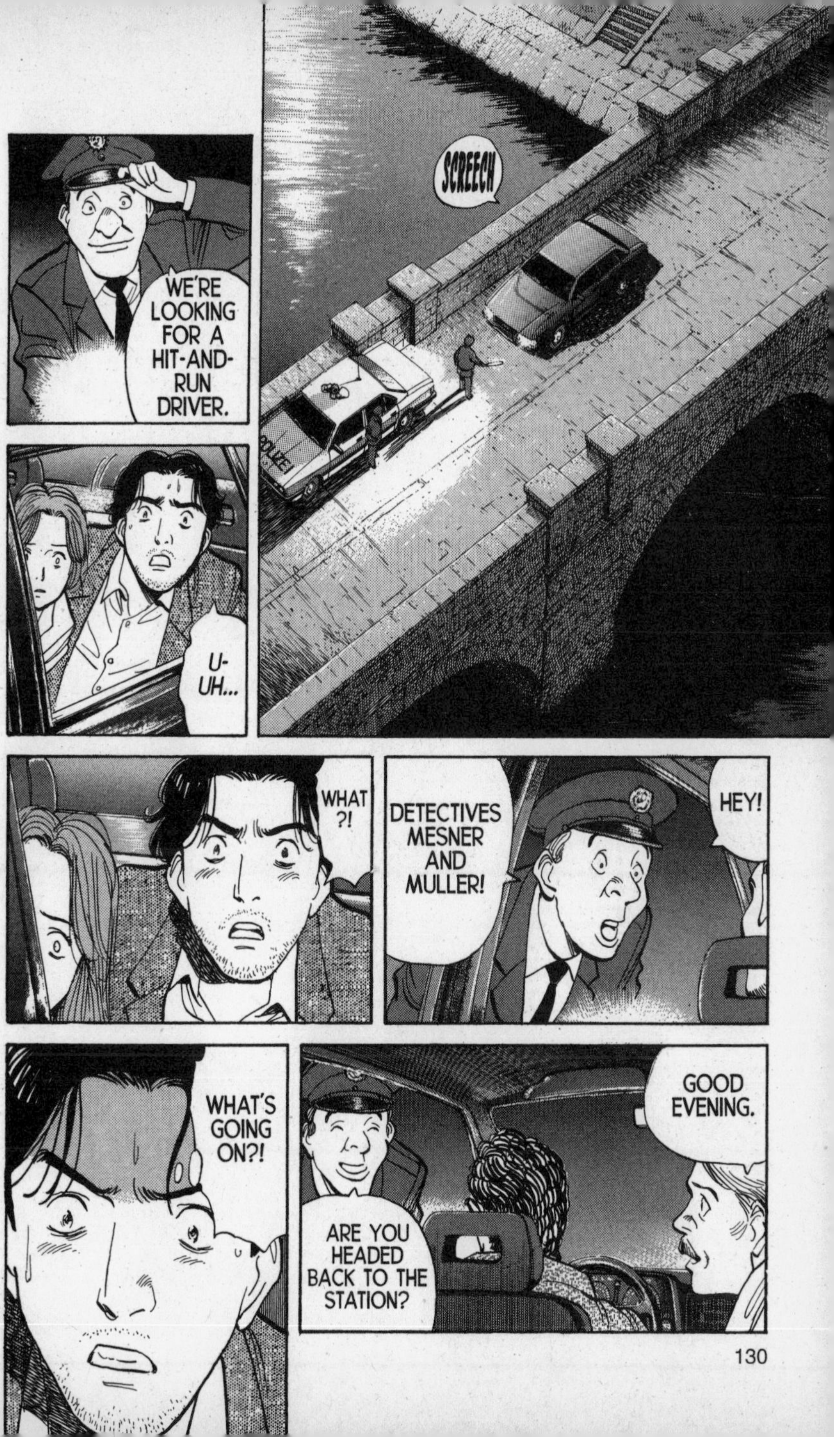
SCREECH
WE'RE LOOKING FOR A HIT-AND-RUN DRIVER.
U-UH...
HEY!
DETECTIVES MESNER AND MULLER!
WHAT?!
GOOD EVENING.
ARE YOU HEADED BACK TO THE STATION?
WHAT'S GOING ON?!

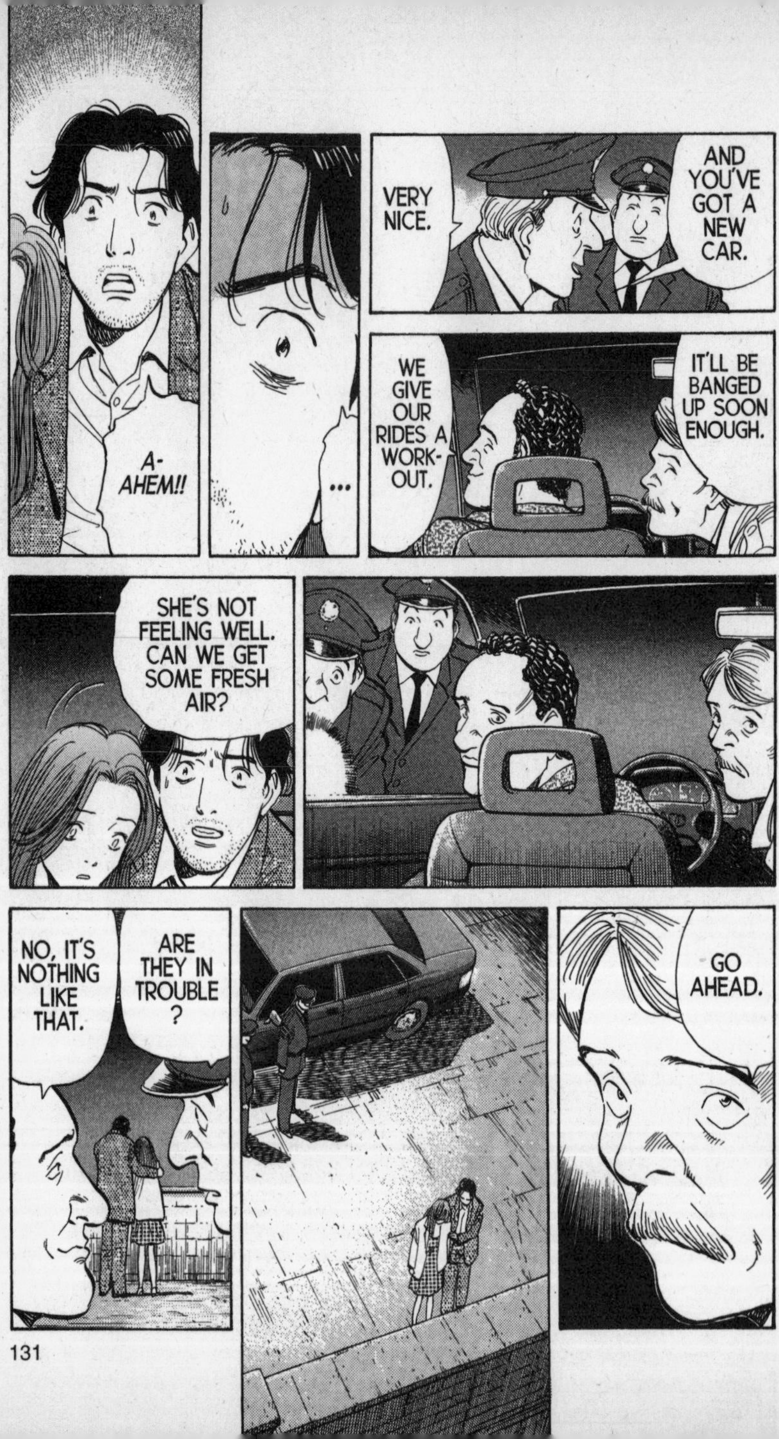
A-AHEM!!
...
VERY NICE.
AND YOU'VE GOT A NEW CAR.
WE GIVE OUR RIDES A WORK-OUT.
IT'LL BE BANGED UP SOON ENOUGH.
SHE'S NOT FEELING WELL. CAN WE GET SOME FRESH AIR?
ARE THEY IN TROUBLE?
NO, IT'S NOTHING LIKE THAT.
GO AHEAD.

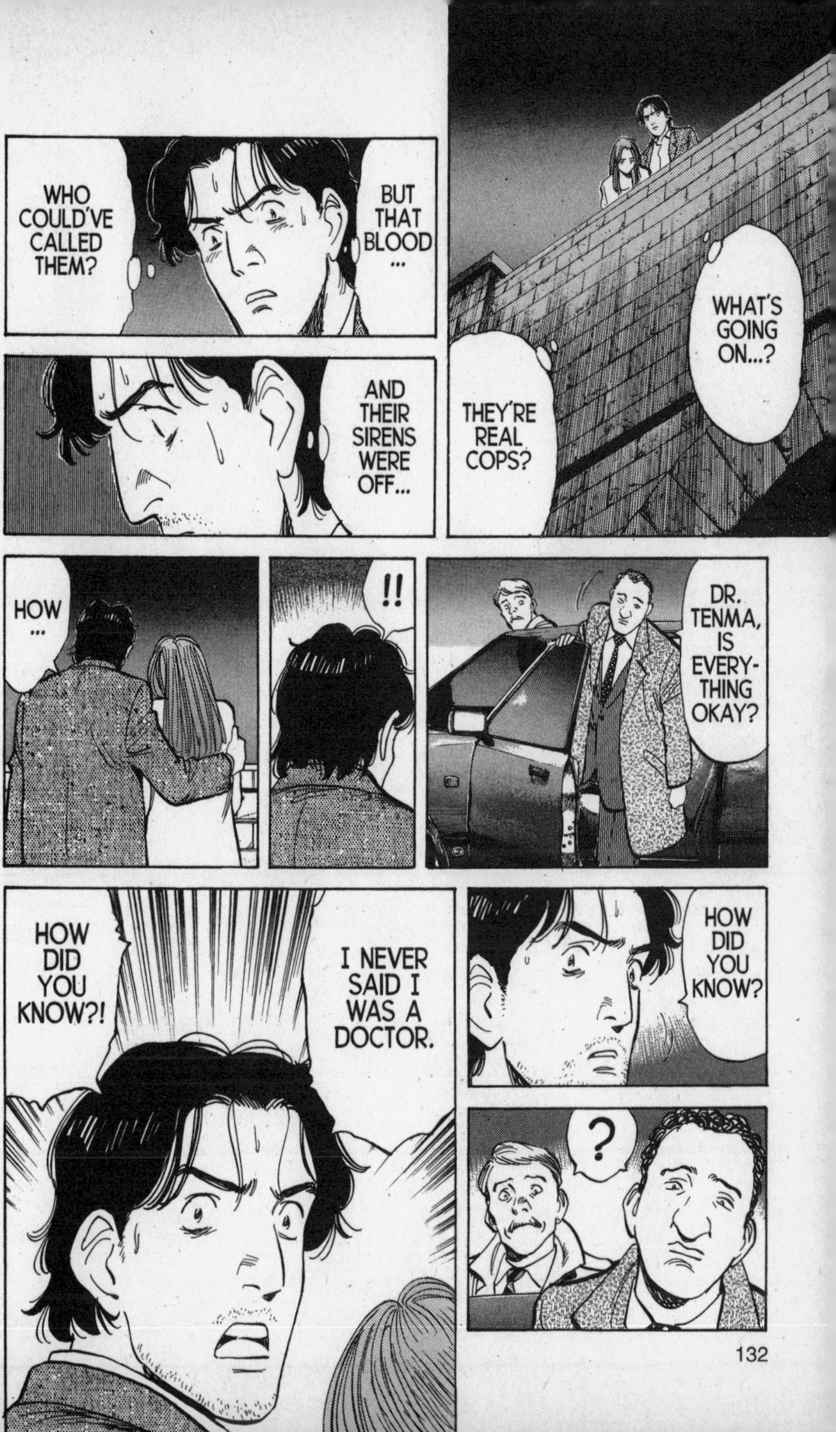
WHAT'S GOING ON...?
THEY'RE REAL COPS?
BUT THAT BLOOD...
WHO COULD'VE CALLED THEM?
AND THEIR SIRENS WERE OFF...
DR. TENMA, IS EVERY-THING OKAY?
!!
HOW...
HOW DID YOU KNOW?
?
I NEVER SAID I WAS A DOCTOR.
HOW DID YOU KNOW?!

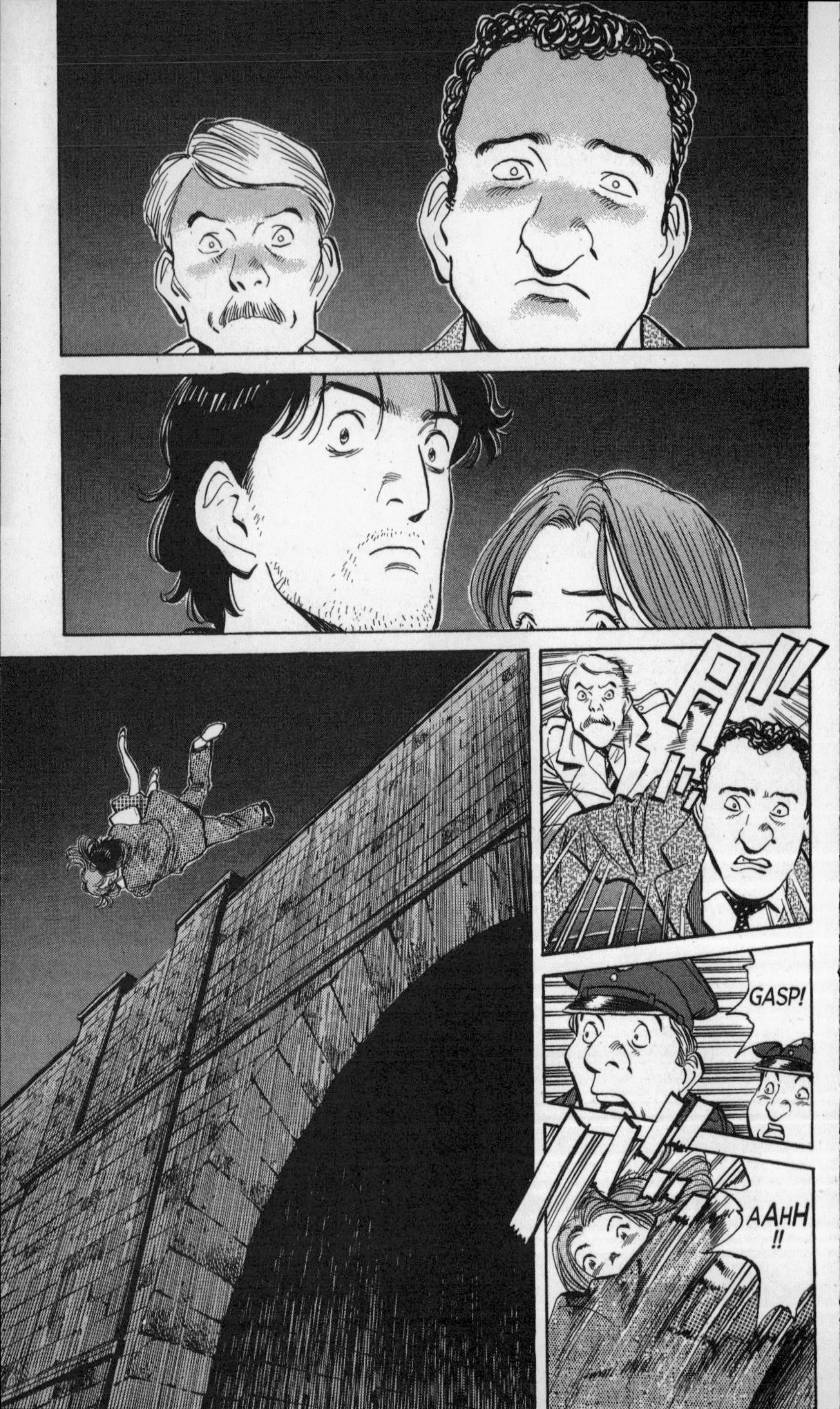
GASP!
AAHH
!!

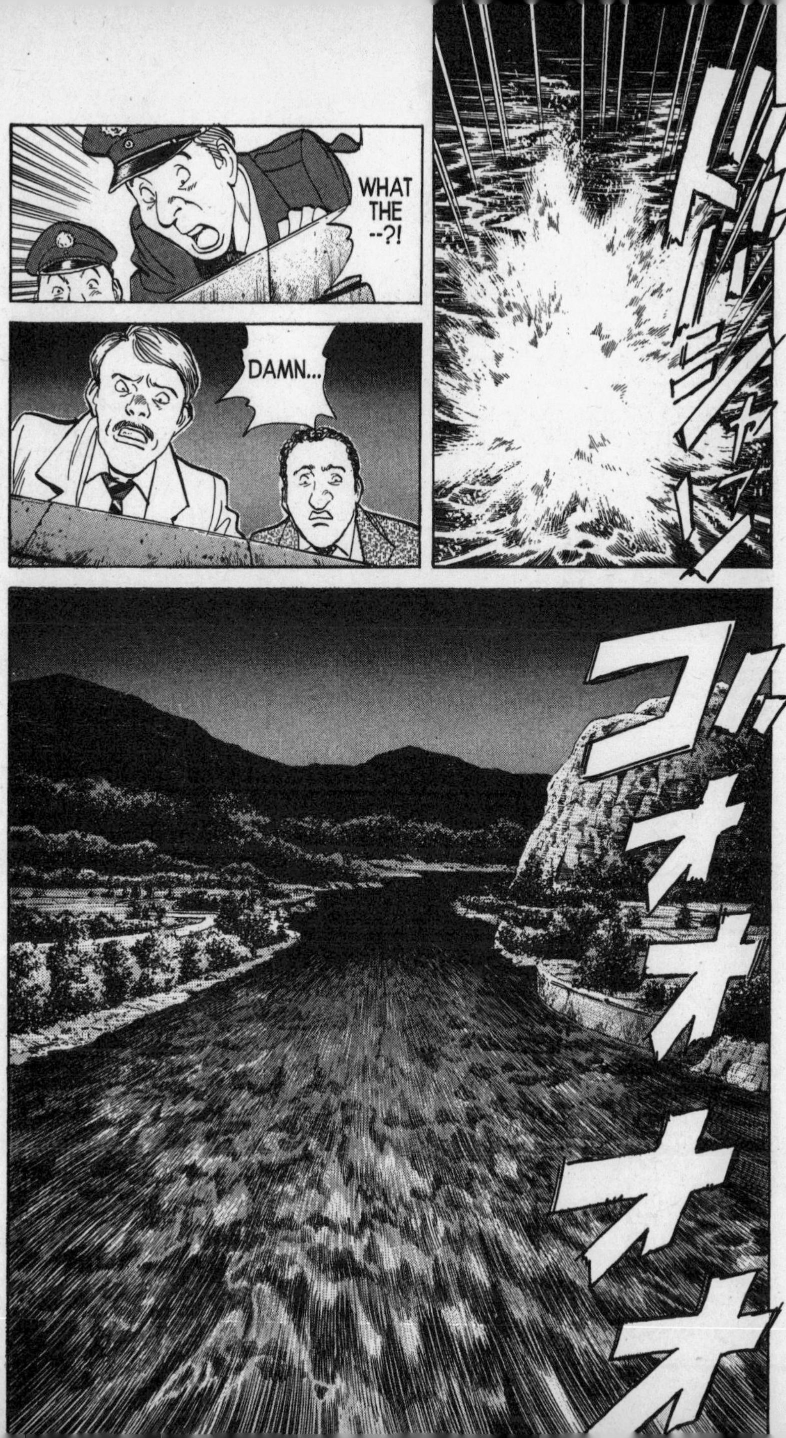
WHAT THE --?!
DAMN...

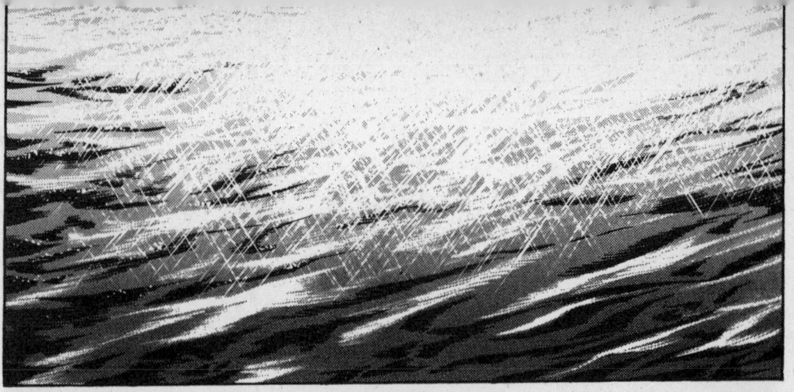

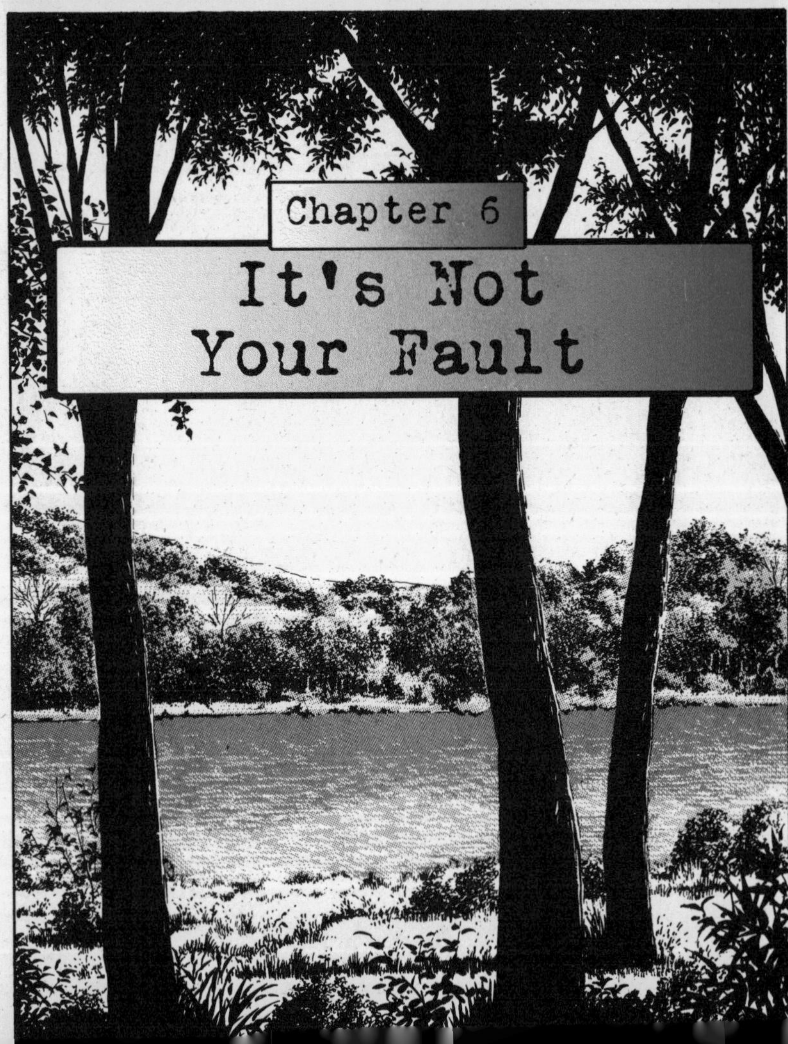

Chapter 6

It's Not Your Fault

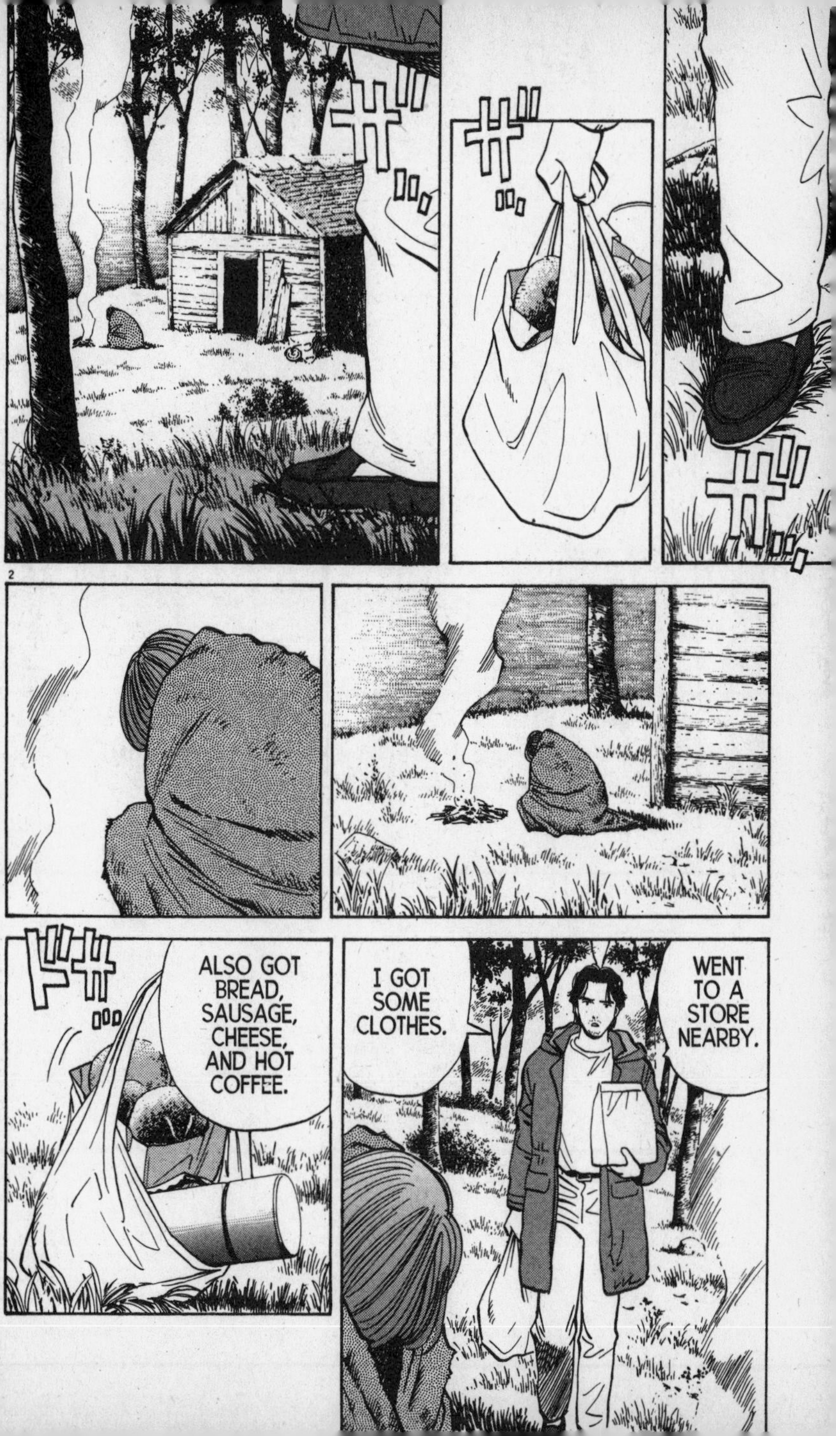
WENT TO A STORE NEARBY.
I GOT SOME CLOTHES.
ALSO GOT BREAD, SAUSAGE, CHEESE, AND HOT COFFEE.

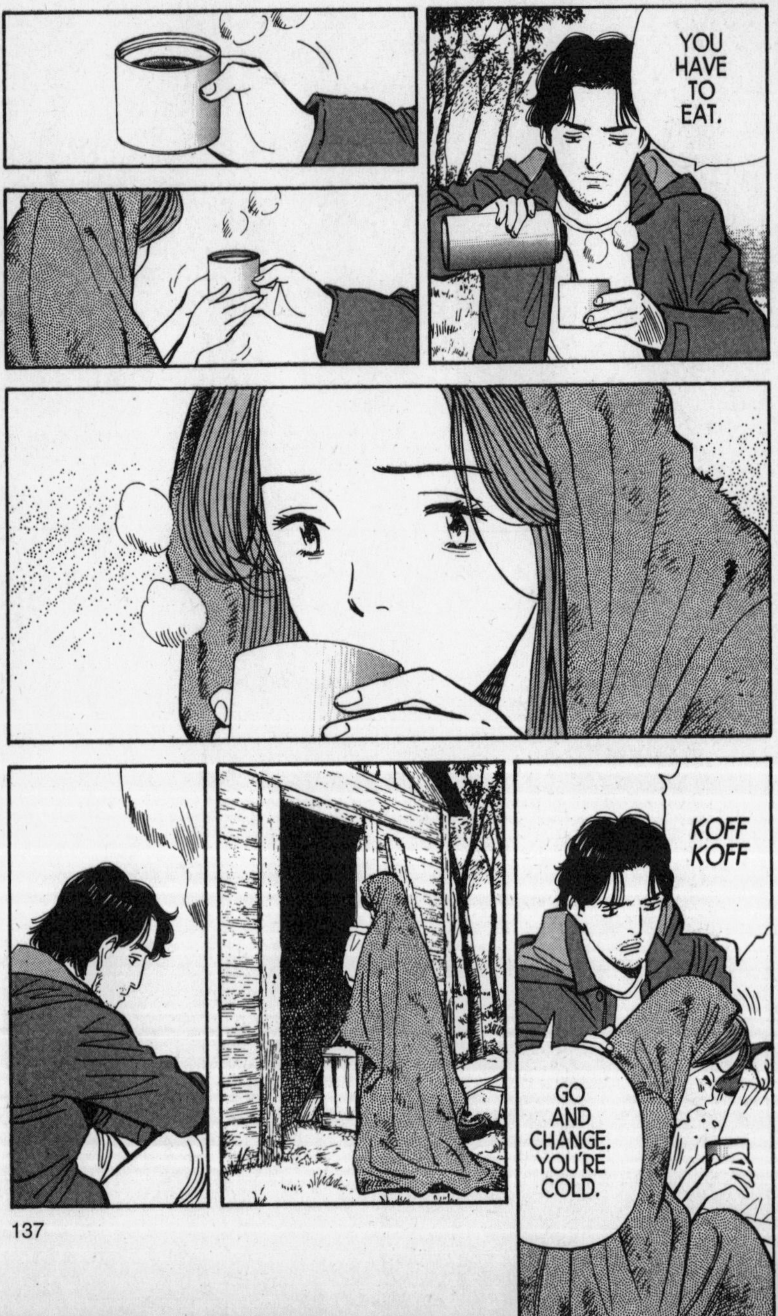
YOU HAVE TO EAT.
KOFF KOFF
GO AND CHANGE. YOU'RE COLD.

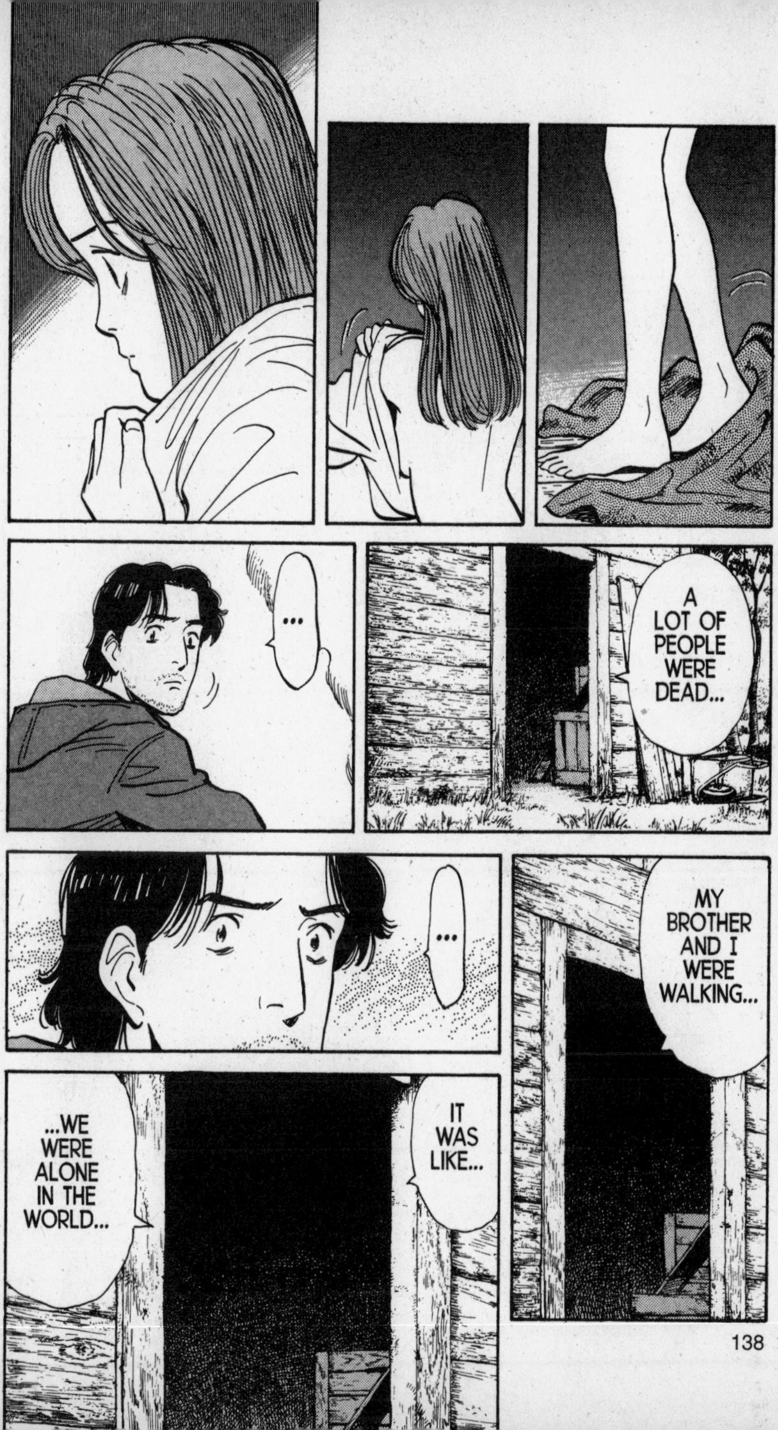
A LOT OF PEOPLE WERE DEAD...
...
MY BROTHER AND I WERE WALKING...
...
IT WAS LIKE...
...WE WERE ALONE IN THE WORLD...

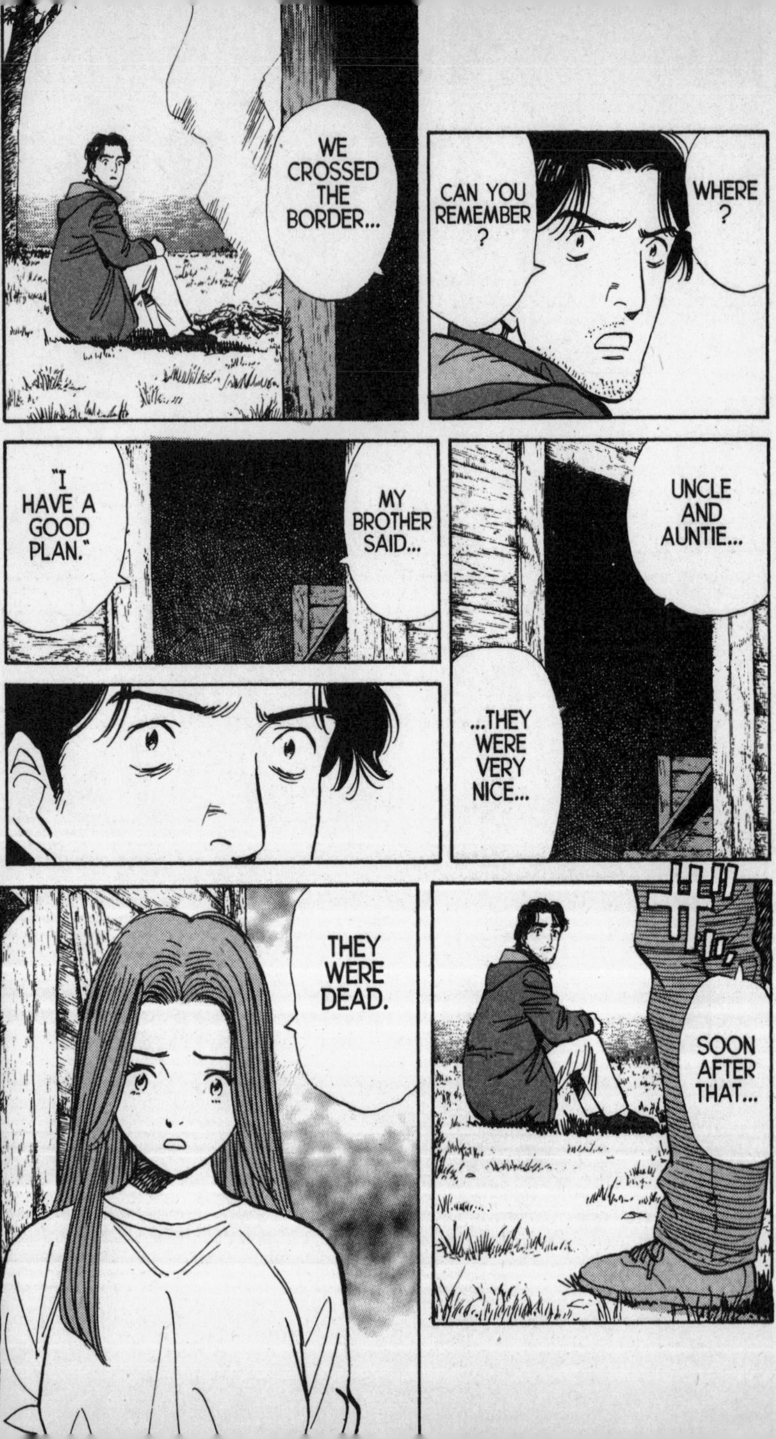
WHERE?
CAN YOU REMEMBER?
WE CROSSED THE BORDER...
UNCLE AND AUNTIE...
...THEY WERE VERY NICE...
MY BROTHER SAID...
"I HAVE A GOOD PLAN."
ザッ
SOON AFTER THAT...
THEY WERE DEAD.

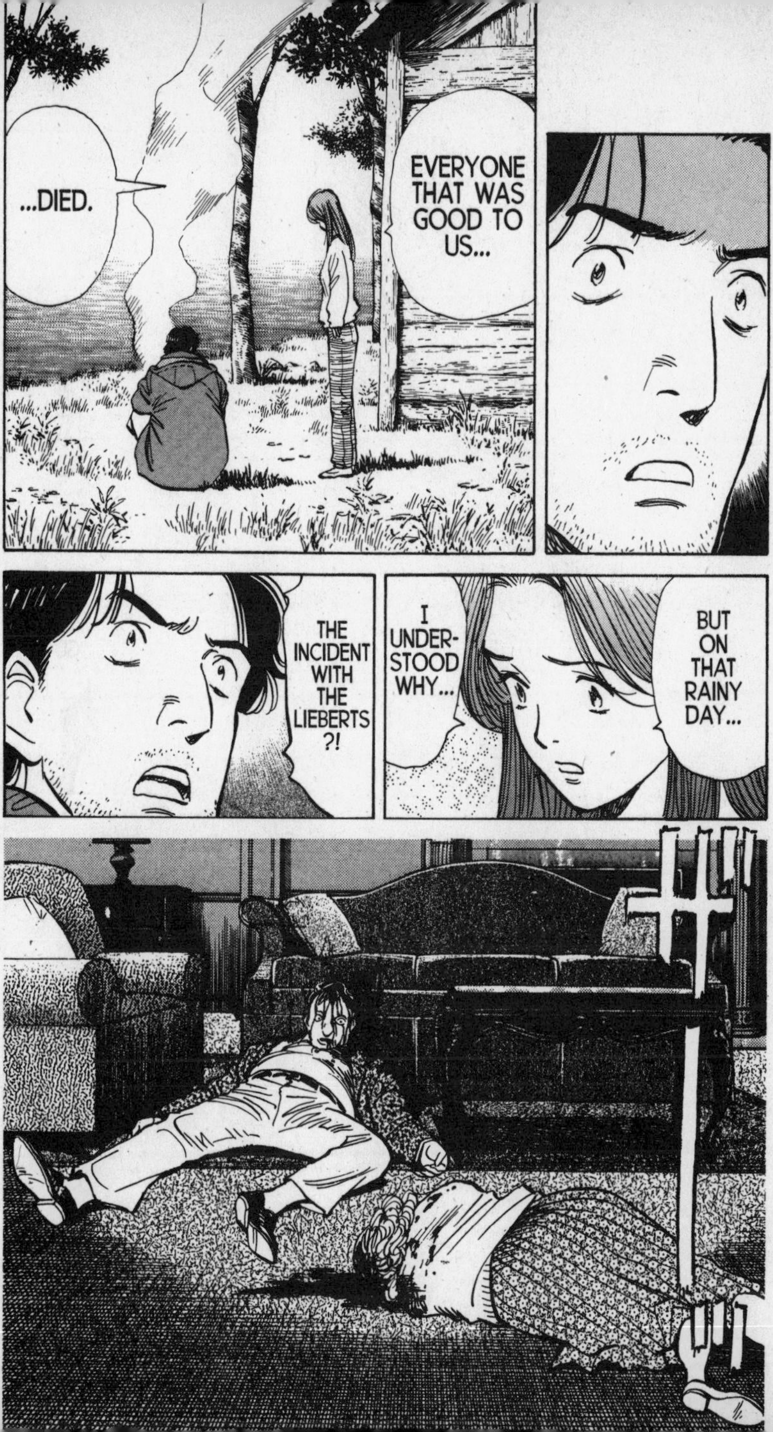
EVERYONE THAT WAS GOOD TO US...
...DIED.
BUT ON THAT RAINY DAY...
I UNDER-STOOD WHY...
THE INCIDENT WITH THE LIEBERTS ?!

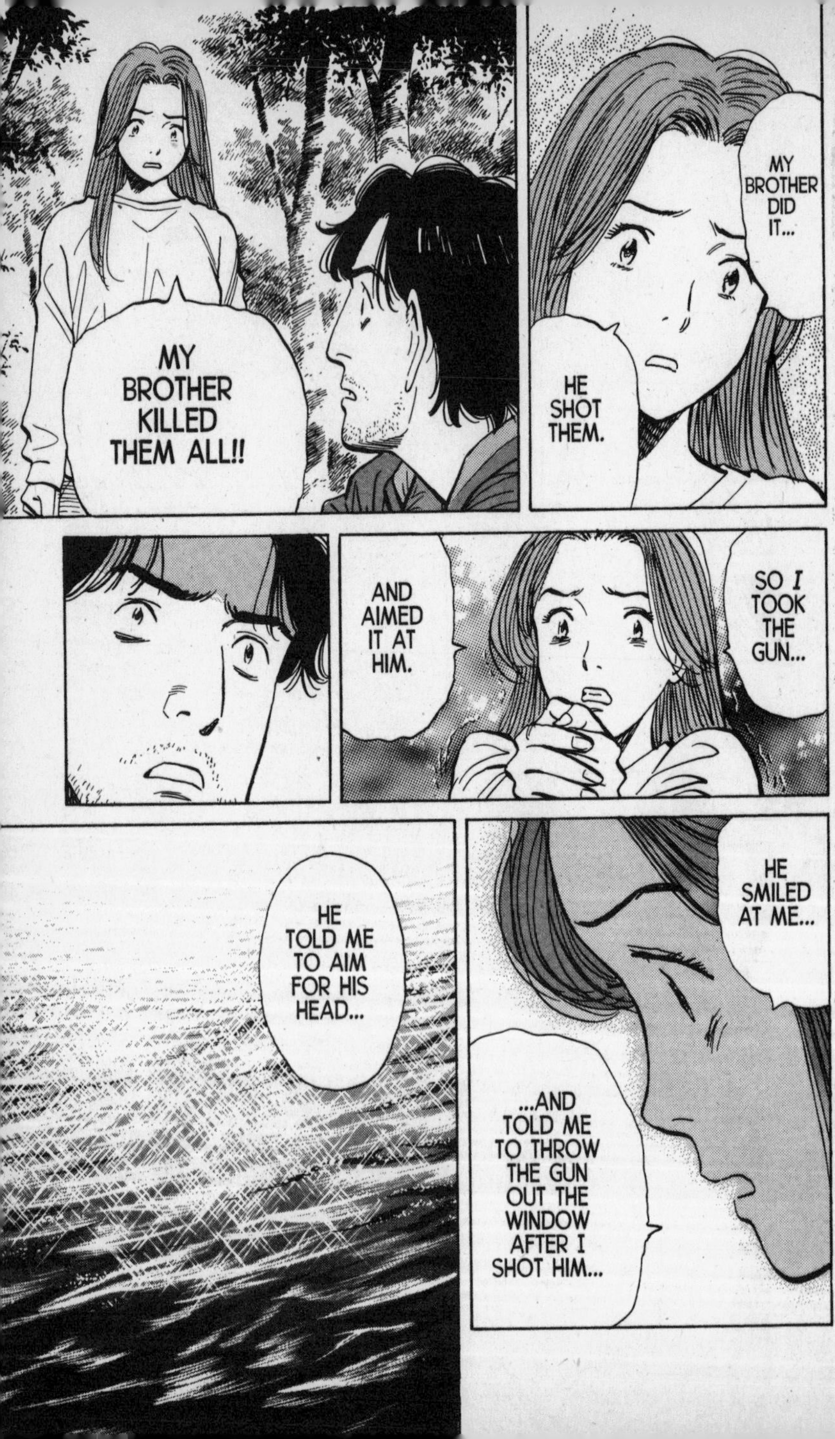
MY BROTHER DID IT...
HE SHOT THEM.
MY BROTHER KILLED THEM ALL!!
SO *I* TOOK THE GUN...
AND AIMED IT AT HIM.
HE SMILED AT ME...
...AND TOLD ME TO THROW THE GUN OUT THE WINDOW AFTER I SHOT HIM...
HE TOLD ME TO AIM FOR HIS HEAD...

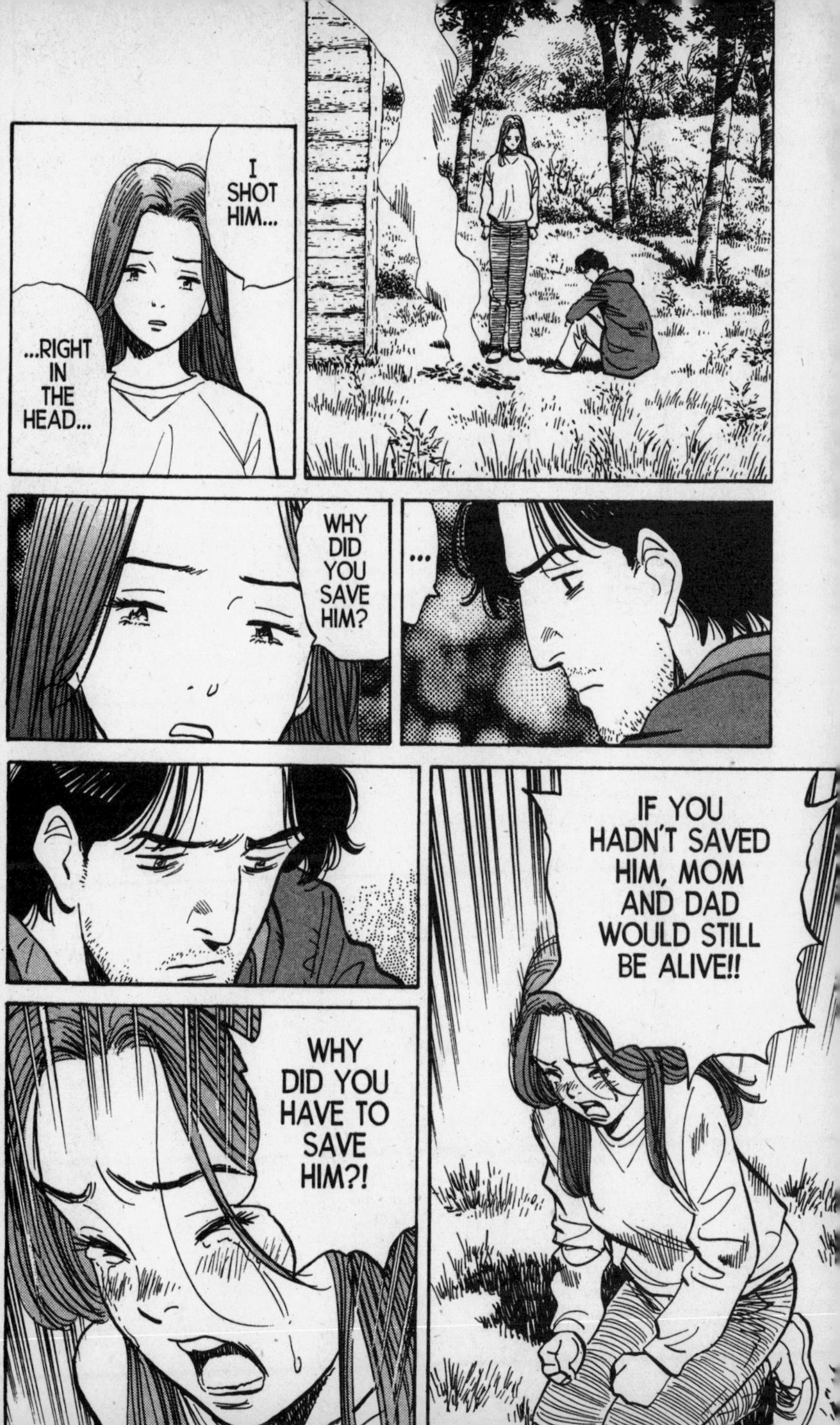
I SHOT HIM...
...RIGHT IN THE HEAD...
...
WHY DID YOU SAVE HIM?
IF YOU HADN'T SAVED HIM, MOM AND DAD WOULD STILL BE ALIVE!!
WHY DID YOU HAVE TO SAVE HIM?!

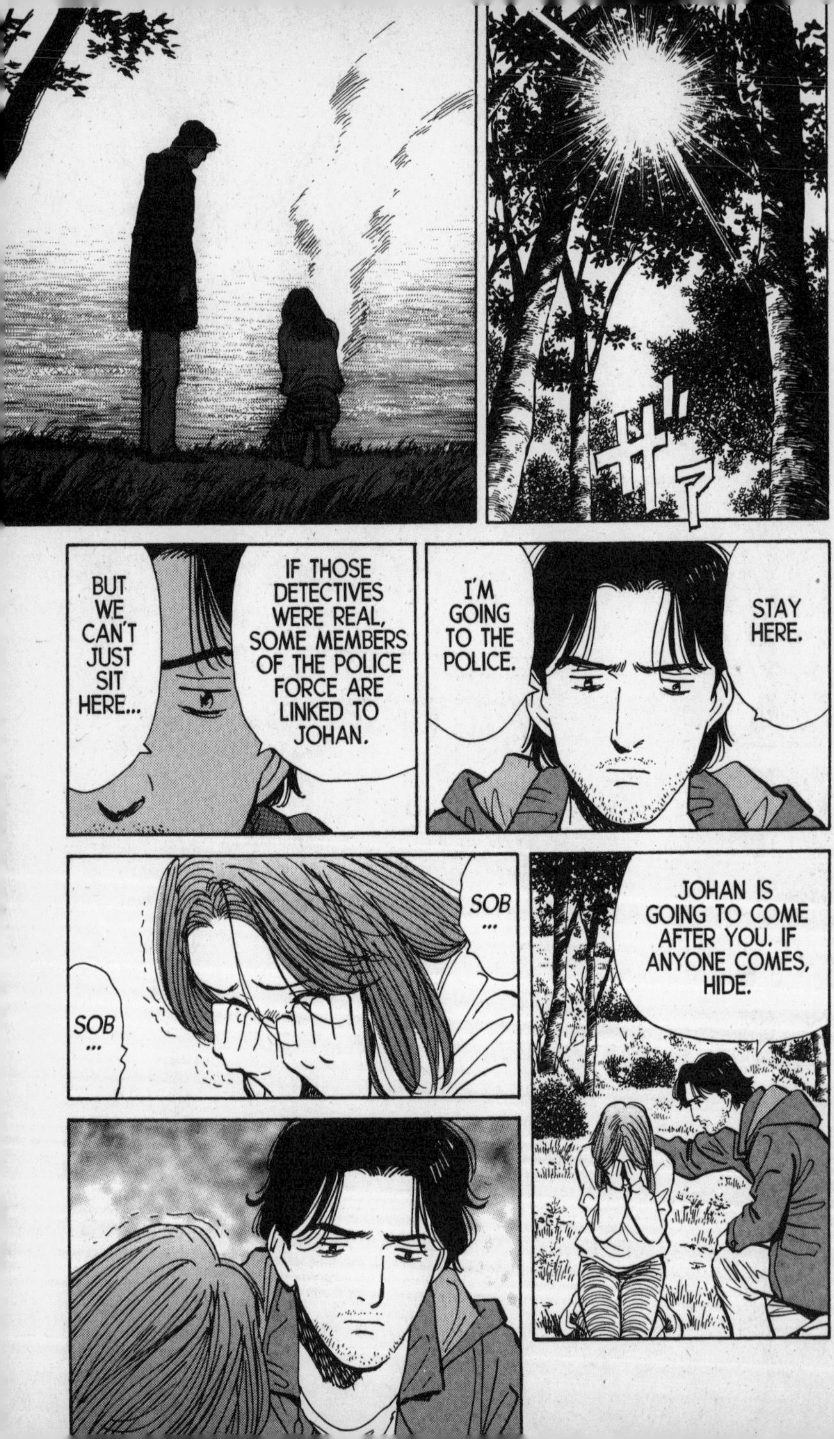
ザァ
STAY HERE.
I'M GOING TO THE POLICE.
IF THOSE DETECTIVES WERE REAL, SOME MEMBERS OF THE POLICE FORCE ARE LINKED TO JOHAN.
BUT WE CAN'T JUST SIT HERE...
JOHAN IS GOING TO COME AFTER YOU. IF ANYONE COMES, HIDE.
SOB ...
SOB ...

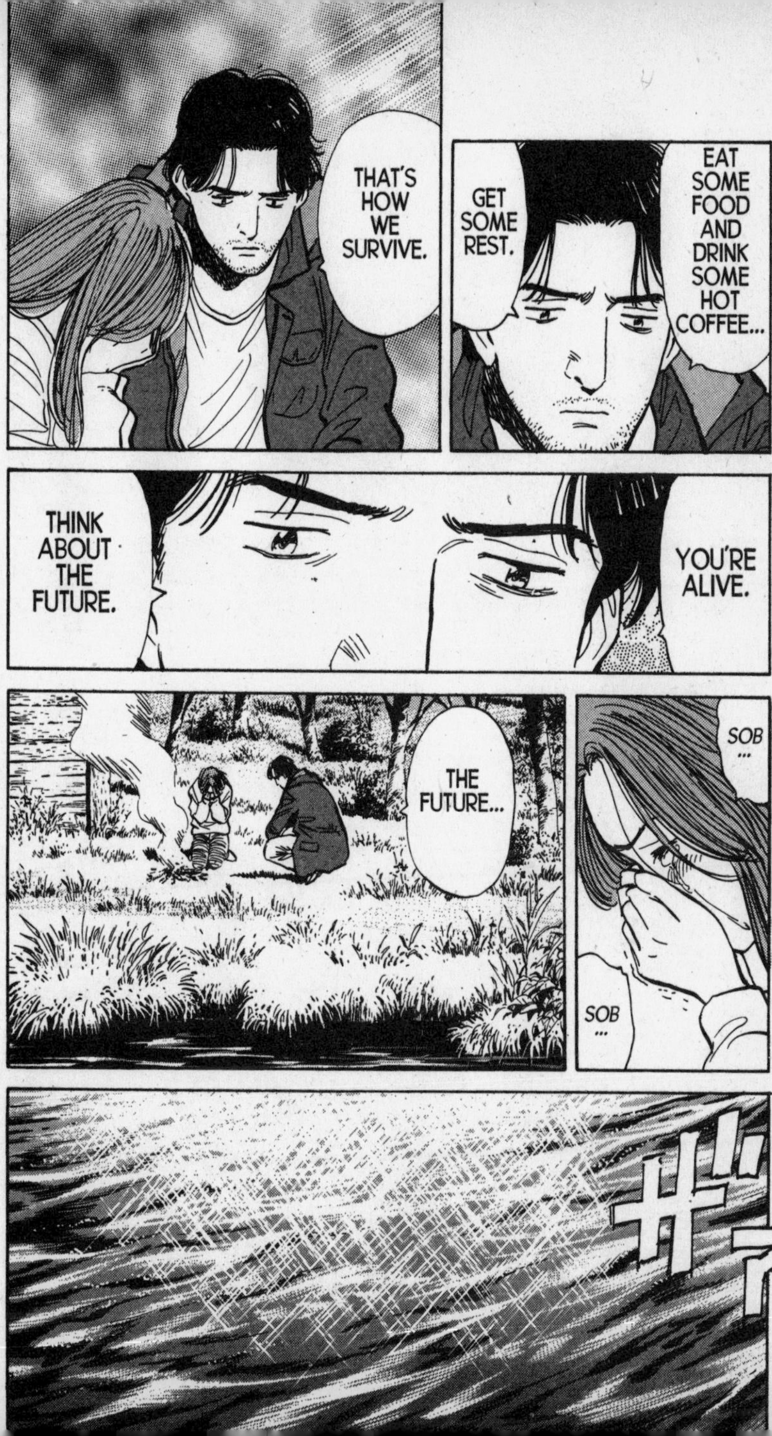
EAT SOME FOOD AND DRINK SOME HOT COFFEE...
GET SOME REST.
THAT'S HOW WE SURVIVE.
YOU'RE ALIVE.
THINK ABOUT THE FUTURE.
SOB...
SOB...
THE FUTURE...
ザァ

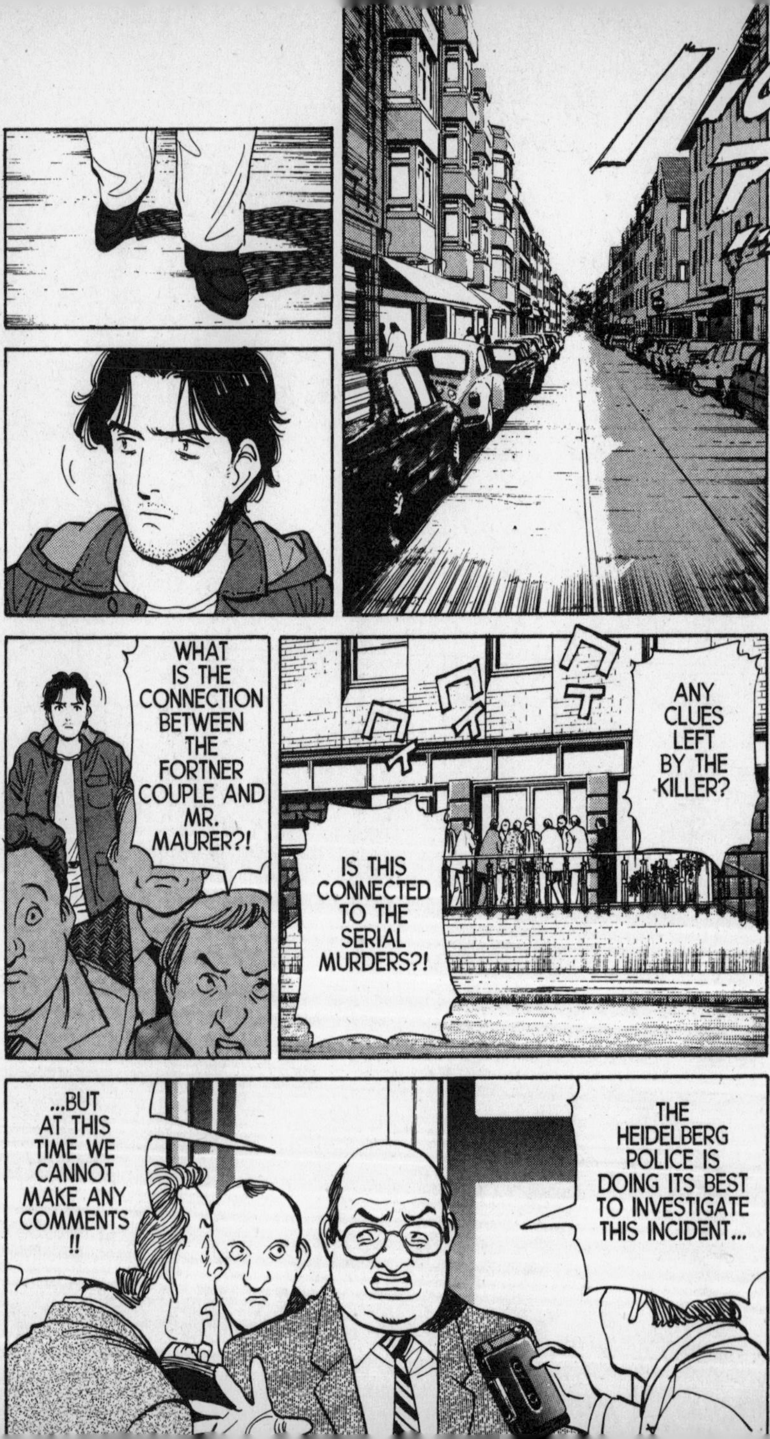
ANY CLUES LEFT BY THE KILLER?
IS THIS CONNECTED TO THE SERIAL MURDERS?!
WHAT IS THE CONNECTION BETWEEN THE FORTNER COUPLE AND MR. MAURER?!
THE HEIDELBERG POLICE IS DOING ITS BEST TO INVESTIGATE THIS INCIDENT...
...BUT AT THIS TIME WE CANNOT MAKE ANY COMMENTS !!

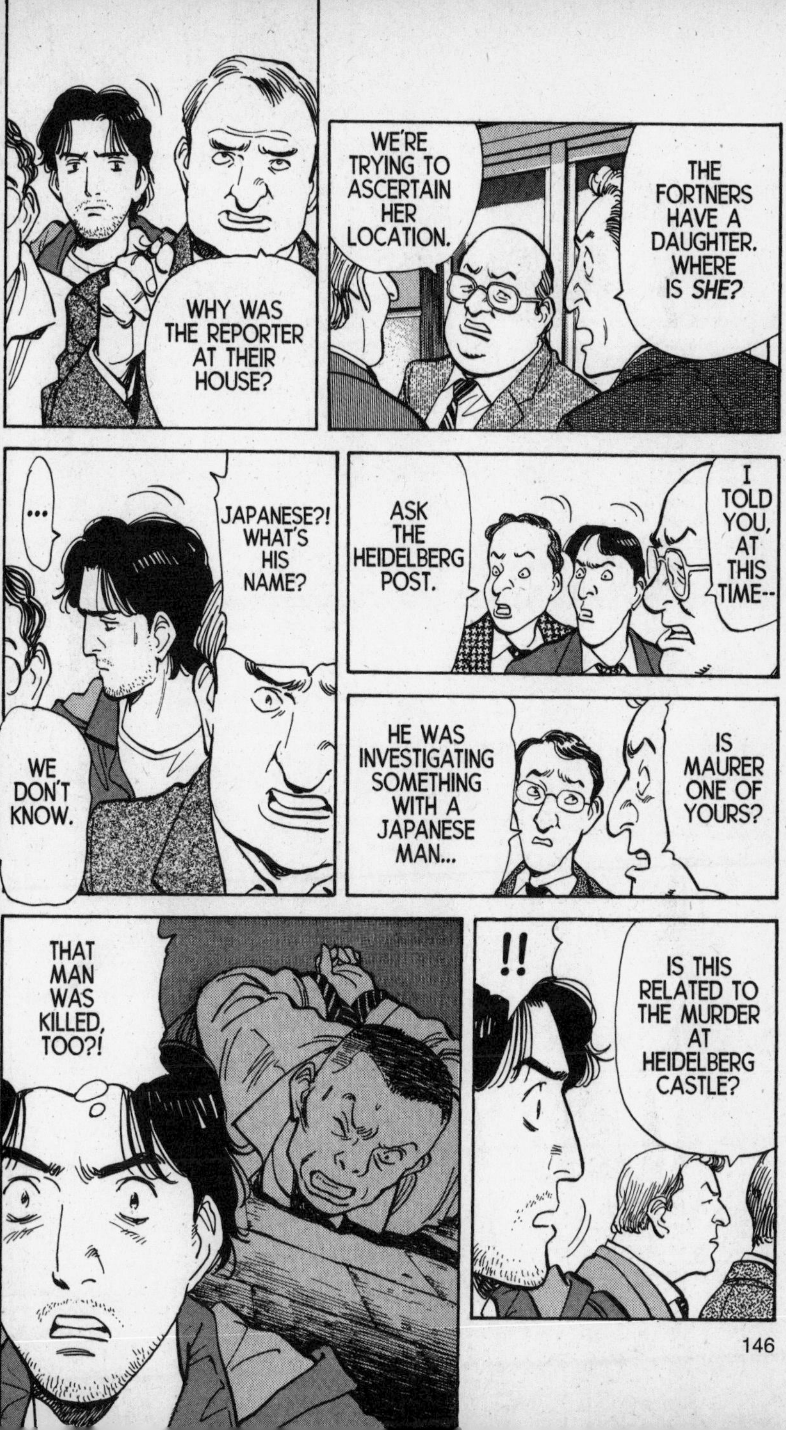
THE FORTNERS HAVE A DAUGHTER. WHERE IS *SHE?*
WE'RE TRYING TO ASCERTAIN HER LOCATION.
WHY WAS THE REPORTER AT THEIR HOUSE?
I TOLD YOU, AT THIS TIME--
ASK THE HEIDELBERG POST.
IS MAURER ONE OF YOURS?
HE WAS INVESTIGATING SOMETHING WITH A JAPANESE MAN...
JAPANESE?! WHAT'S HIS NAME?
...
WE DON'T KNOW.
IS THIS RELATED TO THE MURDER AT HEIDELBERG CASTLE?
!!
THAT MAN WAS KILLED, TOO?!

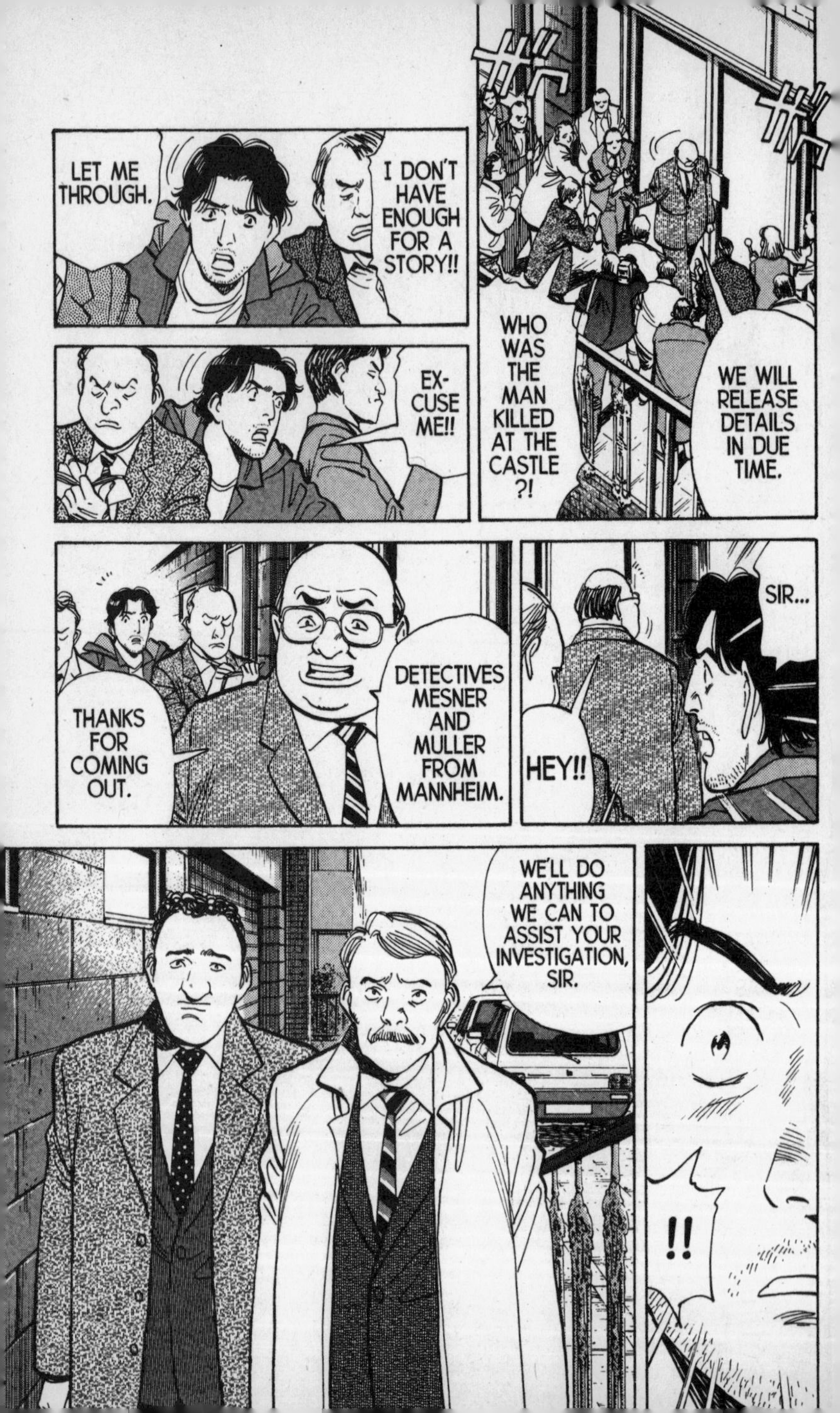
WHO WAS THE MAN KILLED AT THE CASTLE?!
WE WILL RELEASE DETAILS IN DUE TIME.
I DON'T HAVE ENOUGH FOR A STORY!!
LET ME THROUGH.
EX-CUSE ME!!
SIR...
HEY!!
DETECTIVES MESNER AND MULLER FROM MANNHEIM.
THANKS FOR COMING OUT.
!!
WE'LL DO ANYTHING WE CAN TO ASSIST YOUR INVESTIGATION, SIR.

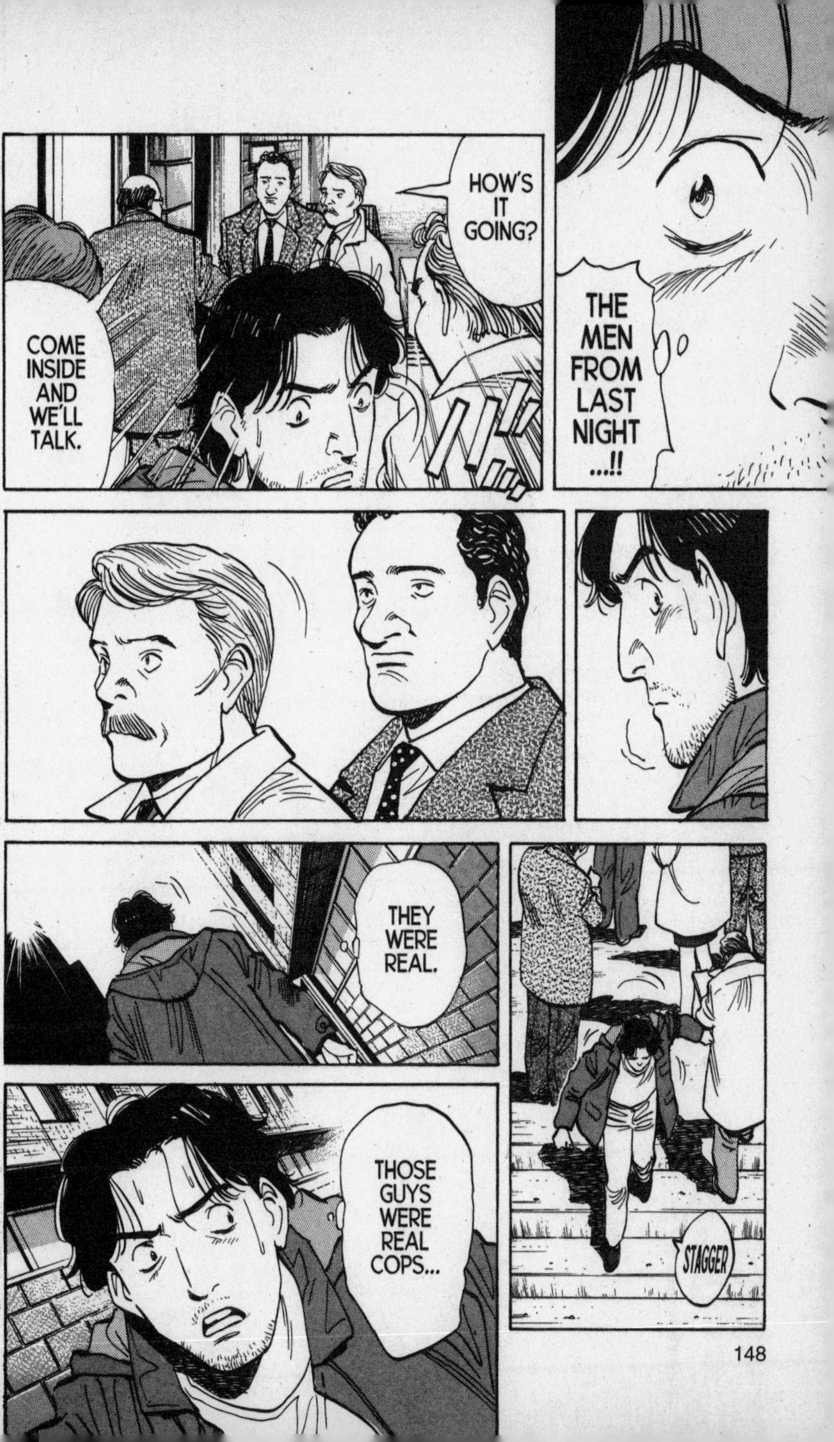
THE MEN FROM LAST NIGHT ...!!
HOW'S IT GOING?
COME INSIDE AND WE'LL TALK.
STAGGER
THEY WERE REAL.
THOSE GUYS WERE REAL COPS...

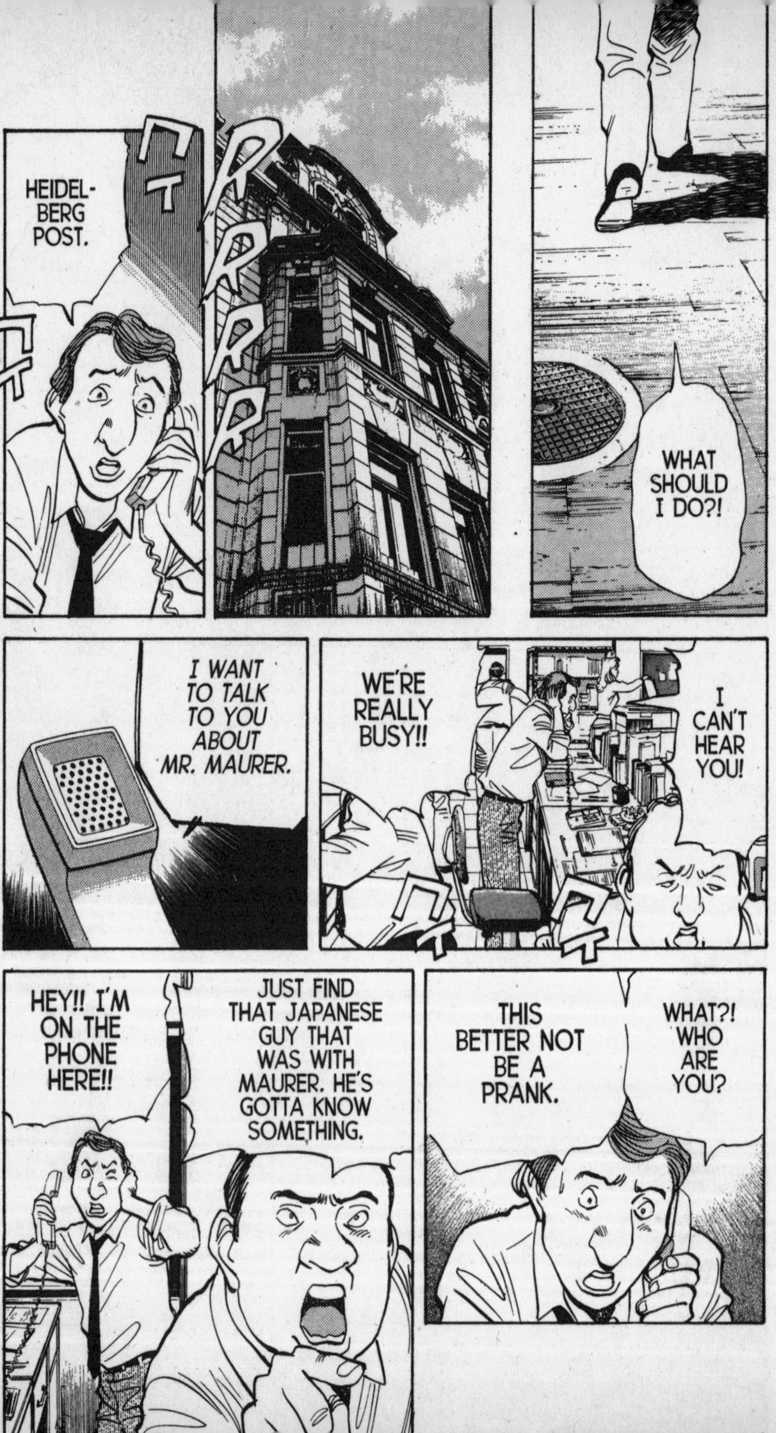
WHAT SHOULD I DO?!
HEIDEL-BERG POST.
I CAN'T HEAR YOU!
WE'RE REALLY BUSY!!
I WANT TO TALK TO YOU ABOUT MR. MAURER.
WHAT?! WHO ARE YOU?
THIS BETTER NOT BE A PRANK.
JUST FIND THAT JAPANESE GUY THAT WAS WITH MAURER. HE'S GOTTA KNOW SOMETHING.
HEY!! I'M ON THE PHONE HERE!!

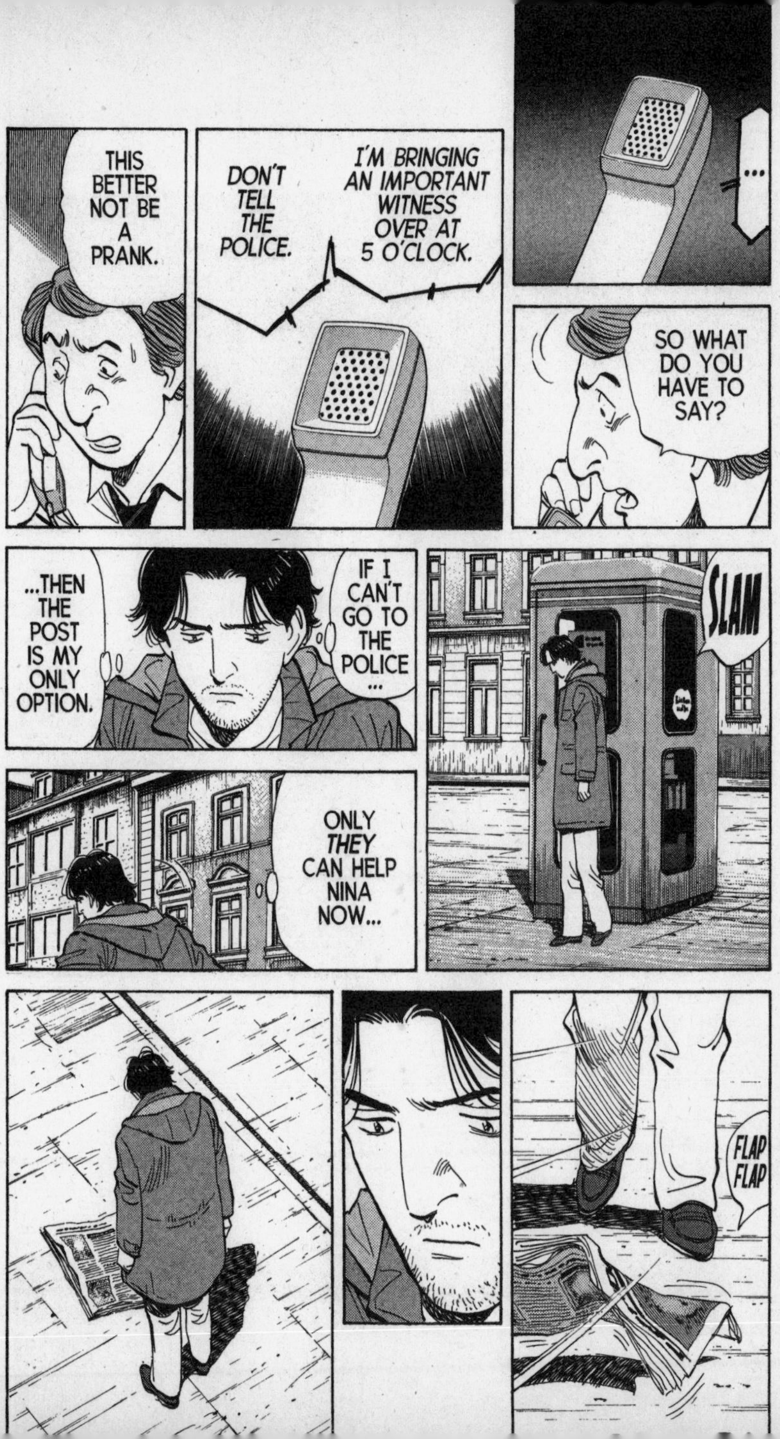
...
SO WHAT DO YOU HAVE TO SAY?
I'M BRINGING AN IMPORTANT WITNESS OVER AT 5 O'CLOCK.
DON'T TELL THE POLICE.
THIS BETTER NOT BE A PRANK.
SLAM
IF I CAN'T GO TO THE POLICE ...
...THEN THE POST IS MY ONLY OPTION.
ONLY *THEY* CAN HELP NINA NOW...
FLAP FLAP

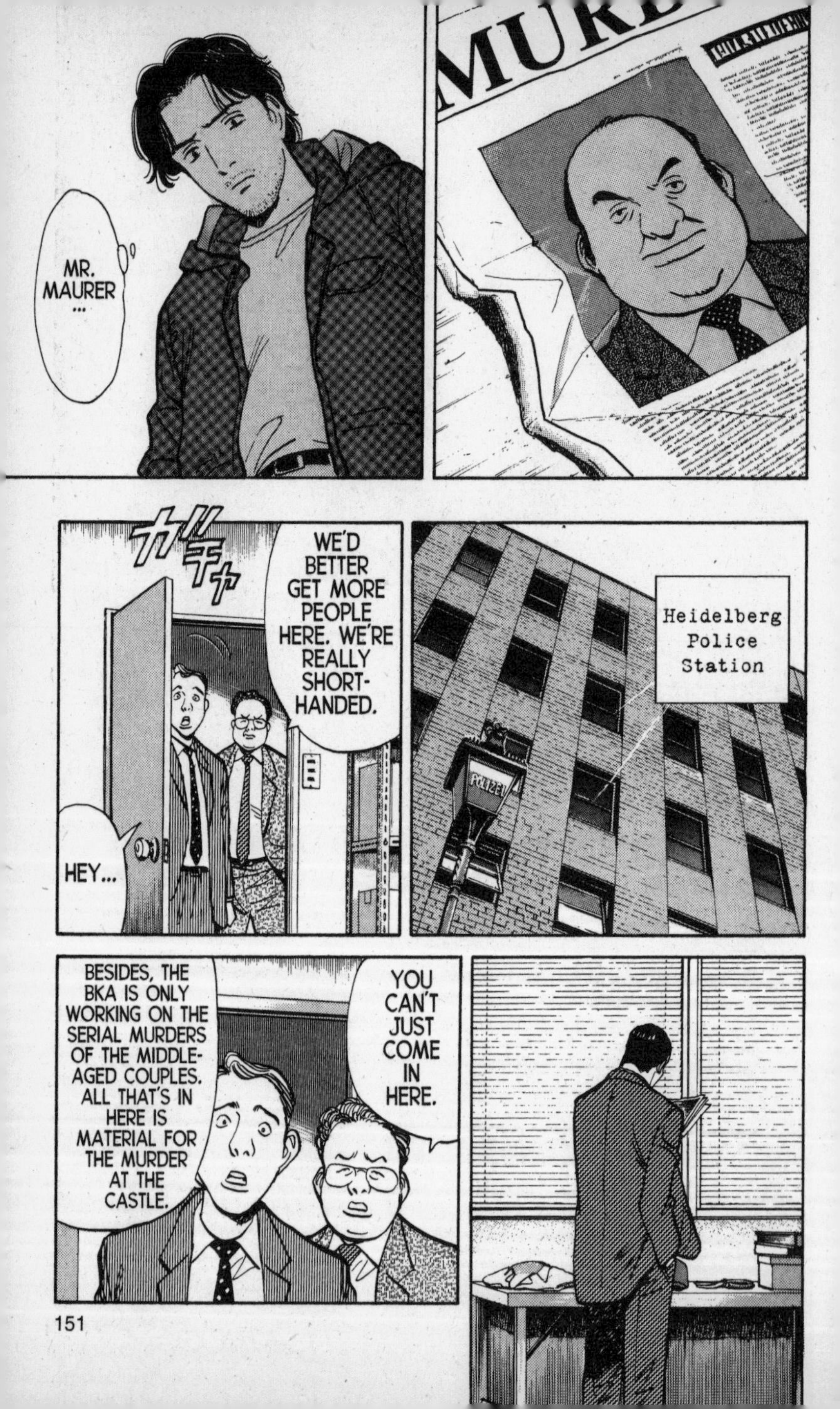
MR. MAURER ...
Heidelberg Police Station
POLIZEI
ガチャ
WE'D BETTER GET MORE PEOPLE HERE. WE'RE REALLY SHORT-HANDED.
HEY...
YOU CAN'T JUST COME IN HERE.
BESIDES, THE BKA IS ONLY WORKING ON THE SERIAL MURDERS OF THE MIDDLE-AGED COUPLES. ALL THAT'S IN HERE IS MATERIAL FOR THE MURDER AT THE CASTLE.

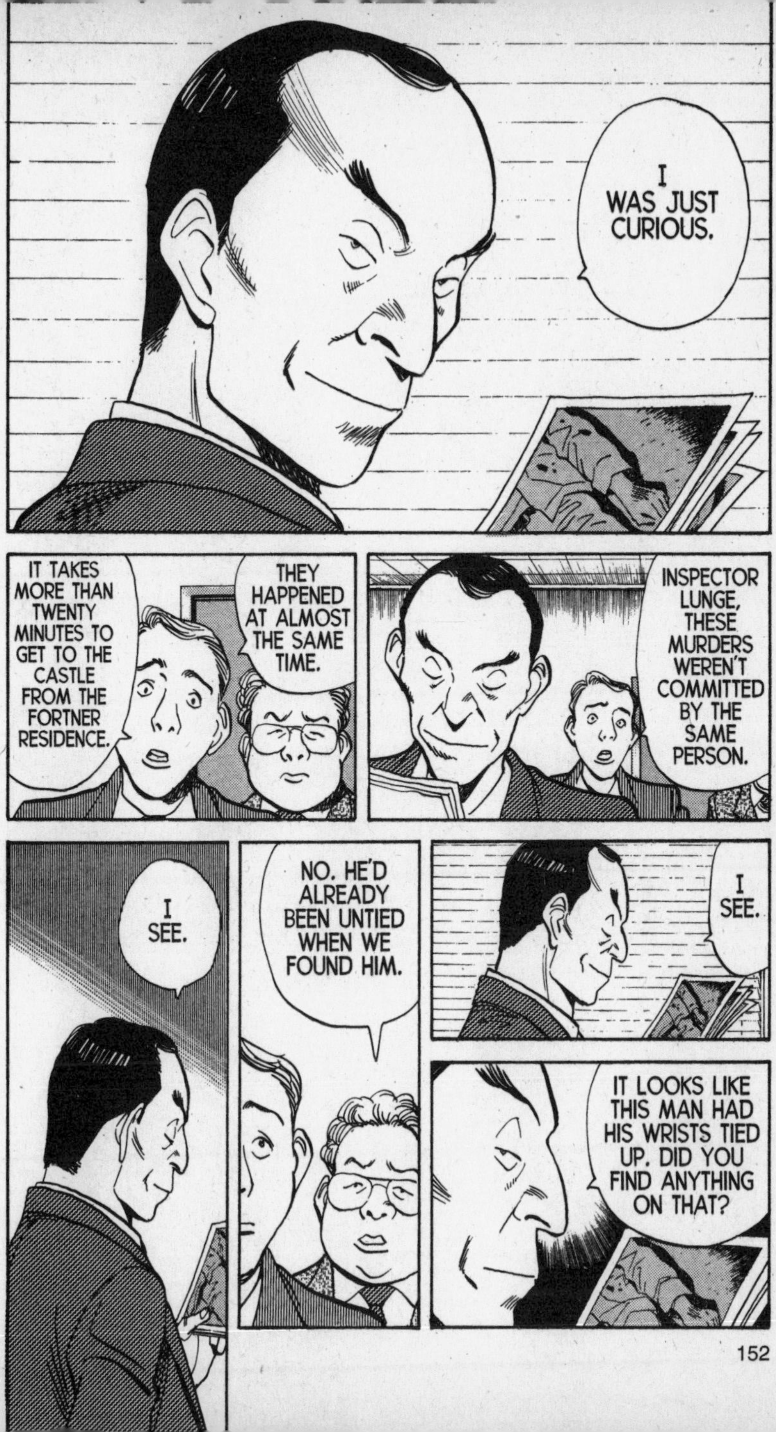
I WAS JUST CURIOUS.
INSPECTOR LUNGE, THESE MURDERS WEREN'T COMMITTED BY THE SAME PERSON.
THEY HAPPENED AT ALMOST THE SAME TIME.
IT TAKES MORE THAN TWENTY MINUTES TO GET TO THE CASTLE FROM THE FORTNER RESIDENCE.
I SEE.
IT LOOKS LIKE THIS MAN HAD HIS WRISTS TIED UP. DID YOU FIND ANYTHING ON THAT?
NO. HE'D ALREADY BEEN UNTIED WHEN WE FOUND HIM.
I SEE.

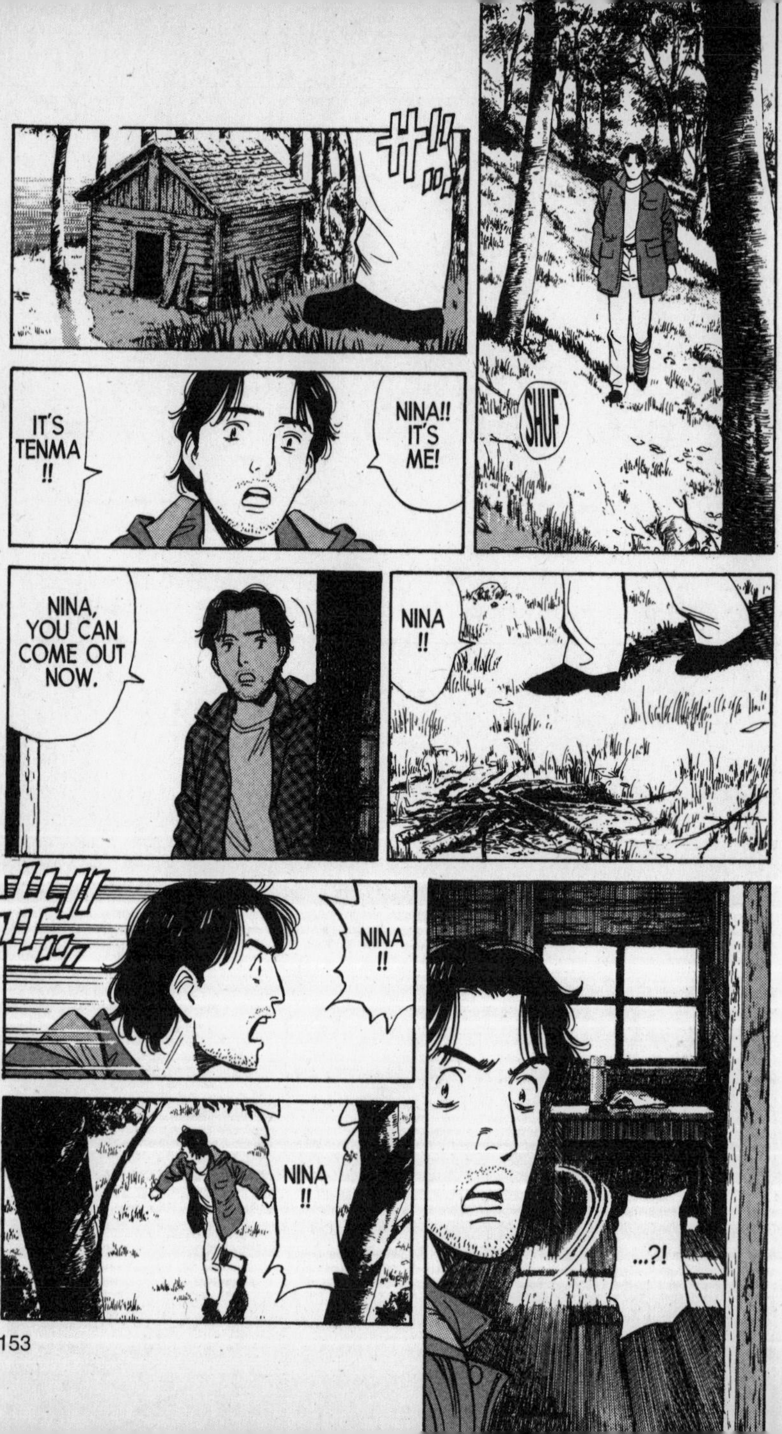
SHUF
NINA!! IT'S ME!
IT'S TENMA !!
NINA !!
NINA, YOU CAN COME OUT NOW.
...?!
NINA !!
NINA !!

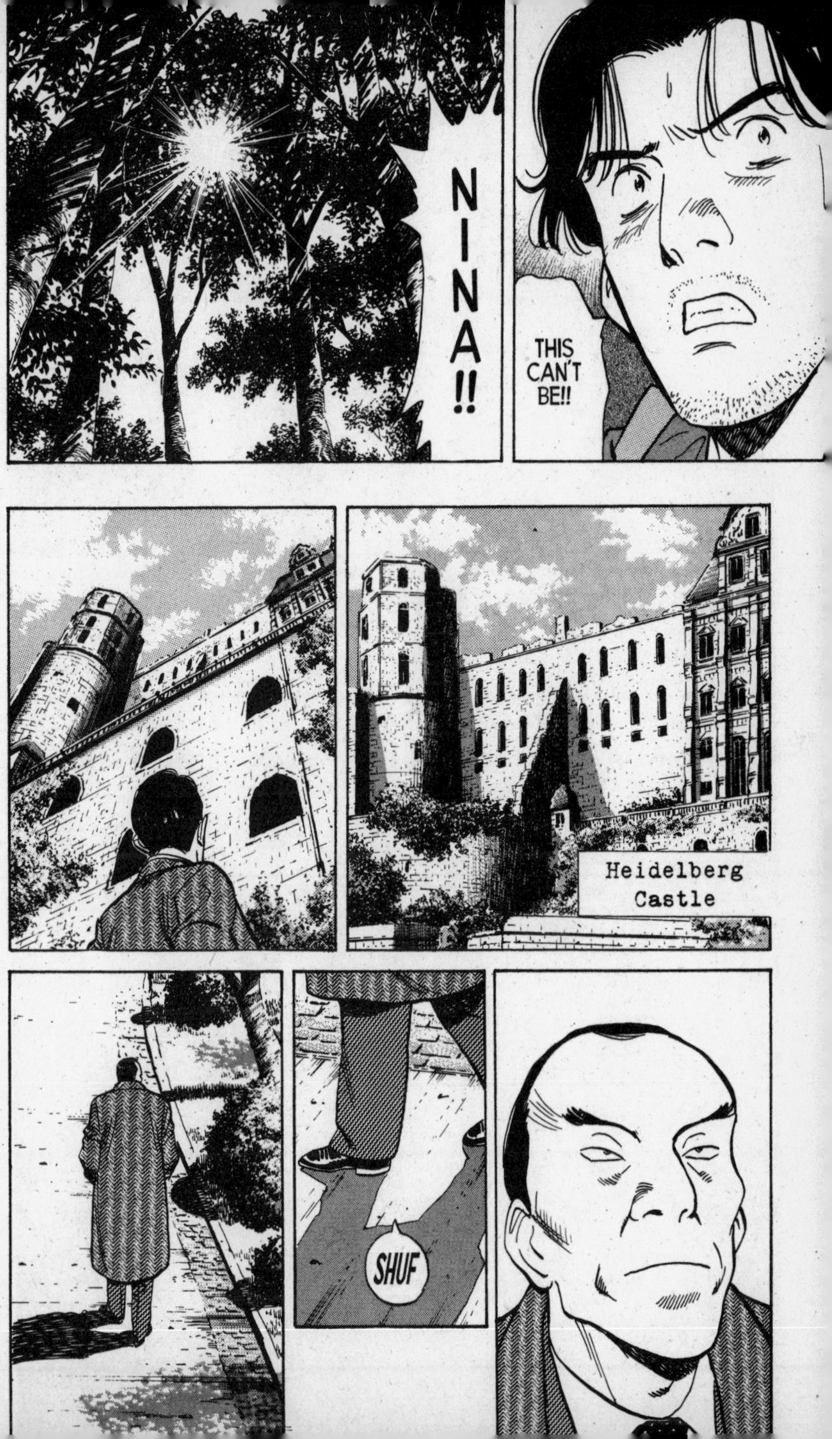
THIS CAN'T BE!!
NINA!!
Heidelberg Castle
SHUF

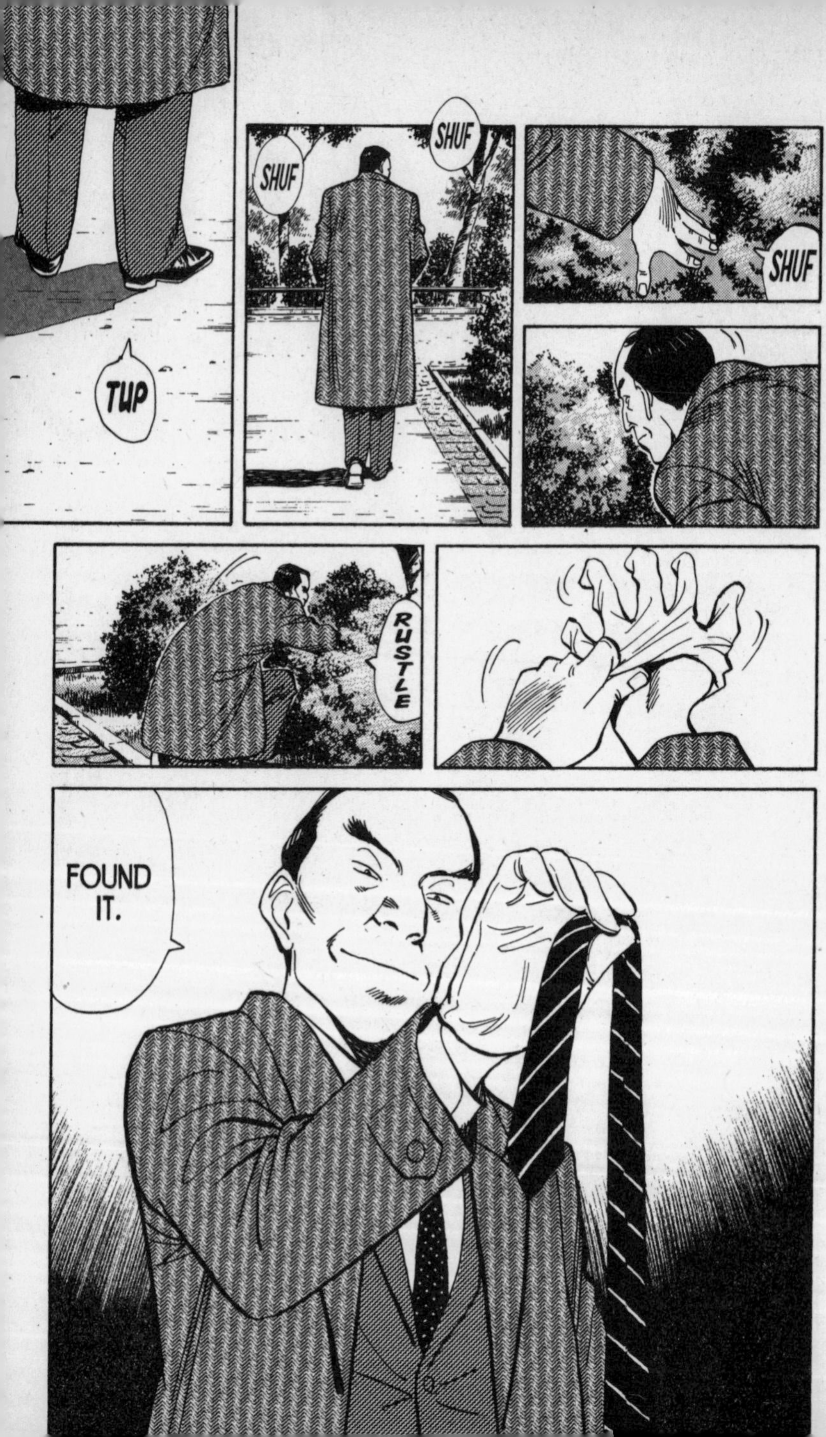
TUP
SHUF
SHUF
SHUF
RUSTLE
FOUND IT.

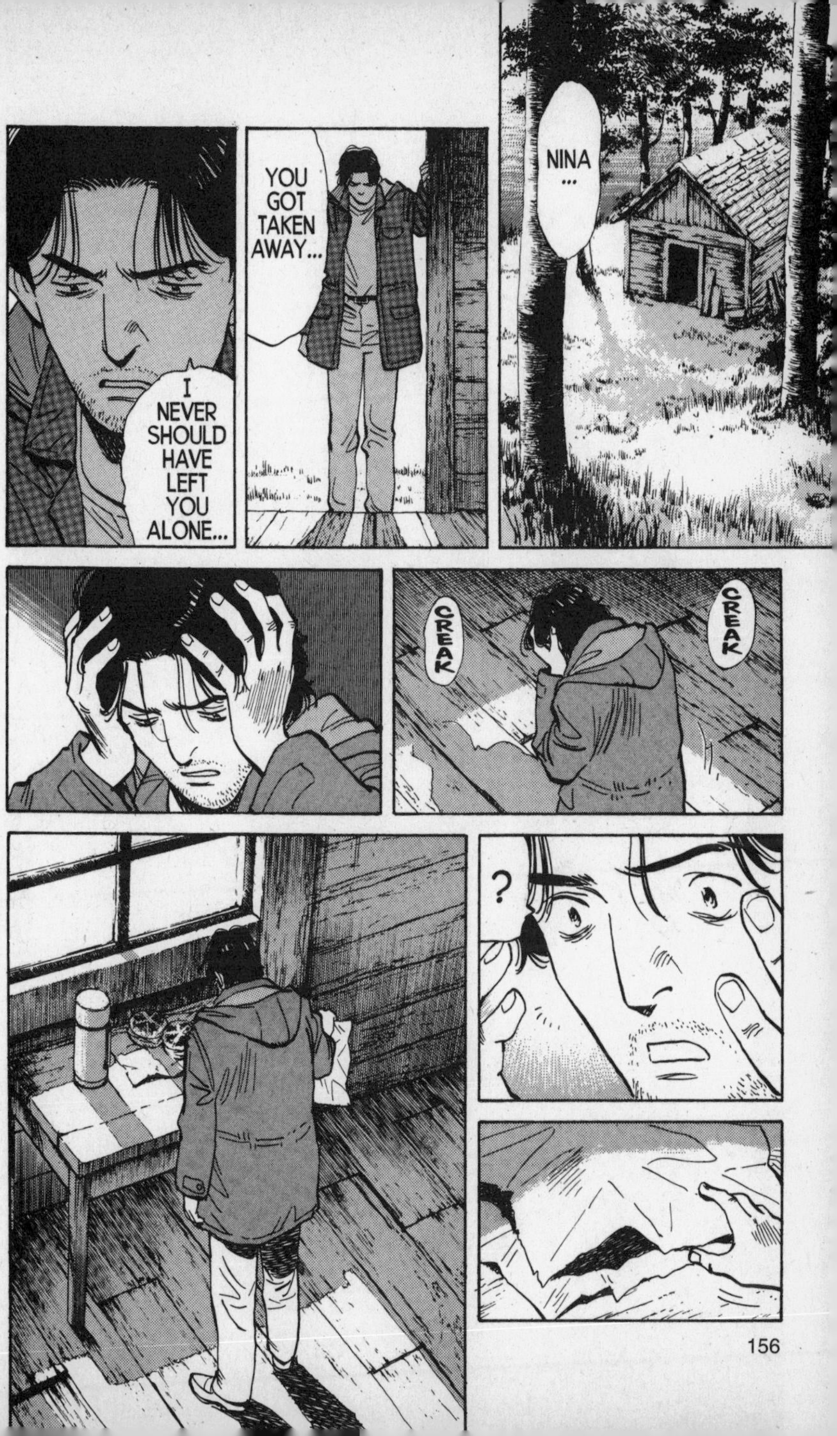
NINA ...
YOU GOT TAKEN AWAY...
I NEVER SHOULD HAVE LEFT YOU ALONE...
CREAK
CREAK
?

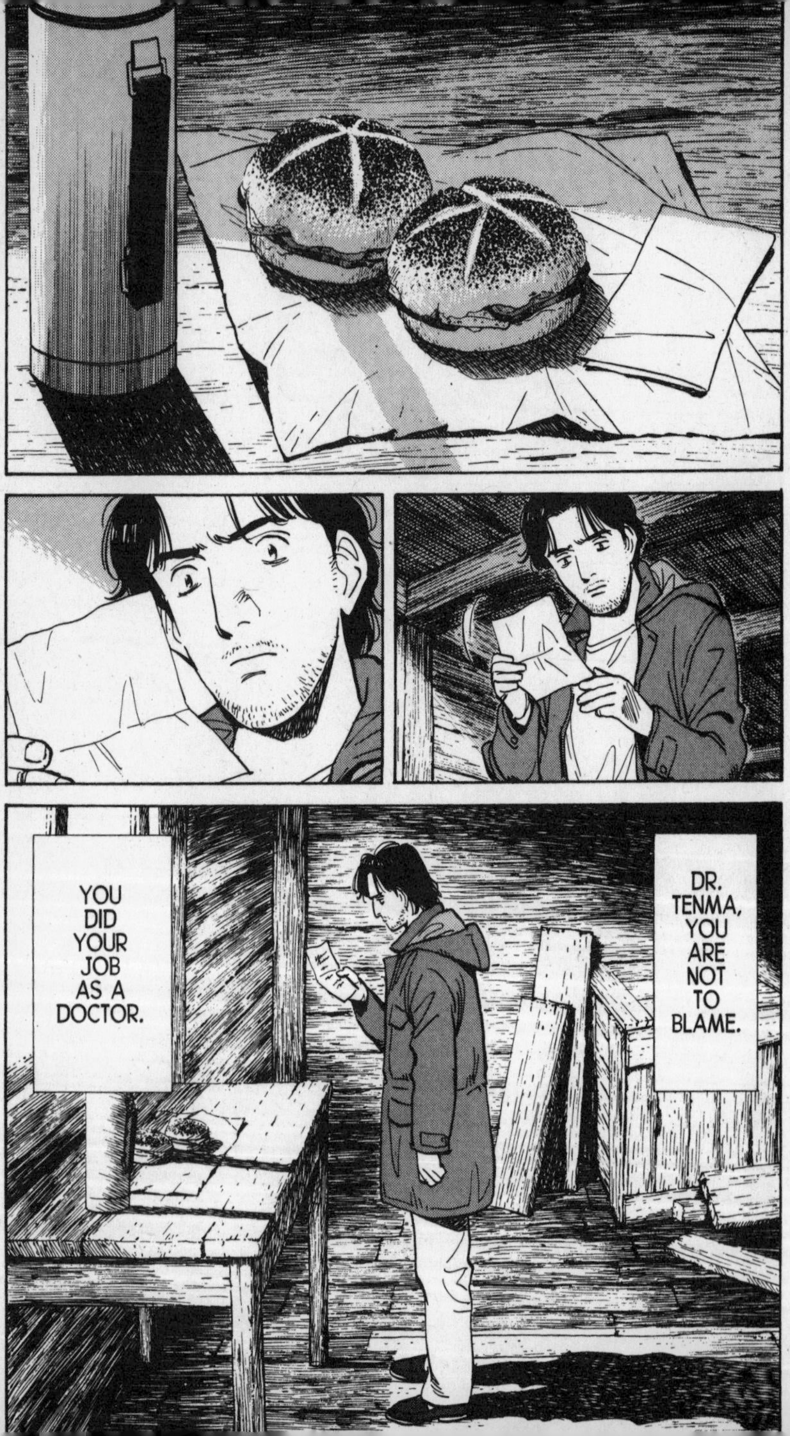
DR. TENMA, YOU ARE NOT TO BLAME.
YOU DID YOUR JOB AS A DOCTOR.

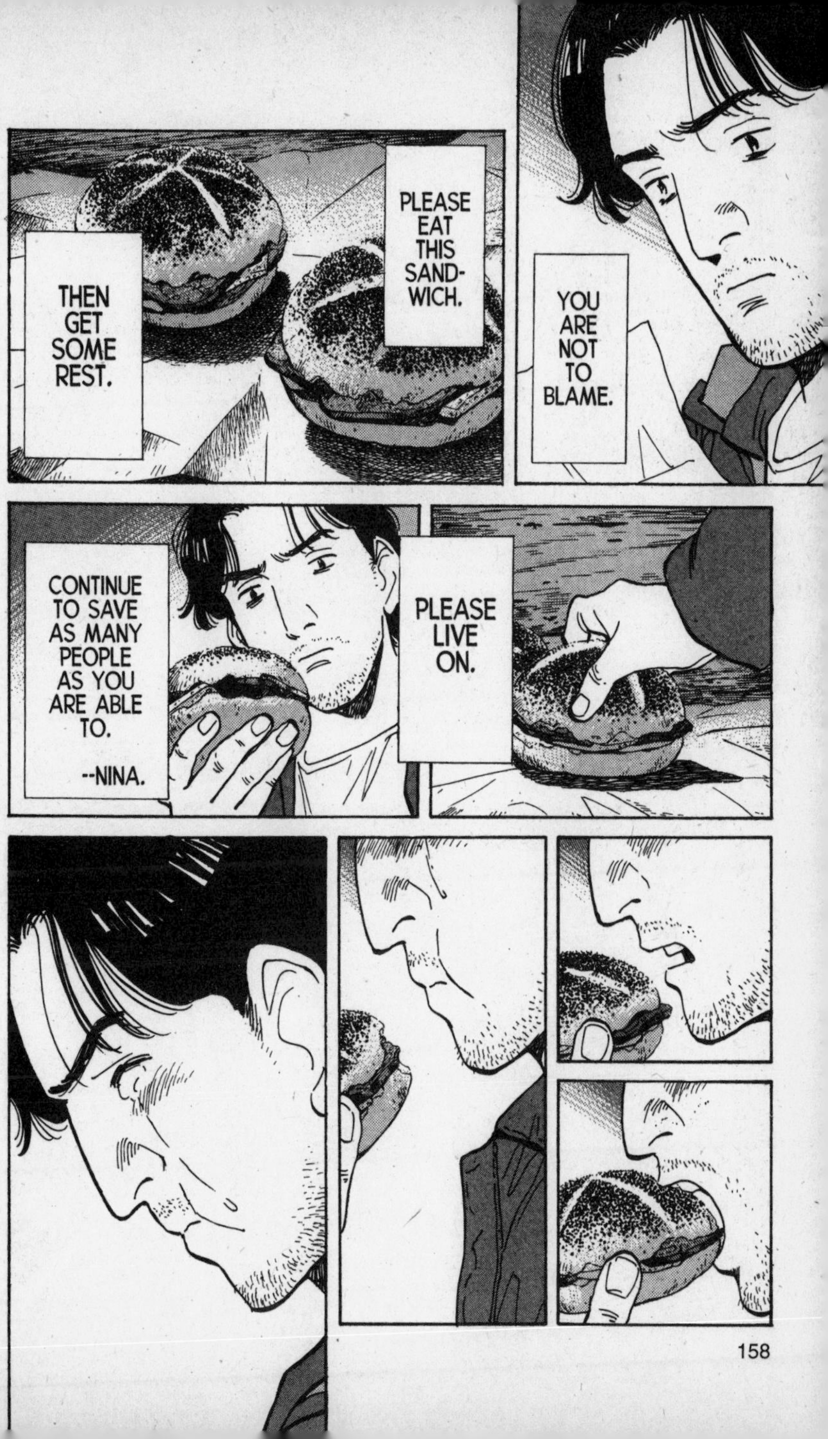
YOU ARE NOT TO BLAME.
PLEASE EAT THIS SANDWICH.
THEN GET SOME REST.
PLEASE LIVE ON.
CONTINUE TO SAVE AS MANY PEOPLE AS YOU ARE ABLE TO.
--NINA.

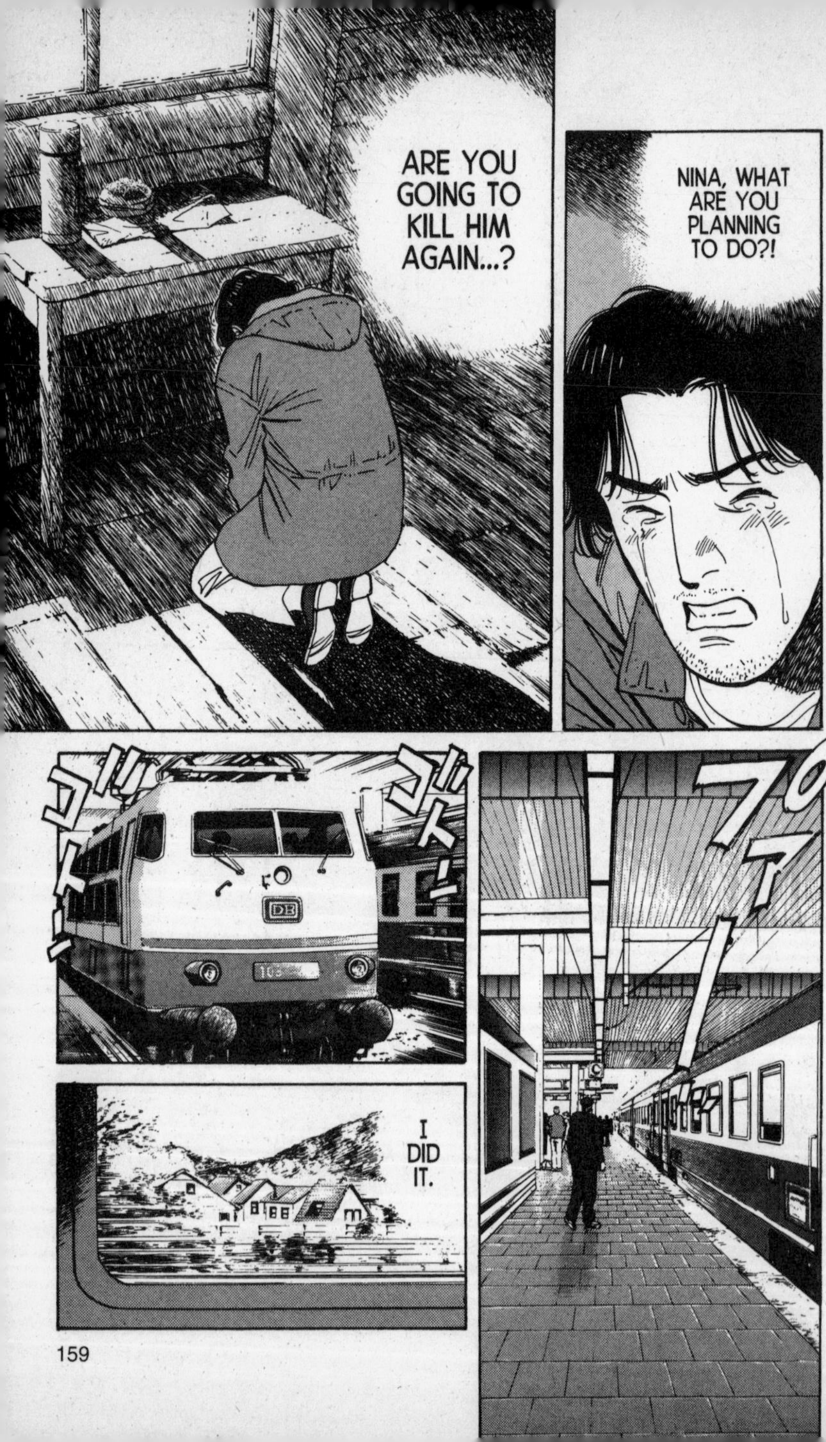
NINA, WHAT ARE YOU PLANNING TO DO?!
ARE YOU GOING TO KILL HIM AGAIN...?
I DID IT.

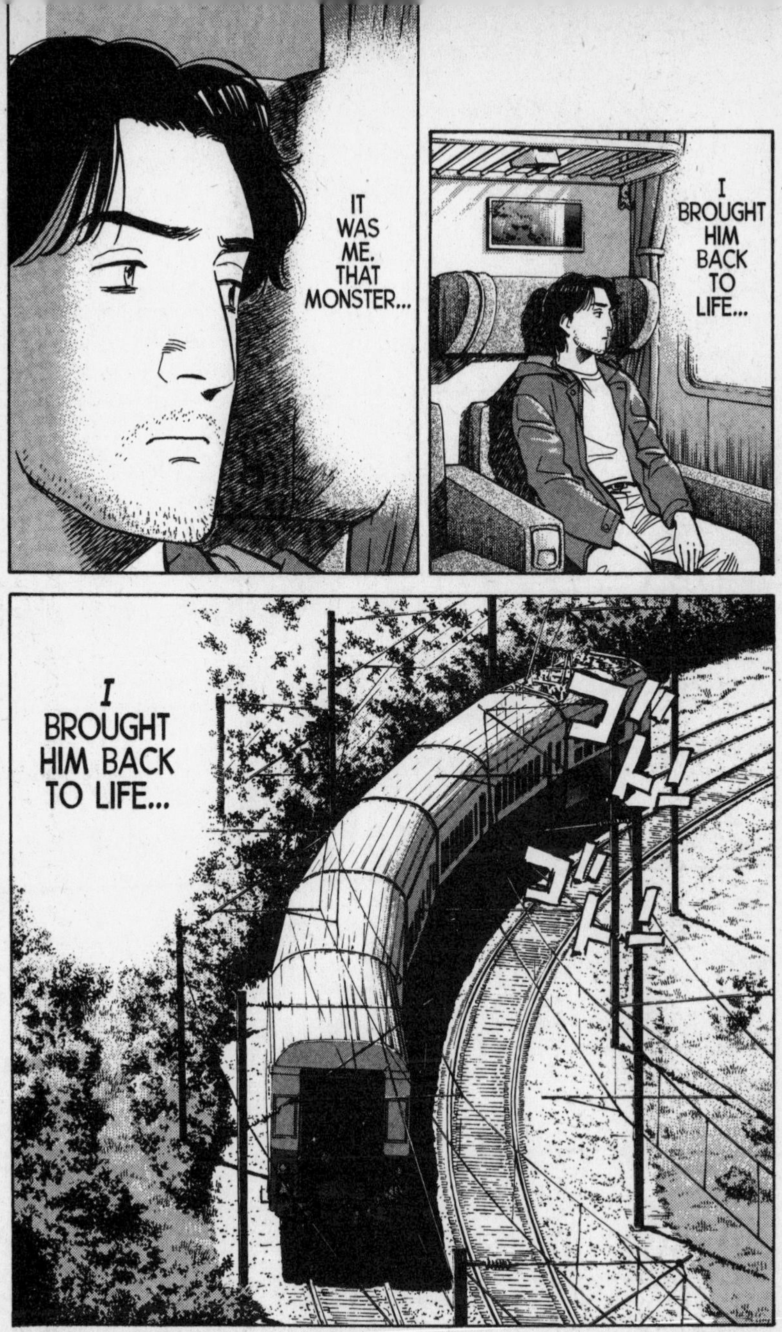
I BROUGHT HIM BACK TO LIFE...
IT WAS ME. THAT MONSTER...
I BROUGHT HIM BACK TO LIFE...
ゴドン
ゴドン

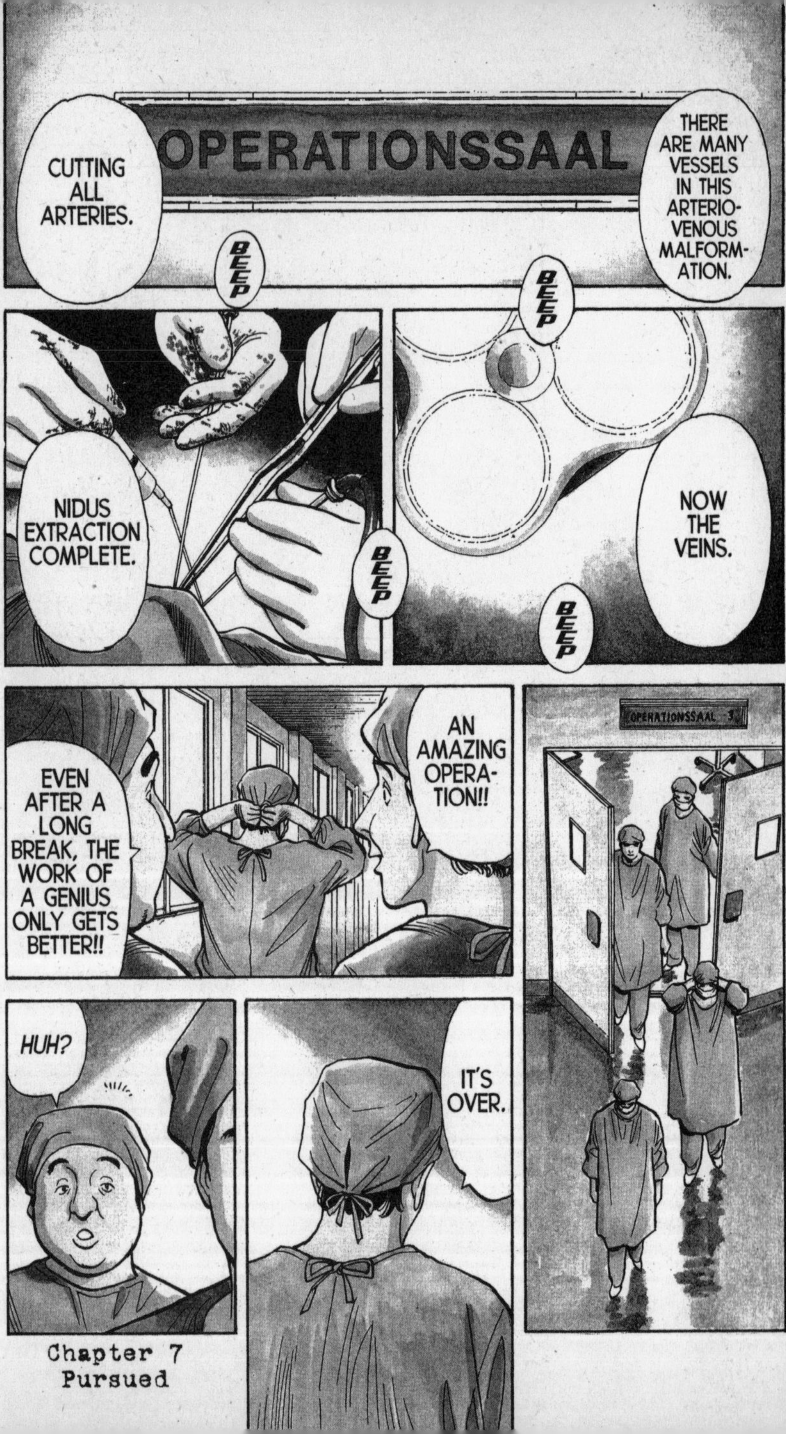
OPERATIONSSAAL
THERE ARE MANY VESSELS IN THIS ARTERIO-VENOUS MALFORM-ATION.
CUTTING ALL ARTERIES.
BEEP
BEEP
NOW THE VEINS.
BEEP
BEEP
NIDUS EXTRACTION COMPLETE.
OPERATIONSSAAL 3
AN AMAZING OPERA-TION!!
EVEN AFTER A LONG BREAK, THE WORK OF A GENIUS ONLY GETS BETTER!!
IT'S OVER.
HUH?

Chapter 7
Pursued

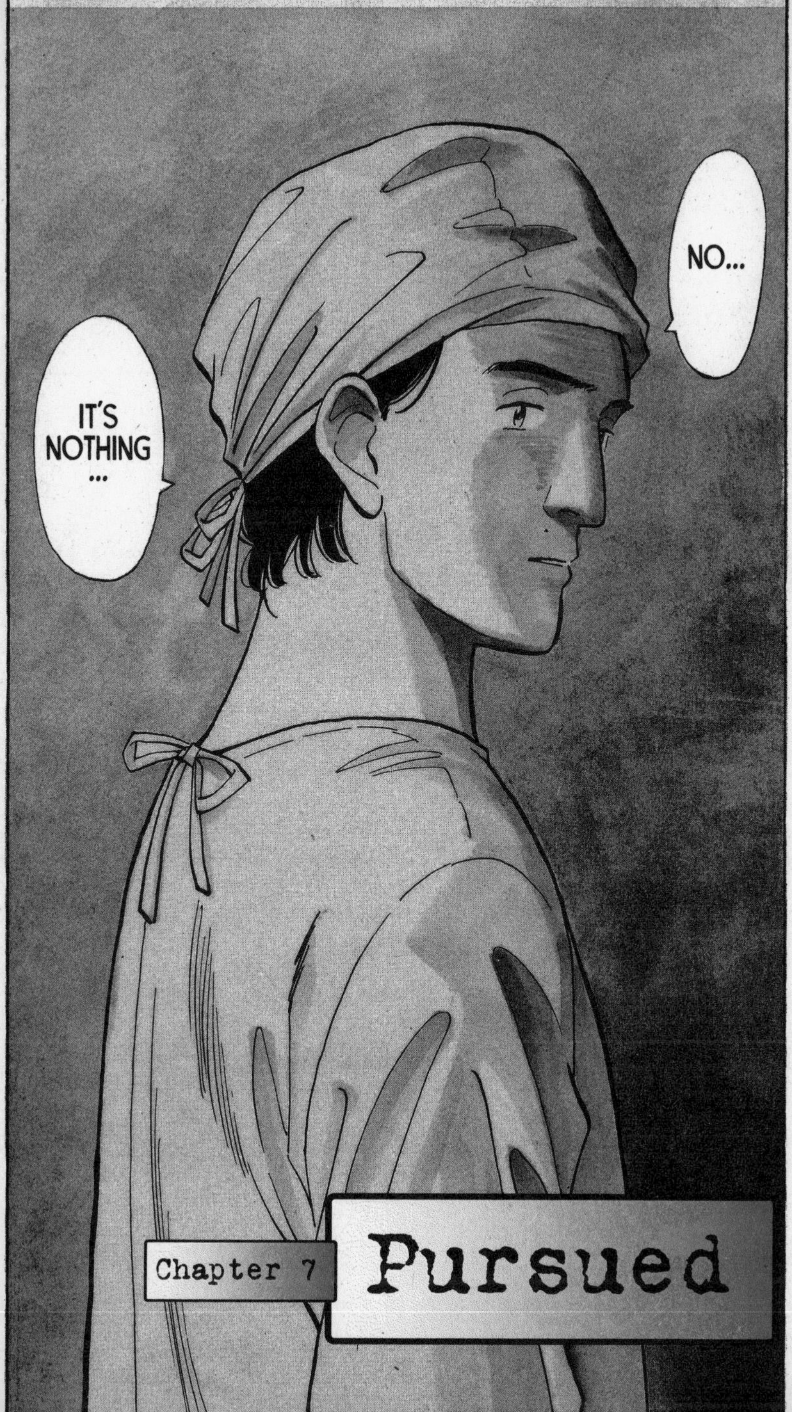
NO...
IT'S NOTHING ...
Chapter 7
Pursued

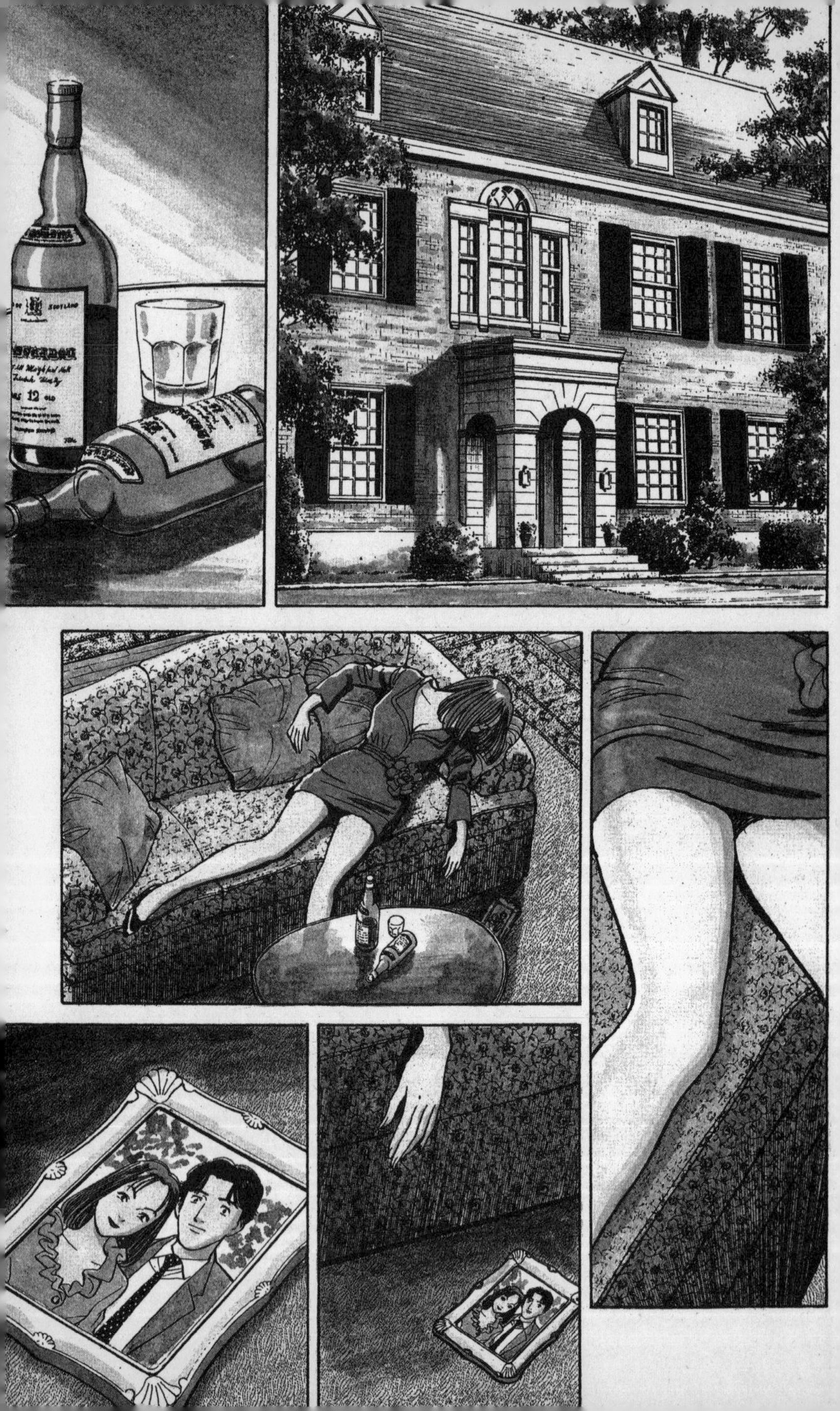

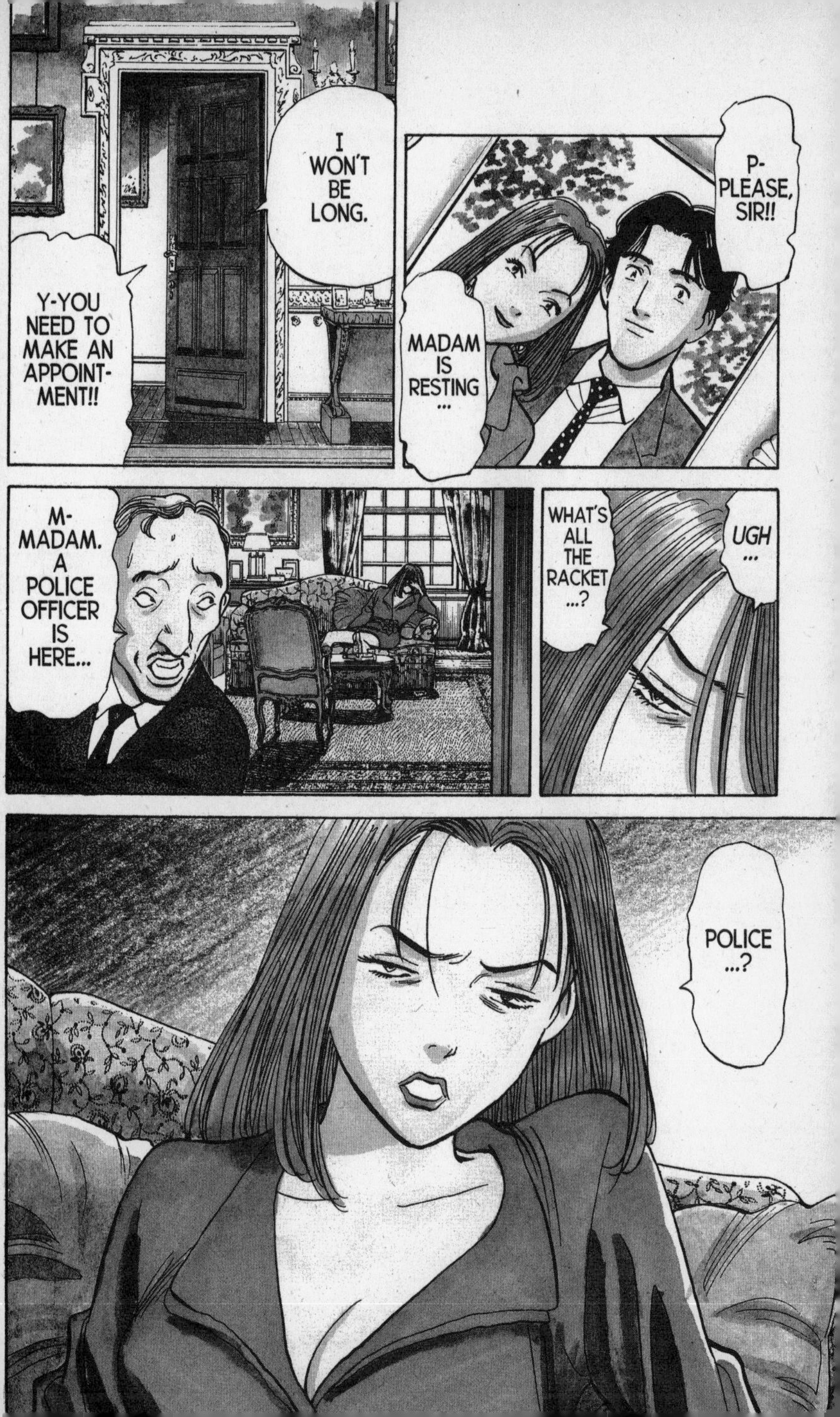
P-PLEASE, SIR!!
MADAM IS RESTING...
I WON'T BE LONG.
Y-YOU NEED TO MAKE AN APPOINTMENT!!
UGH...
WHAT'S ALL THE RACKET...?
M-MADAM. A POLICE OFFICER IS HERE...
POLICE...?

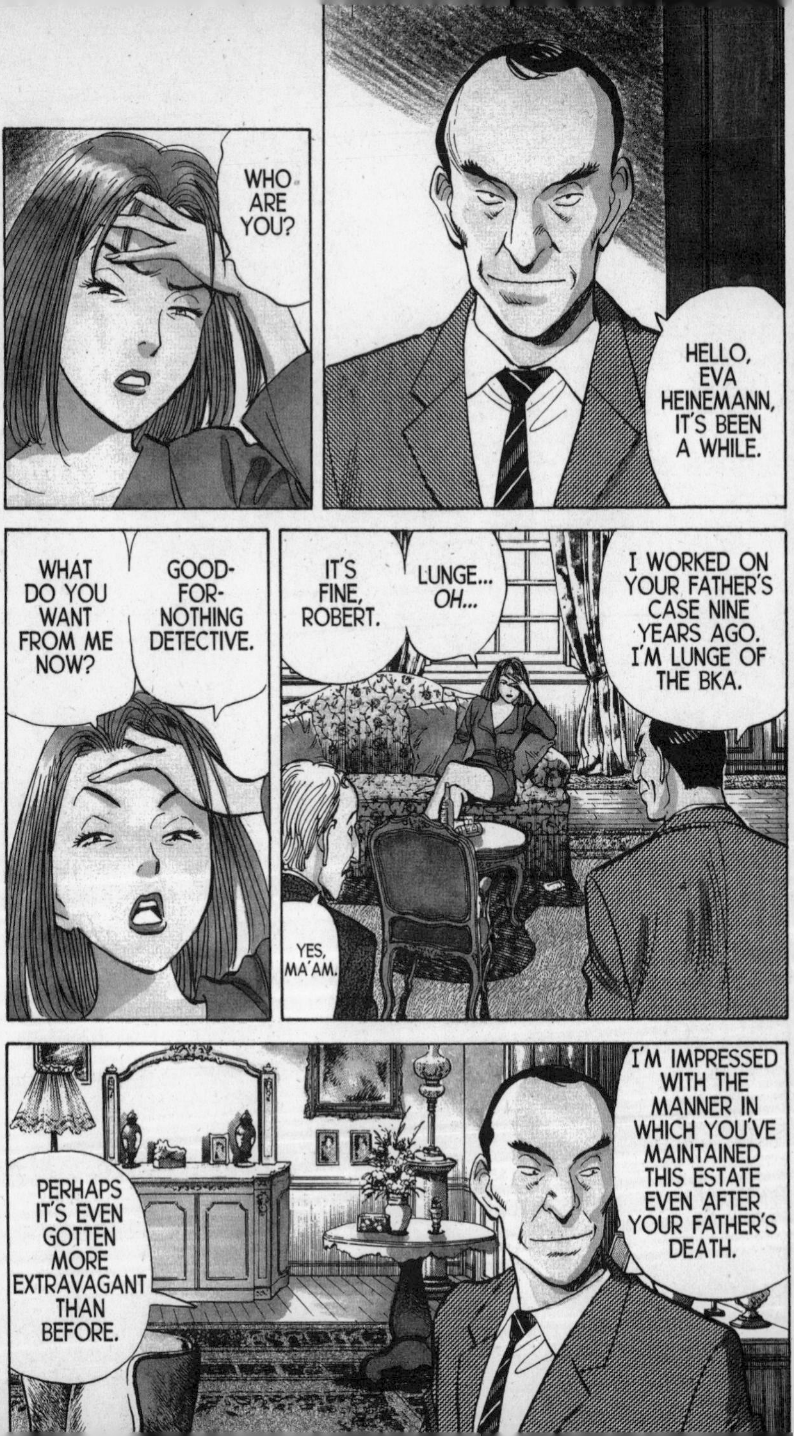
HELLO, EVA HEINEMANN, IT'S BEEN A WHILE.
WHO ARE YOU?
I WORKED ON YOUR FATHER'S CASE NINE YEARS AGO. I'M LUNGE OF THE BKA.
LUNGE... *OH...*
IT'S FINE, ROBERT.
YES, MA'AM.
GOOD-FOR-NOTHING DETECTIVE.
WHAT DO YOU WANT FROM ME NOW?
I'M IMPRESSED WITH THE MANNER IN WHICH YOU'VE MAINTAINED THIS ESTATE EVEN AFTER YOUR FATHER'S DEATH.
PERHAPS IT'S EVEN GOTTEN MORE EXTRAVAGANT THAN BEFORE.

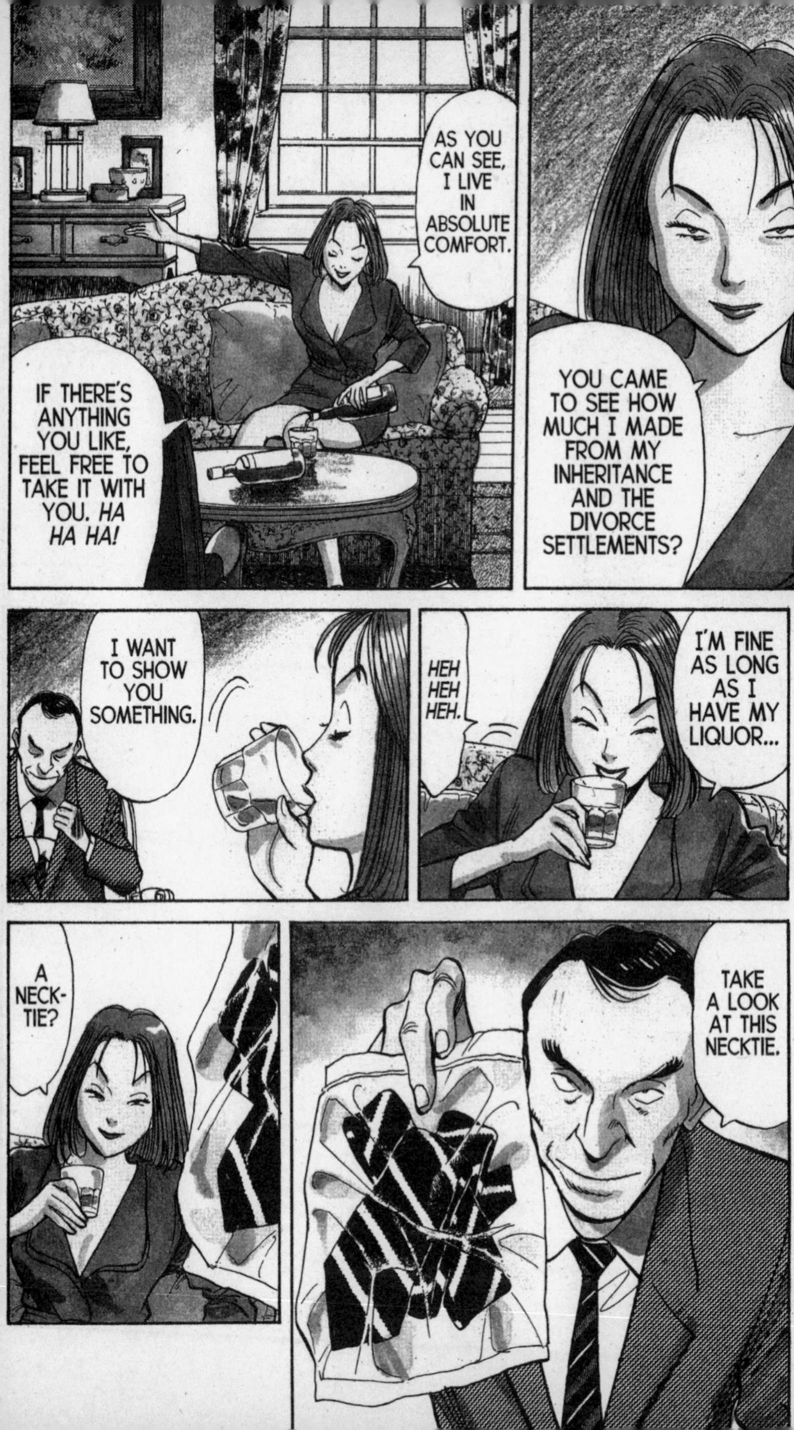
YOU CAME TO SEE HOW MUCH I MADE FROM MY INHERITANCE AND THE DIVORCE SETTLEMENTS?
AS YOU CAN SEE, I LIVE IN ABSOLUTE COMFORT.
IF THERE'S ANYTHING YOU LIKE, FEEL FREE TO TAKE IT WITH YOU. *HA HA HA!*
I'M FINE AS LONG AS I HAVE MY LIQUOR...
HEH HEH HEH.
I WANT TO SHOW YOU SOMETHING.
TAKE A LOOK AT THIS NECKTIE.
A NECK-TIE?

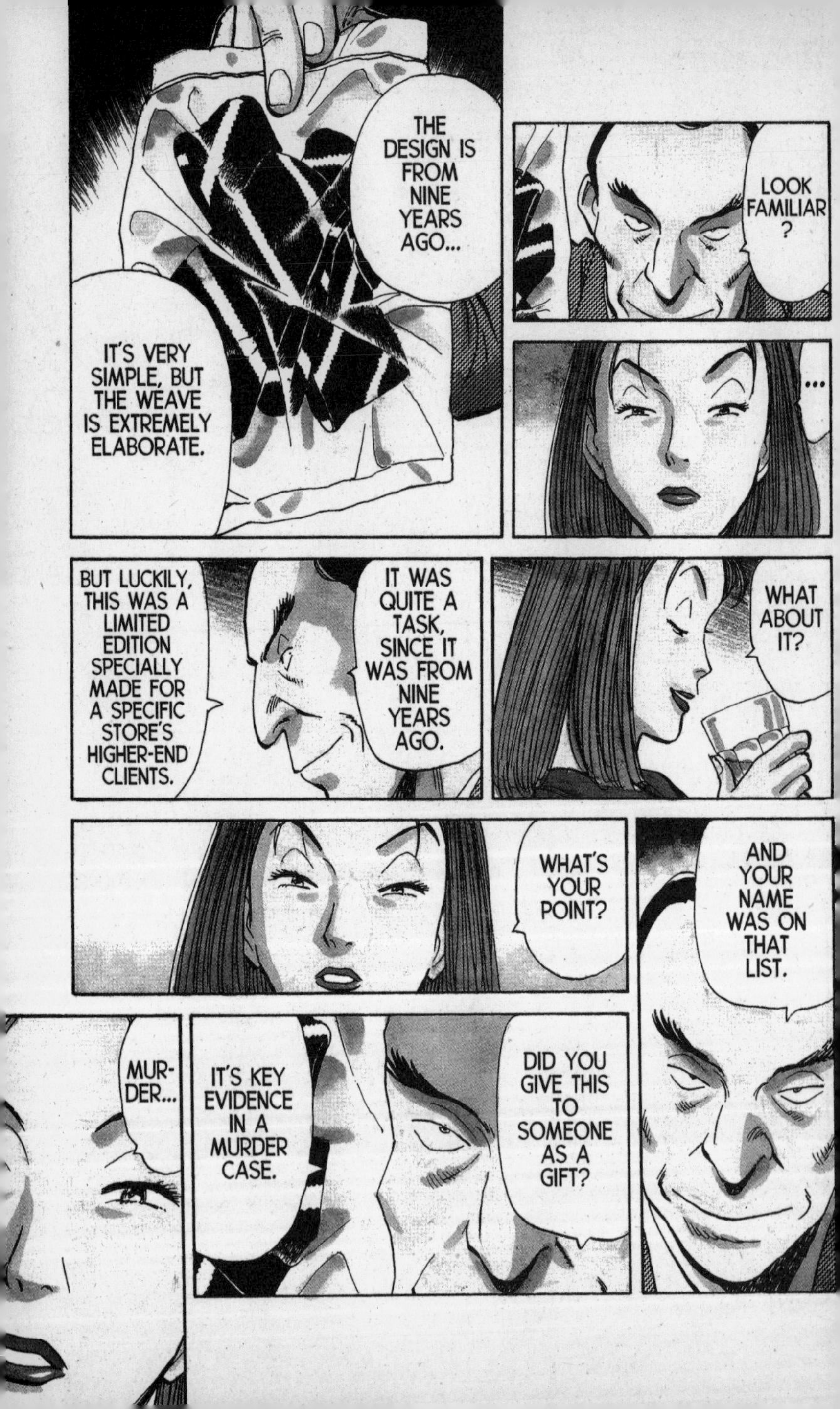
LOOK FAMILIAR?
...
THE DESIGN IS FROM NINE YEARS AGO...
IT'S VERY SIMPLE, BUT THE WEAVE IS EXTREMELY ELABORATE.
WHAT ABOUT IT?
IT WAS QUITE A TASK, SINCE IT WAS FROM NINE YEARS AGO.
BUT LUCKILY, THIS WAS A LIMITED EDITION SPECIALLY MADE FOR A SPECIFIC STORE'S HIGHER-END CLIENTS.
WHAT'S YOUR POINT?
AND YOUR NAME WAS ON THAT LIST.
DID YOU GIVE THIS TO SOMEONE AS A GIFT?
IT'S KEY EVIDENCE IN A MURDER CASE.
MUR-DER...

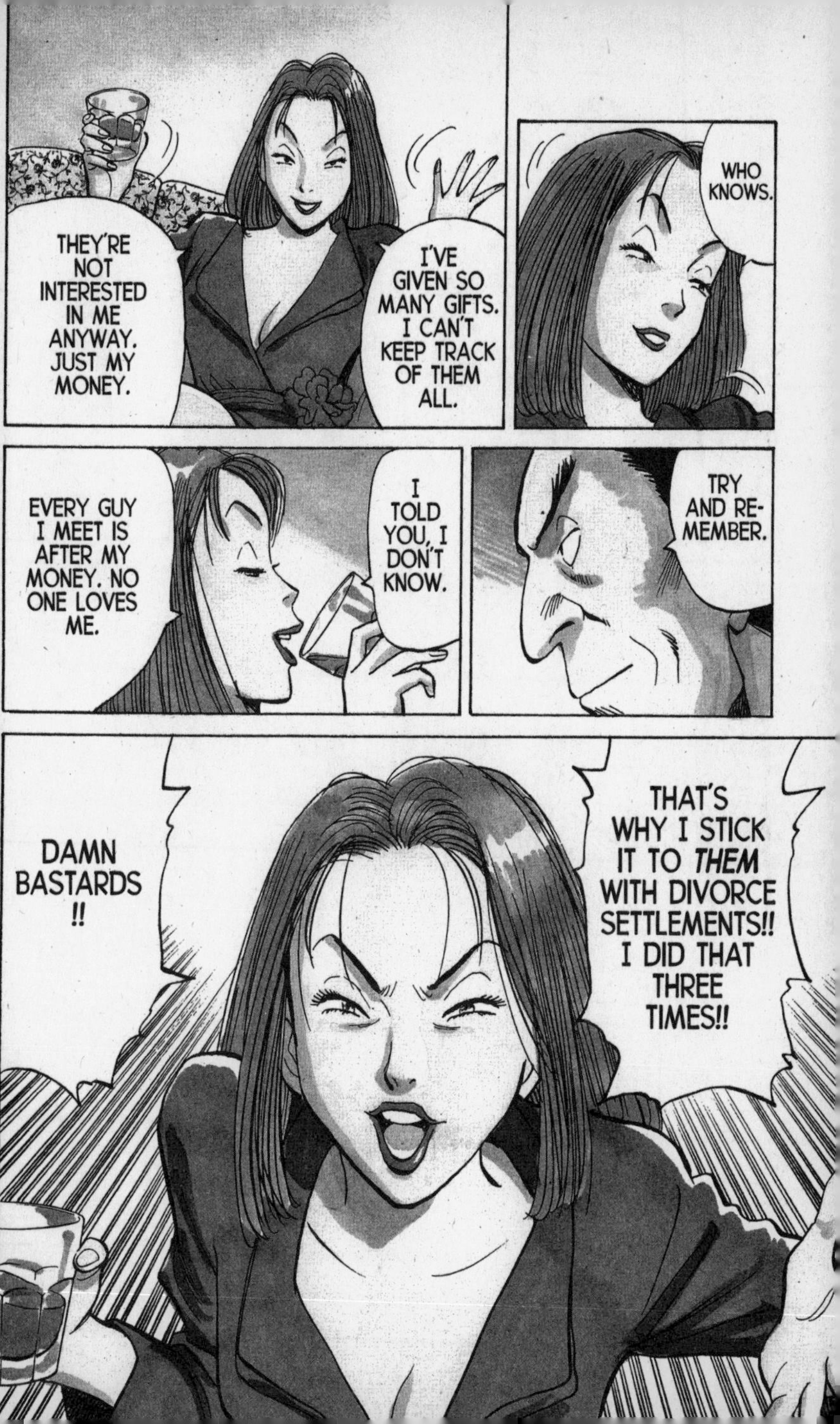
WHO KNOWS.
I'VE GIVEN SO MANY GIFTS. I CAN'T KEEP TRACK OF THEM ALL.
THEY'RE NOT INTERESTED IN ME ANYWAY. JUST MY MONEY.
TRY AND RE-MEMBER.
I TOLD YOU, I DON'T KNOW.
EVERY GUY I MEET IS AFTER MY MONEY. NO ONE LOVES ME.
THAT'S WHY I STICK IT TO *THEM* WITH DIVORCE SETTLEMENTS!! I DID THAT THREE TIMES!!
DAMN BASTARDS !!

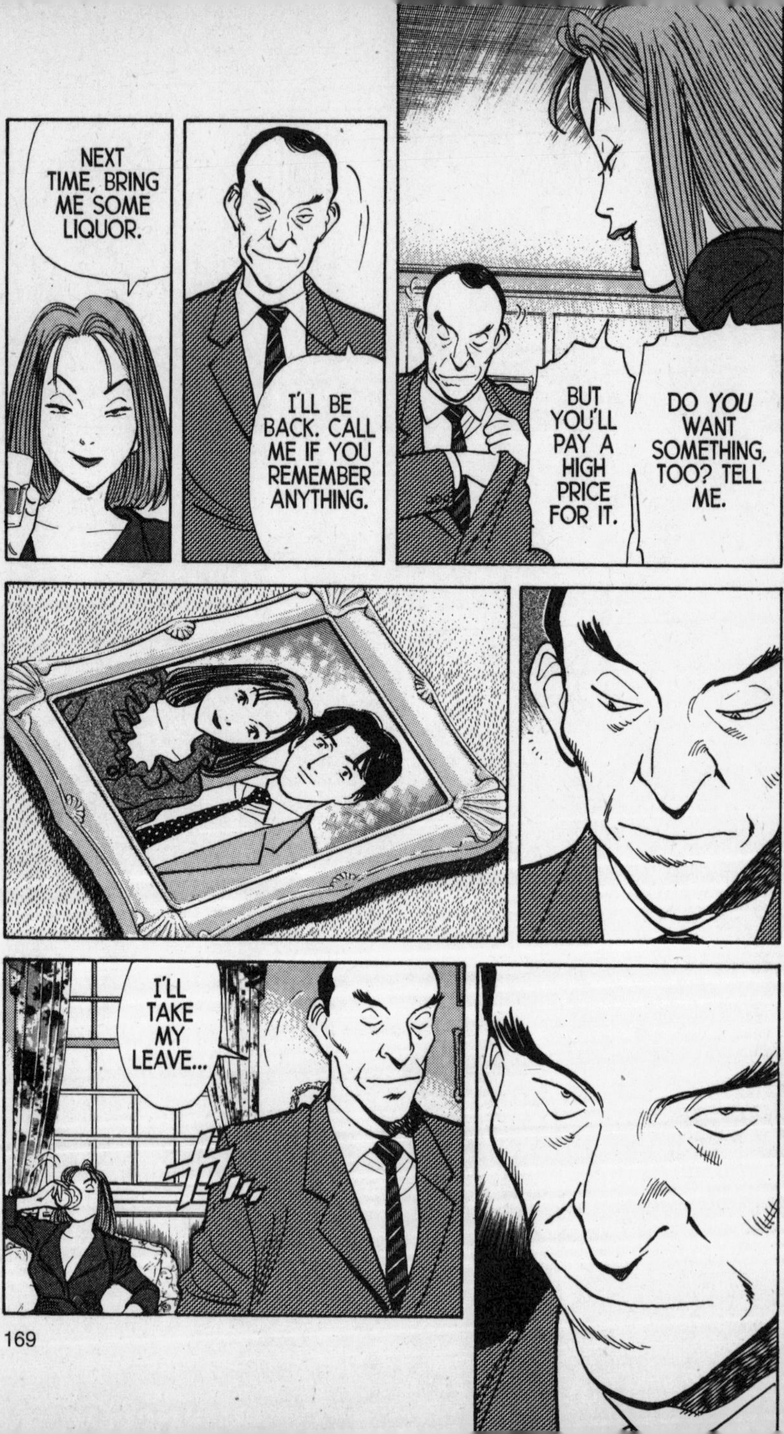
DO *YOU* WANT SOMETHING, TOO? TELL ME.
BUT YOU'LL PAY A HIGH PRICE FOR IT.
I'LL BE BACK. CALL ME IF YOU REMEMBER ANYTHING.
NEXT TIME, BRING ME SOME LIQUOR.
I'LL TAKE MY LEAVE...

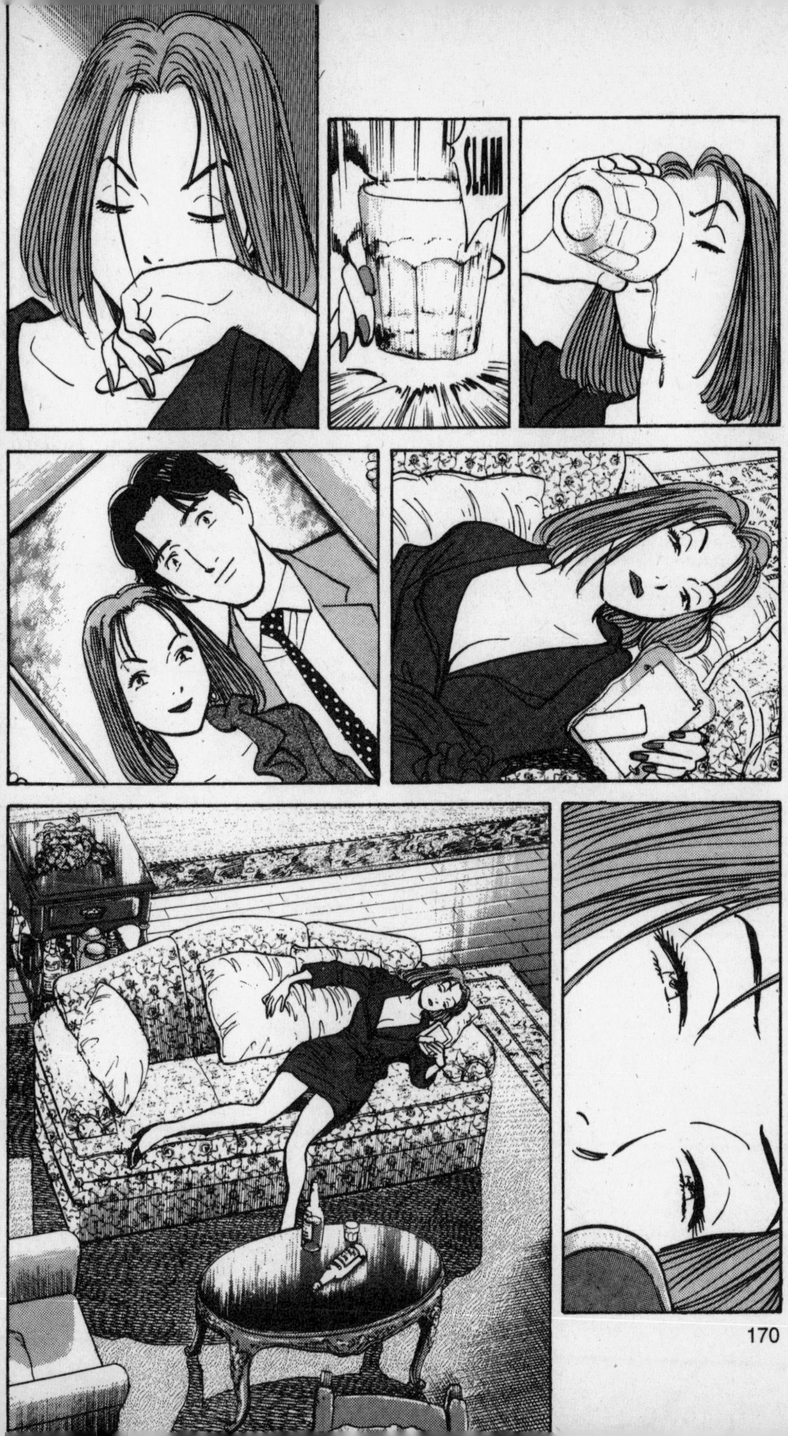
SLAM

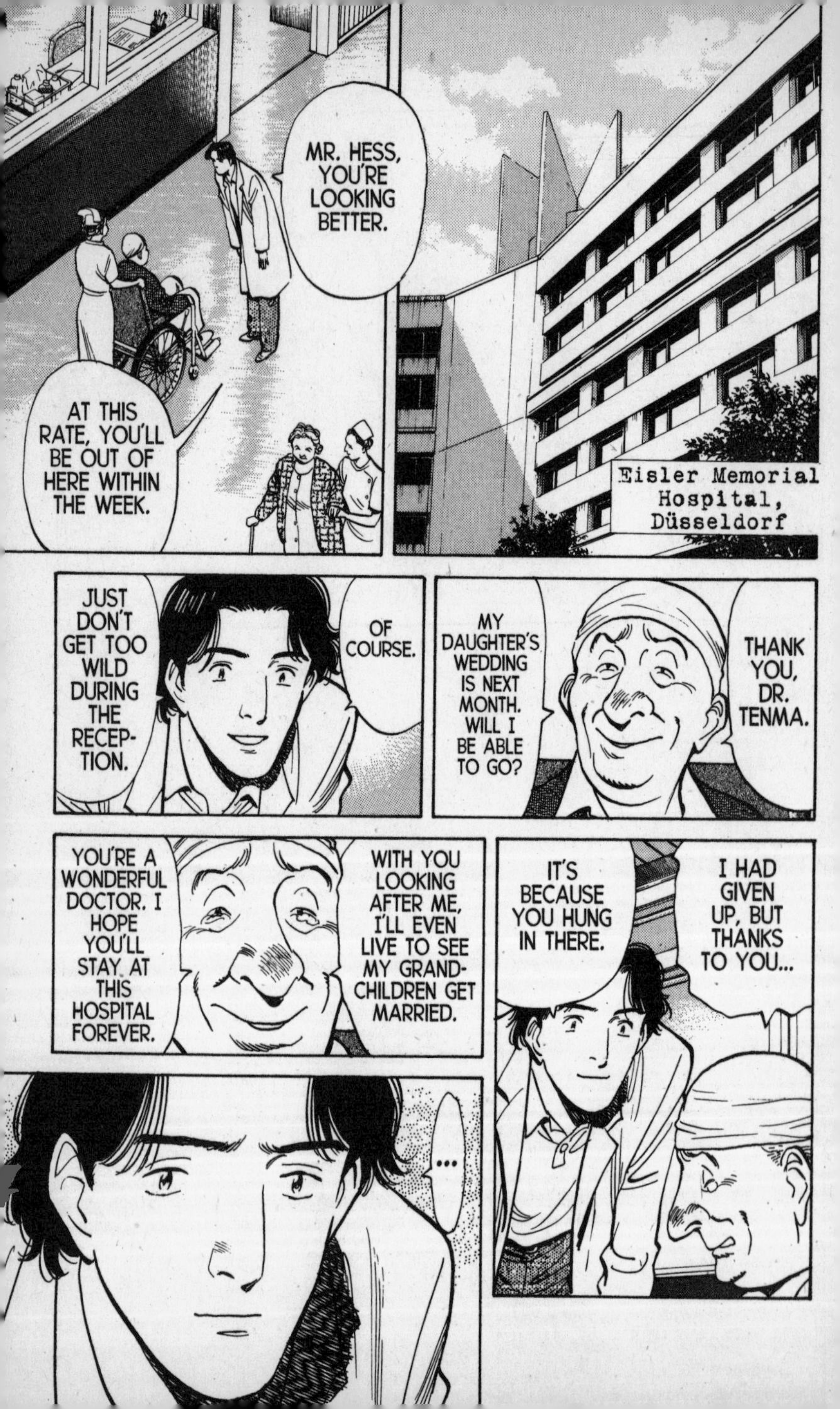
Eisler Memorial Hospital, Düsseldorf
MR. HESS, YOU'RE LOOKING BETTER.
AT THIS RATE, YOU'LL BE OUT OF HERE WITHIN THE WEEK.
THANK YOU, DR. TENMA.
MY DAUGHTER'S WEDDING IS NEXT MONTH. WILL I BE ABLE TO GO?
OF COURSE.
JUST DON'T GET TOO WILD DURING THE RECEP-TION.
I HAD GIVEN UP, BUT THANKS TO YOU...
IT'S BECAUSE YOU HUNG IN THERE.
WITH YOU LOOKING AFTER ME, I'LL EVEN LIVE TO SEE MY GRAND-CHILDREN GET MARRIED.
YOU'RE A WONDERFUL DOCTOR. I HOPE YOU'LL STAY AT THIS HOSPITAL FOREVER.
...

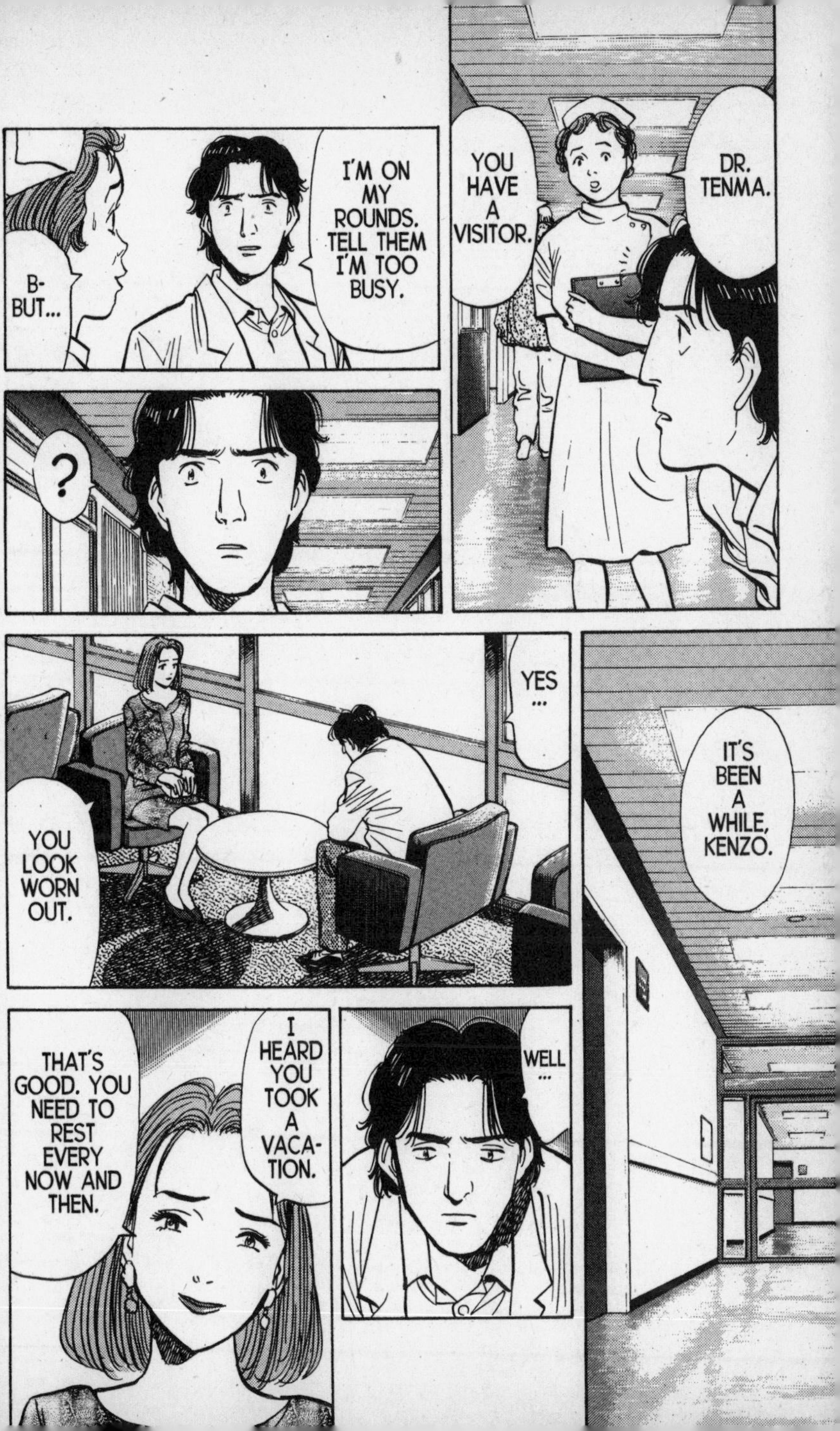
DR. TENMA.
YOU HAVE A VISITOR.
I'M ON MY ROUNDS. TELL THEM I'M TOO BUSY.
B-BUT...
?
IT'S BEEN A WHILE, KENZO.
YES ...
YOU LOOK WORN OUT.
I HEARD YOU TOOK A VACA-TION.
WELL ...
THAT'S GOOD. YOU NEED TO REST EVERY NOW AND THEN.

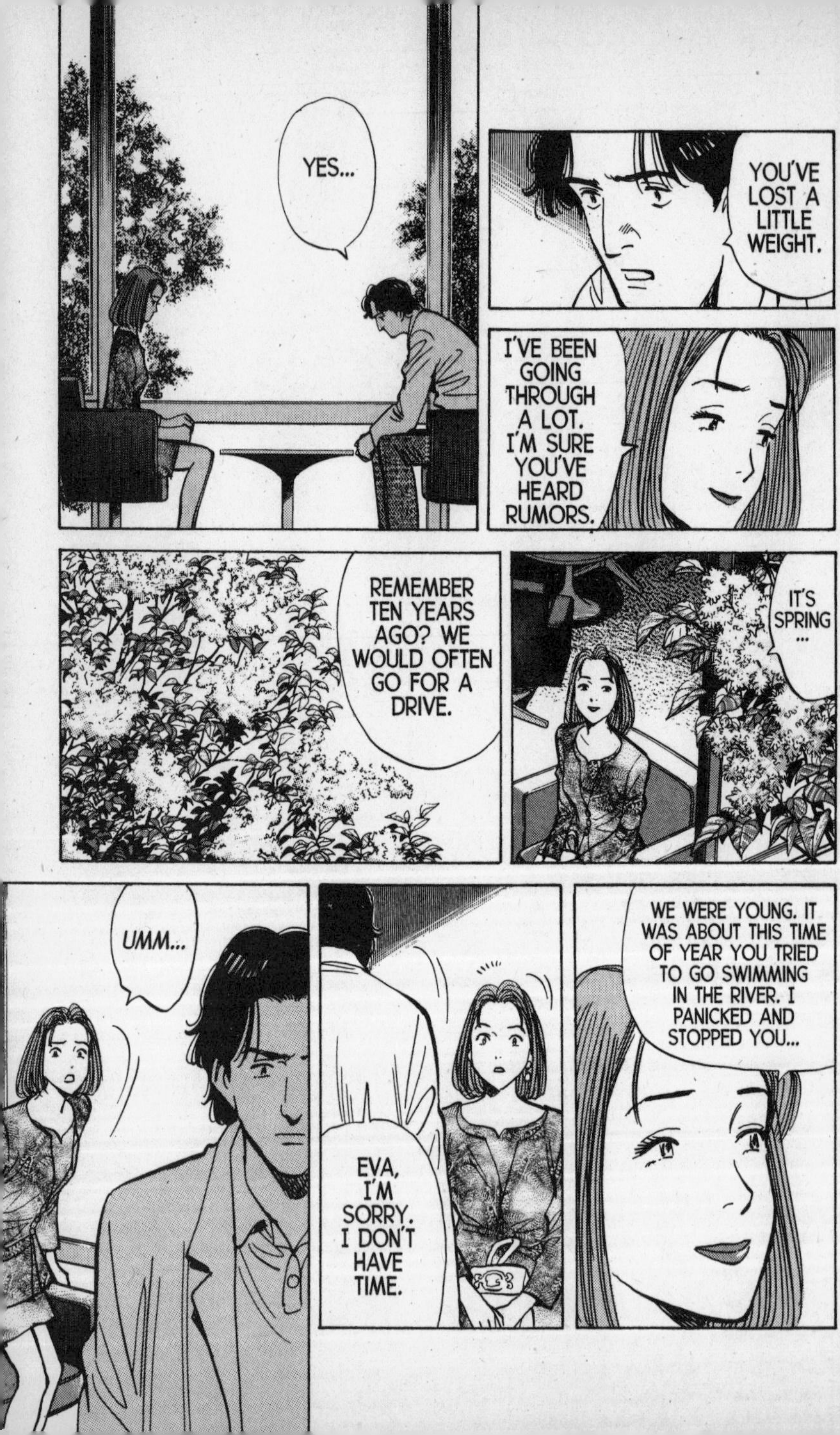
YOU'VE LOST A LITTLE WEIGHT.
I'VE BEEN GOING THROUGH A LOT. I'M SURE YOU'VE HEARD RUMORS.
YES...
IT'S SPRING ...
REMEMBER TEN YEARS AGO? WE WOULD OFTEN GO FOR A DRIVE.
WE WERE YOUNG. IT WAS ABOUT THIS TIME OF YEAR YOU TRIED TO GO SWIMMING IN THE RIVER. I PANICKED AND STOPPED YOU...
EVA, I'M SORRY. I DON'T HAVE TIME.
UMM...

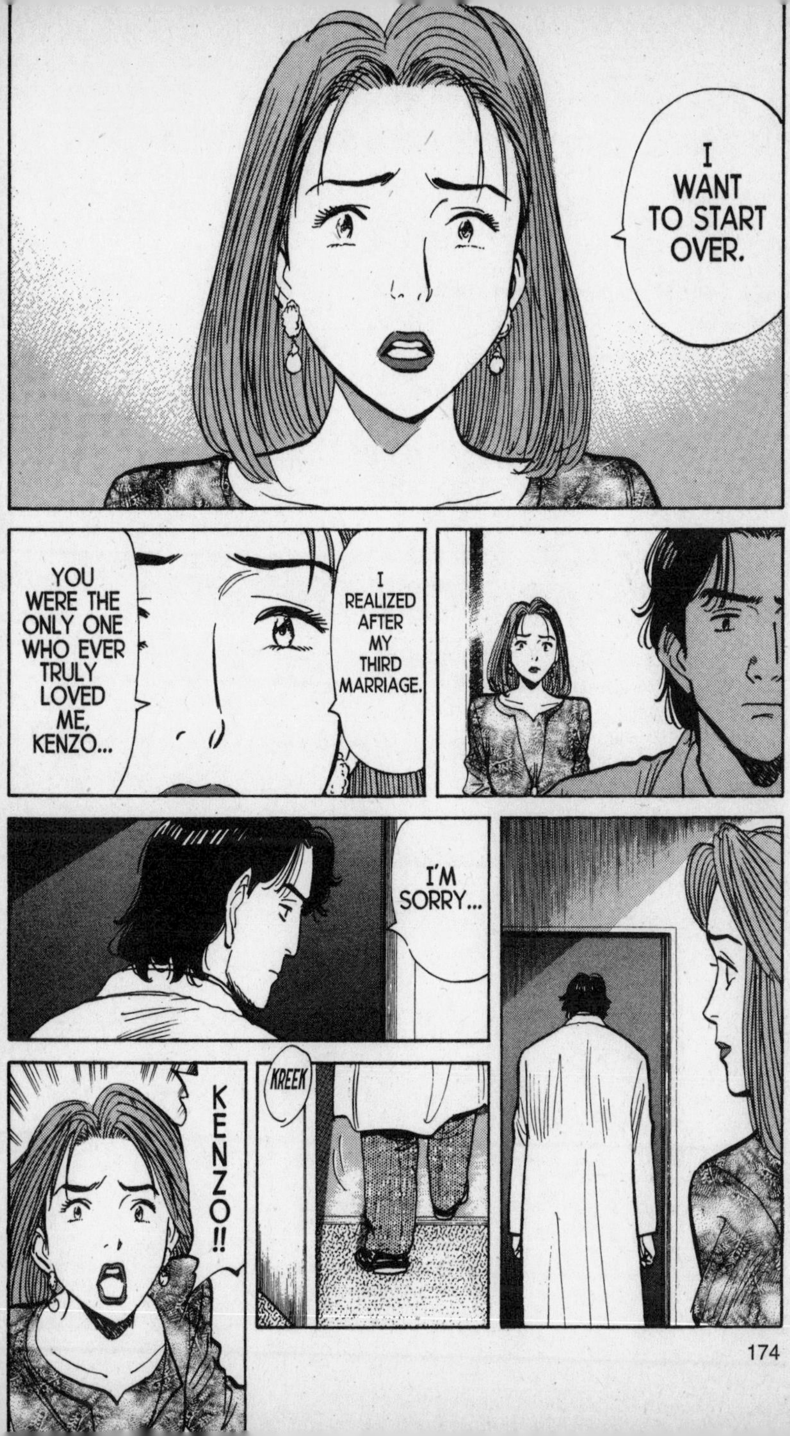
I WANT TO START OVER.
I REALIZED AFTER MY THIRD MARRIAGE.
YOU WERE THE ONLY ONE WHO EVER TRULY LOVED ME, KENZO...
I'M SORRY...
KREEK
KENZO!!

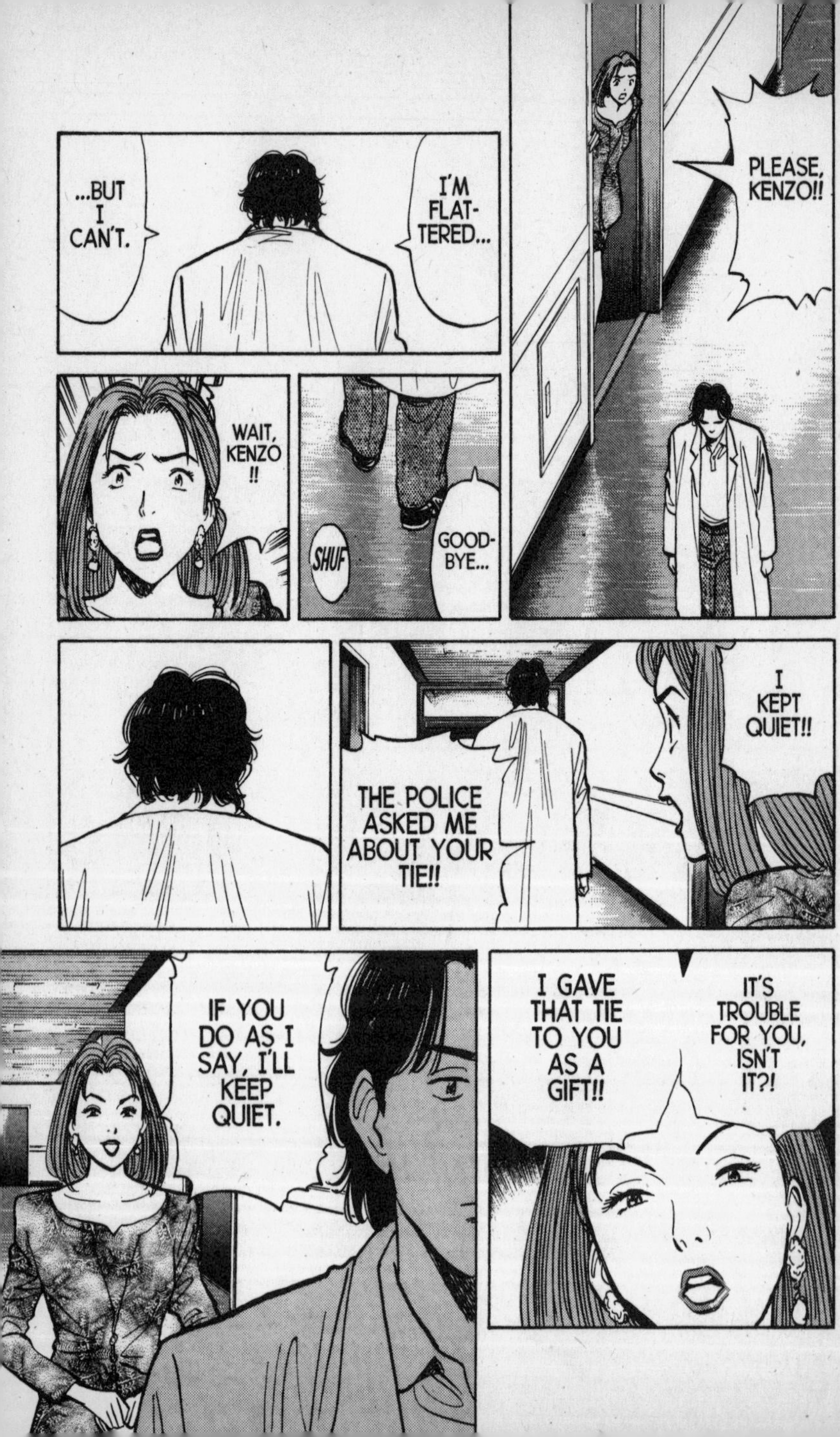
PLEASE, KENZO!!
I'M FLATTERED...
...BUT I CAN'T.
GOOD-BYE...
SHUF
WAIT, KENZO!!
I KEPT QUIET!!
THE POLICE ASKED ME ABOUT YOUR TIE!!
IT'S TROUBLE FOR YOU, ISN'T IT?!
I GAVE THAT TIE TO YOU AS A GIFT!!
IF YOU DO AS I SAY, I'LL KEEP QUIET.

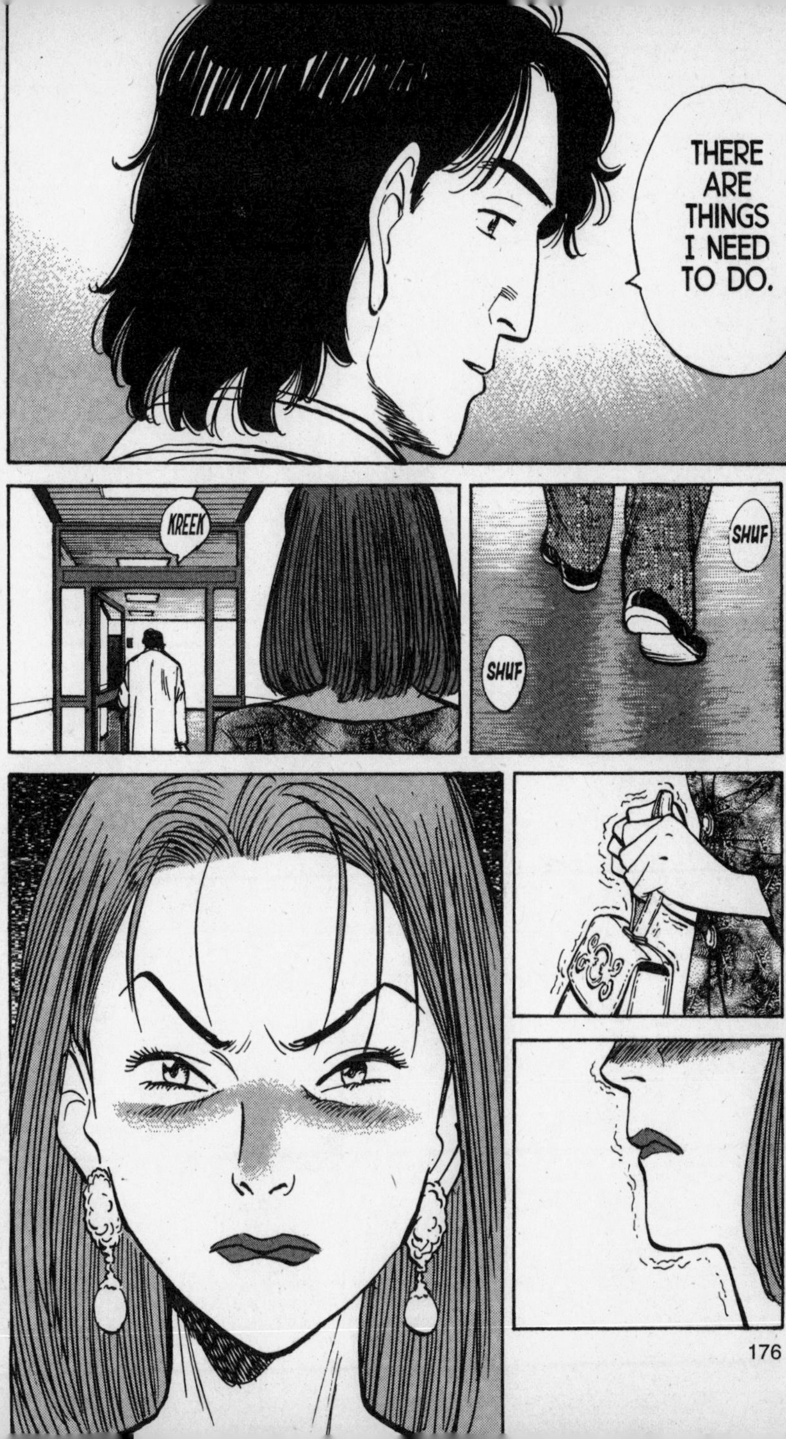
THERE ARE THINGS I NEED TO DO.
SHUF
SHUF
KREEK

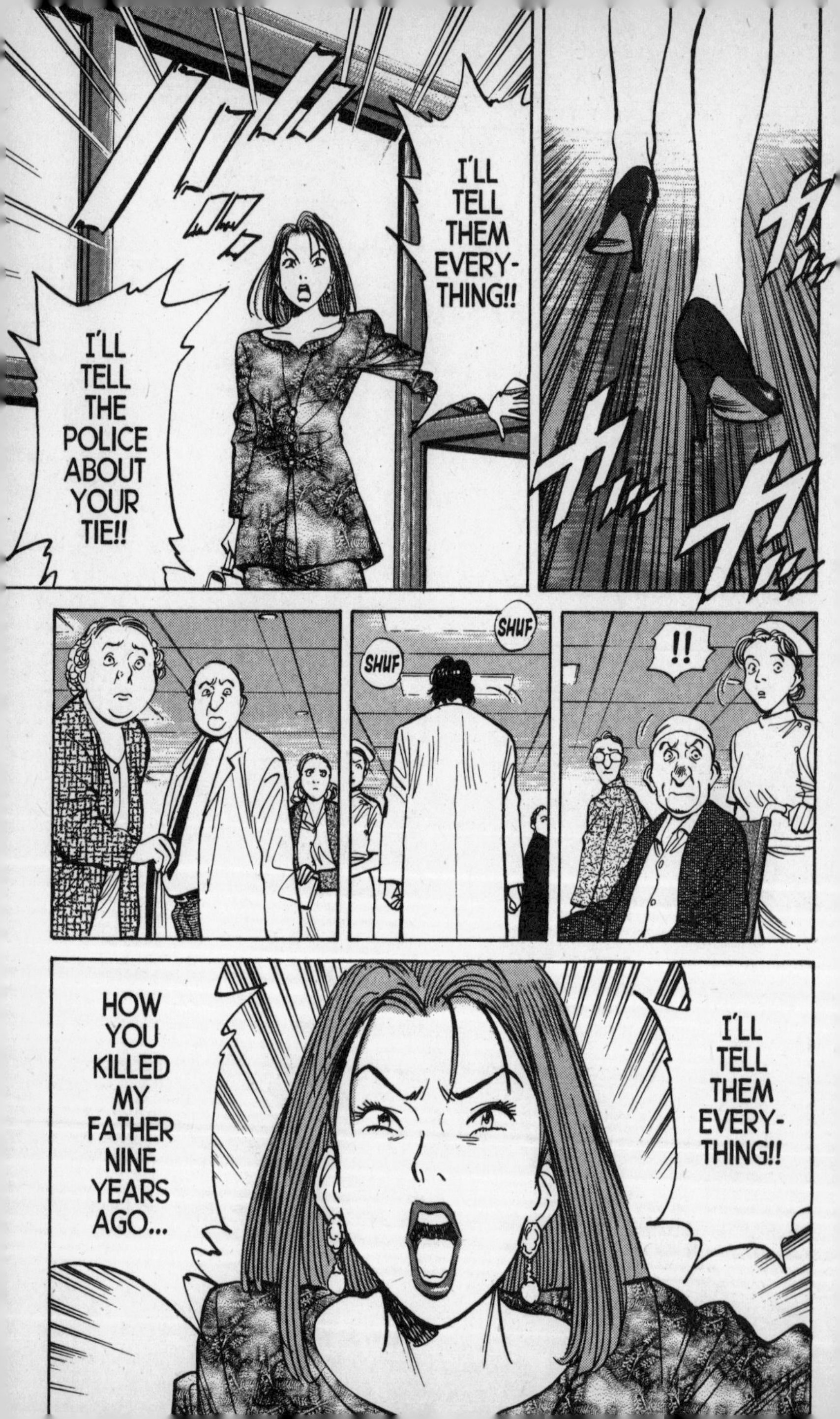
I'LL TELL THEM EVERY-THING!!
I'LL TELL THE POLICE ABOUT YOUR TIE!!
!!
SHUF
SHUF
I'LL TELL THEM EVERY-THING!!
HOW YOU KILLED MY FATHER NINE YEARS AGO...

IT'S ALL YOUR FAULT!!

SHUF SHUF

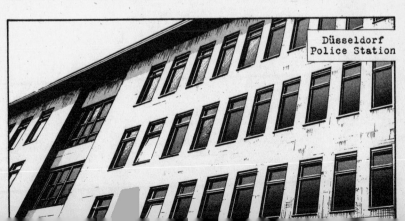

Düsseldorf Police Station

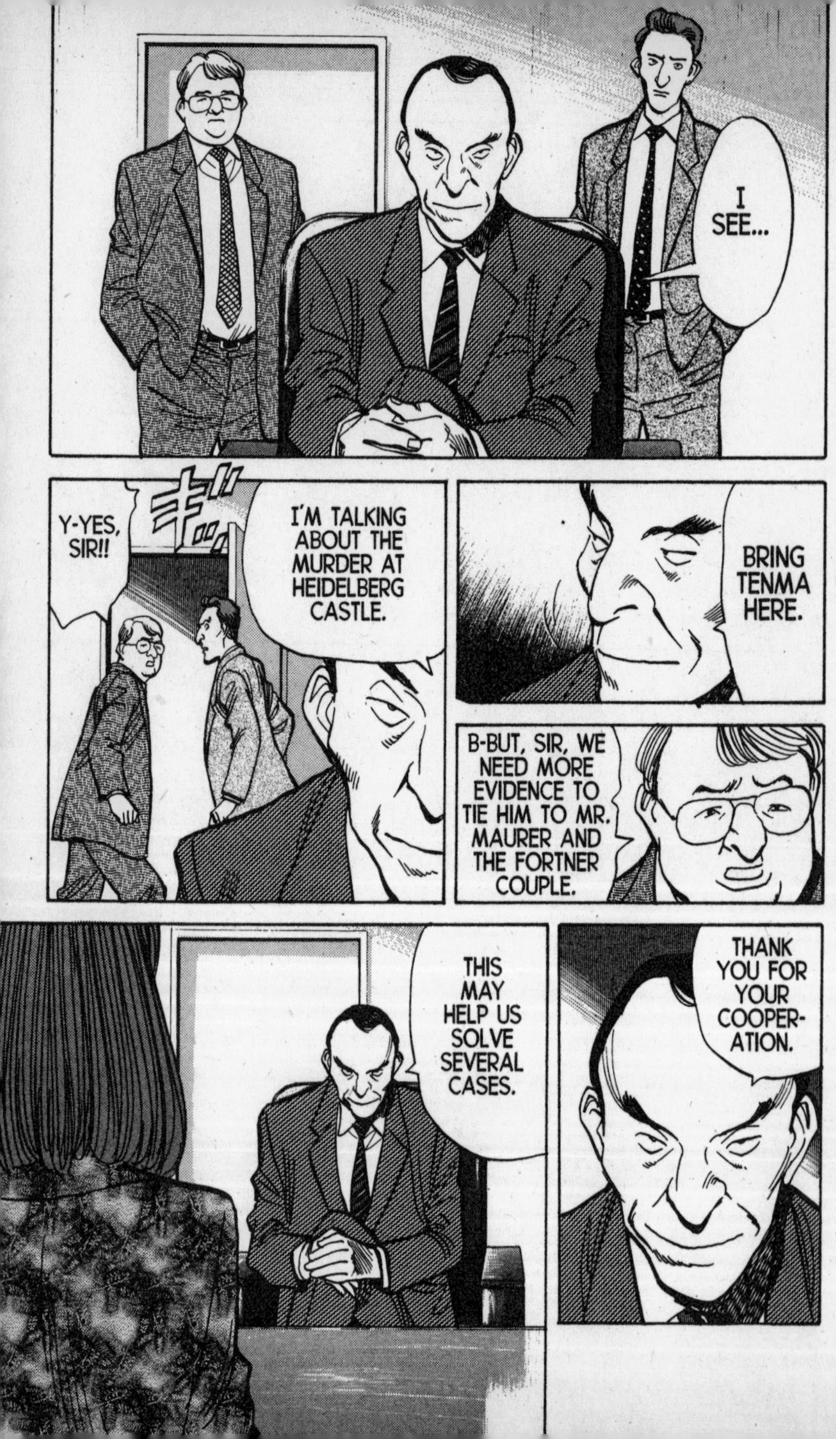
I SEE...
BRING TENMA HERE.
B-BUT, SIR, WE NEED MORE EVIDENCE TO TIE HIM TO MR. MAURER AND THE FORTNER COUPLE.
I'M TALKING ABOUT THE MURDER AT HEIDELBERG CASTLE.
Y-YES, SIR!!
THANK YOU FOR YOUR COOPER-ATION.
THIS MAY HELP US SOLVE SEVERAL CASES.

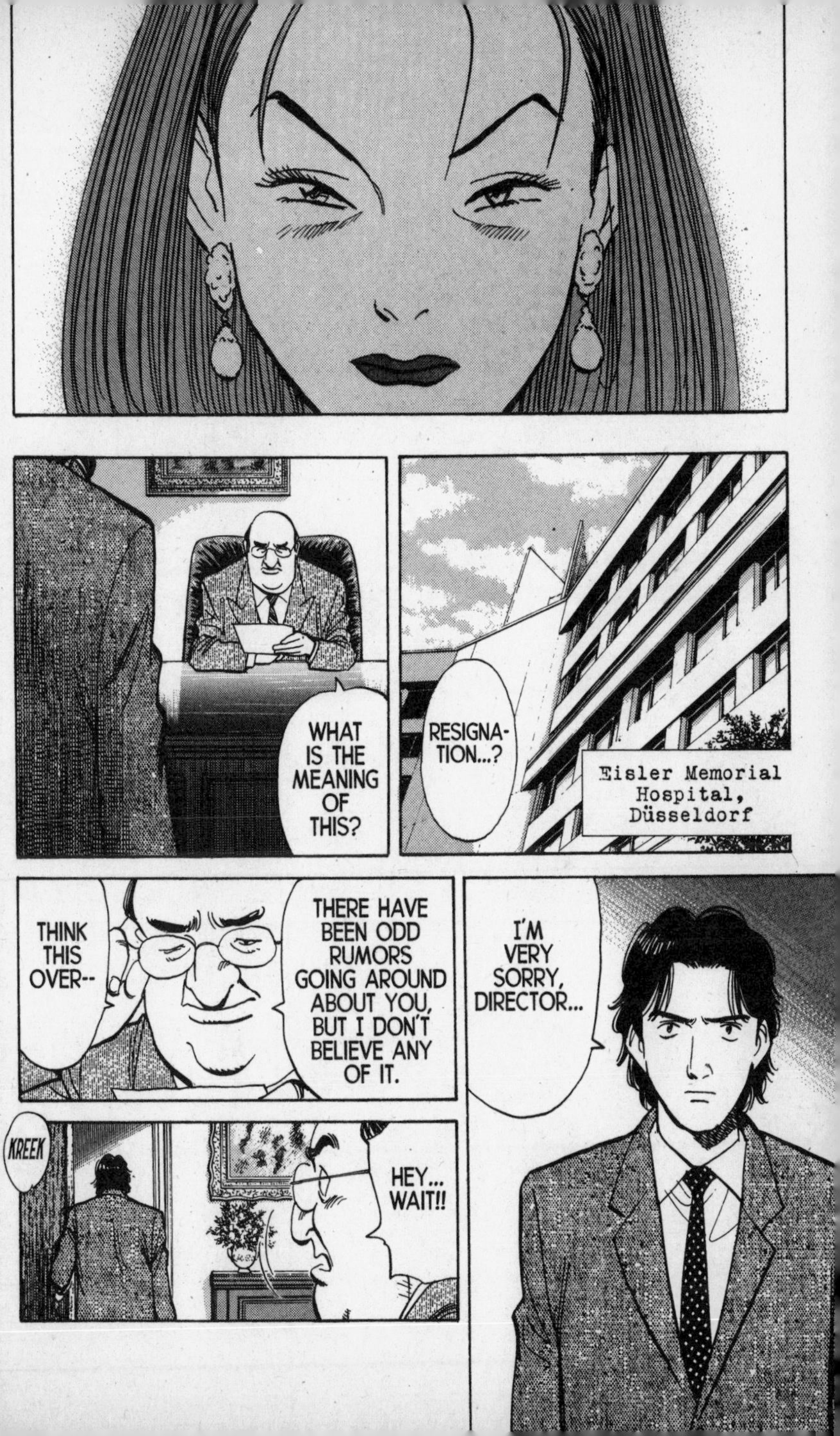
Eisler Memorial Hospital, Düsseldorf
RESIGNA-TION...?
WHAT IS THE MEANING OF THIS?
I'M VERY SORRY, DIRECTOR...
THERE HAVE BEEN ODD RUMORS GOING AROUND ABOUT YOU, BUT I DON'T BELIEVE ANY OF IT.
THINK THIS OVER--
HEY... WAIT!!
KREEK

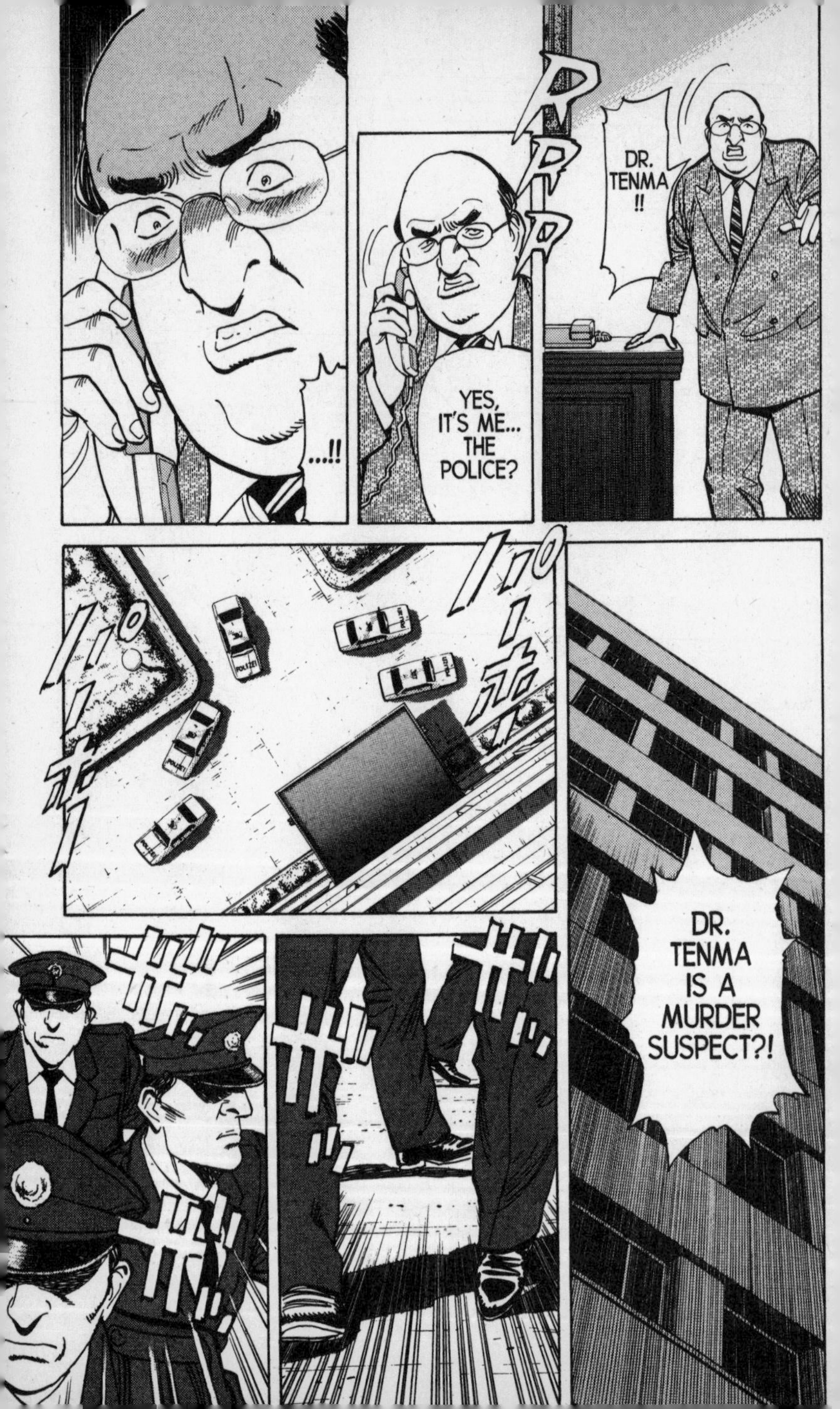
DR. TENMA !!
YES, IT'S ME... THE POLICE?
...!!
DR. TENMA IS A MURDER SUSPECT?!

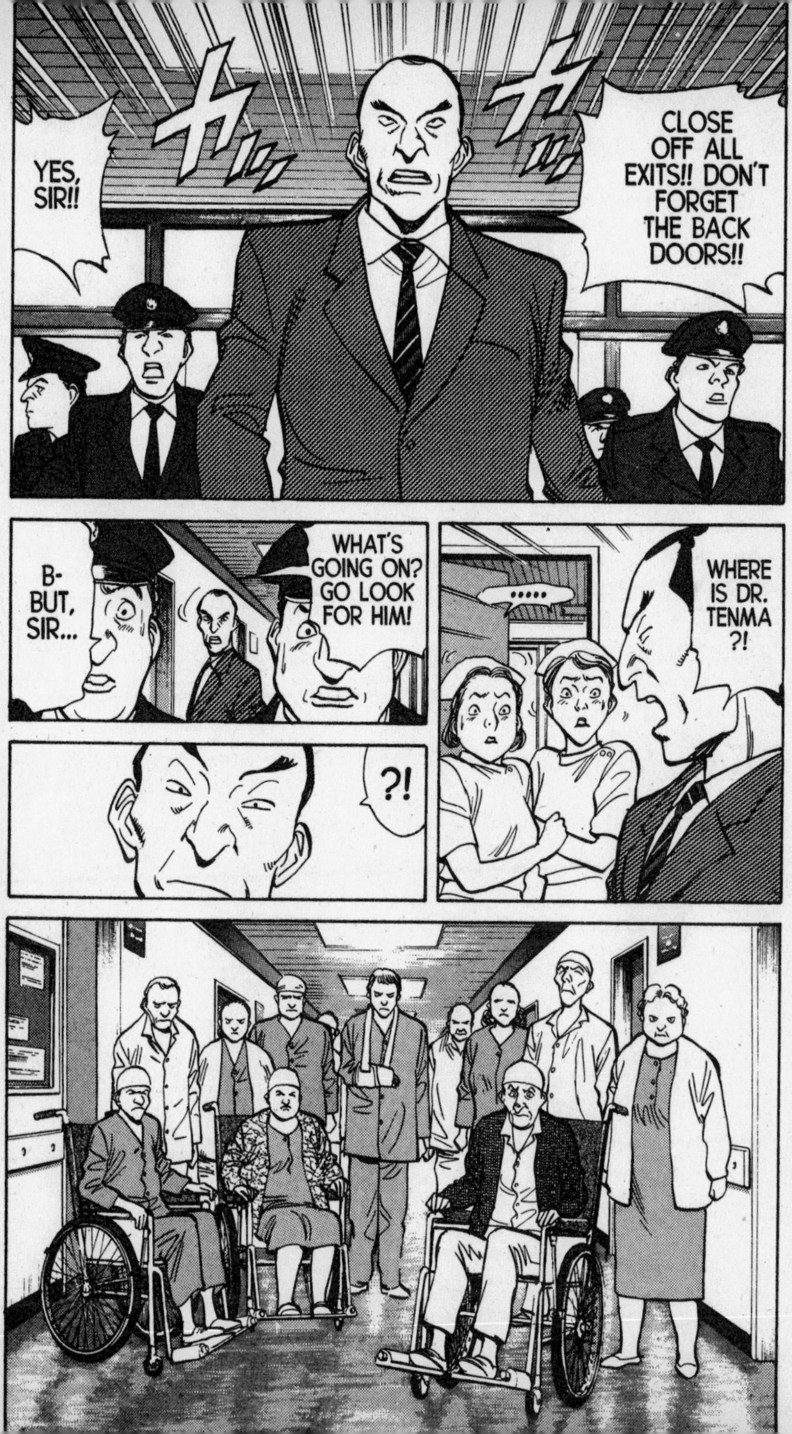
CLOSE OFF ALL EXITS!! DON'T FORGET THE BACK DOORS!!
YES, SIR!!
WHERE IS DR. TENMA?!
.....
WHAT'S GOING ON? GO LOOK FOR HIM!
B-BUT, SIR...
?!

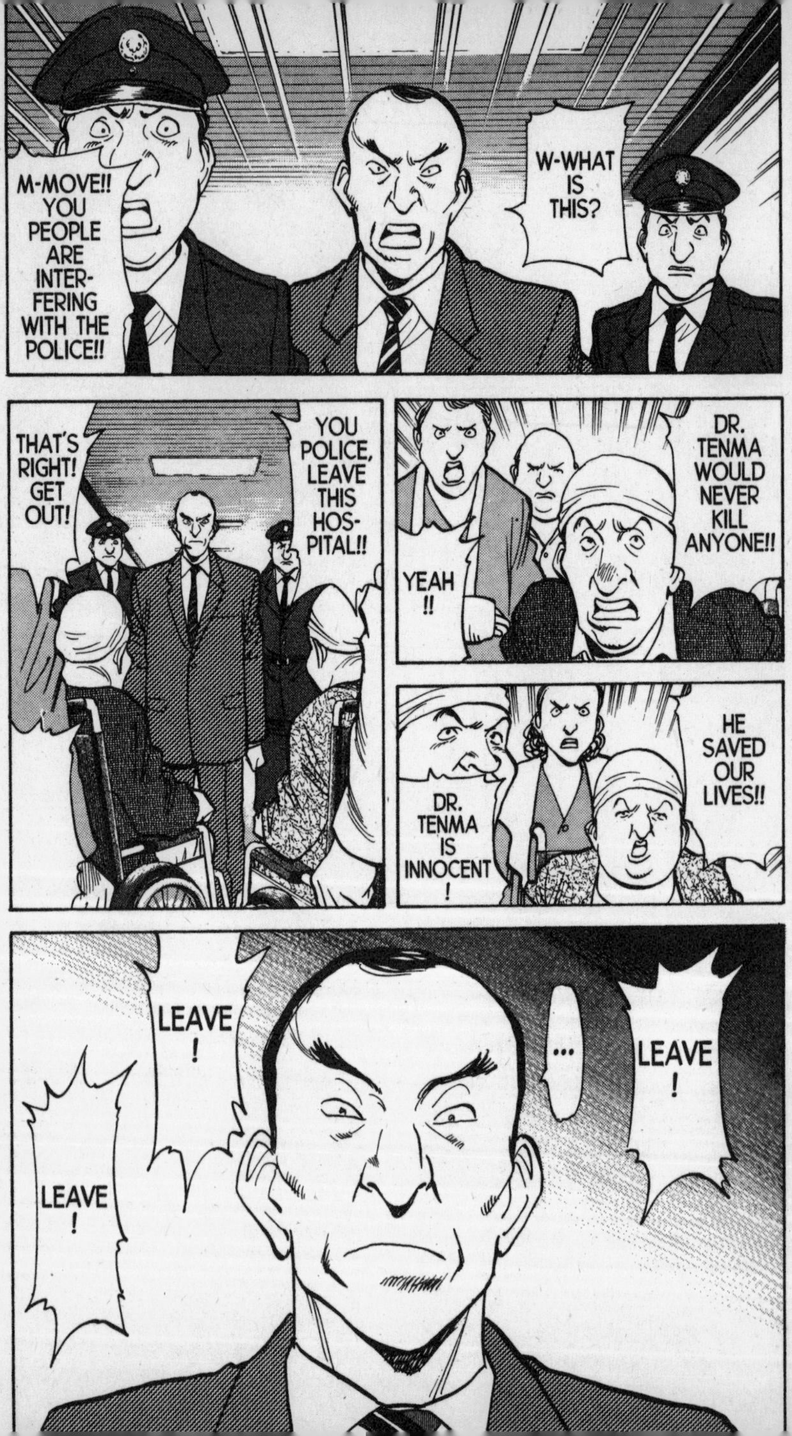
W-WHAT IS THIS?
M-MOVE!! YOU PEOPLE ARE INTER-FERING WITH THE POLICE!!
DR. TENMA WOULD NEVER KILL ANYONE!!
YEAH!!
HE SAVED OUR LIVES!!
DR. TENMA IS INNOCENT!
YOU POLICE, LEAVE THIS HOS-PITAL!!
THAT'S RIGHT! GET OUT!
LEAVE!
...
LEAVE!
LEAVE!

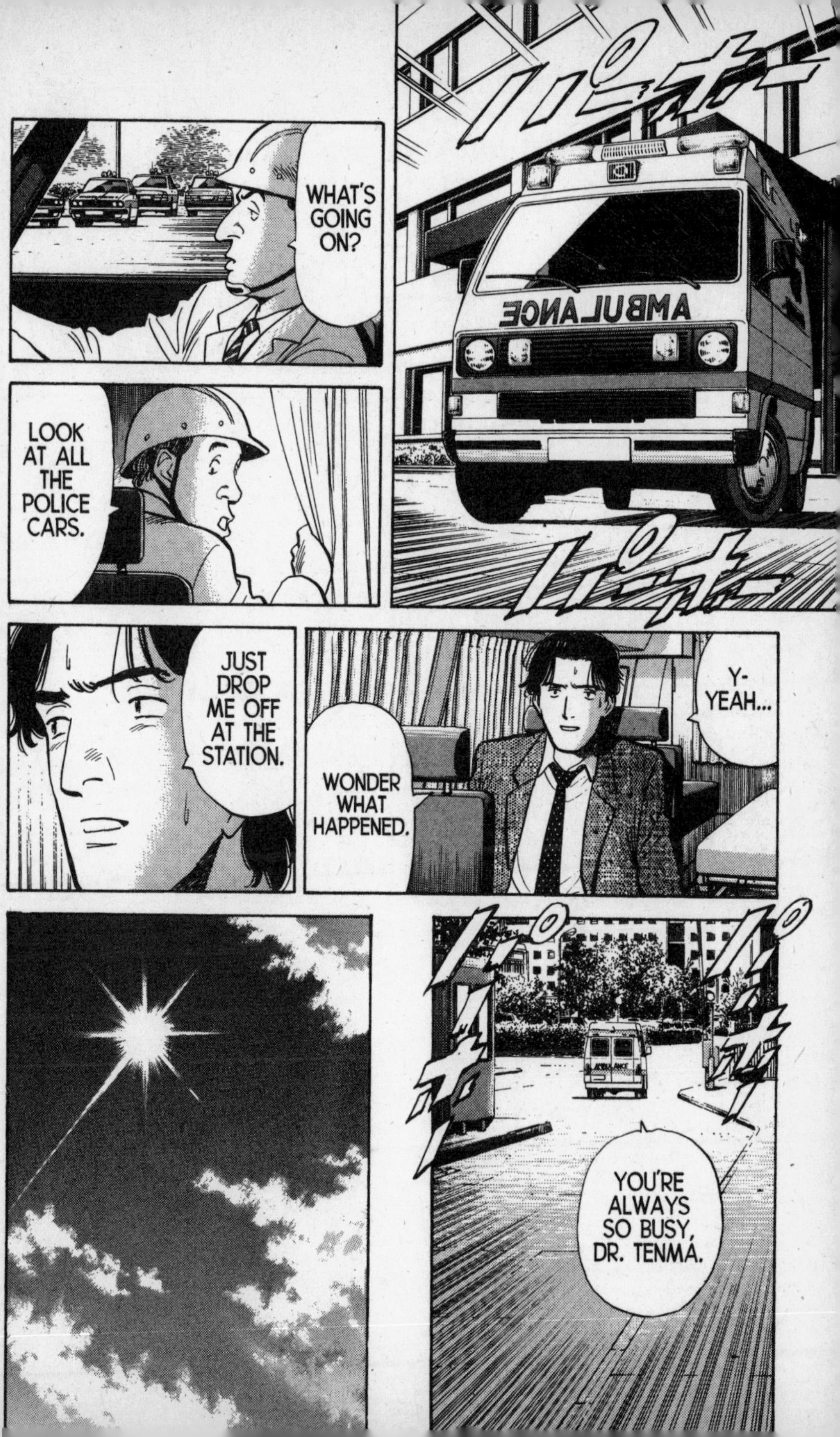
WHAT'S GOING ON?
LOOK AT ALL THE POLICE CARS.
Y- YEAH...
WONDER WHAT HAPPENED.
JUST DROP ME OFF AT THE STATION.
YOU'RE ALWAYS SO BUSY, DR. TENMA.

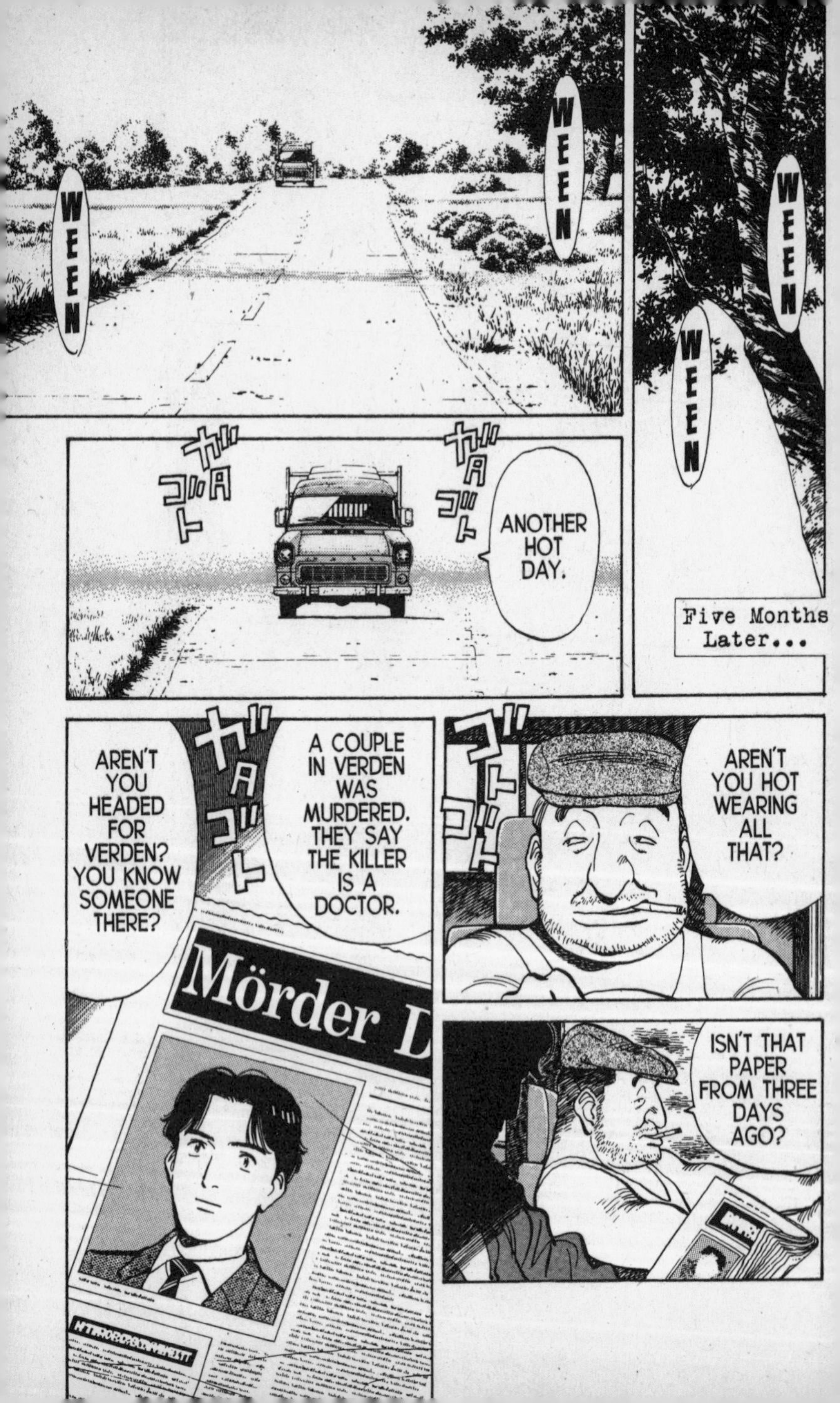
WEEN
WEEN
Five Months Later...
WEEN
WEEN
ANOTHER HOT DAY.
AREN'T YOU HOT WEARING ALL THAT?
ISN'T THAT PAPER FROM THREE DAYS AGO?
A COUPLE IN VERDEN WAS MURDERED. THEY SAY THE KILLER IS A DOCTOR.
AREN'T YOU HEADED FOR VERDEN? YOU KNOW SOMEONE THERE?
Mörder D

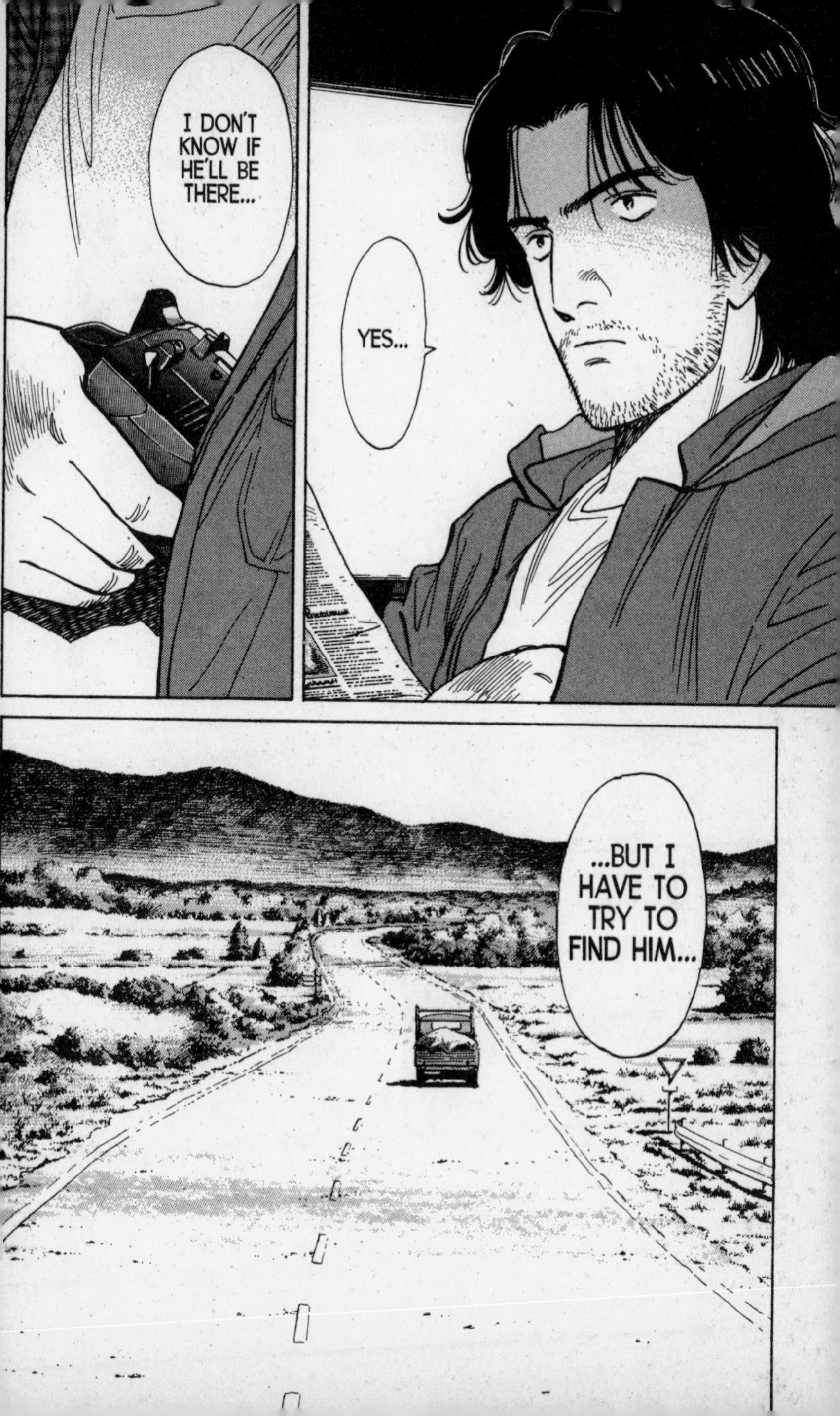
YES...
I DON'T KNOW IF HE'LL BE THERE...
...BUT I HAVE TO TRY TO FIND HIM...

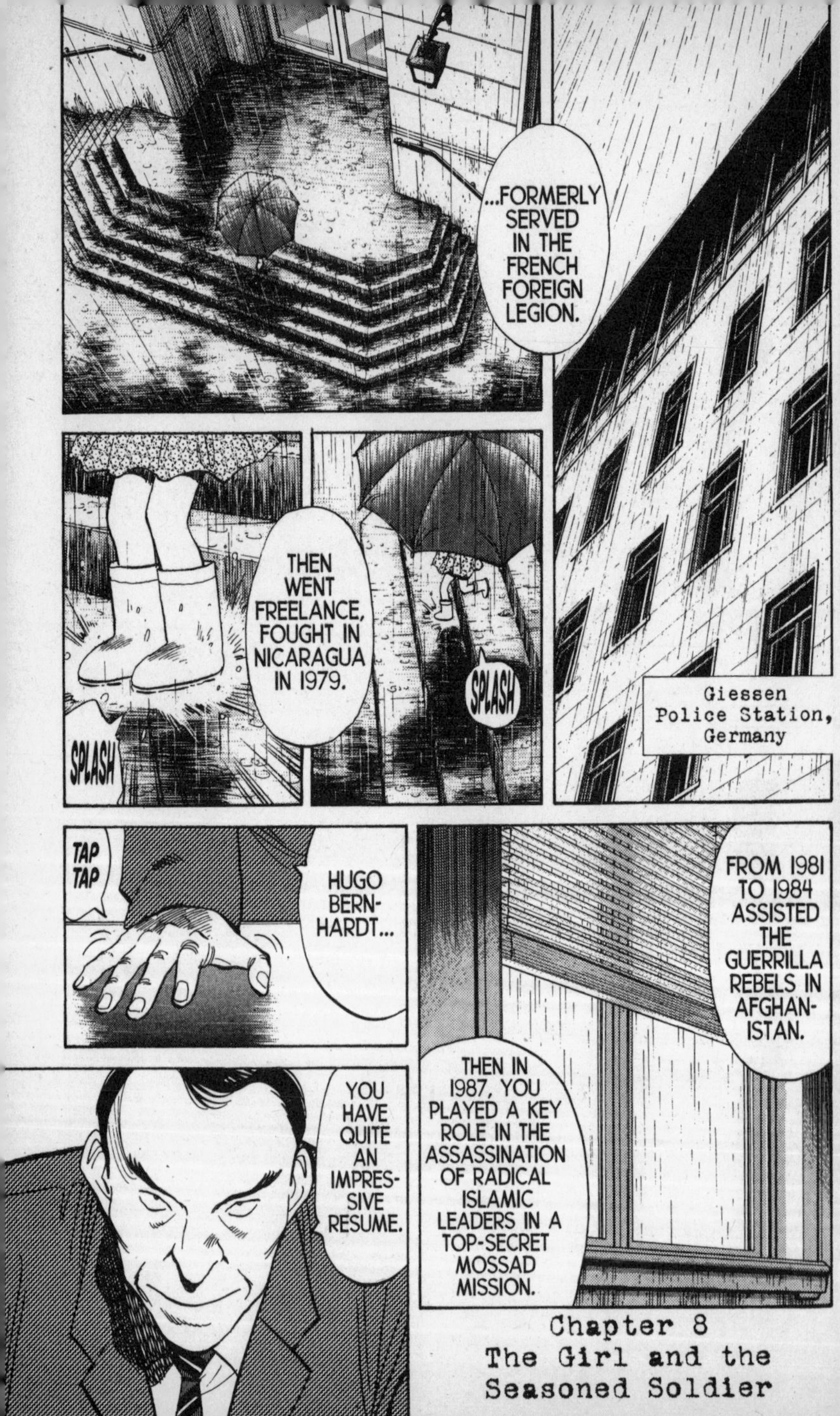
Giessen Police Station, Germany
...FORMERLY SERVED IN THE FRENCH FOREIGN LEGION.
SPLASH
THEN WENT FREELANCE, FOUGHT IN NICARAGUA IN 1979.
SPLASH
FROM 1981 TO 1984 ASSISTED THE GUERRILLA REBELS IN AFGHAN-ISTAN.
THEN IN 1987, YOU PLAYED A KEY ROLE IN THE ASSASSINATION OF RADICAL ISLAMIC LEADERS IN A TOP-SECRET MOSSAD MISSION.
TAP TAP
HUGO BERN-HARDT...
YOU HAVE QUITE AN IMPRES-SIVE RESUME.

Chapter 8
The Girl and the Seasoned Soldier

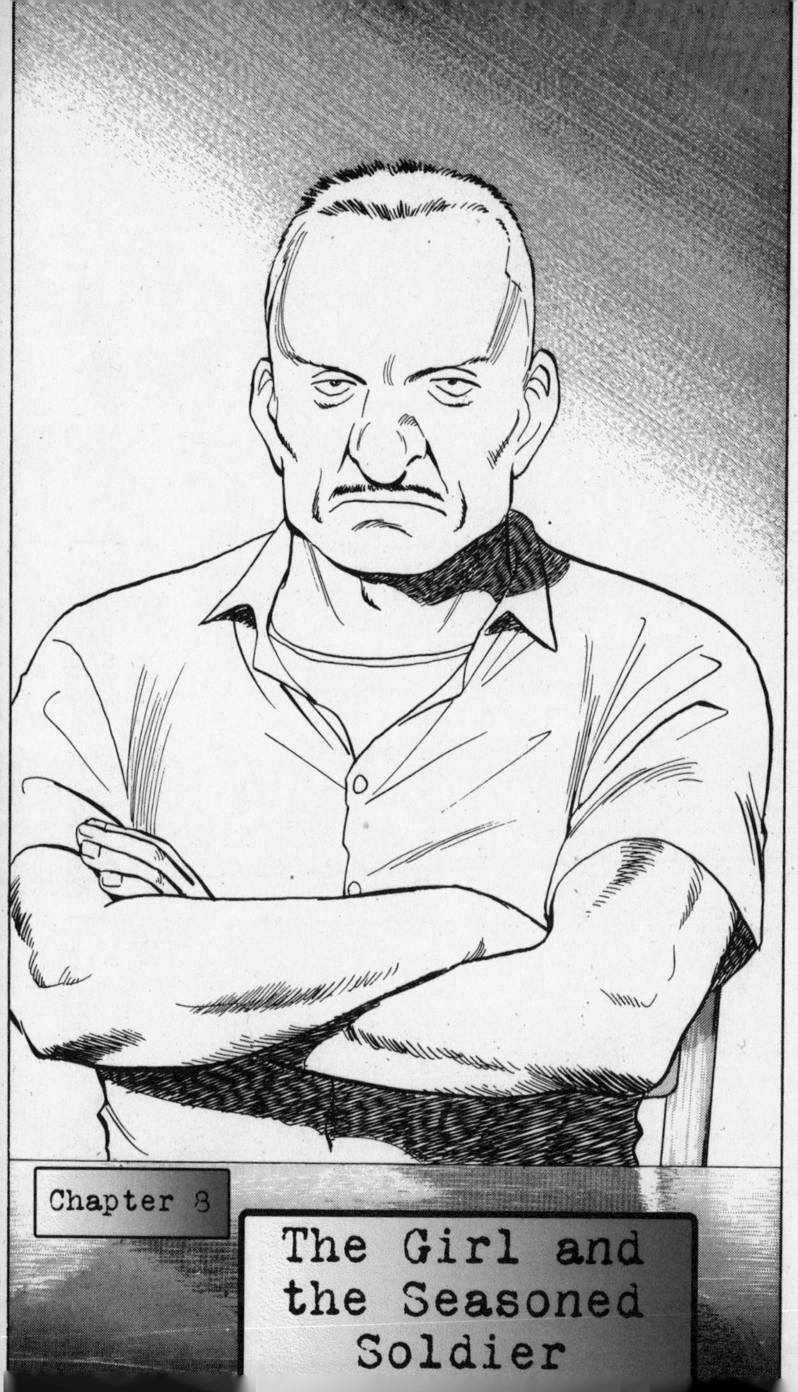
Chapter 8
The Girl and the Seasoned Soldier

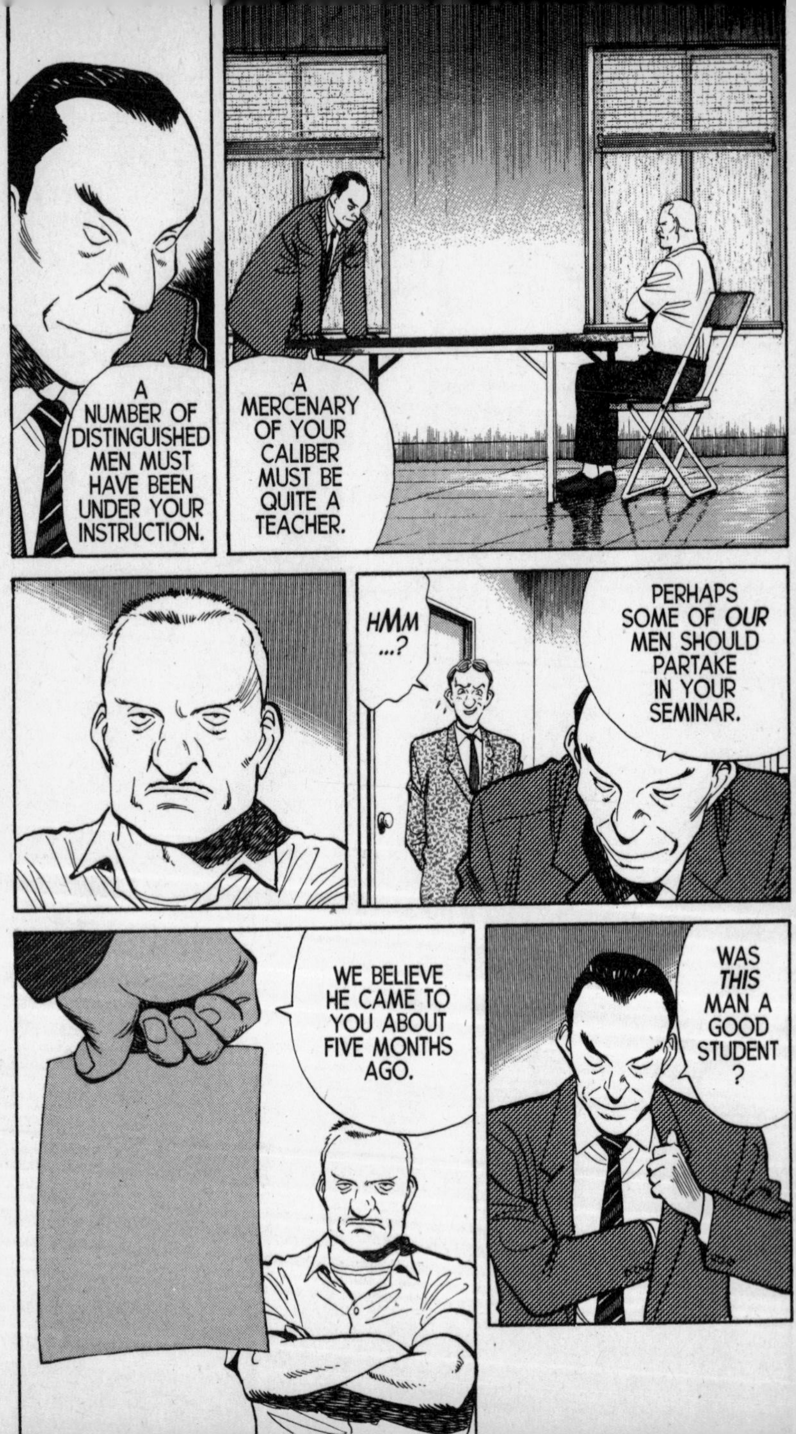
A MERCENARY OF YOUR CALIBER MUST BE QUITE A TEACHER.
A NUMBER OF DISTINGUISHED MEN MUST HAVE BEEN UNDER YOUR INSTRUCTION.
PERHAPS SOME OF *OUR* MEN SHOULD PARTAKE IN YOUR SEMINAR.
HMM ...?
WAS *THIS* MAN A GOOD STUDENT ?
WE BELIEVE HE CAME TO YOU ABOUT FIVE MONTHS AGO.

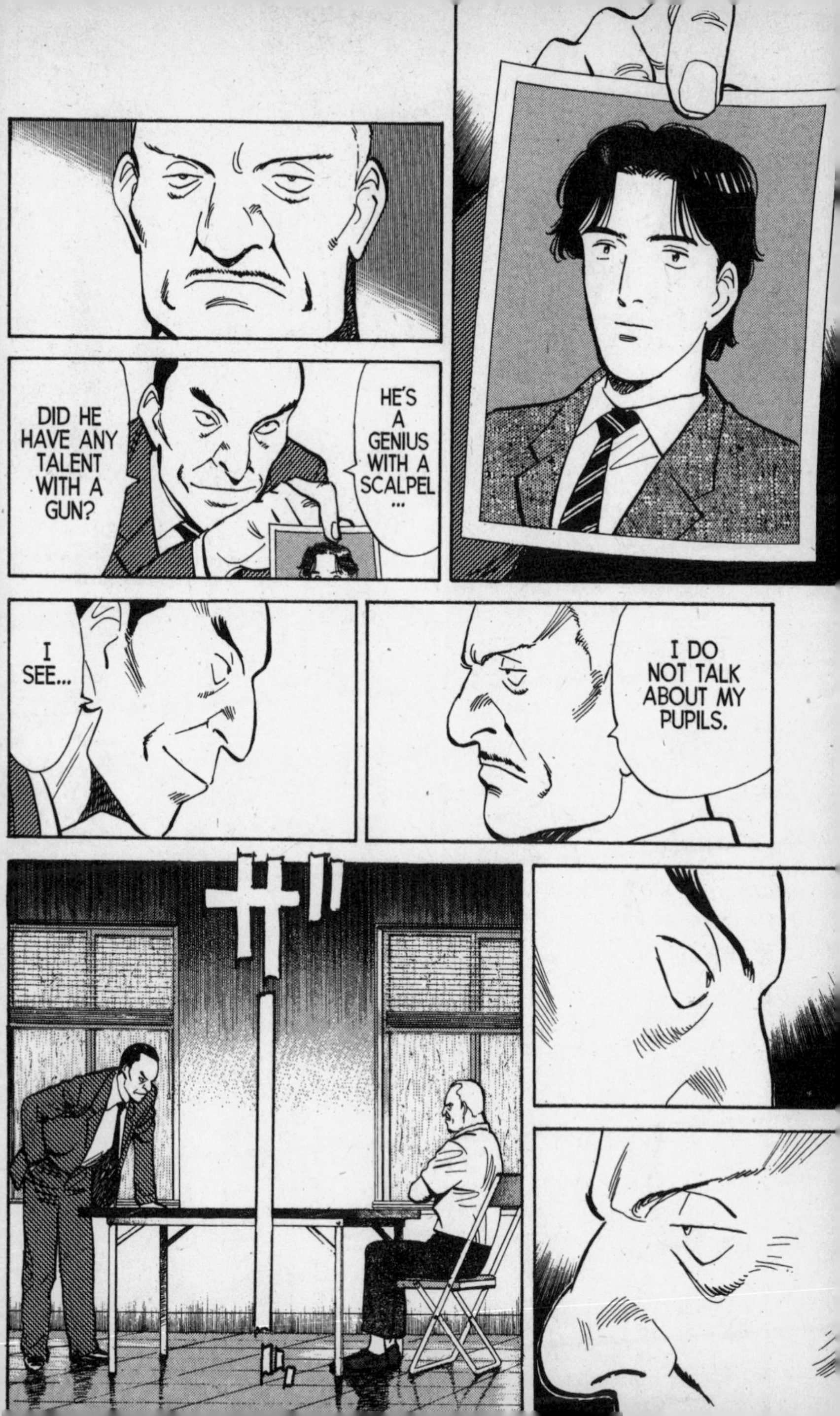
HE'S A GENIUS WITH A SCALPEL...
DID HE HAVE ANY TALENT WITH A GUN?
I DO NOT TALK ABOUT MY PUPILS.
I SEE...

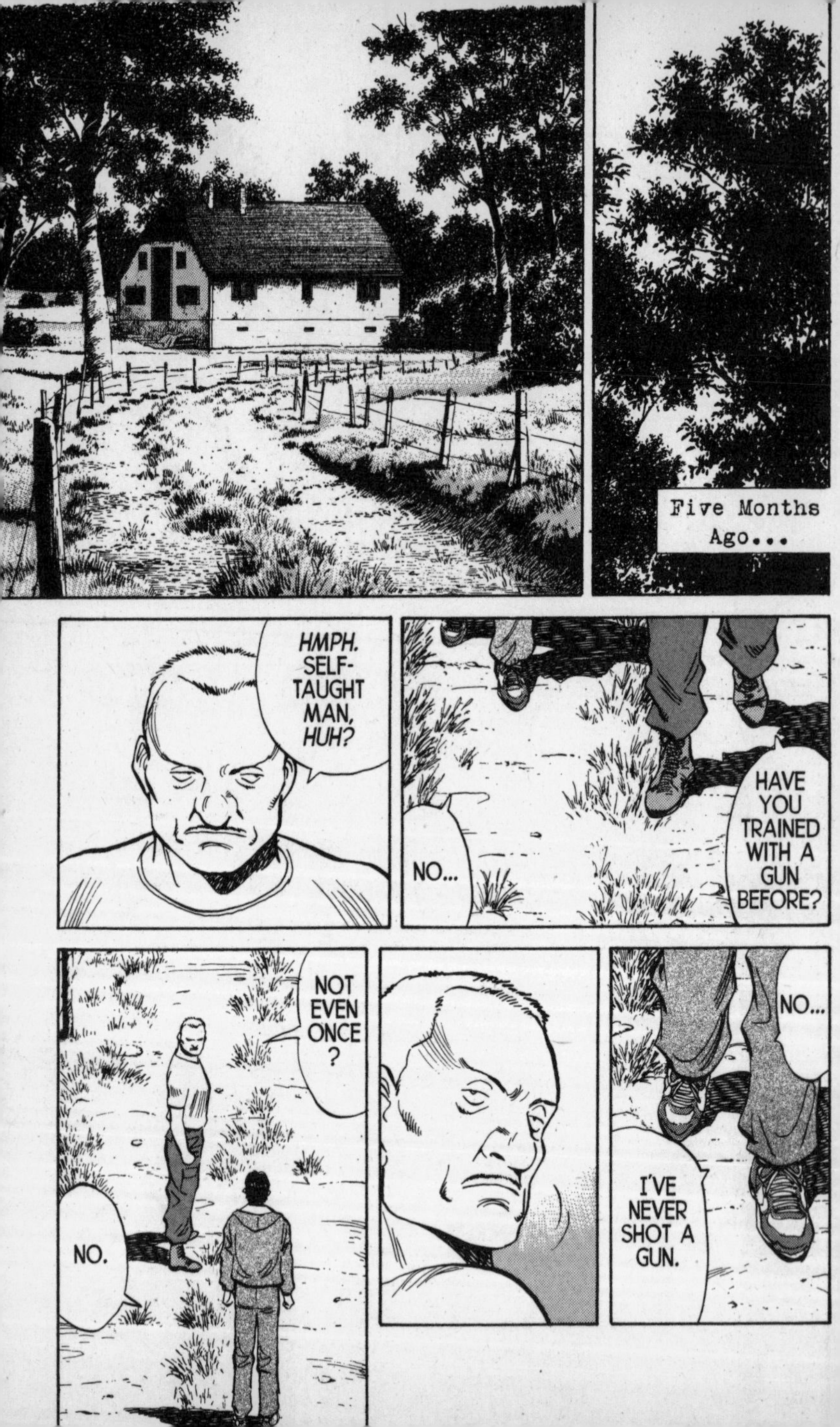
Five Months Ago...
HAVE YOU TRAINED WITH A GUN BEFORE?
NO...
HMPH. SELF-TAUGHT MAN, HUH?
NO...
I'VE NEVER SHOT A GUN.
NOT EVEN ONCE?
NO.

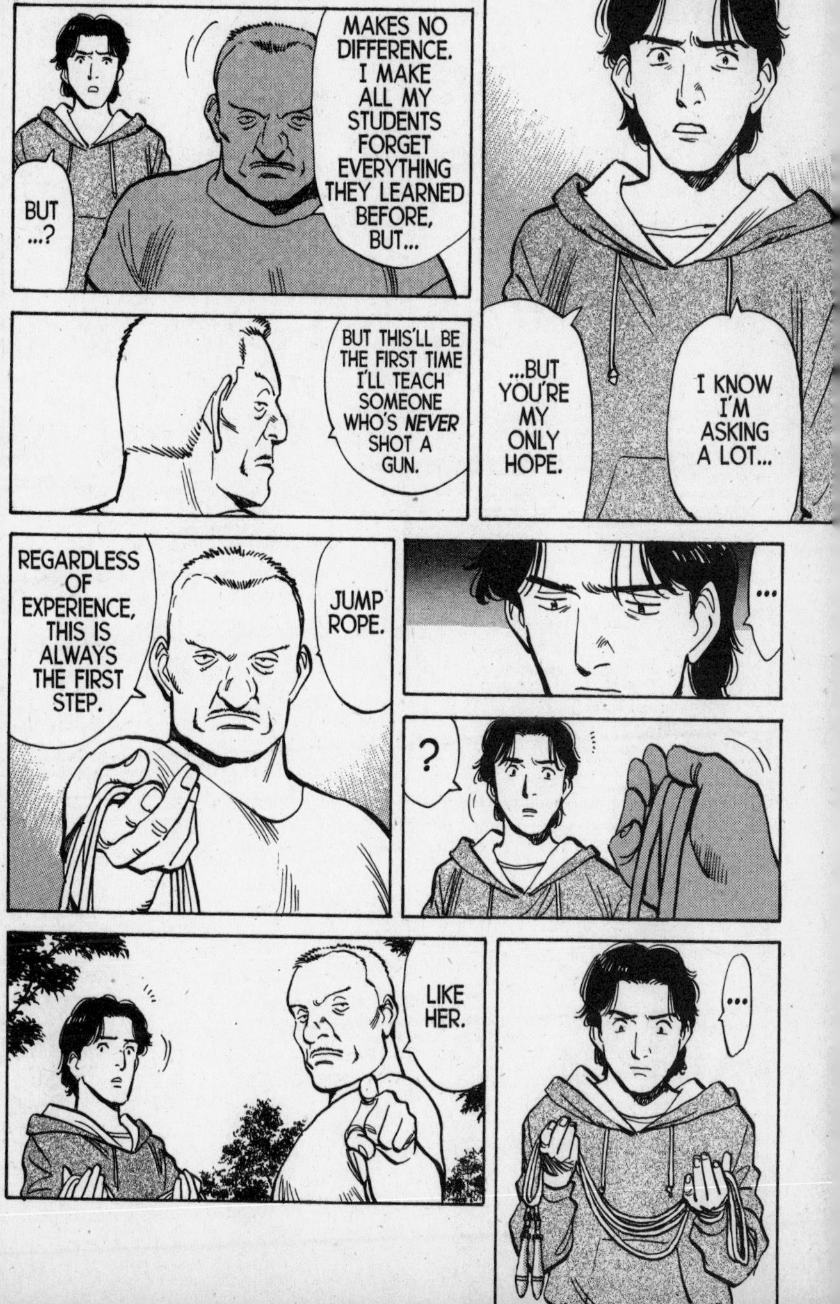
I KNOW I'M ASKING A LOT...
...BUT YOU'RE MY ONLY HOPE.
MAKES NO DIFFERENCE. I MAKE ALL MY STUDENTS FORGET EVERYTHING THEY LEARNED BEFORE, BUT...
BUT ...?
BUT THIS'LL BE THE FIRST TIME I'LL TEACH SOMEONE WHO'S *NEVER* SHOT A GUN.
...
?
JUMP ROPE.
REGARDLESS OF EXPERIENCE, THIS IS ALWAYS THE FIRST STEP.
...
LIKE HER.

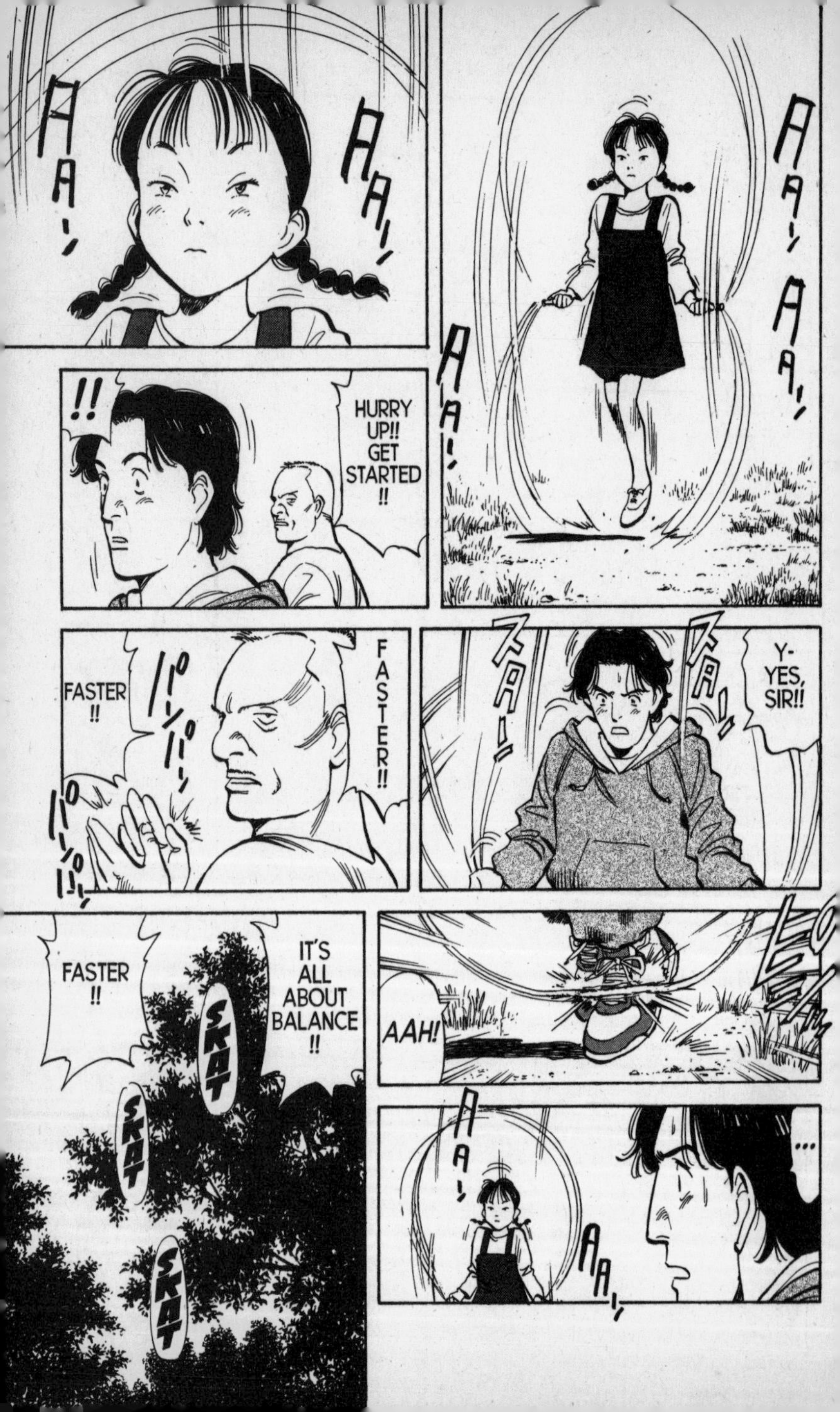

!!
HURRY UP!! GET STARTED!!
Y-YES, SIR!!
FASTER!!
FASTER!!
AAH!
...
IT'S ALL ABOUT BALANCE!!
FASTER!!
SKAT
SKAT
SKAT

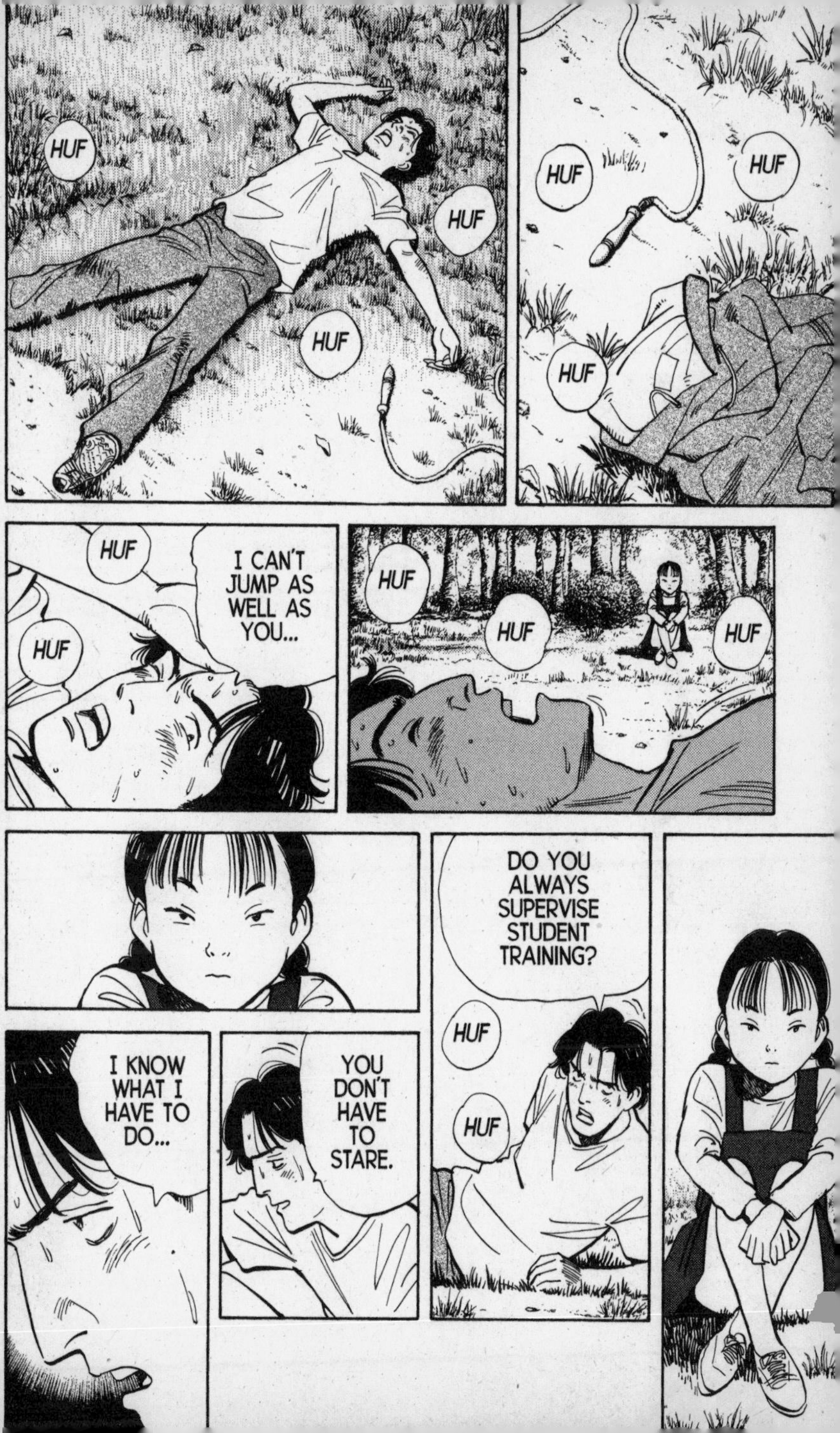
HUF
HUF
HUF
HUF
HUF
HUF
HUF
HUF
HUF
I CAN'T JUMP AS WELL AS YOU...
HUF
HUF
DO YOU ALWAYS SUPERVISE STUDENT TRAINING?
HUF
HUF
YOU DON'T HAVE TO STARE.
I KNOW WHAT I HAVE TO DO...

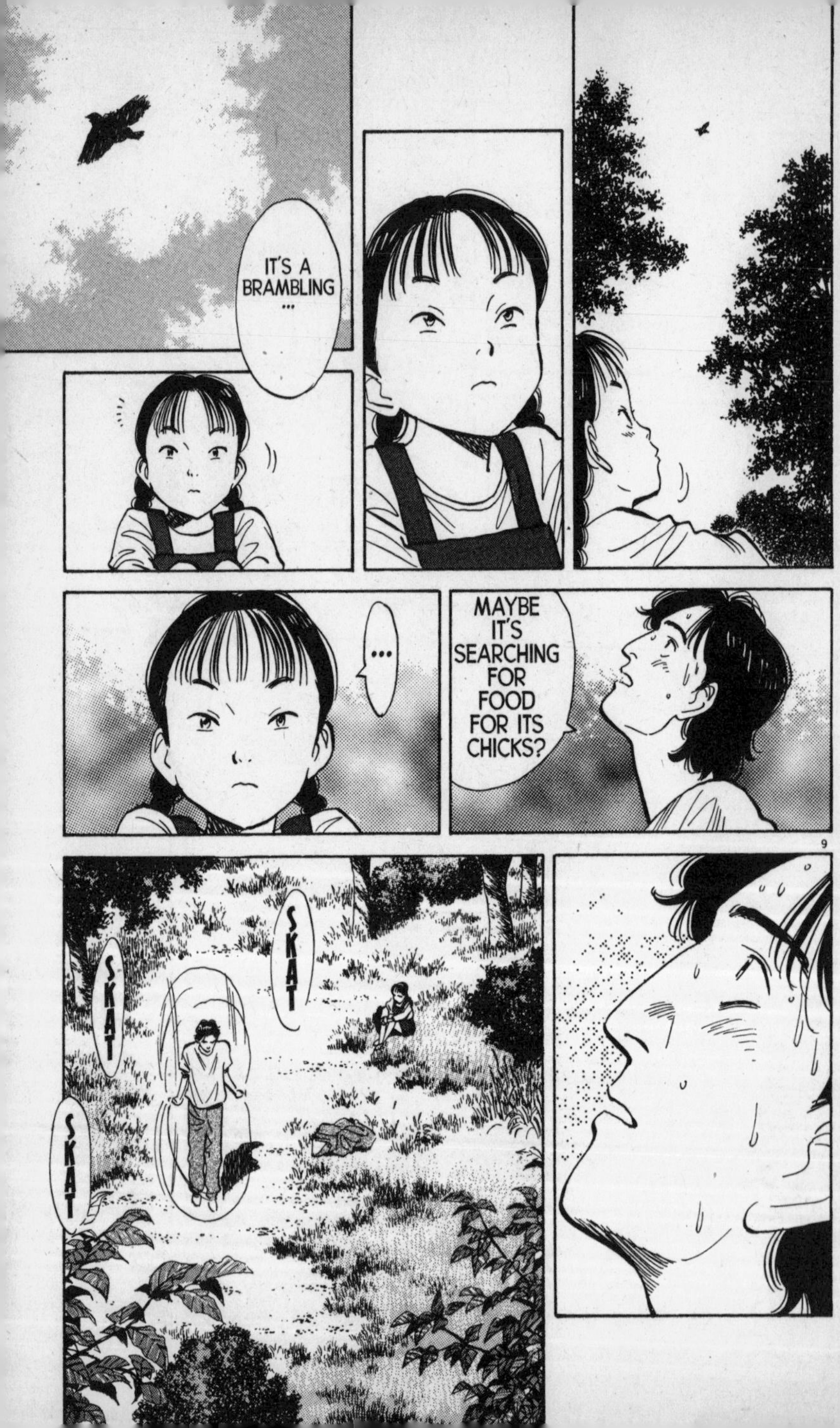
IT'S A BRAMBLING ...
MAYBE IT'S SEARCHING FOR FOOD FOR ITS CHICKS?
...
SKAT
SKAT
SKAT

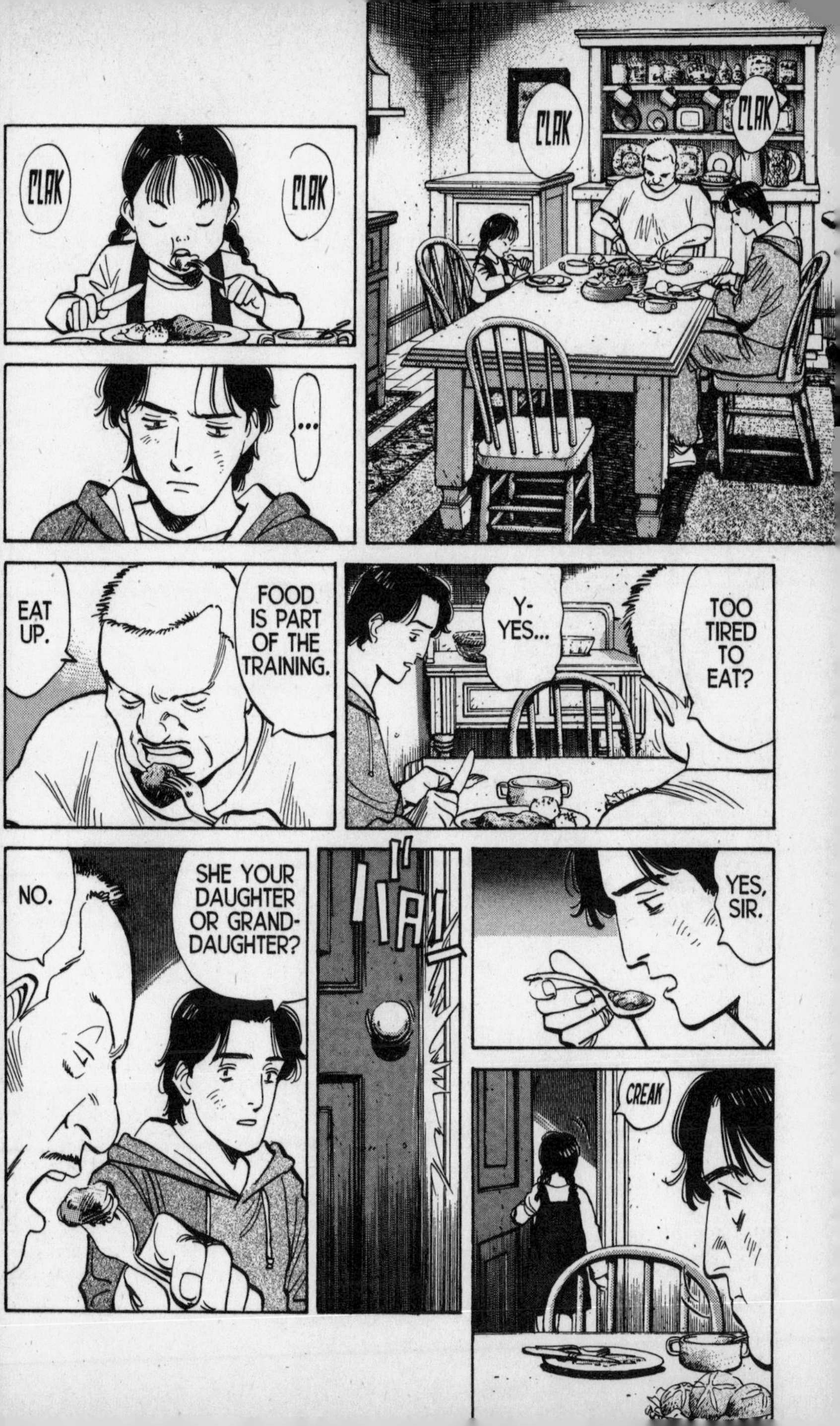
CLAK
CLAK
CLAK
CLAK
...
TOO TIRED TO EAT?
Y- YES...
FOOD IS PART OF THE TRAINING.
EAT UP.
YES, SIR.
CREAK
SHE YOUR DAUGHTER OR GRAND-DAUGHTER?
NO.

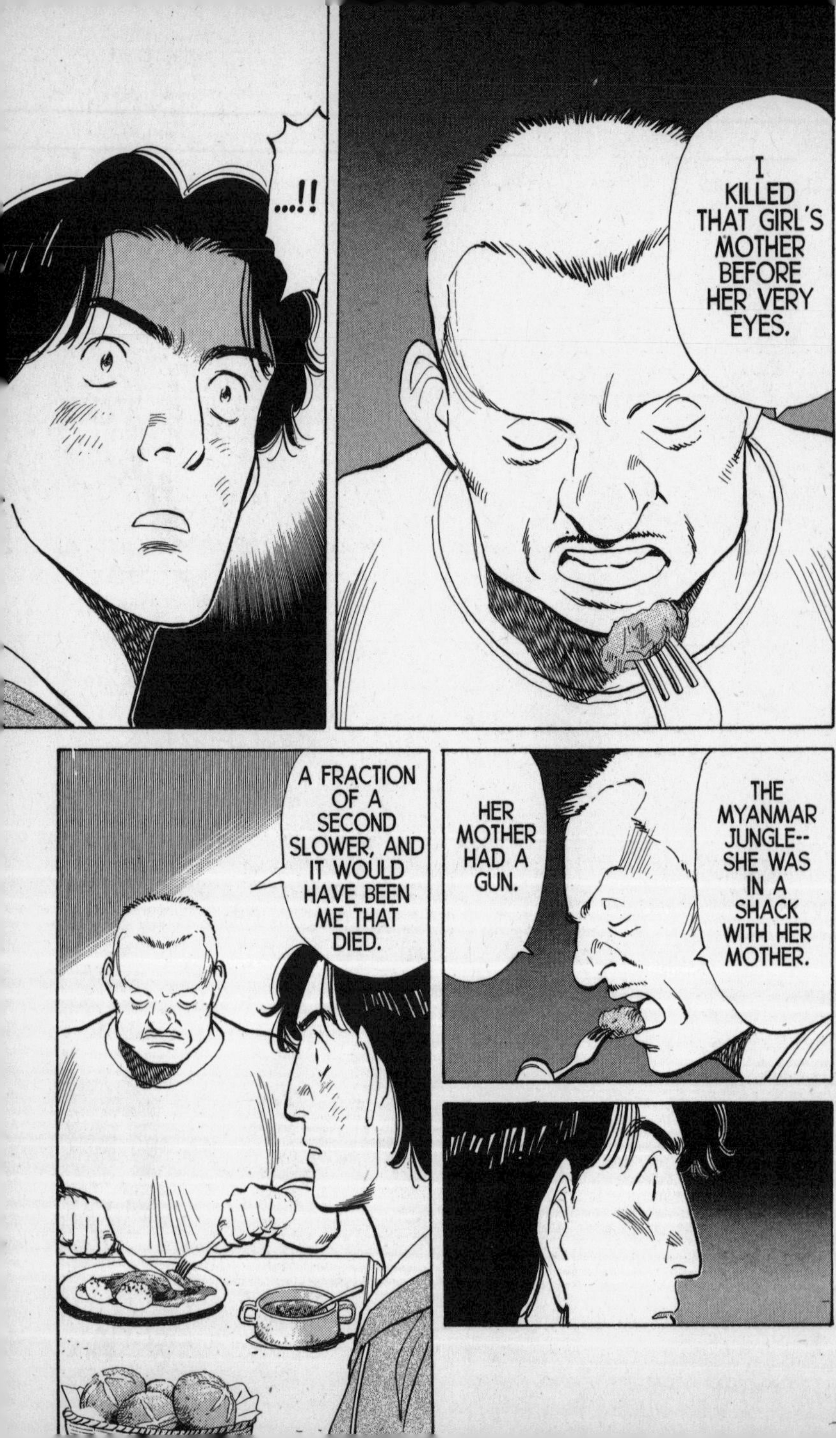
I KILLED THAT GIRL'S MOTHER BEFORE HER VERY EYES.
...!!
THE MYANMAR JUNGLE-- SHE WAS IN A SHACK WITH HER MOTHER.
HER MOTHER HAD A GUN.
A FRACTION OF A SECOND SLOWER, AND IT WOULD HAVE BEEN ME THAT DIED.

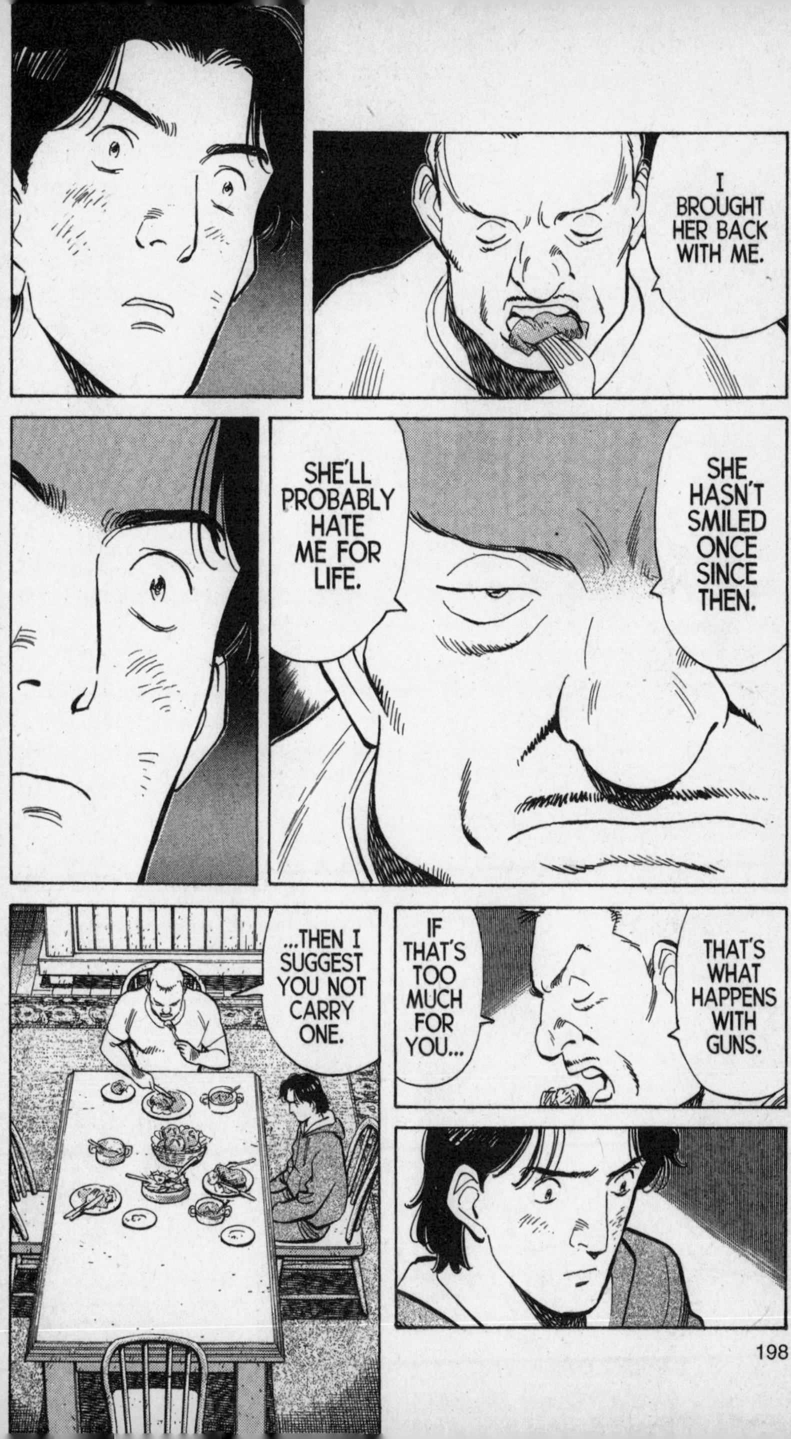
I BROUGHT HER BACK WITH ME.
SHE HASN'T SMILED ONCE SINCE THEN.
SHE'LL PROBABLY HATE ME FOR LIFE.
THAT'S WHAT HAPPENS WITH GUNS.
IF THAT'S TOO MUCH FOR YOU...
...THEN I SUGGEST YOU NOT CARRY ONE.

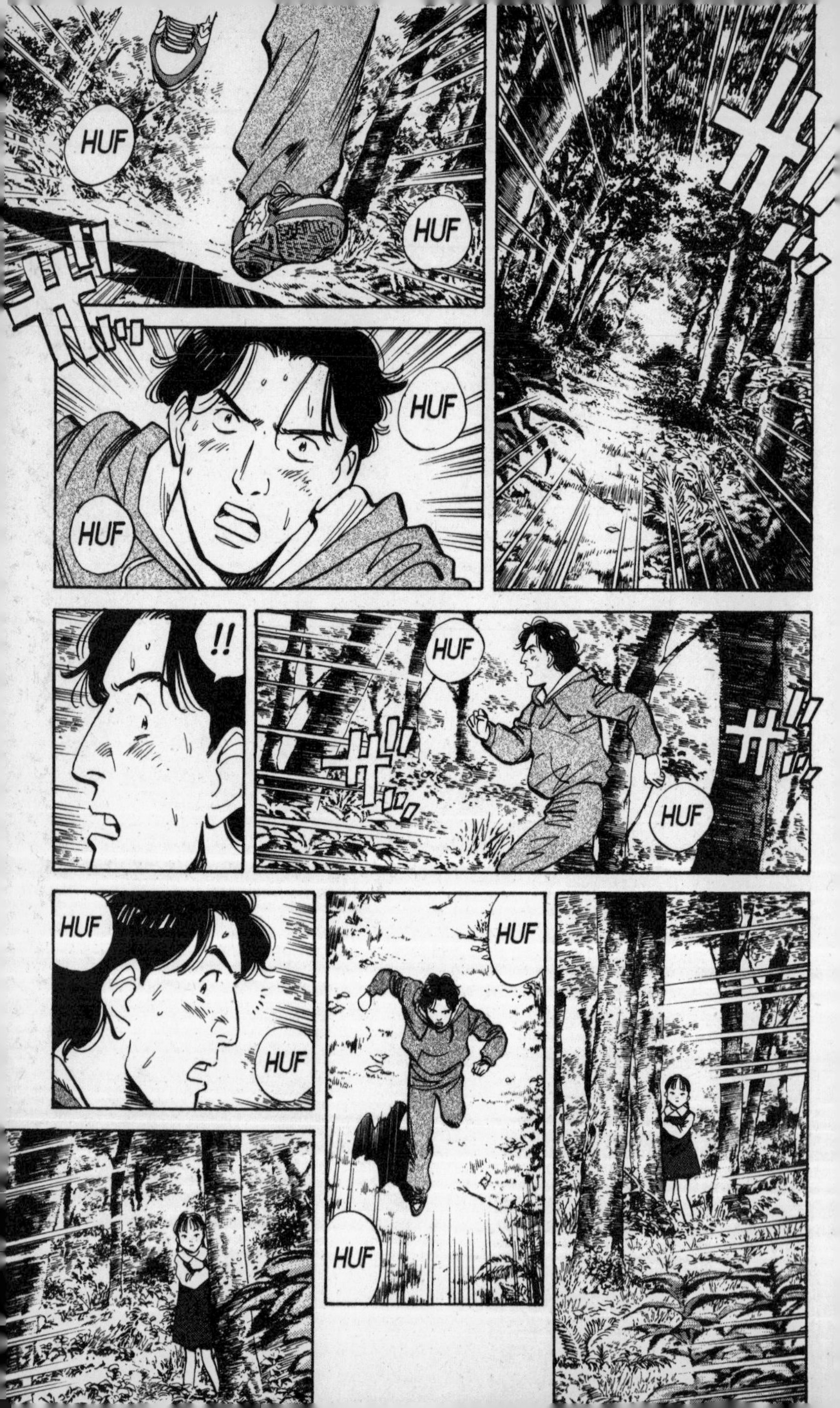
HUF
HUF
HUF
HUF
HUF
HUF
!!
HUF
HUF
HUF
HUF

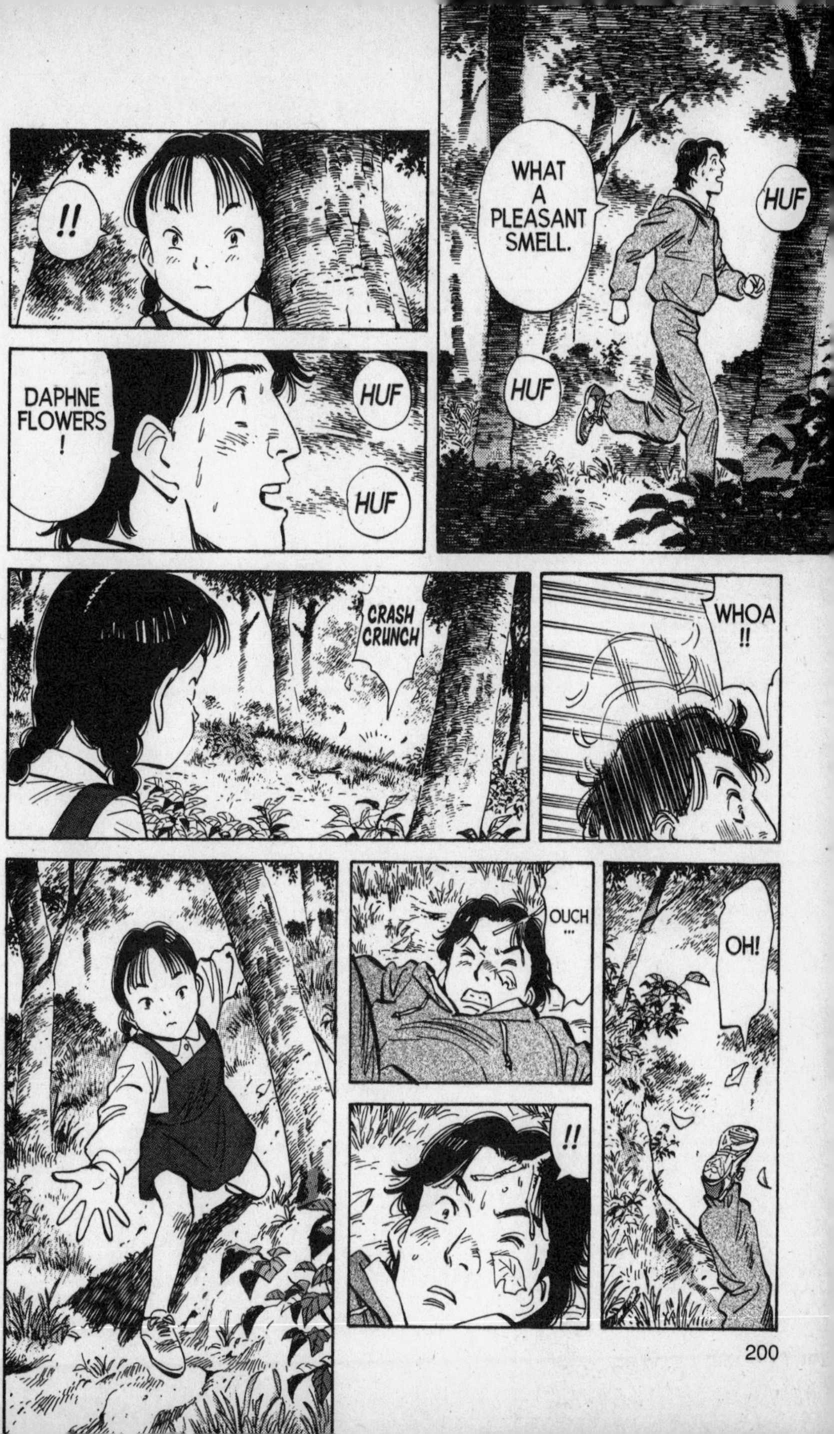
WHAT A PLEASANT SMELL.
HUF
HUF
!!
DAPHNE FLOWERS !
HUF
HUF
WHOA !!
CRASH CRUNCH
OH!
OUCH ...
!!

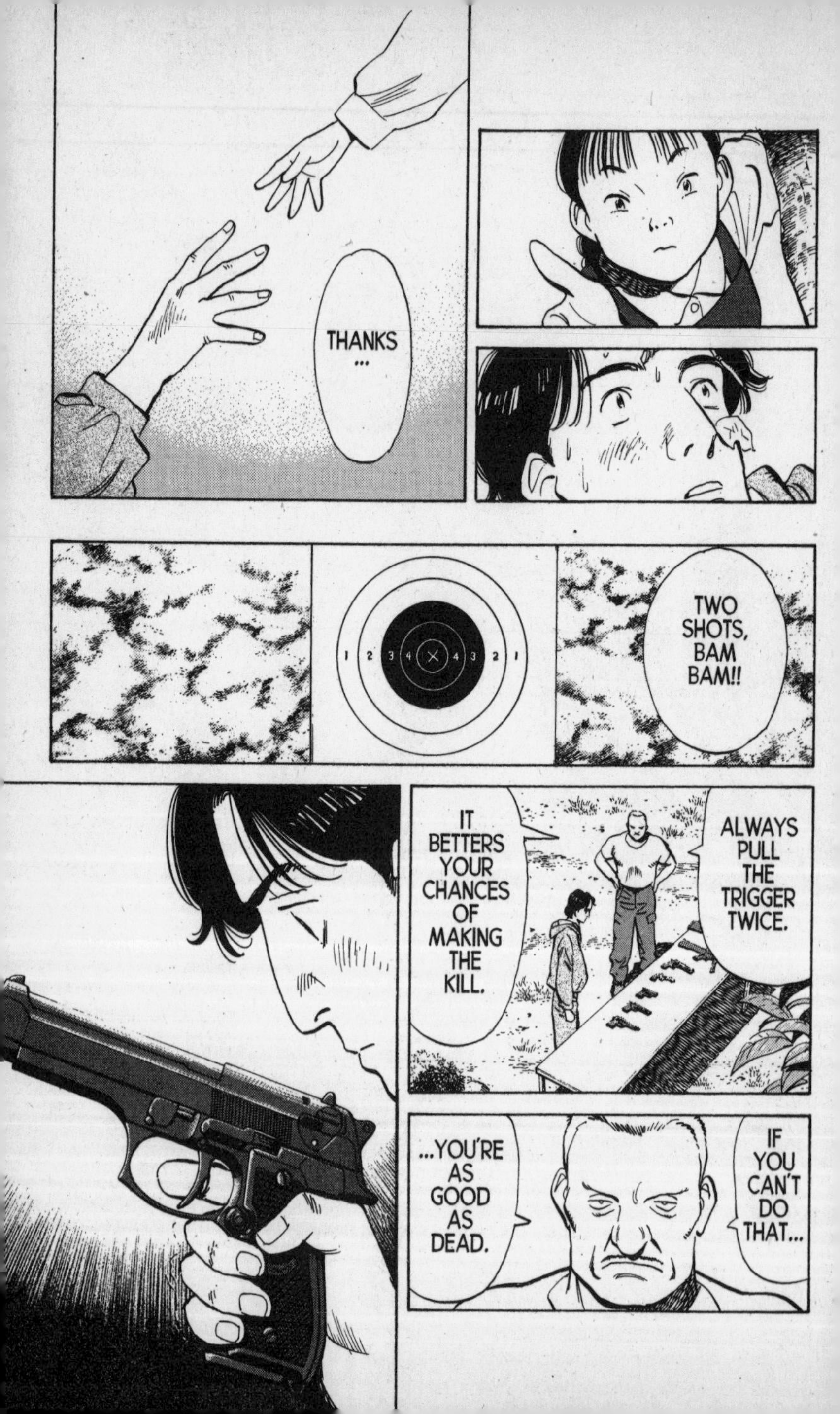
THANKS ...
TWO SHOTS, BAM BAM!!
ALWAYS PULL THE TRIGGER TWICE.
IT BETTERS YOUR CHANCES OF MAKING THE KILL.
IF YOU CAN'T DO THAT...
...YOU'RE AS GOOD AS DEAD.

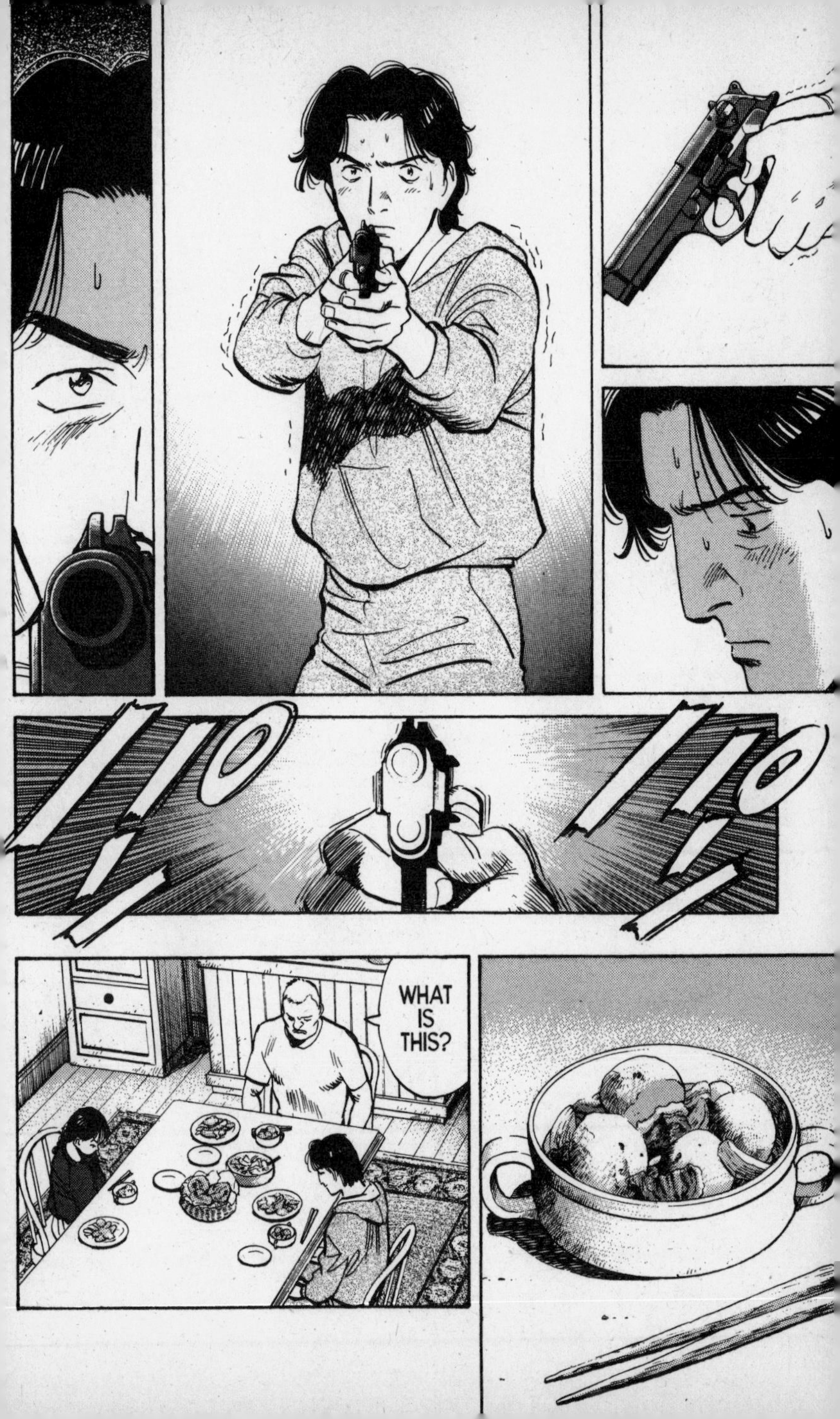
WHAT IS THIS?

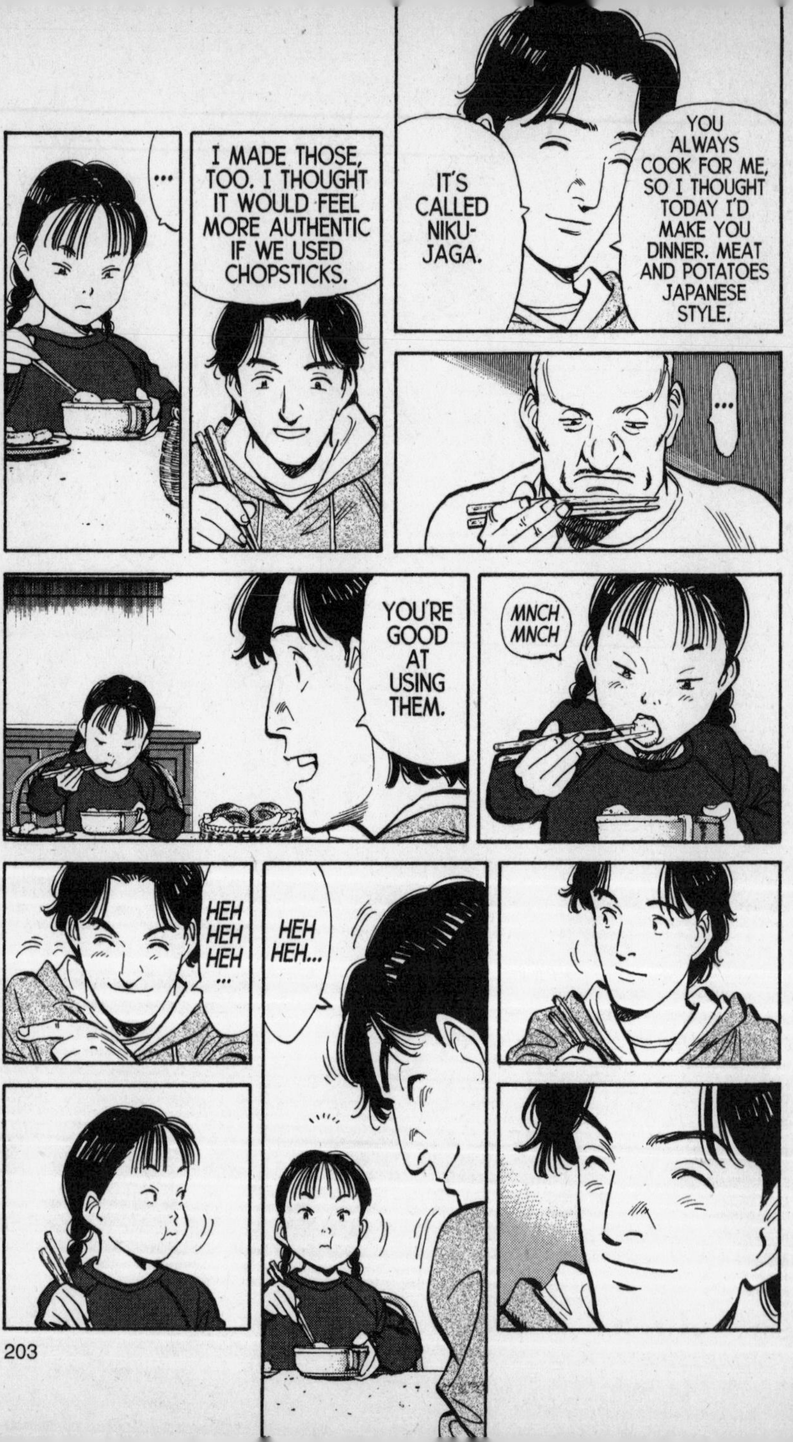
YOU ALWAYS COOK FOR ME, SO I THOUGHT TODAY I'D MAKE YOU DINNER. MEAT AND POTATOES JAPANESE STYLE.
IT'S CALLED NIKU-JAGA.
...
I MADE THOSE, TOO. I THOUGHT IT WOULD FEEL MORE AUTHENTIC IF WE USED CHOPSTICKS.
...
MNCH MNCH
YOU'RE GOOD AT USING THEM.
HEH HEH...
HEH HEH HEH ...

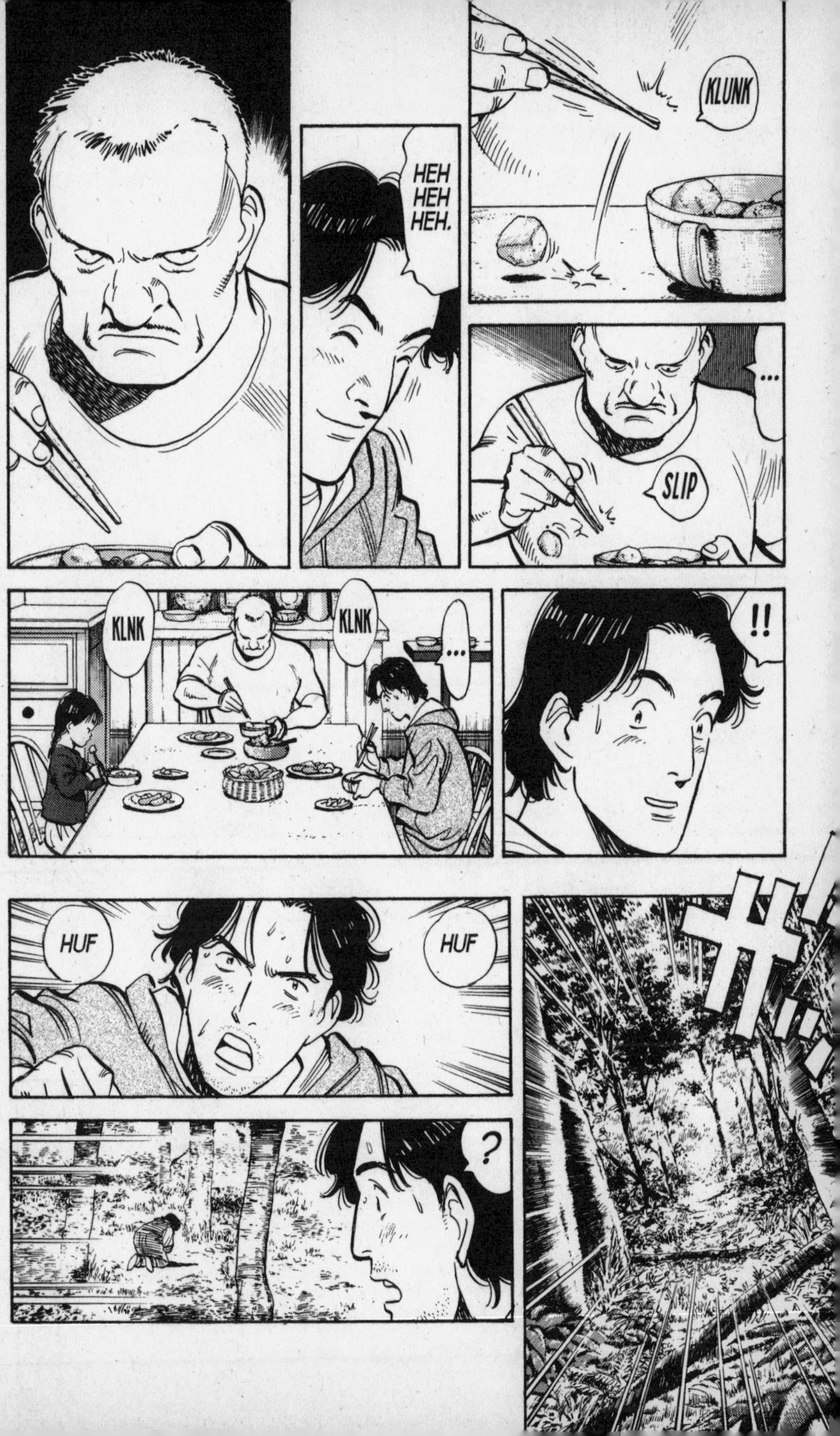
KLUNK
...
SLIP
HEH HEH HEH.
!!
...
KLNK
KLNK
ザ…
HUF
HUF
?

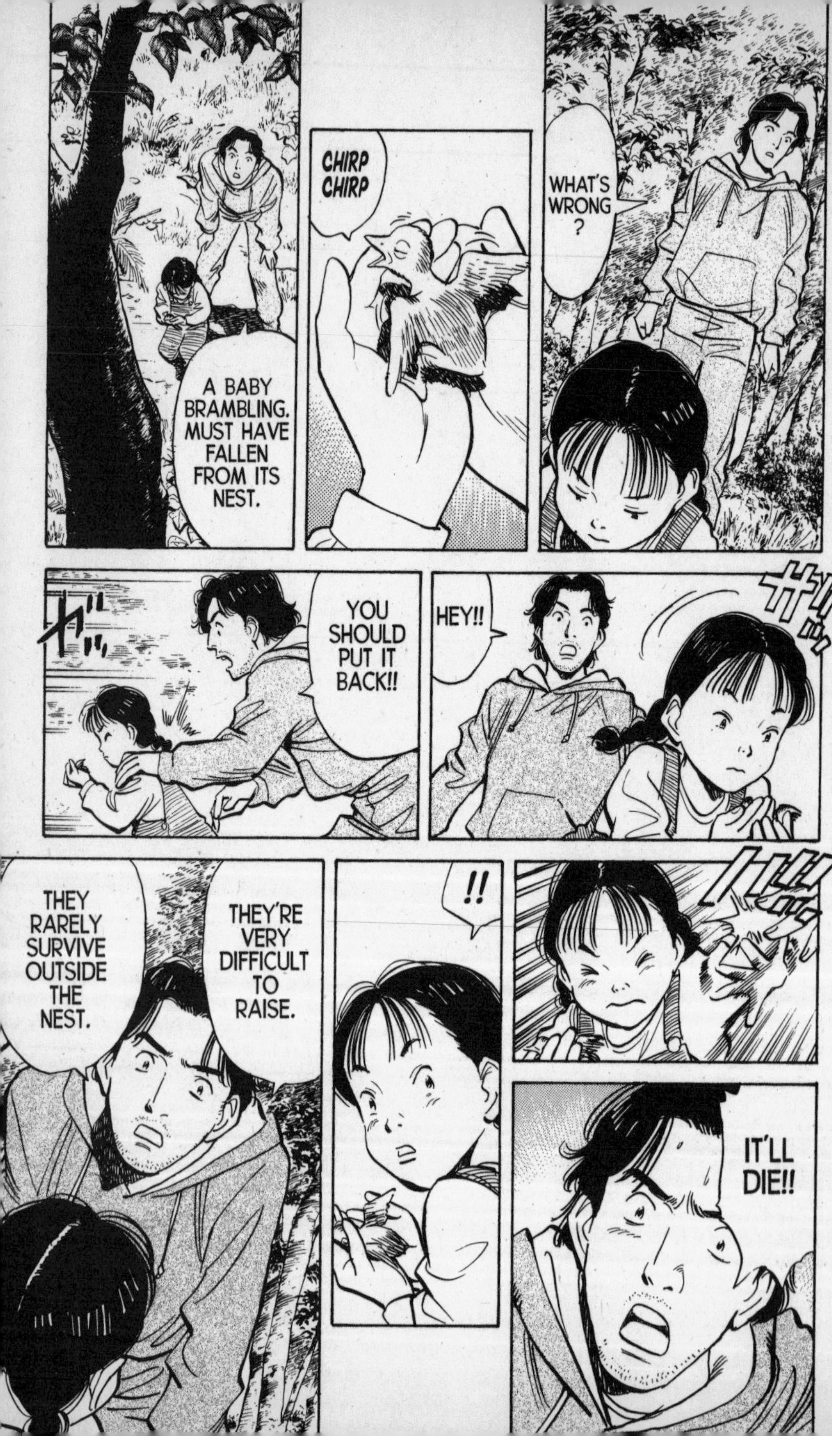
WHAT'S WRONG ?
CHIRP CHIRP
A BABY BRAMBLING. MUST HAVE FALLEN FROM ITS NEST.
HEY!!
YOU SHOULD PUT IT BACK!!
IT'LL DIE!!
!!
THEY'RE VERY DIFFICULT TO RAISE.
THEY RARELY SURVIVE OUTSIDE THE NEST.

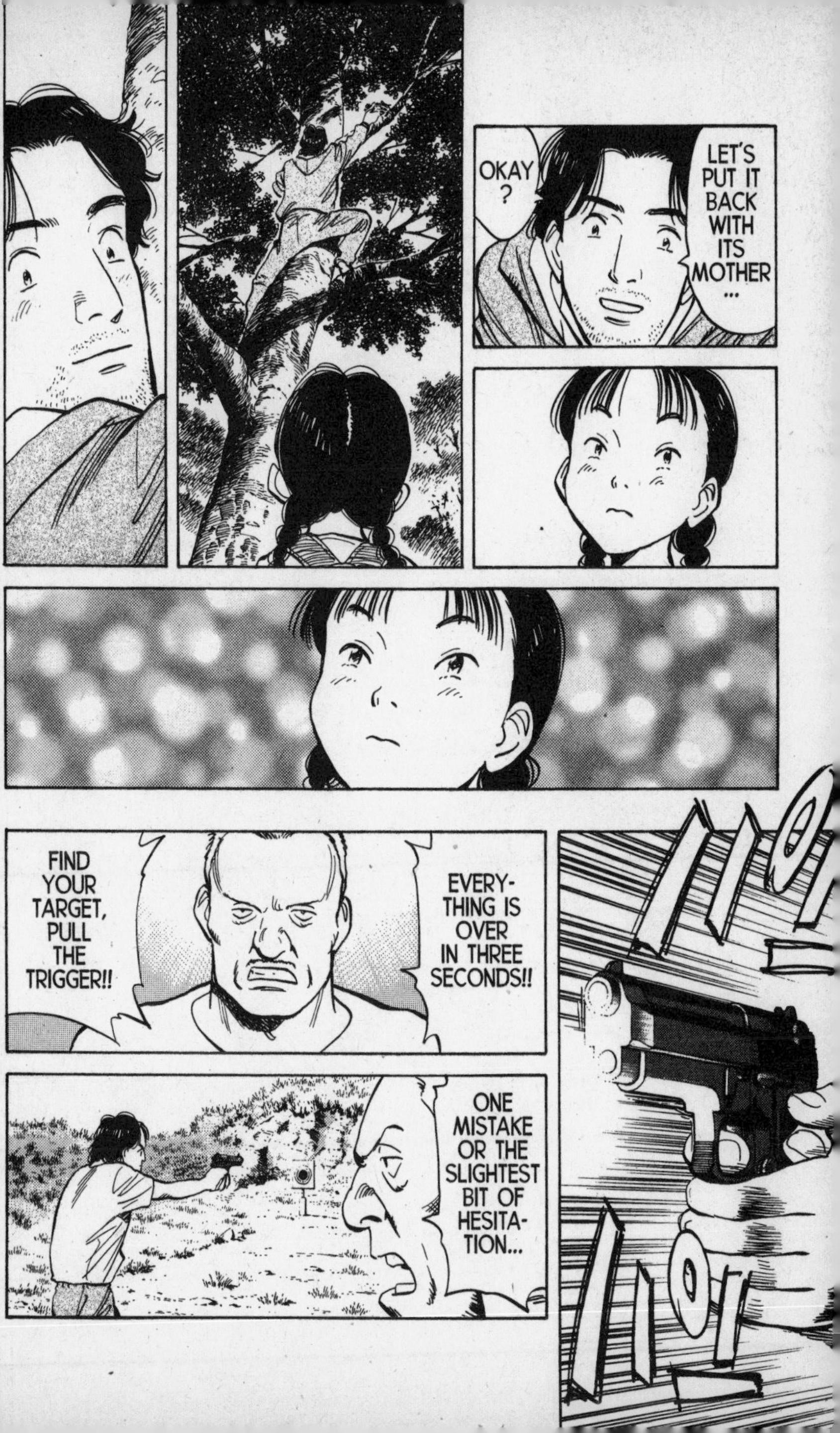
LET'S PUT IT BACK WITH ITS MOTHER ...
OKAY ?
EVERY-THING IS OVER IN THREE SECONDS!!
FIND YOUR TARGET, PULL THE TRIGGER!!
ONE MISTAKE OR THE SLIGHTEST BIT OF HESITA-TION...

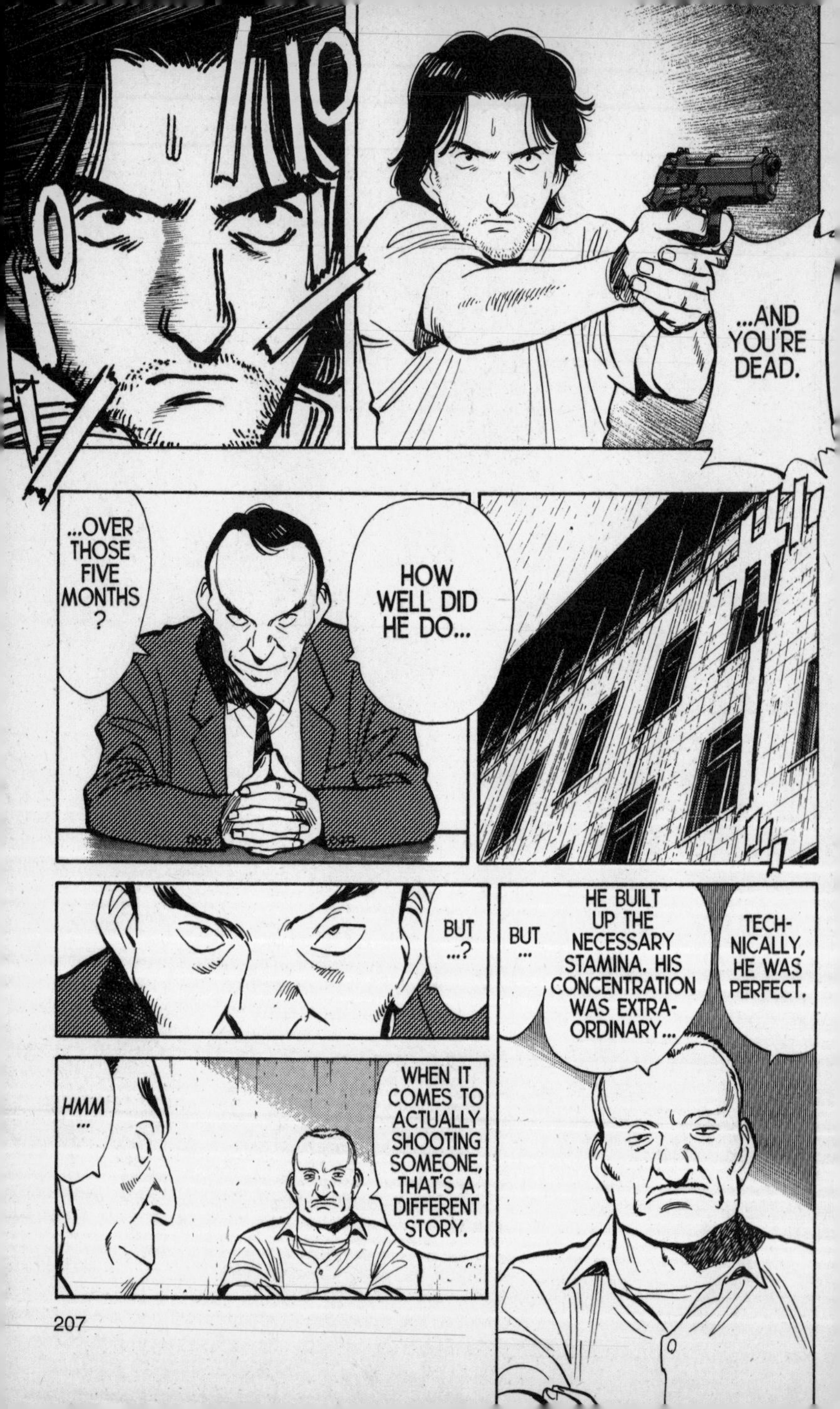
...AND YOU'RE DEAD.
HOW WELL DID HE DO...
...OVER THOSE FIVE MONTHS?
TECH-NICALLY, HE WAS PERFECT.
HE BUILT UP THE NECESSARY STAMINA. HIS CONCENTRATION WAS EXTRA-ORDINARY...
BUT...
BUT...?
WHEN IT COMES TO ACTUALLY SHOOTING SOMEONE, THAT'S A DIFFERENT STORY.
HMM...

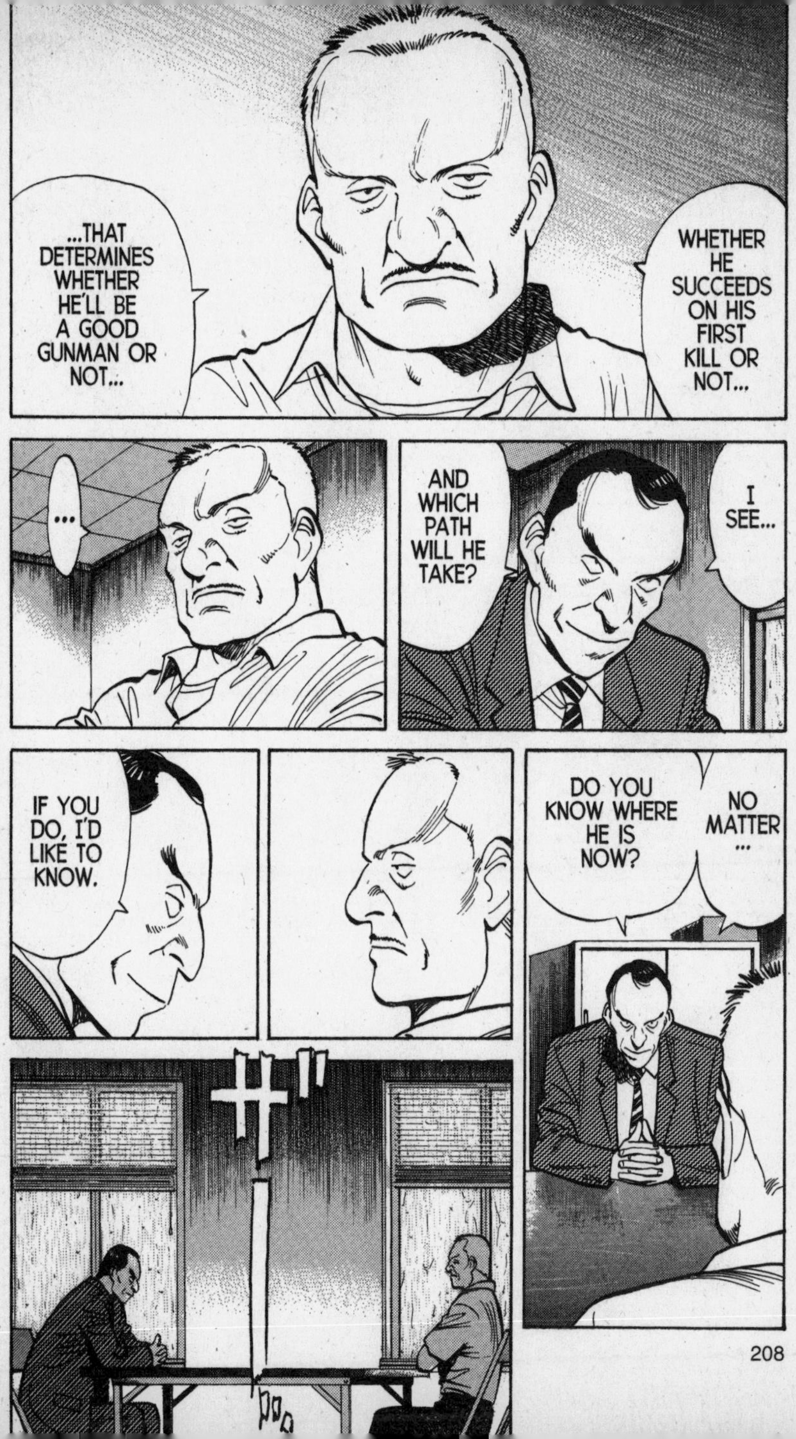
WHETHER HE SUCCEEDS ON HIS FIRST KILL OR NOT...
...THAT DETERMINES WHETHER HE'LL BE A GOOD GUNMAN OR NOT...
I SEE...
AND WHICH PATH WILL HE TAKE?
...
NO MATTER...
DO YOU KNOW WHERE HE IS NOW?
IF YOU DO, I'D LIKE TO KNOW.

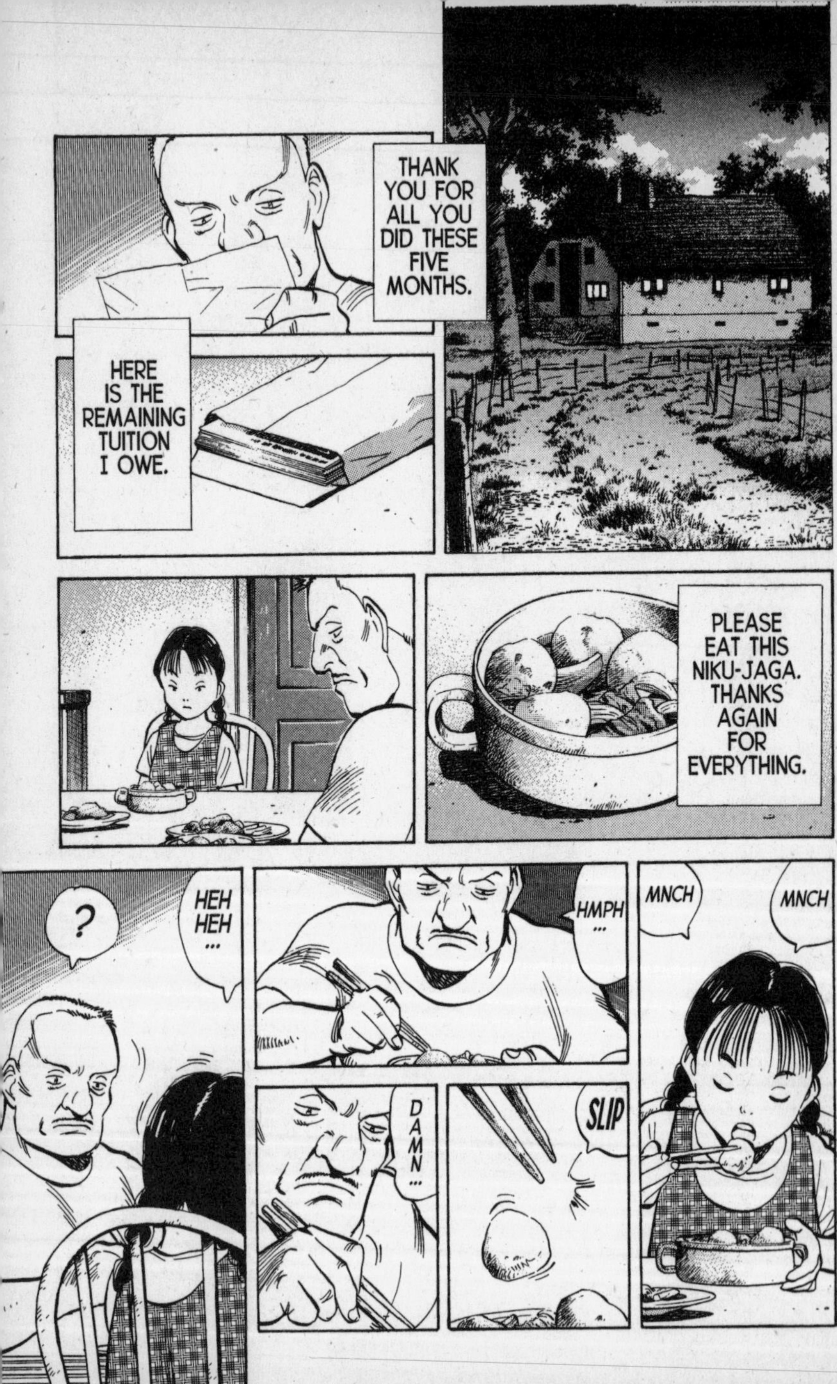
THANK YOU FOR ALL YOU DID THESE FIVE MONTHS.
HERE IS THE REMAINING TUITION I OWE.
PLEASE EAT THIS NIKU-JAGA. THANKS AGAIN FOR EVERYTHING.
MNCH
MNCH
HMPH...
SLIP
DAMN...
HEH HEH...
?

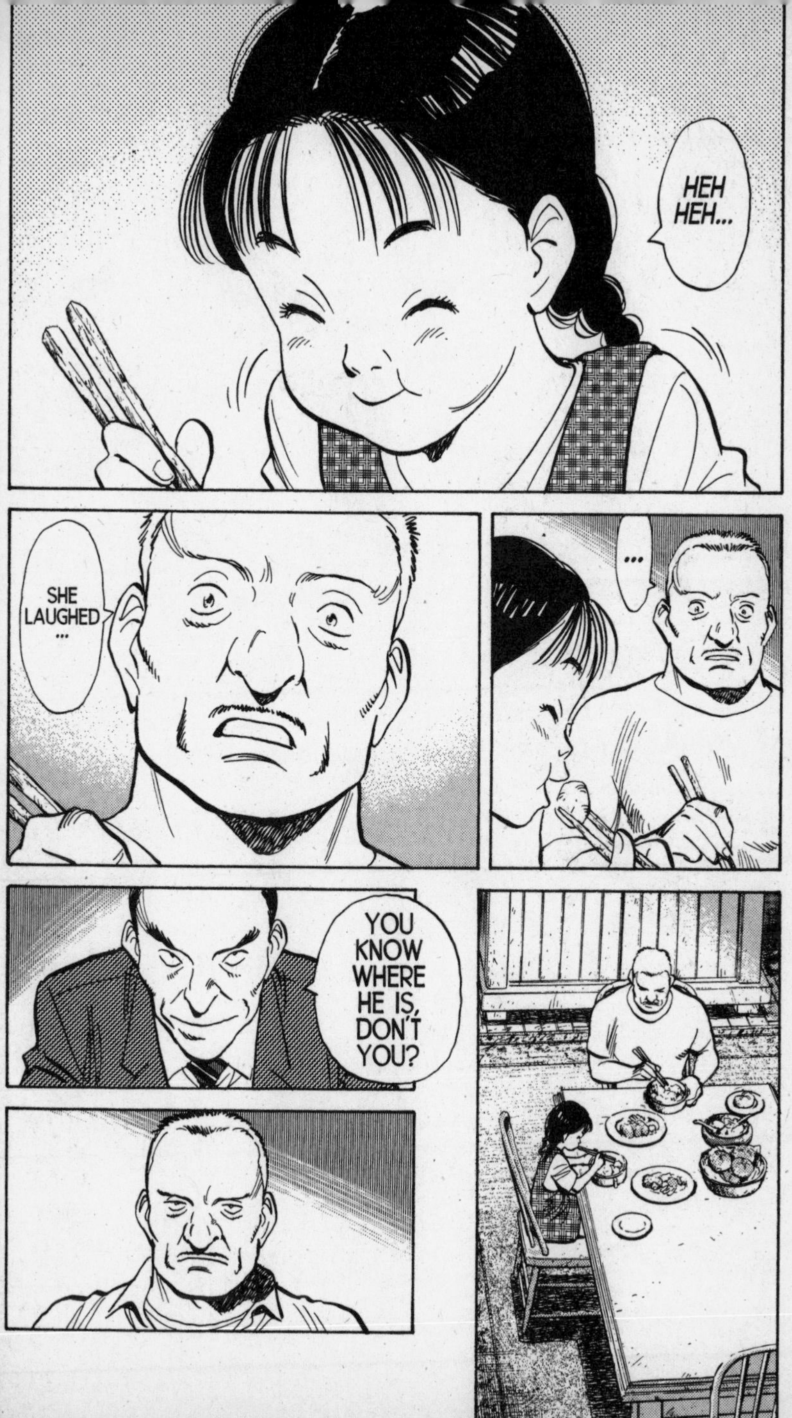
HEH HEH...
...
SHE LAUGHED...
YOU KNOW WHERE HE IS, DON'T YOU?

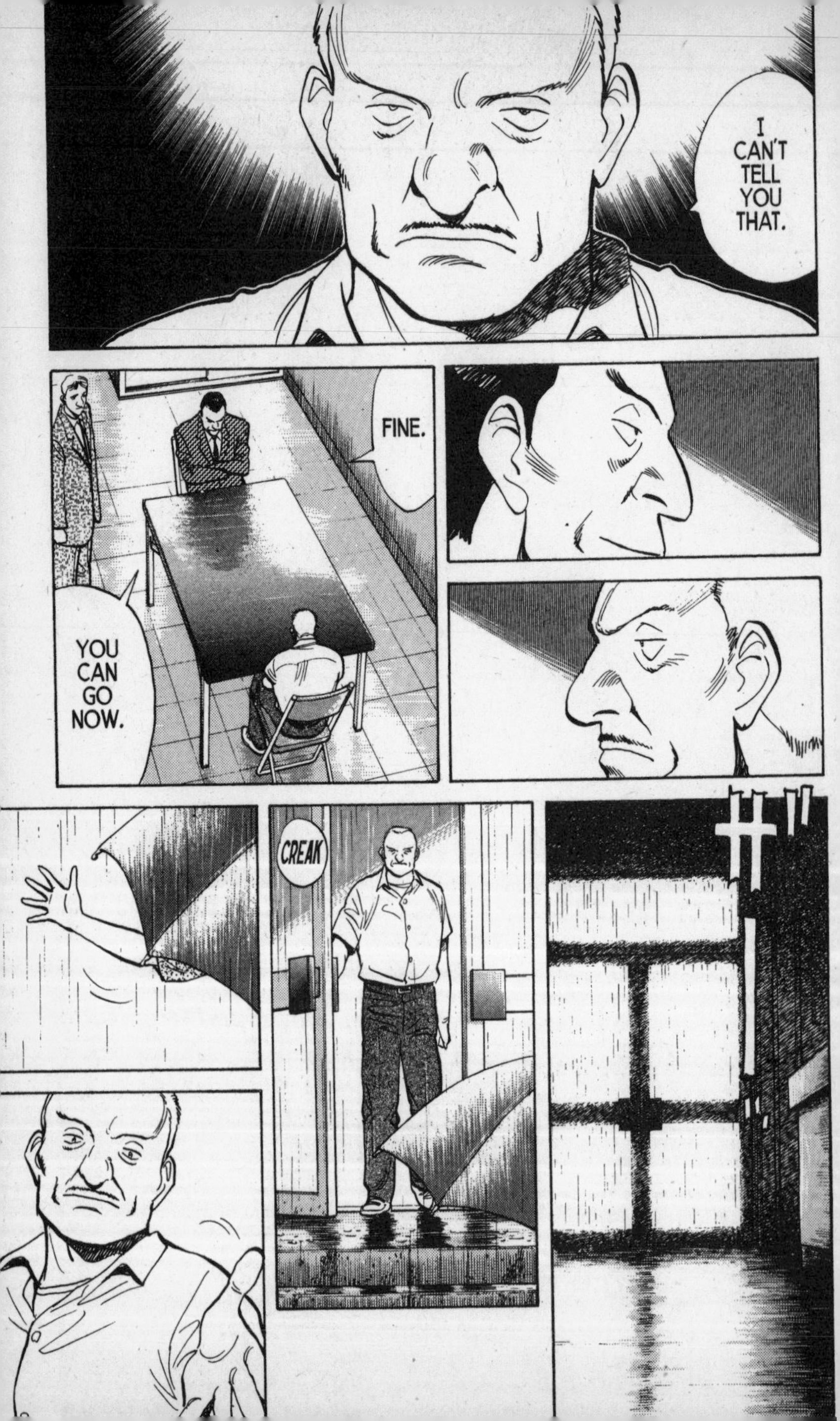
I CAN'T TELL YOU THAT.
FINE.
YOU CAN GO NOW.
CREAK

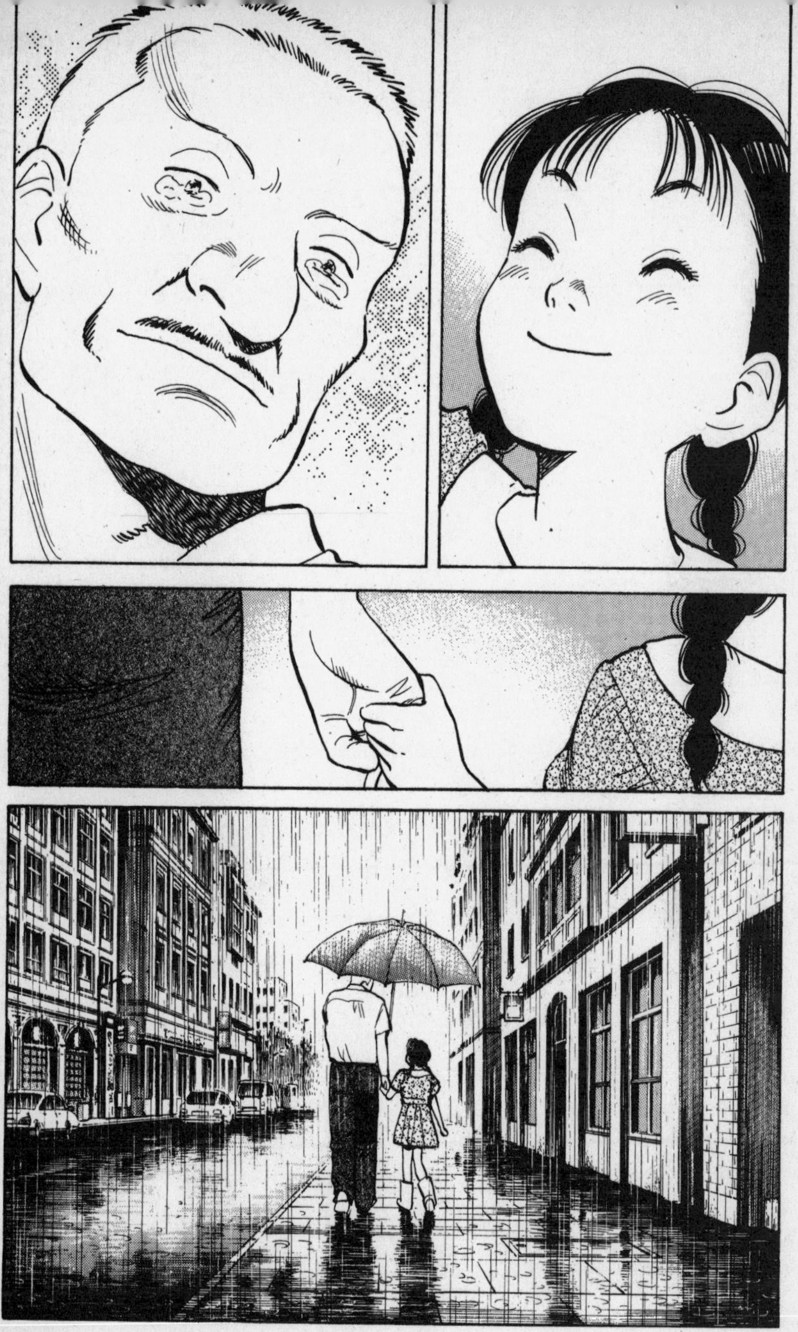

about the author

Naoki Urasawa, born in Tokyo in 1960, is Japan's manga master of the suspense thriller. Critically acclaimed and immensely popular, his award-winning works include *20th Century Boys*, *Master Keaton*, *Pineapple Army*, and *Yawara*.

(push push push)

116.7—FX: Gu gu (push push)

122.1—FX: Da (dash)

122.2—FX: Gacha (kchak)

122.5—FX: Gi (creak)

122.6—FX: Ban (bam)

124.6—FX: Bamu bamu
(slam slam)

124.7—FX: Za (vwoosh)

124.8—FX: Ba (vwoosh)

125.5—FX: Ba (vwoosh)

126.1—FX: Ba (vwoosh)

127.4—FX: Oon (vroom)

128.2—FX: Ba (vwoosh)

129.4—FX: Ba (vwoosh)

133.3—FX: Da (dash)

133.5—FX: Ba (vwoosh)

134.1—FX: Dobashan (splash)

134.4—FX: Go (roar)

Chapter 6

136.1—FX: Za (shuf)

136.2—FX: Za (shuf)

136.3—FX: Za (shuf)

136.7—FX: Dosa (fwump)

139.6—FX: Za (shuf)

140.5—FX: Za (flashback)

144.6—FX: Za (sheen)

145.1—FX: Pa (zoom)

145.4—FFX: Wai wai wai
(crowd chatter)

147.1—FX: Zawa zawa
(crowd chatter)

148.2—FX: BA (fwoosh)

149.3—FX: Wai wai
(crowd chatter)

149.4—FX: Wai wai
(crowd chatter)

151.4—FX: Gacha (kchak)

153.2—FX: Za (shuf)

153.7—FX: Za (shuf)

159.3—FX: Pa (vwoosh)

159.4—FX: Goton Goton
(clikkety clack)

Chapter 7

177.1—FX: Ka ka ka
(klak klak klak)

177.2—FX: Ba (fwoosh)

178.2—FX: Zawa zawa
(crowd noise)

178.3—FX: Zawa zawa
(crowd noise)

178.4—FX: Zawa zawa zawa
zawa (crowd noise)

179.4—FX: Gi (creak)

181.5—FX: Paho Paho (sirens)

181.6—FX: Za za (shuf shuf)

181.7—FX: Za za (shuf shuf)

182.1—FX: Ka ka (klak klak)

184.1—FX: Paho Paho (sirens)

184.6—FX: Paho Paho (sirens)

185.3—FX: Gata goto gata
goto (clank clunk)

185.4—FX: Goto goto
(clunk clunk)

185.6—FX: Gata goto
(clank clunk)

Chapter 8

190.8—FX: Zaa (rainfall)

193.1—FX: Tatan tatan tatan
(skip skip skip)

193.2—FX: Tatan tatan
(skip skip)

193.4—FX: Sutan Sutan
(stomp stomp)

193.5—FX: Pan pan pan pan
(clap clap clap clap)

193.6—FX: Bishi (slap)

193.7—FX: Tatan tatab
(skip skip)

196.8—FX: Batan (slam)

199.1—FX: Za (vwoosh)

199.2—FX: Za (vwoosh)

199.4—FX: Za za
(vwoosh vwoosh)

202.5—FX: Pan pan
(bang bang)

204.7—FX: Za (vwoosh)

205.4—FX: Za (vwoosh)

205.5—FX: Ga (grab)

205.6—FX: Ba (fwoosh)

206.6—FX: Pan pan
(bang bang)

207.2—FX: Pan pan
(bang bang)

207.3—FX: Zaa (rainfall)

208.7—FX: Zaa (rainfall)

211.5—FX: Zaa (rainfall)

glossary

Chapter 1

5.1 —— FX: Da (dash)

5.3 —— FX: Da (dash)

6.4 —— FX: Da (dash)

6.6 —— FX: Ban (slam)

10.1 —— FX: Ba (fwoosh)

10.2 —— FX: Baba
(fwoosh fwoosh)

10.3 —— FX: Ga (grab)

10.5 —— FX: Zudan (slam)

10.6 —— FX: Banban (slap slap)

11.1 —— FX: Za (fwoosh)

11.2 —— FX: Pachi Pachi Pachi
Pachi (clap clap clap)

11.3 —— FX: Pachi Pachi Pachi
Pachi (clap clap clap)

12.5 —— FX: Ba (fwoosh)

12.7 —— FX: Ba (fwoosh)

13.1 —— FX: Ba ba ba
(put put put)

13.2 —— FX: Ba ba ba
(put put put)

13.3 —— FX: Ba ba ba
(put put put)

22.1 —— FX: Ga ga
(munch munch)

22.3 —— FX: Ga ga
(munch munch)

28.3 —— FX: Za (shuf)

29.1 —— FX: Buo (vroom)

29.1 —— FX: Paa (beep)

29.4 —— FX: Paa (beep)

Chapter 2

37.3 —— FX: Batan (slam)

52.4 —— FX: Ba ba ba
(put put put)

53.8 —— FX: Za (shuf)

54.2 —— FX: Za (shuf)

Chapter 3

59.4 —— FX: Batan (slam)

64.6 —— FX: Dosa dosa
(bam bam)

65.1 —— FX: Dosa (bam)

73.2 —— FX: Dota dota
(stomp stomp)

73.3 —— FX: Gacha (kchak)

73.6 —— FX: Da (dash)

75.1 —— FX: Baku baku
(chomp chomp)

75.4 —— FX: Hagu Hagu
(chomp chomp)

Chapter 4

84.6 —— FX: Za (shuf)

86.1 —— FX: Baa (vwoosh)

90.5 —— FX: Baa (vwoosh)

90.7 —— FX: Za (shuf)

92.2 —— FX: Batan (slam)

92.4 —— FX: Don don
(bam bam)

93.1 —— FX: Don don
(bam bam)

95.7 —— FX: Ga (grab)

95.8 —— FX: Da (dash)

96.8 —— FX: Da (dash)

102.7 —— FX: Za (shuf)

103.4 —— FX: Da (dash)

103.6 —— FX: Ba (fwoosh)

103.7 —— FX: Do (thud)

104.4 —— FX: Ga (grab)

104.5 —— FX: Ba (fwoosh)

104.6 —— FX: Dan (slam)

104.7 —— FX: Kan karan (clatter)

105.1 —— FX: Ga (grab)

105.7 —— FX: Gi (tug)

106.6 —— FX: Da (dash)

107.3 —— FX: Da (dash)

108.1 —— FX: Ba (vwoosh)

Chapter 5

111.1 —— FX: Don don
(bam bam)

111.2 —— FX: Don don
(bam bam)

112.1 —— FX: Gacha (kchak)

112.2 —— FX: Gi (creak)

112.3 —— FX: Do (ba-bump)

112.4 —— FX: Do (ba-bump)

115.6 —— FX: Gu gu (push push)

115.7 —— FX: Gu gu gu
(push push push)

115.9 —— FX: Gu gu (push push)

115.10 — FX: Gu gu (push push)

116.1 —— FX: Gu gu (push push)

116.2 —— FX: Gu (push)

116.3 —— FX: Gu gu gu

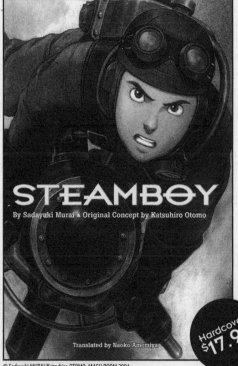